THE RITUAL LIFE OF
MEDIEVAL EUROPE:

PAPERS BY AND FOR
C. CLIFFORD FLANIGAN

volume 52-53 | 2014

Copyright 2014 Mario B. Longtin

Published simultaneously in Canada.
Printed in the United States of America.

First Printing 2014
First Circle Publishing: London, Ontario, Canada
www.firstcirclepublishing.com

ISBN-13: 978-0991976027
ISBN-10: 0991976029

ROMARD: Research on Medieval and Renaissance Drama, vol. 52-53

The Ritual Life of Medieval Europe: Papers By and For C. Clifford Flanigan

Guest Editor	Robert L. A. Clark
Chief Editor	Mario B. Longtin

www.FirstCirclePublishing.com

About ROMARD

Guest Editor vol. 52-53	Robert L. A. Clark Kansas State University, Manhattan, Kansas
Chief Editor	Mario B. Longtin Western University, London, Ontario
Associate Editor	M. J. Toswell Western University, London, Ontario
Copy Editor	Pamela Sheingorn Baruch College and The Graduate Center, CUNY, Emerita
Typesetting and IT	David DeAngelis First Circle Publishing, London, Ontario
Junior Editor	Emily Pickard Western University, London, Ontario

ROMARD wishes to thank Western University for its support through the Scholarly Journals at Western program.

ROMARD (ISSN 0098-647X) is published annually at Western University (London, Ontario). Inquiries concerning publication should be submitted to the Chief Editor at romard@romard.org.

The current annual rate is $25 USD plus shipping for individuals. For all subscription inquiries, including institutional subscriptions and back issue orders, please contact subscriber-inquiries@romard.org. ROMARD may also be purchased online at www.romard.org and on www.amazon.com.

Please visit our website for the latest ROMARD information at www.romard.org.

C. Clifford Flanigan

Contents

	Foreword **Mario B. Longtin, Chief Editor**	1
	Preface **Robert L. A. Clark, Guest Editor**	3
	From Cultic to Cultural Practice: The Human Sciences in the Work of C. Clifford Flanigan **Robert L. A. Clark**	5
	Major Publications and Performances of C. Clifford Flanigan	17
I	In Memoriam C. Clifford Flanigan **Claus Clüver**	23
	Cliffnotes: Performance, Pedagogy, and the Medieval Past **Claire Sponsler**	27
II	*Quid Quaeritis, O Clerici*? A Review of Some Recent Scholarship on the Medieval Latin Music Drama **C. Clifford Flanigan**	35
	Books of Hours and the Construction of Reality in the Fifteenth Century **C. Clifford Flanigan**	61
	Praying the Life of Christ: Late Medieval Devotion in the Light of Ideological Critique **C. Clifford Flanigan**	69

	Private Prayer and the Paschal Cycle: A Low-German *Gebetbuch* in Cultural Perspective **C. Clifford Flanigan**	77
	The Conflict of Ideology in Late Medieval Urban Drama **C. Clifford Flanigan**	85
	Localizing the *Visitatio Sepulchri*: Towards a New Orientation of Medieval Drama Studies **C. Clifford Flanigan**	95
	From Popular Performance Genre to Literary Play and Back Again: The Literary Appropriation of Medieval Vernacular Drama **C. Clifford Flanigan**	103
	Amalarius of Metz and the Ideology of Liturgical Semiotics **C. Clifford Flanigan**	111
	Comparative Literature and the Shifting Paradigms of Literary Study **Claus Clüver and C. Clifford Flanigan**	123
III	Playing by the Book: Performance of Liturgical Drama at Klosterneuburg **Amelia J. Carr and Michael L. Norton**	143
	Framing Medieval Drama: The Franciscans and English Drama **Lawrence M. Clopper†**	153
	Leudast's *Passio* and Sacred Violence in Gregory of Tours **Thomas Goodmann**	163
	Imagining a Medieval Performance: A Phenomenological Approach **Jesse Hurlbut**	179
	The *Miracle of the Pregnant Abbess*: Refractions of the Virgin Birth **Eric T. Metzler**	195
	Athens, Jerusalem, and Fray Luis de León **Ignacio Navarrete**	207

Music, Dramatic Extroversion, and Contemplative Introspection: Hildegard of Bingen's *Ordo Virtutum* **Nils Holger Petersen**	**219**
The Performed Book: Textuality and Social Space in the Cult of Sainte Foy **Kathleen Ashley and Pamela Sheingorn**	**233**
Contributor Biographies	**257**

Foreword
Mario B. Longtin, Chief Editor

I met Robert Clark in Paris in 1999. At that time, I was putting the finishing touches on my PhD thesis, and he was revising the work of his supervisor and friend C. Clifford Flanigan for publication. He and I became good friends, and I was privileged enough to read a few pages of an unpublished article by Clifford Flanigan that Bob was editing. I remember how impressed I was by the sheer enthusiasm and passion that leapt out at me from his writing. I promised myself, and Bob, that I would read more of his thought-provoking work. Almost fourteen years have passed since I discovered Clifford Flanigan's work in Bob's apartment on the *rue Cloche Perse* in Paris. The words of the great man are now ready to work their magic again, and internationally recognized scholars, not to mention first-rate friends, wanted to honor his memory by adding their voice to his. The result is a beautiful equilibrium of humanity and scholarship.

I am thrilled to be publishing this double volume 52-53 devoted to Clifford Flanigan's memory; his influence and importance in the field demanded a volume of ample dimensions.

This volume in honor of Clifford Flanigan assumed several shapes, and adopted many forms and styles through the years, following the seasons. In order to prevent delaying the publication of the present volume, we elected to leave the endnotes in the form they were in when we inherited the manuscript. We limited our interventions to ensuring that the details provided in the endnotes were correct and that the references displayed were clear and traceable. Apart from the endnotes, the volume conforms to our style and practices. Our copyeditor Pam Sheingorn's expertise was instrumental in bringing the manuscript to the high standard expected by our readers. We can't thank her enough for the work she devoted to this volume.

This project would not have been possible without the patient diligence for which our Junior Editor Emily Pickard is known. It would take too long to list all of the technical challenges surmounted by David DeAngelis, our technical specialist. Emily and David played absolutely essential roles in bringing this project to fruition, and I am pleased to recognize their exceptional contribution here.

I would also like to take this opportunity to thank Robert Clark for trusting the ROMARD team with this important volume and for assuming the role of guest editor with such grace. David DeAngelis, Emily Pickard, and I enjoyed working with Bob on this very special project. Each of us has been privileged to contribute to the publication of this volume honoring Clifford Flanigan.

* * *

Just before this volume went to press, we learned of the sad news of the passing of Lawrence M. Clopper. With our deepest sympathy, we offer our condolences to his friends, colleagues, and family.

Preface

Robert L. A. Clark, Guest Editor

The present volume in honor of C. Clifford Flanigan was a long time in the making. The idea of a commemorative volume containing a selection of Cliff's unpublished papers together with articles by his colleagues and former students was conceived soon after his death. In the weeks that followed his death, several people helped to locate and access Cliff's files. Lawrence Clopper, aided by Cliff's son Patrick, gathered materials at Indiana University, including files from Cliff's computer. Cliff's former wife Beverly Flanigan sent a large box of papers as well as the photograph of Cliff that we have used. Finally, Raglind Binkley, the widow of Cliff's collaborator Thomas Binkley at the Early Music Institute at Indiana, shared the recording of the talk that Cliff gave for Binkley's students, part of which I have transcribed in the introduction. This volume would not have been possible without the help of these individuals at what was a very difficult time.

Five sessions of papers, "Ritual, Performance and Culture: In Honor of C. Clifford Flanigan," were organized by Kathleen Ashley, Lawrence Clopper, and Clifford Davidson for the International Congress on Medieval Studies at Kalamazoo in 1995. Revisions of several of those papers are included in this volume, and to these several other articles were later added. An agreement to produce the collection was reached with an editor, but unfortunately that project did not come to fruition. I am deeply grateful to Mario Longtin for agreeing to publish the volume in *ROMARD* despite the fact that the project had lain dormant for a number of years. Longtin and his editorial team, David DeAngelis and Emily Pickard, worked indefatigably at converting and editing the files, some of which were available only in outdated or corrupted versions. Wim Hüsken also helped edit earlier versions of the files. I'm especially grateful to Pamela Sheingorn for her careful proofreading of the entire volume. Despite the passage of time, all of the original contributors agreed to remain in the collection. Their articles appear here with only minor revisions. Their support of this project for a period of almost two decades is eloquent testimony to their devotion to a remarkable scholar and friend.

From Cultic to Cultural Practice: The Human Sciences in the Work of C. Clifford Flanigan
Robert L. A. Clark

> "It seems evident to me that there is no knowledge without prejudice, no interpretation without presupposition."
>
> – C. Clifford Flanigan[1]

The sudden death of Clifford Flanigan on October 27, 1993, came as an enormous shock to his many students, colleagues, and friends. It occurred literally in the middle of a visit to the Indiana University campus by the distinguished historian Peter Brown, who gave two lectures there in the Patten Lecture Series. Professor Flanigan had introduced Brown at his first talk and was, according to one person who was present, at "the top of his form."[2] The day in between Brown's two lectures was devoted to meeting students and going to classes, as is typical of the Patten, and Cliff was accompanying Brown and several students for lunch in the Tudor Room in the Indiana Memorial Union. While they chatted and waited for their table, Cliff was felled by a massive heart attack. He died instantly. Needless to say, this brutal event created shock waves that went out into the Bloomington community and beyond, although the news did not reach some of Cliff's students who were buried in the library working on their dissertations. Thus, they learned of his death from Peter Brown, who had decided to go forward with his second lecture as scheduled and spoke to "the memory of Clifford Flanigan."

The present volume is an effort on the part of some of those whose lives were touched by Cliff to fill the terrible void that was created on that dreadful day "in between." It gathers together eight of Professor Flanigan's unpublished papers, another piece he wrote in collaboration with his colleague Claus Clüver, and seven papers by colleagues and former students. His unpublished conference papers, written between 1988 and 1992 for presentation at the annual meeting of the Modern Language Association, the International Congress on Medieval Studies (Western Michigan University) and the Indiana University Medieval Symposium, show a characteristically vigorous working through of positions and ideas broached in his published work and suggest the direction his scholarship might have taken had he but lived.[3] And yet, it seems somehow appropriate that the final writings of his that we possess should be his conference papers. For in both his scholarly and pedagogical engagements, as Claire Sponsler emphasizes in her eloquent and moving memoir of Professor Flanigan as teacher-scholar, it is the performative dimension that is so strikingly present in his various and varied activities – so much so that the distinction between scholarship and pedagogy is an inadequate one in Cliff's case. As his colleague Sheila Lindenbaum remarked after his death, Cliff "operated within an oral culture,"[4] a culture that embraced the classroom, the discussion group (whether around a table or on line), collaboration with colleagues (including the historical reconstructions of medieval and early modern rituals and dramas in conjunction with Thomas Binkley) and, of course, the scholarly conference. Acutely and uncommonly aware of the institutional contexts and constraints of our professional practice, Cliff never wrote or reflected on any topic without challenging the prejudices and presuppositions – including his own – evoked in my epigraph. In his case, this practice took the form of an impassioned, body-and-soul polemical engagement for which the scholarly conference provided the ideal venue. And while he frankly detested the Modern Language Association convention for its heavy-handed institutionalization and hype of academic "stars," he relished the collegial and liminal atmosphere of the International Congress on Medieval Studies at Kalamazoo and the intimacy of the Indiana University Medieval Symposium, which he was instrumental in establishing.

Clifford Flanigan was a comparatist, both by virtue of his academic position and by disposition. His earliest articles, "The Roman Rite and the Origins of the Liturgical Drama" and "The Liturgical Context of the *Quem Quaeritis* Trope," both published in 1974, are characterized by a comparatist perspective and also by an emphasis on context, as indicated by the title of the latter piece.[5] In his prize-winning article on the Roman rite, it is the comparative study of religion, as exemplified by the work of Mircea Eliade, brought into conjunction with the broad context of Western church history and the more specialized history of the liturgy, which provides the theoretical framework for his investigation. The literary historical approach that had dominated the field, though not entirely eschewed, is considerably deemphasized. Ultimately, of course, he would come to reject the literary approach altogether as one which, along with historicism, had in his view done the most to hinder the proper understanding of the significance of ritual and drama in the lives of medieval subjects.[6] Rather, it was "the liturgical life of medieval Europe," a phrase twice used in the introductory paragraphs of his first article on the Roman rite, that was and would remain the central issue in his work, that is, what was the cultural and ideological role of the drama and rituals of the Middle Ages for the communities that invested themselves in these practices?

In later years, Cliff was somewhat sheepish about having written an article about the "origins" of liturgical drama. As an indication of the ground that he would traverse in the fifteen years after the appearance of his groundbreaking article, a polemical intervention that he made on an electronic discussion list, probably ANSAX-L, in 1990 or 1991, is especially telling:

> Even if we knew the "origin" (whatever that is) of the "drama" (whatever that is), what would we know? Why would we care? What would it tell us that makes any difference? Nothing, I think. A Platonist, with his belief that "as it was in the beginning, is now and ever shall be," might of course think differently. These remarks come from someone who published an essay 15 years ago on "The Roman Rite and the Origins of the Liturgical." I might add that I not only have come to think that questions of origins are useless (and worse, ideologically insidious) but that the notion of "liturgical drama" is wholly a construction of nineteenth-century scholarship that really needs to be abandoned since it is neither descriptive of a medieval phenomenon nor a useful concept that speaks to our hermeneutical situation at the end of the twentieth century.

But Cliff had more than one "take" on the search for origins in his work and in that of others. In a somewhat less polemical piece of writing, his anniversary appraisal of "Karl Young and the Drama of the Medieval Church," published in RORD in 1984, he shifted the search for "origins" to the search for the cultural milieu that gave rise to the liturgical music-drama. In reference to the work of the art historian Carol Heitz, he wrote:

> Here the quest for origins has shifted from a specific text or practice and a definite moment to an intellectual and socio-cultural milieu …. My own earlier study similarly sought the origin of the drama in the cultic climate which prevailed in northern Europe after the replacement of the Gallican rite by the Roman rite.

We have thus arrived at the second phase of Professor Flanigan's scholarship in which the approach, still contextual, sought to place liturgical and dramatic practices in specific local, social, and cultural settings. A watershed moment in this second phase came on May 7, 1982, when he read a paper at Kalamazoo with the deceptively innocent-sounding title: "The Medieval English Mystery Cycles and the Liturgy." In Kathleen Ashley's words, in this paper Cliff "attempted to use ritual theory and anthropological relativizing to discuss the sacred medieval drama."[7] This approach was inspired in part by his reading of the social historian Charles Phythian-Adams, particularly the piece on "Ceremony and the Citizen: The Communal Year at Coventry."[8] Cliff's paper has, unfortunately, not been found, but he returned to Phythian-Adams's work in his review of scholarship, an exercise in which he excelled, in "Comparative Literature and the Study of Medieval Drama," published four years after his Kalamazoo paper. There, he writes:

> Studies of local history like Phythian-Adams's make clear that removing a play from its context and separating it from all of the other ceremonies, games and dramatic activities of which it was the climax and which […]

it surely included within itself, will lead to a seriously distorted view of medieval urban culture and of the function of the plays within that culture.[9]

These would appear to be reasonable assertions, but they were not received as such, to put it mildly, by some who heard his paper. Indeed, there was a hysterical outburst from those who, quite correctly, sensed that the paradigms were shifting beneath their feet. I was present on this occasion and recall that Cliff seemed genuinely delighted by the response his provocative paper received, and rightly so, for he had succeeded in engaging his colleagues in a debate on the usually unarticulated assumptions underwriting the historicist and literary approaches to the study of medieval theater.

Professor Flanigan's long engagement with cultural anthropology, first mentioned in his 1974 article on the *Quem Quaeritis* trope, doubtless culminated in his critique of Victor Turner's concept of liminality and Bakhtin's theory of the carnivalesque, which appeared in 1990 in Kathleen Ashley's collection, *Victor Turner and the Construction of Cultural Criticism*. His enthusiasm for the work of Turner and Geertz is well attested to in his publications but, as important as the work of these anthropologists was for his own work, it was perhaps Phythian-Adams's example, combined with reception theory, that was most crucial. Cliff's synthesis of these two approaches was typically brilliant in its simplicity: to the emphasis on the local context, he added the localization of specific human communities and human subjects, each of whom brought to a dramatic or ritual performance their own horizon of expectations. This is the perspective he brought to the Fleury playbook in his 1984 essay on that manuscript. It is also the perspective in his 1988 Kalamazoo paper published here and from which I take my epigraph, "Localizing the *Visitatio Sepulchri:* Towards a New Orientation of Medieval Drama Studies." The notion of context is all important in this paper and works on several levels: the codicological context of the *Visitatio* in the *Regularis Concordia*; the monastic context of the "scripts for living" contained in that customary; the problematic position of the *Visitatio* within the context of medieval drama studies; the potential of the latter, not yet realized, to occupy a more vital position within the context of the human sciences. It is a marvelous piece of writing which bears quoting here:

> Clearly, then, in the *Regularis Concordia*, the *Visitatio Sepulchri* is one of innumerable practices to be imitated in order to cultivate and reinforce the roles which the customary assigns to those who would play a part in its own version of the drama of the monastic life. It is not motivated by a desire to create or put on a play, or by a desire to teach religious truths …. Seen in the context of that document, the *Visitatio Sepulchri* has nothing to do with the beginnings of modern drama, and one could only think otherwise by arbitrarily removing it from that context. That, of course, is exactly what every editor and every interpreter concerned with the text has done.

Cliff returned in the final phase of his work to the texts and issues with which he had begun, although he also developed in a series of papers, published here, an interest in private prayer to which he brought the perspective he had honed in his study of the drama. Other papers and articles followed, on liturgical processions, on the "monastic family," on Amalarius of Metz, and what was to be his final article, "The Biblical Apocalypse and the Medieval Liturgy," first given as a lecture at the Indiana University Institute of Religious Studies and published in the 1992 volume edited by Richard Emmerson and Bernard McGinn, *The Apocalypse in the Middle Ages*. As mentioned above, some of the papers published in this volume were given at the Indiana Medieval Symposium, of which he was truly the founding father. At the first symposium in 1988, Cliff delivered the paper, "The Conflict of Ideology in Late Medieval Urban Drama." In this tightly argued and typically polemical piece, Cliff expressed with perhaps unparalleled concision his credo to the effect that historicist and new critical practices had to be abandoned in favor of vigorous ideological critique, and, to make his point, he offered as an example a new critical reading of the *Second Shepherd's Play* by a drearily earnest New Critic. In her contribution to this volume, Claire Sponsler recalls this memorable moment:

> At one point in his paper he was lambasting some critic for doing an old-fashioned and naive reading of a medieval text. You could feel the tension rising in the room as people listened. Then, Cliff revealed that the critic he was attacking was an earlier incarnation of himself. And the room dissolved into laughter and relief. I thought it was an interesting moment on many levels: testimony to Cliff's masterful oratorical skills and ability to manipulate an audience …. It also said something about his ironic self-awareness – an ability to see himself in a historical context.

These are rare qualities indeed, and they will ensure that future generations of scholars will return to the work of Clifford Flanigan, precisely because of the way he challenged the ways we think, and do not think, about what it is that we do as scholars.

An equally significant aspect of Professor Flanigan's contributions as a teacher-scholar was his collaboration with Professor Thomas Binkley of the Early Music Institute at the Indiana University School of Music. It is clear that Cliff viewed his work in these nine productions, created in a burst of creativity in a little over three years' time and in which he played a variety of roles (scriptwriter, dramaturge, ritual director, director, and performer), as an integral part of his scholarship as listed on his *curriculum vitae* right after his published work.[10] Part of his role, as he saw it, was to instill in the student-performers something of the excitement he himself felt to represent and *render present* these dramas and rituals for a contemporary audience, to make them live again as they had for the medieval communities for and by which they had been created. To this end, in 1982 he spoke at length to the student-performers who were to undertake the formidable task of staging *The Greater Passion Play* from the *Carmina Burana* Manuscript, the first of his collaborations with Thomas Binkley. Fortunately, at least part of his remarks was recorded, of which I can provide here only a few excerpts.[11]

> Let me say before I begin, however, that you're at a beginning, and a beginning in which I am only indirectly involved but about which I'm exceedingly excited. In fact, I've been associated with the study of medieval drama for close to fifteen years now, and I can't think of any time when I've been as excited as I am about what you're going to be doing... [Flanigan proceeds to use the words "exciting" and, for the third time, "excited" in his opening remarks.]

There follows extensive commentary on the text and the manuscript, including: the manuscript's pagination after its rebinding in the sixteenth century and the "miraculous" rediscovery of seven missing leaves at the turn of the century (with reference to Binkley's facsimile on display in front of the participants); general remarks about medieval music; a brief discussion of the origin of the terms "medieval" and "Middle Ages," with cautionary remarks about having "a kind of condescending or simplistic notion about this period .... [W]e want to remember that every age has its own complexities." He then moves on to the Latin music-drama, but not without evoking the problematic question of continuity between medieval and modern drama, with reference to the *Quem Quaeritis* trope; the equally problematic question of continuity between classical and medieval drama; whether or not Seneca's plays were ever "performed in the way that we think of a performance of a play"; oral reading as practiced in Late Antiquity; Hroswitha's dramas; and, finally, twelfth-century music-drama! Here, I quote his remarks at greater length so that readers may better hear his unique voice using somewhat less academic language to convey his phenomenal erudition and sophisticated theories about ritual to a group of primarily undergraduate music student-performers:

> Now, I'd like you to think with me a minute about rituals, about what happens in a ritual or in a piece of liturgy. [Here, he briefly evokes the work of Mircea Eliade.] Now what happens in a ritual? And what is a ritual supposed to do? These are questions we really need to give some consideration to. Well, a ritual is inherently mimetic. There is certainly a dimension of acting and of imitation that is present in a ritual. If we take just, say, perhaps the most common ritual of Christianity, the Eucharistic action, there is at the high moments of that action a very clear-cut sense of imitation. [Here, he summarizes the actions of the traditional mass.] So there is something mimetic about that ritual and about lots of other rituals as well. Now we might think that that mimesis, or that imitation, has its function to teach somebody something. But, while rituals do in fact teach people things, for most of the Middle Ages, the emphasis on this kind of imitation in ritual actions and words is not didactic; it's not to teach something, because in medieval Christianity, and indeed in religions around the world, rituals are efficacious. They are believed to do something. They're not mere words or mere teachings. Rituals effect that action which they imitate. They make it happen again, and hence, when the celebrant breaks the bread and blesses the wine, and the congregation eats and drinks, they are, on the one hand, doing what happened on the

night of the Last Supper, but doing it in such a way that they believe that it's not a mere imitation that's taking place but that their actions are joined to the actions of the first participants. There's a sense in which every celebration of the Eucharist, then, makes that first Eucharist happen again, makes it happen in our midst. We become partakers in that action. [Here, he summarizes the early Christian teaching about baptism with reference to Paul's *Letter to the Romans*.] The point I only want to make here is that rituals are efficacious imitations. They are believed by the community to effect that which they imitate. The community that performs the ritual believes that ritual – and here I speak again not only of Christian rituals but of rituals in general – has the power to effect a transformation of time and space. When I do the action – there are several ways to say this but to make it simple – when I do the action, I am brought in such connection with the archetypal action that I'm imitating that I am now in – this place has become, without ceasing to be the place that it is – it has also become the upper room in Jerusalem. So we live in a time, a ritual time, which is our time but at the same time there's another time that's present.

To drive home his point that rituals are not didactic, mimetic exercises, Flanigan now gives an extended reading analysis of the *Regularis Concordia* including, of course, the *Quem Quaeritis* trope, then continues:

Let's think about what's happening here. Here come the three monks [sound of Flanigan's feet pacing], down some aisle, someplace in the church, not necessarily… in fact, emphatically not the main altar. And they come upon another monk – there's not much realism here – these three monks are associated with the women who, the text tells us, visited Jesus' tomb early on Easter morning. They're doing it just about the time that the women visited Jesus' tomb, but of course they're not women, they're monks. They have no realistic costumes, although there's perhaps a gesture in that direction. They walk around, they're looking for something, they encounter a character who says: "Whom are you seeking?" And the Biblical account is more or less played out. Well we have here all the characteristics of a ritual. Not a play, again, to put on a play, it's not a play to instruct. These are actions here which seek to make it happen again, to make it happen in our midst, in order that we, who live in the tenth century, can be connected to those great archetypal acts of salvation that took place in the first century. You see – and we'll come back to this when we talk about the Benediktbeuren play in just a moment – one of the persistent questions that arises in the Christian tradition, to which a number of very different answers have been given, is: here are the events in the first century that somehow are considered saving events, and here I am in the tenth. Well, what's my connection here with those events back there? And the primary answer in the early Middle Ages is a ritual one. By doing what they did, I can make those actions present here. I can connect myself to them. They can be my actions, and I can receive the salvation once proper to the women, or to the disciples, or whoever we're talking about. And that's made clear, I think, in the final rubric of this text we've just been talking about, because the last line is: "The Lord is risen from the sepulcher, who hung for us on the Cross." And then the last rubric says: "When this antiphon is finished, let the prior, rejoicing with them at the triumph of our king, in that he rose having conquered death, begin the hymn *Te deum laudamus*." And here it's very clear. *Te deum laudamus* is sung of course – it's the way Matins ends every Sunday. So we always expect to end that way, but at the same time we sing this text, *Te deum laudamus*, because we've heard the announcement of the Resurrection. We've heard it and it's happened in our midst, and we respond.

Shortly after this point, before Cliff managed to circle back to the Benediktbeuren play as he had promised, the recording stops. One can only imagine how the student-performers may have integrated this staggering amount of information, how *their* performance may have been shaped by *his*. However, those who were fortunate enough to see the production in Bloomington during Holy Week, as was I, doubtless recall the tour de force performance provided by the student-performers, especially the long Marian lament at the foot of the cross.[12] Fortunately, several of the Binkley-Flanigan reconstructions were recorded and have now been reissued on CD by the Musical Heritage Society.[13]

Cliff's last published article but one was his essay on "Medieval Latin Music-Drama," which appeared in 1993 in Eckehard Simon's volume, *The Theatre of Medieval Europe*. As it appears in the Simon volume, it is but a truncated version of what is perhaps his most sustained piece of polemical writing on the scholarly tradition and practice in his major field of interest. In the original version, printed here, it bears a somewhat different title, part of which disappeared in the printed version. The original included a question, one that Cliff asked over and over again of his predecessors, of his colleagues, of his students, and of himself: "*Quid Quaeritis, O Clerici?*" If one may say that this questioning of our questioning is Cliff's legacy to us, it is no mean gift.

* * *

An important part of Clifford Flanigan's legacy is the community of scholars who were profoundly impacted by his teaching and his scholarship, and the scholars who have contributed to this volume are a small but representative sample of this community. Their essays cover a broad range of topics but all, in their way, pay homage to the remarkable teacher-scholar who was Clifford Flanigan.

Claire Sponsler, one of his doctoral students at Indiana University, evokes in her piece, "Cliffnotes: Performance, Pedagogy, and the Medieval Past," Cliff's powerful presence, both in the classroom and at the podium, his superb oratorical skills, and his ability to not just describe rituals such as the *Visitatio Sepulchri* but to transform a classroom of students into participants in the rite. Claus Clüver, Cliff's colleague in the Department of Comparative Literature at Indiana, opens the volume with his "In Memoriam" and also provides the bridge to the essays by the other contributors as co-author of a piece written in collaboration with Cliff, "Comparative Literature and the Shifting Paradigms of Literary Study," originally conceived as the introduction to a new handbook intended to replace Newton P. Stallknecht and Horst Frenz's *Comparative Literature: Method and Perspective*. Clüver and Flanigan's piece is provocative and indeed polemical in its call for a complete rethinking of the discipline that would require it to set aside such notions as national canons and even the construct of literature itself in favor of a meaningful engagement with literary and reception theory, popular culture, imagology, and interliterary and interarts relations, among other types of discourse. It is still a bracing manifesto more than twenty years after it was written, and it certainly is to be regretted that this volume with its revolutionizing approach to the field did not see completion.

It should perhaps not come as a surprise that the articles by the other contributors to the volume espouse, each in its own way, the broad, interdiscursive approach set forth by Clüver and Flanigan. In "Playing by the Book: Performance of Liturgical Drama at Klosterneuburg," Amelia Carr and Michael Norton study the latest version from Klosterneuburg of the *Visitatio Sepulchri*, the office to which Clifford Flanigan, like other scholars of Latin music-drama, returned time and again. They embed this late version of the *Visitatio* in a rich and multilayered context, paying special care to the many liturgical books that the execution of the office would have necessitated. Their careful reading is all the more compelling for the fact that the scribe, Oswald Ostner, copied the manuscript as a form of penance while in prison. Carr and Norton bring out the tensions that Clifford Flanigan and others have noted in the *Visitatio*, occupying as it does a kind of middle ground, "at once spectacle and communal enactment" and, in the case of Ostner's copy, reflecting a personal *parti pris* for the pre-Tridentine office he had known as a youth.

In "Framing Medieval Drama: The Franciscans and English Drama," Lawrence Clopper, Cliff's colleague at Indiana, argues that the affective piety of the Franciscans frames medieval English biblical drama, despite the often-cited prohibitions of clerical participation in lay dramatic performances. Observing parallels with the Pseudo-Bonaventuran *Meditations on the Life of Christ* and Franciscan iconography, he writes that the Franciscans are both absent from and present in the English cycle plays, with the clearest indication of Franciscan influence occurring in the *N-Town* plays. There, unlike in the northern cycles, Christ explicitly chooses poverty and refuses all riches, as in the "Marriage of Joseph and Mary," and, in the "Woman Taken in Adultery," is constructed as mendicant preacher. Clopper allows that these are fleeting indications but suggests that the Franciscans were nonetheless the "writers behind the writers" who produced the *N-Town* plays.

Thomas Goodmann's article, "Leudast's *Passio* and Sacred Violence in Gregory of Tours," analyzes an episode from Gregory of Tours' *History of the Franks*, a text he first read in one of Cliff's classes. Goodmann asks why the career of a relatively minor figure should receive such expansive attention from Gregory, what "kind of work" his account performs in the *Historiae francorum*. Examining prior scholars' treatments of the episode and drawing on René Girard's concept of desire, Goodmann reads the

Leudast episode as a series of crises or anxieties that undergird both Gregory's text and the social and cultural situation of the Franks that he relates. He concludes that Leudast's violent demise "resolves the problem of its anti-social subject who poses a threat to social differences," even as it empowers the author as the "instrument of social order in the *History of the Franks*." Ultimately, Leudast "is terribly useful to the Bishop's effort to make sense out of his world."

In "Imagining a Medieval Performance: A Phenomenological Approach," Jesse Hurlbut reconstructs from archival records the ceremonial entry of Charles, Count of Charolais, into Dijon in October 1461. His account of this medieval "performance" painstakingly pieces together the myriad details of the expense accounts for this event, which he includes as an appendix to his article. Drawing on the semiotics of theater as developed by Marvin Carlson and others, Hurlbut also has recourse to Wolfgang Iser's concept of reading as aesthetic response in his shaping of both details and lacunae into a coherent "reading" of the performance. While stressing that his reconstruction is fragmentary, Hurbut notes that "the discovery of each new dramatic element in the terse language of the accountant increases our overall understanding of the event," an event which he has doubly restored to us in his edition of the archives and in his "reading" of them.

Like Thomas Goodmann, Eric Metzler first read the text on which he writes in one of Cliff's classes. In "The *Miracle of the Pregnant Abbess*: Refractions of the Virgin Birth," Metzler analyzes the version of this popular legend that was performed as a processional play in Lille. Comparing the Lille version with its source, the *Speculum Historiale* of Vincent de Beauvais, he notes that the play adds important details about the birth of the abbess's child. Like the Virgin Mary, she gives birth painlessly but, unlike Mary, her virginity is miraculously restored. Metzler argues that the play, although it forces the analogy with Mary, also emphasizes the fallen state of the abbess and, by extension, of all women except Mary, concluding that the play "redeems women but reminds us once again that women are essentially fallen creatures through their sexuality and can only be holy by denying their sex."

In writing his article, "Athens, Jerusalem and Fray Luy de León," Ignacio Navarrete also returned to texts that he read with Cliff Flanigan, applying the principles of interpretation expounded in works by Bultmann, Curtius, and Auerbach to the commentary on the Song of Songs by Luis de León. Navarette characterizes Fray Luis's commentary as an attempt to "recover the literal, Hebrew meaning of the Song of Songs, through a philological, rhetorical, and performance-oriented analysis." It is the last of these three that Navarrete focuses on with regard to Fray Luis's difficulties in explaining some of the metaphors in the Song of Songs that seem like "breaches in decorum." Ultimately, however, it is metaphorization, at first a hindrance to interpretation, which "makes it possible for readers to appropriate and talk about the literature of another time and culture."

With Nils Holger Petersen's piece, "Music, Dramatic Extroversion, and Contemplative Introspection: Hildegard of Bingen's *Ordo Virtutum*," we return to the interpretation of Latin music-drama. Although this play has long been read by scholars as a kind of morality play, perhaps intended for the edification of the nuns who were in Hildegard's care, Petersen argues that it is more promising to read the *Ordo Virtutum* in its liturgical context without, however, ignoring its dramatic possibilities, however problematic or anachronistic its status as "drama" may be. In his interpretation, Petersen analyzes the unusual structure of the *Ordo Virtutum* and its two mutually-reinforcing modes of liturgical action, celebration and narration, in order to understand its meaning for the "assembly of the congregation, *hic et nunc*." Thus, for the nuns, "the play would have been experienced – and no doubt meant – as a play, a ritual about themselves as well as the whole world, a play about the meaning of the conventual life of Hildegard's virgins," even while it offered to the laity the possibility to "share (earlier) pious ideals which had been the prerogative of monks and clerics."

The final essay in the volume, "The Performed Book: Textuality and Social Space in the Cult of Sainte Foy," by Kathleen Ashley and Pamela Sheingorn, seeks to contextualize the representation of books and other forms of writing at the monastery at Conques, the heart of Sainte Foy's cult. They argue that the community at Conques was a textual community, most notably founded on the *Liber miraculorum*, begun by Bernard of Angers and completed by anonymous monks. The centrality of books in the hagiographic construction of Foy and also in the liturgy that celebrated her cult is reflected and reinforced by the images of reading and writing that appear in the fabric of the church: the scrolls and open books held by the angels and apostles at the crossing; and the writing on the tympanum of the Last Judgment. These representations encouraged the monks, local laypeople and pilgrims to feel a connection to the cult by embedding them in a rich "visual and textual matrix of meanings." Combined with the performed books of Foy's cult, the images worked to create and sustain the broad and varied community that evolved around the saint.

Notes

1. "Localizing the *Visitatio Sepulchri*: Towards a New Orientation of Medieval Drama Studies," p. 92 in this volume.
2. The text of Flanigan's remarks has not been found in his papers. It is entirely possible they were delivered extemporaneously, as he was a brilliant public speaker.
3. Among the works in progress listed on his *curriculum vitae* were collaborative projects with Gabor Klaniczay (*Saint Margaret of Hungary: The Vita by Marcellus and Selections from the Investigations into Her Sanctity*) and Thomas Binkley (*The Greater Passion Play in the Carmina Burana: An Edition, Translation, Transcription, and Commentary*); a translation with commentary of the Frankfort Passion Play; and a guide to issues and resources for Medieval Latin Music Drama.
4. Personal communication.
5. For complete citations of Professor Flanigan's work, see the list of works cited, "Major Publications and Performances of C. Clifford Flanigan," in this volume.
6. See in particular "*Quid Quaeritis, O Clerici*? A Review of Some Recent Scholarship on the Medieval Latin Music Drama," pp. 31-56 in this volume. As he would emphasize again and again, the "discursive practice which we call 'literature'"[6] was decidedly a non-medieval practice ("Localizing," p. 92).
7. Personal communication.

8. Phythian-Adams, Charles, "Ceremony and the Citizen: The Communal Year at Coventry, 1450-1550," in *Crisis and Order in English Towns, 1500-1700*, Peter Clark and Paul Slack [eds.], (Toronto: University of Toronto Press, 1972), 57-85.

9. See "Comparative Literature and the Study of Medieval Drama." *Yearbook of Comparative and General Literature* 35 (1986): 56-104, quoted here at pp. 92-93.

10. See list of works cited.

11. I wish to thank Thomas Binkley's widow Raglind Binkley for providing me with a recording on audio-cassette of Flanigan's remarks. Unfortunately, only one side of the cassette was used. In private correspondence, Ms. Binkley wrote that Tom had probably turned the cassette over but forgotten to press the record button again!

12. Surprisingly, the four performances that followed at the Cloisters Museum in New York City stirred controversy in the Jewish community of New York on account of "anti-Semitic" aspects of the play. For a balanced account of the controversy, including Thomas Binkley's response, see the article, "Passion Play Text Stirs Controversy," by Harold C. Schonberg, long-time music critic of the *New York Times*, which appeared in that publication on July 20, 1982: http://www.nytimes.com/1982/07/20/theater/passion-play-text-stirs-controversy.html.

13. See list of works cited.

Major Publications and Performances of C. Clifford Flanigan

Publications

"The Roman Rite and the Origins of the Liturgical Drama." *University of Toronto Quarterly: A Canadian Journal of the Humanities* 43 (1974): 263-84.

"The Liturgical Context of the *Quem Quaeritis* Trope." *Comparative Drama* 8 (1974): 45-62. Reprinted in *Studies in Medieval Drama Presented to William L. Smoldon on His Eighty-Second Birthday*. Edited by Clifford Davidson. Kalamazoo: Western Michigan University, 1974, 45-62.

"Biblical Angels and English Shepherds: The Gospel Tradition in the Second Shepherds' Play." In *Biblical Images in Literature*. Edited by Roland Bartel et al. Nashville: Abingdon, 1975, 297-307.

"The Liturgical Drama and Its Tradition: A Review of Scholarship 1965-1975, Part I." *Research Opportunities in Renaissance Drama – Medieval Supplement* 18 (1975): 81-102.

"The Liturgical Drama and Its Tradition: A Review of Scholarship 1965-1975, Part II." *Research Opportunities in Renaissance Drama – Medieval Supplement* 19 (1976): 109-36.

"The Fleury Playbook and the Traditions of Medieval Latin Drama." *Comparative Drama* 18 (1984): 588-602. Reprinted in *The Fleury Playbook: Essays and Studies*. Edited by Thomas P. Campbell and Clifford Davidson. Kalamazoo: Medieval Institute Publications, 1985, 1-25.

"Karl Young and the Drama of the Medieval Church." *Research Opportunities in Renaissance Drama* 27 (1984): 157-66.

"Comparative Literature and the Study of Medieval Drama." *Yearbook of Comparative and General Literature* 35 (1986): 56-104.

"Teaching the Medieval Latin 'Drama': Reflections Historical and Theoretical." In *Approaches to Teaching Medieval Drama*. Edited by Richard K. Emmerson. New York: Modern Language Association of America, 1990, 50-56.

"Liminality, Carnival, and Social Structure: The Case of Late Medieval Biblical Drama." In *Victor Turner and the Construction Criticism*. Edited by Kathleen M. Ashley. Bloomington: Indiana University Press, 1990, 42-63.

"Medieval Latin Music-Drama." In *The Theatre of Medieval Europe: New Research in Early Drama*. Edited by Eckehard Simon. Cambridge: Cambridge University Press, 1991, pp. 21-41.

"The Biblical Apocalypse and the Medieval Liturgy." In *The Apocalypse in the Middle Ages*. Edited by Bernard McGinn and Richard K. Emmerson. Ithaca: Cornell University Press, 1992, 231-52.

"Medieval Liturgy and the Arts: *Visitatio Sepulchri* as Paradigm," in *Liturgy and the Arts in the Middle Ages. Studies in Honour of C. Clifford Flanigan*. Edited by Eva Louise Lillie and Nils Holger Petersen. Copenhagen: Museum Tusculanum Press, 1996, 9-35.

"Liturgy As Social Performance: Expanding the Definitions" (with Kathleen Ashley and Pamela Sheingorn). In *The Liturgy of the Medieval Church*. Edited by Thomas J. Heffernan and E. Ann Matter. Kalamazoo: Medieval Institute, 2005, 635-52.

Radio

The Story of Abelard and Heloise. Written with Thomas Binkley, commissioned by the Swedish Broadcast Service and twice broadcast in 1984.

Stage

Historical Reconstructions of Medieval and Renaissance Rituals and Dramas, in conjunction with Thomas Binkley, School of Music, Indiana University. For all of the performances listed below, Clifford Flanigan prepared the performance script and served as dramaturge and, as noted below, in additional capacities.

The Greater Passion Play from the *Carmina Burana* Manuscript. Bloomington and New York City, March 1982; repeated in Bloomington, March 1983.[1]

"A Mass from Notre Dame de Paris in the Twelfth Century." Ritual Director and Cast Member. International Congress on Medieval Studies, May 1982, Kalamazoo, and Bloomington, 1982.[2]

The Play of the Ascension of Jesus from the Chester Cycle of Mystery Plays. Bloomington and International Medieval Drama Festival, Toronto, May 1983.

"A Baroque Mass from Seventeenth-Century Bavaria." Director. Bloomington and American Musicological Society, Louisville, October 1983.

"Sunday Vespers from the Eton Choir Book." Bloomington and Indianapolis, February 1984.[3]

The Plays of the Annunciation and Visitation of the Virgin Mary from the Wakefield Cycle of Mystery Plays. Bloomington and International Medieval Drama Festival, Toronto, May 1985.

"A Bach *Gottesdienst*." Director. Bloomington, October 1985.

"A French Candlemas of the Fifteenth Century." Ritual Director and Cast Member. Bloomington and Indianapolis, 1986.

"Four Plays of Saint Nicholas from the *Fleury Playbook*." Bloomington and International Medieval Congress, Kalamazoo, May 1986.

Notes

1. A recording of this performance was published by the Musical Heritage Society, New York City; by Focus Records, Indiana University Press; and, in Europe, by Harmonia Mundi Records.
2. A recording of this performance was published by the Musical Heritage Society, New York City; by Focus Records, Indiana University Press; and, in Europe, by Harmonia Mundi Records.
3. A recording of this performance was published by Focus Records.

Part I

In Memoriam C. Clifford Flanigan
2 August 1941 – 27 October 1993[1]
Claus Clüver

Clifford Flanigan died suddenly on 27 October 1993 at the age of 52. An Associate Professor in Comparative Literature at Indiana University, he probably left his strongest impact on certain areas of Medieval Studies; but his stimulating work reached far beyond. He was a genuine scholar-teacher, and most who came in touch with him inevitably became his students. When they heard about his death quite a few friends sent messages, many of them containing superlatives; it could not be otherwise. I shall use only one: Cliff was my best friend.

The most difficult word in this statement is the word "was." The afternoon before his death, I had a lengthy conversation with him. It was about the immediate past, and very much about the future. It brought to mind the scene of his return from his stay in Denmark as a Fulbright lecturer, when my wife and I met him at the Indianapolis airport, dressed in a European suit, uncommonly elegant, tired and yet buoyant with enthusiasm about what he had been able to accomplish, the recognition he had received, the work he was planning to do. That scene significantly marks the one end of my memories of Cliff. The other goes back to the Flanigans' first Christmas in Bloomington, which they spent at our house with Patrick the toddler, delighted by real candles in the Christmas tree. Driving out of town to cut a Christmas tree for each family is among my first memories of Cliff.

For details of his life before he got to Bloomington I have turned to Beverly Flanigan. This is largely her account:

> *Charles Clifford Flanigan was born August 2, 1941, in the heart of Baltimore, Maryland, the only child of Charles and Anna Flanigan, whose forebears had come to America from Germany and Ireland in the middle of the last century. He attended an accelerated middle school and City College, a public but selective high school, graduating at sixteen. As a boy he loved to play "high church" with his closest friend, Charles McClean (now an Episcopal priest); so it seemed natural that they both go to a pre-theological junior*

college (in Bronxville, New York), then to Concordia Senior College in Fort Wayne, Indiana, and finally to Concordia Theological Seminary in St. Louis, Missouri, where Cliff got a Master of Divinity degree in 1967.

In his last years at seminary he was becoming disillusioned with matters of theology and dogma, but he loved to study Latin, Greek, and Hebrew, church history, and liturgy. In fact, the "saving grace" of the seminary years were the baroque organ concerts and the then-new liturgical revival in the Lutheran church. He enjoyed ritual and ceremony and eagerly celebrated religious holidays: Easter and Passover, Christmas and Hanukkah, Our Lady's Day and Twelfth Night, as well as all the saints' days he knew of: St. John's, St. Stephen's, St. Patrick's, St. Michael and All Angels, St. Bridget's, St. Nicholas', St. Lucia's, St. Joseph's, St. Benedict's, St. Sulpicius'…

He had begun to take graduate courses in Comparative Literature and medieval languages at nearby Washington University while still in seminary, and finally he decided to forgo ordination and pursue doctoral studies full time, studying under Liselotte Dieckmann, Herbert Lindenberger, and William Matheson, among others. His dissertation, on the origins of medieval Latin drama in church ritual, was completed in 1973; meanwhile he had accepted a teaching position in the Comparative Literature Program at Indiana University.

Cliff came to Indiana with a large collection of records, a fascination with archetypal criticism and Northrop Frye, and an enthusiasm for teaching. His theoretical orientations changed, but not his engagement with theory. And he was always surrounded by students, even though some of us were faculty members at our respective institutions. He was an enthusiastic and inspiring teacher, using his courses to work out many of the ideas which he then presented at conferences and in publications. In 1987 he was awarded the Frederick Lieberman Award for Distinguished Teaching. In 1994, a number of his former students, now academics elsewhere, returned to Bloomington to participate in a symposium held in his honor – a sign of the profound loyalties he used to create. Another symposium in his memory was held by former colleagues at the 30th International Congress on Medieval Studies at Kalamazoo, May 1995. I remember vividly the glee with which he reported the discussions following his presentations at Kalamazoo and elsewhere, presentations where his applications of recent critical theory to matters medieval apparently caused some consternation but helped to change the discipline.

Cliff's love was liturgy, but he promoted the study of early monastic culture in all of its variety and vigor. What made his work important and innovative was his insistence on approaching medieval studies in the light of recent critical theory and in a truly transdisciplinary perspective. And while displaying rigorous scholarship in his writing and teaching, he was also deeply involved in restoring life to medieval texts in performance, notably in collaboration with Thomas Binkley, director of the Early Music Institute. Perhaps the most spectacular of these productions was their restoration of *The Greater Passion Play* from the *Carmina Burana* manuscript, presented not only in Bloomington but also in New York. Others – there were nine altogether – were taken to the annual International Congress on Medieval Studies at Kalamazoo or to festivals at Toronto.

His first publication, "The Roman Rite and the Origins of the Liturgical Drama," won him the Elliott Prize of the Medieval Academy of America in 1976. In the last few years before his death he published articles in three distinguished collections of essays: "Liminality, Carnival, and Social Structure: The Case of Late Medieval Biblical Drama," in *Victor Turner and the Construction of Cultural Criticism*, edited by Kathleen Ashley; "Medieval Latin Music Drama," in *The Theatre of Medieval Europe*, edited by Eckehard Simon; and "The Biblical Apocalypse and the Medieval Liturgy," in *The Apocalypse in the Middle Ages*, edited by Bernard McGinn and Richard Emmerson. Earlier publications of particular importance were "The Fleury Playbook and the Traditions of Medieval Latin Drama and Modern Scholarship" in *The Fleury Playbook: Essays and Studies*, edited by Thomas Campbell and Clifford Davidson, and his extensive and provocative "Forschungsbericht" on "Comparative Literature and the Study of Medieval Drama" published in 1986 in the *Yearbook of Comparative and General Literature*.

His scholarly work brought him honors and opportunities, such as an NEH Fellowship that allowed him to spend a year in Cambridge, Massachusetts. What he himself felt to be the greatest opportunity in his career turned out to be its conclusion: the invitation to serve as the Senior Fulbright Lecturer at the Institute for Church History of the University of Copenhagen in the spring semester of 1993, which involved giving lectures in several countries. He returned with plans for collaborative projects with old and new Scandinavian colleagues and friends, and the messages received from there indicate that his brief stay provided an uncommon stimulus.

It is not possible even to touch on the many and varied areas in which Cliff was engaged and where he made a (frequently profound) impact. I should mention his involvement with the Biblical Studies Institute, the Honors Division, the Medieval Studies Institute, and the Medieval Studies Reading Circle, which he founded. He became fascinated with computers and served the department and the university well with his newly developed specialty; several of us, his colleagues, were early introduced to FinalWord, the program he then swore by. For the "Bibliography on the Relations of Literature and Other Arts" published annually in the *Yearbook of Comparative and General Literature* he created a complicated and comprehensive special database, the secret keys of which he took with him. In recent years he channeled his drive for restoration and renovation to the house he had bought and which has been completely transformed not only through his own labors but those of many loyal students. The loyalty was mutual, of course; he was always available for them – and for any seminarian who came from Louisville or elsewhere and needed special tutoring. Perhaps the words e-mailed to me by our colleague Gil Chaitin from Strasbourg are as good a summary as any: "I appreciated Cliff's willingness to help me out when I ran into problems with my computer (which was often), no matter how busy he was; he was one of the few scholars and colleagues I knew whose teaching and writing were genuinely innovative (I'm referring to the theoretical aspects of his work that I was capable of judging); and above all, he was a genuinely decent man".

Cliff Flanigan was beginning his twenty-third year on the faculty when he died. His ashes were taken to Baltimore, where there was a simple ceremony in the nursing home where his mother lived. Patrick then took the urn to the cemetery and placed it (I am again citing Beverly Flanigan):

> ... *on the burial site, next to Cliff's father's grave in a plot full of uncles and aunts, on a hilltop surrounded by lovely oak trees in a cemetery called (Cliff loved the symbolism) "Druid Ridge". The committal service was brief, we strewed carnations around the urn, and it was over.*[2]

Notes

1. The following is an amplified version of the obituary published in 1994 in the *Yearbook of Comparative and General Literature*, which was based on a biographical presentation by Claus Clüver read at a memorial celebration for Clifford Flanigan on 13 November 1993 and on the memorial resolution written by Claus Clüver and Lawrence Clopper for distribution to the Faculty of Indiana University.

2. Beverly Flanigan informed me in a letter dated 12 August 1999 that "his mother has now died too, last fall. She was so sad and lonely after Cliff died, yet she survived him by five years. So Cliff is buried beside both his parents, and since he had no siblings, only Patrick remains."
In 2010, Patrick and his wife attended the annual "C. Clifford Flanigan Graduate Colloquium," which in that year opened a series of events celebrating sixty years of Comparative Literature at Indiana University. The program also featured an exhibition honoring the work of four distinguished deceased colleagues: Matei Calinescu, Henry H. H. Remak, Mary Ellen Solt, and Cliff.

Cliffnotes: Performance, Pedagogy, and the Medieval Past
Claire Sponsler

At the time of his death in the fall of 1993, Clifford Flanigan had taught for twenty-one years at Indiana University, offering by my reckoning some ninety courses reflecting his broad range of interests in such diverse topics as church ritual, medieval drama, anthropology, and contemporary theory. Legendary both for the abiding interest he took in his students and for the daunting but exhilarating scope of his knowledge, which seemed to cover every nook and cranny of scholarship, Cliff to a remarkable degree defined himself and his position within academia as a teacher. Such was his devotion to teaching, both in and outside of the classroom, with students and colleagues alike, that it often took precedence over his published written work. As a consequence, his contribution to scholarship resides in large part in his ever-widening circle of influence on the work of others through the public forum of the classroom and through contacts with colleagues at conferences as well as in private exchanges.

To a surprising extent Cliff "performed" his scholarly work, using formal and informal pedagogies as ways of engaging with and actively producing the past with which he was fascinated. Although this essay is intended to honor the memory of the remarkable teacher Cliff was, I also wish to develop an argument as well. This argument has to do, as my title suggests, with the relationship between performativity, teaching, and the construction of the medieval past.

I begin with the personal, with the person, I should say, of the teacher and scholar as an embodied subject. Feminist critics have insisted on the need to acknowledge that we necessarily speak, and before speaking come to know ourselves, as embodied subjects, as entities who inhabit a corporeal form that shapes and controls our voices just as it is in turn shaped by external forces. The sheer physicality of Cliff's being has to be the starting point for any appreciation of his pedagogy. There was never a way of avoiding the fact that Cliff was a mind and voice enfleshed. In fact, his teaching deliberately deployed the communicative possibilities of the body. Information flowed through the expressive channels of Cliff's being, as when, facing a group of students who knew nothing of biblical stories, he would perch on the edge of his desk, lean out towards them, and chuckle while booming out, "What's the matter with you people?

Didn't you ever go to Sunday school?" Or when, caught up in the passion of an idea he would lurch across the front of the classroom, gesticulating wildly, crossing his eyes, grimacing, sometimes even spitting, a madman, captivated by knowledge and struggling to express it. Witnessing such moments, one received two impressions. The first was of the almost demonic power of ideas that could so forcibly take control of someone, literally possessing him and holding him in its grip. The second was of a formidable intellect straining mightily against the inadequacies of language.

Through a compelling bodily rhetoric of gestures and movements, Cliff's teaching demonstrated what he himself strongly believed, that ideas were potent but that meaning always exceeded the signifiers available to express it. Faced with the inadequacy of language, Cliff used his body as an actor would, aware of the impact it could make, conscious of how it could say things that words could not. One former student remembers a medieval drama seminar in which Cliff was demonstrating how liturgical time and real time fused in the procession around the church and towards the altar. Cliff was pacing through the classroom and among the students, looking down very intently at the floor; then, dramatically, he raised his eyes at the key moment to look at his desk/altar at the front of the room. Suddenly the classroom was transformed into the medieval church Cliff was evoking as the performance conjured up the "reality" of the medieval past.

On reflection, it seems to me that what this performance, and others like it, perhaps best conveyed was not, however, the "reality" or presence of the medieval past, but rather the strength of desire for an irremediably lost object. As Paul Zumthor says in *Speaking of the Middle Ages*," we speak well only about those things ... we love. ... Every relationship we maintain with a text involves some latent eroticism. Only this dynamism puts the critical reader in a situation comparable to that of the medieval reader or listener, whose whole body, not only his visual and auditory faculties, was engaged in the reception of the text".[1] An erotics of reading, which Zumthor sees as the hallmark of medieval textual response, also informed Cliff's teaching. In our affectless postmodern world, Cliff was a master of affect. He craved response from texts and from listeners. Like any good performer he fed off of the flow of energy in the classroom and desperately needed to create that flow. His pedagogy was based on a unique ability to personalise the abstract and impersonal. He relished making the intellectual emotional, charging it with excitement. For Cliff, knowledge and texts were exciting; they were meant to provoke, to incite, to inspire. Not to react to them passionately thus represented a failure of reading or of knowing, or more, seriously, a refusal of the erotic gestures of the text and the past.

If Cliff had the actor's sense of bodily movement, he also had the oral poet's sense of narration. He loved a good story and knew how to tell one for maximum effect. He instinctively knew which narratives mattered and would seize the imagination. His stories functioned as exempla, standing as pithy examples to be told over and over again. In fact, repetition was a distinctive feature of Cliff's narrative technique. Like a minstrel or preacher, he had a repertoire of tales that he could retell at will, often prefaced by some comment like "I'm sure I've told you this before." Despite their reiteration, or perhaps because of it, his stories retained their force and even gained from their repeated retellings. Cliff liked to tell the story of a classmate of his who wore an artificial leg, held on through conscious and alert control of his muscles. This classmate was easily bored, in Cliff's recounting of it, especially by tedious lectures, and when bored, easily fell asleep, thus with some frequency releasing his limb to drop with a loud bang to the floor, alarming everyone else in the room and startling himself awake, at which point he would lean over, reattach his leg and begin the whole cycle over again. This story, whose veracity I somehow never thought to question but which now strikes me as wildly improbable – could such a thing really have ever happened? – was recycled by Cliff to illustrate a variety of points as the occasion demanded – from the need to be a lively lecturer to the unending trials of teaching to the tactics of covert protest available to students. Cliff was by disposition completely at home in orality, a trait that not incidentally made him a living conduit to a preprint culture so difficult to access.

Cliff's pedagogical performances also aimed at putting an intimate face on history. For Cliff the past was never abstract or disembodied; instead it was personal and located in the individual self. Thus he could derive great delight from imagining the motives of someone like Peter Abelard, for example, motives which for Cliff were usually grounded in the well-known complexities of human longing, self-aggrandizement, and self-delusion. Good at deflating pretensions in an affectionate way that humanized the voice behind the ideas, Cliff could make someone like Abelard come to life, leaping over eight hundred years of history to make the affairs of a twelfth-century scholastic every bit as compelling as the latest scandal about a university president. If Cliff was a demystifier who delighted in pulling back the curtain on fake-gods, he also loved a good mystification: he once confessed that he always called on students to read aloud certain passages from the *Aeneid* because he was incapable of reading them himself without weeping.

This constant and characteristic intellectual movement back and forth between cultural affirmation and cultural critique was reflected in the way that his pedagogical performances always emphasized the margins, the borders, the unsafe boundaries where powerful emotions lurk. Tears, blood, and sighs made up the stuff of Cliff's syllabi as he worked his way through the rituals of the church or the intricacies of the liturgy. So too did farts, turds, and belches, as he followed sacred rites into their various, often irreverent, rewritings and reshapings. This emphasis on margins was intentional, since for Cliff, "understanding" medieval culture meant recognizing its alterity and its marginality. His insistence on the shameful and excessive processes of the body deliberately drew attention to the signs of danger, which Mary Douglas has amply described, that mark off highly charged areas of culture – the taboo, the forbidden, the hot zones. Part of Cliff's desire for the Middle Ages was precisely that it has come to represent for us now, in the technocratic post-industrial West, a liminal space, a danger zone that can call into question the grounds of our being. Cliff would, of course, have been the first to see this liminal past as a constructed Middle Ages and would have vociferously argued against assuming the existence of any "innate" or natural or essential Middle Ages; nonetheless, he liked the notion of the Middle Ages as Other, as stepping off point for self-analysis and social criticism.

If Cliff's teaching could be seen as a form of acting, then it was always clear that he had a vast repertoire of scripts to draw on. His knowledge, covering as it did fields as diverse as scholasticism, Church ritual, the theater, nineteenth-century German philology, contemporary theory, computers, and detective fiction, was wide-ranging and synthetic. But it also was always controlled by his strong belief in the necessity of adopting a critical, self-reflective, and interrogatory stance towards discourse and history, and he aimed his courses at developing similar skills in his students. A one-hour lecture focusing on *The Voyage of St. Brendan* might range over such related topics as St. Patrick and the development of Irish Christianity, monasticism, St. Martin of Tours, penitential doctrines, and the ascetic tradition. Typical exam questions and exercises asked, for example, that students interpret the N-Town play of *The Woman Taken in Adultery*, considering it in relation to a) other English cycle plays, b) a medieval Latin play, c) a French play, d) the Frankfurt Passion Play, and e) *Mankind*, all while developing a controlling thesis about the N-Town play – I am not making this up – in five to eight typed pages. Far from being mere exercises in pedantry, such assignments encouraged students constantly to think in the broadest possible terms about any individual cultural production and about their relation to it, to think, in fact, of themselves not just as passive spectators but as potential actors performing and revising history's scripts.

Cliff's performative teaching style also embodied the intellectual history of medieval studies, at any given moment lending voice to the themes, ideals, and fantasies that have guided the appropriation and analysis of the Middle Ages from the Renaissance to the present while also putting each under erasure, subjecting it to critique and to an ironic distancing. This is to say that Cliff's method was at heart hermeneutic: he moved through various modes of interpretation and understanding but always circled around to a critique of them. He had absorbed the poststructuralist notion that centers no longer hold, while also recognizing that we are always involved in producing centers no matter how temporary, contingent, or illusory we know them to be. Thus, when being told by a student about an absolutely essential but excruciatingly tedious monograph on an obscure topic, Cliff could snicker and say: "Must have been written by some German." Simultaneously dismissive and affirmative, such remarks revealed both an intimate knowledge of and affectionate regard for the work of earlier generations of scholars and a delighted awareness of the mutability of knowledge, an awareness that was generous enough even to encompass his own work and to imagine its fate a hundred years from now.

I once witnessed an especially dramatic enactment of this principle of mutability. It was during the course of a conference paper in which Cliff began by excoriating scholars of medieval drama – who made up his audience – for their untheorized and naive adherence to a formalist model of interpretation. As the tension in the room rose higher by the minute, Cliff moved to a detailed critique of what he presented as a particularly flagrant example of the misguidedness of such an approach. The members of the audience, wondering which among them was being pilloried, writhed in their seats. At that moment, Cliff suddenly revealed that the essay he had been attacking was his own, written by him some fifteen years earlier. The relief in the room was perceptible. And the point had been made. Daring to risk their anger by implicating them in his critique, then letting them off the hook, Cliff visibly demonstrated to his listeners – made them actively feel – the force of what might otherwise have been a detached intellectual argument about the contingent nature of knowledge. Such recognition of the inexorability of history, of the way the central could become the marginal, was for Cliff not a source of despair but a condition of the production and consumption of knowledge, by definition a perishable commodity.

I have been suggesting here that as a master of the arts of theatricality, Cliff used his teaching style to mirror his understanding of medieval culture and, more broadly, his assumptions about processes of historical and intellectual inquiry. He "performed" the medieval past at the same time as he "performed" the complex processes of historical retrieval and reconstruction. Cliff's teaching style was grounded on the conviction that knowledge is constructed, or, more strongly, performed and reperformed. Knowledge enters into channels of communication regulated by desire; hence to keep knowledge alive means to make people want it and to make them want to participate in its construction and production. Like those of medieval culture, Cliff's most thoroughly characteristic modes of expression – his orality and performativity – depended on a live audience for their workings; but they were also particularly vulnerable to loss and forgetting. There is for me an extreme poignancy in realizing that despite the major contributions made by his written scholarship Cliff's true significance as an intellectual is tied inextricably to the memories of those who listened to him. More often than not, he entered into the circulation of knowledge in the most defenseless way, not with the power and permanence of print to back him up, but with his voice and body as the tools at hand to convey ideas and plead for their endurance.

I come around now, at the end of this reflection, to a recognition of my own involvement in the various processes I have been describing. Not the least of what I have been attempting to do is to intervene in the flow of history, to narrate and thus fix, however temporarily, for myself and for others, a particular story about a particular scholar and teacher. Certainly this is a nostalgic project. But it is also a project that aims at understanding the position of the individual subject within the vast, frightening, always changing, devouring field of knowledge and its dissemination. Surely those of us involved in these enterprises of collecting, understanding and transmitting ideas and information cannot avoid thoughts about the futility of our chosen social roles. Nor can we escape a sense of our inevitable complicity with hegemonic forces that co-opt us, despite our resistance. Cliff's example provides no release from that grim knowledge. But it does offer, I would like to believe, the valuable evidence of one individual's generous, alert, and heart-felt negotiation of those epistemological and ideological tangles: one who threw himself exuberantly, boldly, and full of desire into the breach, not flinching in the face of the loss, the perishability of the self, the ephemerality of knowledge.

One of the best examples of Cliff's pedagogy can be found in an essay he wrote on teaching the Latin liturgical drama. In typical Flanigan fashion, the essay begins with magisterial breadth by chronicling the entire history of medieval drama studies in three densely written yet grippingly readable pages that chart but also debunk the widely accepted story of the "birth" of drama in the Latin liturgy. The essay then alights on one perfect example that brings into vivid focus the essay's central argument about how and why the drama of premodern Europe should be taught: looking at the *Visitatio sepulchri* in the *Regularis concordia*, which is considered to be the "first" Latin "drama," Cliff compares two versions of it – the version found in David Bevington's widely used anthology of medieval drama, in which the *Visitatio* looks like a stand-alone "drama" with division of spoken parts for actors, and the version found in the *Regularis* (from the British Library manuscript Cotton Tiberius A.III) in which the *Visitatio* blends seamlessly with the surrounding liturgy and looks nothing like a "play" but instead like the chanted church service it was. The essay ends not by berating scholars for having gotten their drama history "wrong," but by suggesting how the differences between the Bevington edition and the *Regularis* original can be used to show students both the alterity of the past and the complex and contestatory practices through which that past is constructed and understood. In Cliff's conclusion to the essay I hear again his passion for teaching, a passion with the highest of stakes and the most enduring of legacies:

> Finally, our teaching must be governed by some larger purpose than teaching the facts of literary history or the fostering of an appreciation of past practices. Most of our students will not become and do not wish to become experts in the medieval drama. But they need to see how the difficulties of interpreting these texts and the strategies by which these difficulties are tentatively but never definitively overcome are similar to the difficulties and strategies we use with all texts, including the texts of our own lives.[2]

Notes

1. Paul Zumthor, *Speaking of the Middle Ages*, [transl.] Sarah White, Lincoln, 1986, p. 22.
2. C. Clifford Flanigan, "Teaching the Medieval Latin 'Drama': Reflections Historical and Theoretical", in Richard Emmerson [ed.], *Approaches to Teaching Medieval English Drama*, New York, 1990, pp. 50-6. Quoted from p. 56.

Part II

Quid Quaeritis, O Clerici? A Review of Some Recent Scholarship on the Medieval Latin Music Drama
C. Clifford Flanigan[*]

There are many ways to write a review of scholarship. Most obviously, the writer can go to the library, use the standard bibliographies to generate a listing of everything published on the subject assigned to him, and simply report on these findings. The advantage of approaching the task in this way is that it avoids a number of complications, above all, the need to draw lines of demarcation which separate the assigned topic from some other topic. The difficulty is that these boundaries are in fact never clear. The bibliography of literary studies published annually by the Modern Language Association of America, for example, lists approximately twenty items published in the past decade which, arguably, are primarily concerned with medieval Latin music drama. The tentativeness of my language in the previous sentence indicates how problematic even a simple search can become. Indeed, the problematic nature of this enterprise has been made all the more difficult by the recent decision of the MLA bibliographers to list scholarship on medieval Latin texts together with scholarship on works of vernacular literature of the geographical area in which the Latin text was written. The battle raging for several earlier decades, especially in Germany, over whether medieval Latin works should be lumped together to form a separate "medieval Latin literature" or should rather be assigned to individual national literatures has been settled by the arbitrary decision of professional bibliographers and computer experts.

This problem, whatever its significance, is only the proverbial tip of the iceberg for anyone attempting to survey the scholarship on Latin music drama. Useful as they are, bibliographies provided by agencies like the MLA are never complete; when I wrote an exhaustive survey of the scholarship on the Latin music drama a decade ago, I discussed more than one hundred items, only twelve of which were listed in the MLA bibliography. The primary reason for this seeming lack of attention to the

---

[*] Unpublished version of an essay that appeared in a thoroughly revised version in Eckehard Simon [ed.], *The Theatre of Medieval Europe: New Research in Early Drama*, Cambridge, 1991, pp. 21-41. Reproduced by permission of estate of C. Clifford Flanigan.

medieval music drama is that the MLA bibliography is devoted to "literary" studies, and much of the work undertaken on our subject has been carried out within the framework of other disciplines, especially musical history and liturgiology. The standard bibliographies in these areas must therefore be consulted. When one attempts to undertake this task and bring together the work of scholars in disparate academic disciplines on what might appear to be "the same subject," new difficulties arise. There is first of all the extremely unfortunate fact that literary scholars usually fail to consult the work of their musicological counterparts; similarly, few historians of music are known for their enthusiasm for literary scholarship. A more fundamental problem is that different disciplines operate by different and often incommensurate paradigms, so that the issues which engage the "literary" scholar in his study of the Latin music drama are often of little interest to musicologists; of course the opposite is true as well. As for the professional student of the liturgy, he or she is usually somewhat informed about literary scholarship and generally aware of musicological studies relevant to his discipline, but since basic journals and handbooks on the history of the liturgy are often absent from even the most complete academic libraries in the United States (liturgiology, a librarian once told me, is a "Catholic" subject that has little place in the American public university), these studies have generally had little impact on the way that either musicologist or literary scholar has thought about the music drama. However, in the past decade liturgiological studies have influenced research on the music drama.

To be sure, all subject matters raise these kinds of interdisciplinary issues, though few do so with the same intensity as the medieval Latin music drama. In naming literary studies, musicology, and liturgiology, we have by no means exhausted the disciplinary interests in our subject, for art history, monastic history, historical theology, and the history of medieval Christian spirituality are as self-evidently concerned with our topic as they are. A thorough exploration of the studies significant for our understanding of the Latin music drama would certainly need to include a survey of work in these areas, one which would go well beyond books and articles which explicitly discuss the music drama. Furthermore, as I have argued elsewhere, the study of anthropology and the history of non-Christian religions are cogent to our concern.[1] So are economic and political history. From the broad perspective sketched here the task of reviewing scholarship on the music drama becomes an enormous and impossible task. Certainly I cannot here – or elsewhere – offer a comprehensive view of the scholarship or of the understanding of the drama which emerges from it.

More modestly, then, I return to the person I am, and the kinds of work that are possible for me: I am a teacher and researcher in literary studies, with a strong interest in musical history, liturgical studies, and, more recently, performance practices. Like many contemporary students of literature, I have become intensely interested in theory, not merely "literary theory" as it was once understood as a handmaiden to literary interpretation in days when Wellek and Warren's *Theory of Literature* dominated Anglo-American literary studies,[2] but theory as Jonathan Culler has more recently suggested, as a cross-disciplinary interest in systems of cultural production and reception.[3] Contemporary theoretical interests have made, as far as I can see, no impact on the study of the medieval Latin music drama, and this situation is unfortunate. It is unfortunate because recent theoretical developments in a number of different disciplines have addressed the inherent limitations of an object's being considered within the bounds and assumptions of a single disciplinary paradigm. They have done so not in order to urge students to become more "interdisciplinary," though the effect of the new theoretical concerns has been that many scholars have begun to ignore earlier disciplinary barriers. Rather, the new theory encourages us to reflect on and call into question the epistemological ground rules which have governed our discourse on subjects like the Latin music drama. Equally importantly, practitioners of the new cross-disciplinary theoretical studies have begun to identify the ways that our own self-interests and self-identity are inscribed in our academic discourse about such subject matters. Furthermore, though much of the stimulus to the new theoretical efforts has come from structuralism and other formal enterprises, theory today has become radically historical in the ways that it demands we conceive of our subject matter and of ourselves. Such a point of view has great potential for helping us to understand how the study of the medieval Latin music drama got to its present state and for opening new avenues of research for the future. As will soon become apparent, my reviewing of some of the major works of scholarship on the dramatic ceremonies of the liturgy has been significantly shaped by a number of the basic concerns of contemporary theory.

In the essay that follows, I will attempt to review and critique some important recent work on the music drama in such a way that its presuppositions will become evident. I will also try to allude to some new directions that we might take in the future study of our subject. In order to keep this work within a reasonable length, I will focus on a few book-length studies and allow references to important journal articles to appear in the course of my critique of these books. Since 1965 the following major book-length studies and editions of the Latin music drama have appeared: Walther Lipphardt's six-volume edition of the *Lateinische Osterfeiern und Osterspiele*,[4] O. B. Hardison's *Christian Rite and Christian Drama in the Middle* Ages,[5] Helmut de Boor's *Die Textgeschichte der lateinischen Osterfeiern*,[6] and Johann Drumbl's *Quem quaeritis: Teatro Sacro Dell'alto Medioevo*.[7] In addition to these, which are treated extensively below, there have been published the following books: Fletcher Collins's *Medieval Church Music Dramas: A Repertory of Complete Plays*, and by the same author, *The Production of Medieval Church* Drama;[8] I have discussed these books at some length in my previous review of scholarship and will not therefore consider them.[9] Also published in the time period under consideration here were Diane Dolan's *Le drame liturgique de Pâques en Normandie et en Angleterre au moyen âge*[10] and Blandine-Dominique Berger's *Le Drame liturgique de Pâques*.[11] The former of these two studies is a first-rate exercise in textual history and musical paleography but, given the scope of the present essay, is too technical to be considered here. The latter fails to do much more than rehash the Young-Hardison debate without adding substantially to it; I have not specifically alluded to this book in the pages that follow.

As the above titles indicate, in recent years, as in the past, most of the discussions of the Latin music drama have centered on the Easter texts. An earlier draft of this paper included a consideration of the scholarship on the non-Easter plays, but I have omitted it here because of space limitations. Though highly important, the relatively small amount of recent scholarship dedicated to these music dramas mostly shows the same trends that are manifest in the discussion of the Easter *Quem quaeritis*. I should at least mention in the body of my essay, however, a book-length collection of studies which appears to me to be the most useful of the recent studies on music dramas other than the *Visitatio Sepulchri* and the texts associated with it: *The Fleury Playbook: Essays and Studies*, edited by Thomas Campbell and Clifford Davidson. The relevant pages of manuscript 201 in the Orléans Municipal Library are conveniently reproduced in this book along with eight studies by as many hands.[12]

Before turning to an extended consideration of the studies to be considered here, I need to say a word about the essay's most obvious omission: a discussion of William L. Smoldon's *The Music of the Medieval Church Dramas*, published in 1980, seven years after Smoldon's death.[13] In the lustrum before its appearance, this book was perhaps the most anticipated of all studies on the Latin music drama. Smoldon devoted several decades to the study of the music of these texts, a subject that no one else had taken up before him. Late in his life he entered into a spirited controversy with Hardison and promised to provide proof from the musical score of the *Quem quaeritis* that the dialogue had originated as a trope.[14] If Smoldon ever possessed such proof – a highly unlikely possibility in light of David Bjork's study – it went to the grave with him. He left a long uncompleted manuscript that required (discussed below) extensive editing, a task for which Oxford University Press engaged Cynthia Bourgeault. Ms. Bourgeault attempted to complete the manuscript as Smoldon would have desired and to correct the literally hundreds of factual errors which it contained. Despite her best efforts, however, the finished product is riddled with mistakes. Furthermore, it represents a state of scholarship on the drama which has long been superseded. Smoldon apparently conceived of his book as a companion to Young's *The Drama of the Medieval Church*.[15] Had it appeared in the decade following the publication of that monumental endeavor, it would have made a genuine contribution and perhaps steered the study of the music drama in a direction quite different from the one it took. But the book that finally appeared in 1980 is really a book of the 1930s and 1940s. Even such a fundamental reference book as Dom Hesbert's edition of the *Corpus Antiphonalium Officii*[16] was not used by Smoldon. The publication of Smoldon's book was a labor of love by Smoldon's colleagues and friends, by Ms. Bourgeault, and by the Oxford Press itself. They conceived of it as a lasting tribute to its author. One would like to respond enthusiastically to Smoldon's book and to pay it the tribute of spirited disagreement. But time had passed it by long before it finally appeared in print. Sad to say, the most charitable response to it is silence; it will not be further discussed here.

I

The recent study of the medieval Latin drama begins with two seminal works, O. B. Hardison's *Christian Rite and Christian Drama in the Middle Ages: Essays in the Origin and Early History of the Modern Drama*, published in 1965, and Helmut de Boor's *Die Textgeschichte der lateinischen Osterfeiern*, published in 1967. Both of these books are important because, whatever their weaknesses, they opened new and profitable directions for the study of the Latin drama by explicitly rejecting broadly accepted assumptions of earlier scholarship. Hardison's book is widely acknowledged in both American and European scholarship; to what can only be the disgrace of American and French scholarship, de Boor's work has unfortunately been virtually ignored except by investigators writing in German. It will be useful to begin our overview of scholarship by considering the chief claims of each of these pioneering books. We begin by setting out briefly the different but related premises of Hardison's book:

1. Hardison claims that a late nineteenth- and early twentieth-century bias against religion caused almost all scholars of the Latin and vernacular medieval drama to underplay religious and liturgical elements in their work and to place apparently peripheral "secular" elements at the center or near the center of their inquiry. For this reason liturgical phenomena were frequently regarded as dramatic in nature.

2. Hardison demonstrates that the earlier fundamental studies of the medieval Latin drama, such as those by Chambers,[17] Young, and Craig,[18] were based on a tacit acceptance of the model of evolutionary development adapted from the biological sciences and that the unacknowledged acceptance of this paradigm by these authors caused them to arrange and describe texts in a linear and regular order which, as they themselves acknowledged, contradicted the surviving manuscript evidence.

3. Hardison believes that the study of the Latin music drama must be grounded in an understanding of the early medieval liturgy. In his book he offers an extended summary and paraphrase of the commentaries of Amalarius of Metz, the most influential Carolingian student of the liturgy, and he offers Amalarius' allegorical interpretation of the liturgy as a model for understanding the *Quem quaeritis* dialogue.

4. In sharp disagreement with most of his predecessors, Hardison asserts that the *Visitatio Sepulchri* ceremony did not develop out of the *Quem quaeritis* trope to the Easter introit. For Hardison the Latin drama has its origins in the Vigil Mass of Easter; he speculates that when the Vigil underwent a transformation in the eighth and ninth centuries which adapted it to monastic use the *Quem quaeritis* became a free-floating ceremony which was inserted in various places in the liturgical cursus.

5. Hardison claims that the vernacular dramatic traditions were not the products of a logical development out of the complex plays in Latin but that they had their beginnings in a tradition entirely separate from the liturgy. French plays at least, he argues, may have existed much earlier than the dates of our surviving evidence.

The present study is not the place to discuss all of these claims. Let it only be noticed that in positing undocumented events in liturgical history and groups of dramatic traditions unattested by manuscript evidence, Hardison repeated and compounded the same kind of error which he criticized in his predecessors and, it must be added, on the basis of far less first-hand acquaintance with medieval liturgical manuscripts. Similarly, as I hope to show in a forthcoming study, Hardison fails to place Amalarius' work in an historical perspective and to consider it in light of a broader medieval theory of semiotics. For this reason his reading of Amalarius' texts and his application of them to texts of the "liturgical drama" seem, to put the best construction on matters, problematic.

More important than such somewhat detailed concerns, however, are the ways that Hardison's book points the direction that most scholarship on the music drama would take. First of all, he insists on the importance of the liturgy and of liturgical scholarship for any adequate investigation in this area, though paradoxically Hardison seems unaware of most twentieth-century professional liturgiological studies. Hardison's emphasis on the liturgy and on the liturgical nature of the Latin dramas differs sharply from the majority of earlier scholarship, which viewed the liturgy only as a point of departure for the study of the "drama." Yet here Hardison's work seems more revolutionary than it is, for it, like the studies which followed, did not question the common assumption that liturgy and drama, whatever characteristics they share, are essentially (or by nature) different. Hardison seeks to show how liturgy was transformed into something that is not liturgy, even while calling into question Young's line of demarcation that was based on the test-case of impersonation. Indeed, one might argue that Hardison does little more than set the line of demarcation at a slightly different spot than it had earlier occupied and invent new terminology to characterize phenomena on either side of the line he has created. For Hardison the terms "drama" and "liturgy" describe entities which have a fixed being with characteristics that are, small details notwithstanding, recognizable by all.

Related to Hardison's distinction between liturgy and drama is his notion of the "paraliturgical," a term or concept which is found or implied in almost all studies of the music drama considered here. Like so many terms, its meaning seems so self-evident that its underlying and unexpressed presuppositions are seldom raised to the level of consciousness. The term tacitly suggests that there is, as Young said directly, "an official liturgy" of the medieval church which is fixed and universal. In addition to this "official liturgy" there are additional elements to be found in liturgical books which are local in origin or practice and therefore "optional," at least when considered in light of the "universal" elements which are, by definition, not optional. Thus the "liturgical drama" is paraliturgical and can and must be considered as something other than "liturgy" in its purest form. That something else, as far as the last century of scholarship is concerned, is "drama." But liturgical scholarship makes clear that such a claim is based on very little medieval evidence. It seems predicated on a post-Tridentine (and pre-Vatican II) conception of liturgy, one which presupposes the use of printed books and a central enforcing agency whose task it is to see that there are no deviations from any officially sanctioned practice. The well known account of the failure of the Carolingian attempt to create a "pure" Roman mass book for use in all of northern Europe is an excellent example of how little most practitioners of the early medieval liturgy had in mind the distinction between the "official liturgy" and the "paraliturgical." More basically, the enormous diversity which an even casual examiner of almost any set of surviving liturgical books readily notices directly contradicts this distinction, one which has nonetheless largely determined the shape of the majority of the scholarship on the music drama. Thus Hardison, even as he criticized Young and Chambers for being children of their time and uncritically accepting evolutionary presuppositions, imposed a different set of presuppositions on the fundamental levels of his own model and therefore produced a view of his subject matter which is theoretically and historically questionable.

The point of these observations is not that scholarship should be without such presuppositions. Though positivists have often claimed otherwise, history ultimately subverts every claim to objectivity. But what is at stake here is the need to recognize that all hermeneutic constructs are human and social constructs; they are epistemological models, not reflections of the way things "really are." Neither liturgy nor drama exists in nature; at least they do not unless one holds to an unreformed platonic metaphysics. We can never know our reality except through the construction of heuristic models, yet these models which are to serve interpretive purposes also inevitably and unavoidably distort. This observation is so basic to the human sciences that one is embarrassed to make it in the present context. Yet the entire history of the scholarship on the medieval music drama seems to fail to recognize that these circumstances always prevail.

Let me mention two ways in which Hardison's unarticulated metaphysical assumptions, coupled with his failure to take history seriously – especially history written in languages other than English – misled him. Hardison argues at great length that the *Visitatio* ceremony did not begin as a trope to the introit. Historically speaking, this is, perhaps, a questionable claim; but more important than whether Hardison was "right" or "wrong" on this issue is, I think, the need to call attention to the conceptual framework, often tacit, which appears to have brought him to this position. At least two assumptions are likely at work here. Firstly, Hardison seems to have assumed that "the official liturgy" did not include the tropes that were regularly performed in monastic houses in the ninth and tenth centuries (indeed, apart from a handful of exceptions, the Council of Trent explicitly forbade their use). For Hardison, then, tropes are envisioned as at best ornamental growths on the liturgy; as such they could not be for him the source of a drama which was liturgical in its origins – and therefore its "nature." But how can the notion that tropes are not fully "liturgical" be justified? Certainly not by examining medieval service books, which do not know of a division between "official" and "unofficial" parts of the rite. I would guess that the chief source of Hardison's historically untenable notions about liturgy and troping is to be found in his apparently unquestioned assumptions about liturgy as a "natural" phenomenon, one which in its "pure" state excludes unessential (or accidental) ornamentation. Had he taken in hand the several different liturgical books needed to perform the office or the mass in the tenth century and attempted to reconstruct the experience of the worshipers who used them, he might well have come to a different and, historically speaking, more satisfactory conclusion about the liturgical function of tropes.[19]

But there is a second and perhaps even more disturbing explanation for Hardison's too facile dismissal of tropes. As a literary scholar, Hardison utterly ignored all recent scholarship on the practice of troping; indeed all of his information about this subject seems to have been derived from the work of his literary predecessors, whom he in other matters so vigorously criticises. Of course, writing in 1965 Hardison could not take advantage of the work which Ritva Jonnson[20] and her Stockholm colleagues at the *Corpus Troparum* are making available to us; nor could he have benefited from the trope scholarship which is being generated by it. At the time that Hardison was writing *Christian Rite and Christian Drama*, however, there were important musicological studies of the practice of troping. Had he consulted them, Hardison might have been saved from his facile dismissal of tropes and the distortions which have arisen from his refusal to consider the results of musicological scholarship.

This is a matter far more serious than the long tradition of disciplinary narrow-mindedness in which Hardison was merely following the unfortunate practices of Chambers, Young, and other literary researchers. Part of the blame for the general lack of knowledge about the history and practice of medieval music on the part of literature students of the *Quem quaeritis* must lie with musicological scholarship, which in 1965 and down to the present shows few signs of wishing to address an audience beyond its own narrow disciplinary confines. But musicological narrowness cannot justify the complete lack of consideration of the musical texts of the *Quem quaeritis* in *Christian Rite and Christian Drama*. Hardison's tacit assumption – shared, as we shall see, by most writers on this subject – seems to be that the Latin music drama is essentially a drama that happened to be sung, and that therefore its musical text is of secondary importance in comparison with its verbal text. Of course, like his predecessors, Hardison acknowledged the musical aspects of these texts, but because he was interested in these texts as drama, he apparently believed that his lack of knowledge about medieval music in general, and the musical aspects of these texts in particular, would not hinder his understanding of them or their history. Indeed, he apparently felt that he could safely hypothesize about these texts on the basis of their verbal text alone because their words were the primary determinative factor of their existence. This is a more than questionable assumption, to say the least. On what possible basis could one claim that these texts are more verbal than musical? The question, of course, can be reversed and addressed to musicologists who have been almost as parochial as Hardison and his literary colleagues, only in the opposite direction. Failure to consider the tension which exists between literary scholars and musicologists on this issue has colored and, in my view, to a marked degree decisively distorted and hindered most of the scholarship produced on the Latin music drama in the twentieth century.

Of course, the literary scholars will claim that they are incompetent to consider the music, and musicologists have shown by practice, if not always by explicit disclaimer, that their knowledge of the way that verbal sign systems function is often limited. But what is remarkable is that the tacit yet determinative assumptions of value which both musicologists and literary scholars have made are quickly passed over as if for each they are self-evident and not worthy of critical reflection. Each has appropriated the music drama to the paradigms of his discipline and often with a show of force made it conform to them. Again, the point here is not that we can avoid disciplinary paradigms but that we should be aware that they have no ontological validity and that they can at best only answer the questions we put to the texts under study on the basis of the heuristic assumptions built into the paradigms. At the very least both literary scholars and musicologists need to recognize the limitations of their paradigms and to acknowledge that the results which they offer are valid not for the music drama itself (if for no other reason than that we can never know anything "in itself") but for the music drama as constructed by the musicological or literary paradigm. One would need at the minimum to acknowledge that alternate accounts of the music drama can be given by the use of alternate paradigms and to recognize modestly but explicitly that no one paradigm can more rightly claim to explain the "reality" of the music drama than another. Perhaps the most useful preparation that the next author of a study on the Latin drama can undertake is a thoughtful reading of Thomas Kuhn's *The Structure of Scientific Revolutions* and the controversy which has surrounded it.[21] I blush to make such an obvious suggestion, but I cannot but be struck by the epistemological naïveté which has characterized all major studies of our subject.

II

Much that has been said in criticism of Hardison's book can with equal validity be applied to the other studies scrutinized here. Certainly this is true for de Boor's *Textgeschichte*, a work which in its own right is as seminal as Hardison's. De Boor's contribution is twofold. On one hand, he sought to do what Young had said was impossible: to write a textual history of the *Visitatio Sepulchri*. In the process of producing his textual history, de Boor offers a characterisation of that body of texts which, at least on some counts, differed considerably from that of his predecessors. Though he was perhaps the most distinguished student of medieval German literature of his generation, de Boor, much to his credit, insisted that the quarter-century of study which his project consumed had taught him that the *Visitatio* could not be approached with the usual methods of "Literaturwissenschaft" because it was an ecclesiastical ceremony, not a "work of art." As we shall see, however, there is a persistent if unarticulated tendency in de Boor's work to somehow recuperate the *Visitatio* offices as literary art. De Boor's textual investigations build on the work of the earlier German scholars of the music drama, above all that of Carl Lange,[22] in making a clear-cut distinction between *Feier* and *Spiel*. By *Feier* de Boor means, "All that is intended for use in the framework of ecclesiastical ritual"; *Spiel*, on the other hand, means "a text which is out of place in the liturgical realm, regardless of whether it was written in Latin or the vernacular, whether it was written by clerics and presented inside the church or was produced with the cooperation of the laity in an outdoor place".[23] Elsewhere de Boor tells us that in the *Feier*, in contrast to the *Spiel*, "the clergy do not represent sacred figures; they 'fulfill' them, they become them".[24] With such statements de Boor seems to break decisively with older literary paradigms and to employ the language of liturgiology to locate the *Visitatio* in a set of assumptions far removed from Young's distinction of imitation and impersonation.

However, on closer examination de Boor's departure from literary models can be exposed, not surprisingly, as only an apparent one. In the first place, he is as oblivious to the *Visitatio* as a musical phenomenon as are all of his literary predecessors. Indeed, he believes that he can establish a textual tradition on the basis of verbal text alone, thus ignoring in all of those texts which preserve both melody and words half of the surviving text. De Boor justifies this practice by admitting his own incompetence in medieval musicology. We can hardly fault a literary scholar for lacking musicological expertise, but we can and must criticise the facile setting aside of the musical evidence. The assumption that governs de Boor's undertaking of the music drama is all too clear: for him, as for Hardison, the *Visitatio*, and by implication all liturgy, is essentially and ontologically a verbal phenomenon; music is only a secondary and accidental feature, presumably because it cannot be the bearer of "meaning" the way that verbal sounds can. Thus de Boor, like Hardison, tacitly valorizes the dominance of a literary paradigm in the study of the dramatic offices even in the very act of arguing against it.

But there is even more at stake in de Boor's methodology than this wholly unwarranted and mostly unreflective rejection of musical communication. De Boor, like Hardison and Drumbl and virtually every other student of the music drama who is not a musicologist, understands drama as a literary phenomenon. Such an understanding of any drama, ancient or modern, sung or spoken, is anathema to most contemporary students of drama. Our colleagues in university departments of theatre and drama, and certainly academically trained men and women of the professional theatre, employ a paradigm for understanding and enacting dramatic texts which is at least partially incommensurate with those unreflectingly used by their literary counterparts. Students of the medieval drama, including the Latin music drama, can ill afford to ignore it. As any student who emerges from the first class in Drama Studies can tell you, drama is essentially action and only secondarily words. Such a view would suggest that an interpretation of the *Visitatio* and similar texts which is authentically dramatic would privilege and reconstruct the actions required for its performance and make them the object of a semiotic inquiry. Furthermore, it would attempt to understand these actions in light of the phenomenological, structural, and semiotic models which increasingly dominate the theory and practice of dramatic studies. At the very least even literary and musicological scholars should read, mark, learn and inwardly digest such elementary manuals as Bernard Beckerman's *Dynamics of Drama* or Keir Elam's *The Semiotics of Theatre and Drama* and produce studies which test the relevance of these models for our subject.[25] Needless to say, such studies hardly exist, although a few readings of the more elaborate music dramas make gestures in this direction. Even here, however, the dominant mode of reading is literary.

This lack of studies which privilege gesture over word is all the more lamentable in light of recent developments in both ritual studies in general and in the history of Christian liturgy in particular, for from the perspective of these disciplines action, not verbal expression, is the primary component of the cultic. Rituals are believed to be efficacious by their practicing communities because they are mimetic gestures, not in the first place because of the words they contain. Indeed, using these perspectives, one might argue that the words that appear in a multitude of different ways in a great variety of the *Visitatio Sepulchri* offices are there to enhance the imitative function of the gestures or to provide a commentary on them. De Boor, like Hardison and the other scholars discussed in this essay, goes a long way in discrediting the old notion that the music drama had as its *raison d'être* the instruction of an ignorant laity. Yet in the end none of these literary scholars can shake off the dominance of the verbal sign which is the presupposition of their discipline in order to give adequate consideration to non-verbal semiotic systems.

But let us turn here to the primary concern of de Boor's book, the establishment of a textual history of the "Easter offices and dramas." De Boor's attempt to justify this project over the cautious objections of his predecessors merits some consideration. Genuine liturgical phenomena, de Boor explains, cannot fully be the subject of traditional textual history. But the *Quem quaeritis* trope and the *Visitatio Sepulchri* can be studied in this manner because they both "live within the liturgy," yet neither is indispensable to it. This peculiar position gives them a "freedom of movement" which the official liturgy does not possess. Because of this freedom, the *Visitatio* could be altered in different ways; it could be abbreviated or expanded or otherwise changed in order to make it fit the special needs of different occasions. It is this openness to change, de Boor claims, which makes a textual history of the *Visitatio* possible. In this way de Boor founds his whole enterprise on the dubious notion of the paraliturgical. Of course it is true that the *Quem quaeritis* trope and the *Visitatio* were sometimes added to a community's ritual books from sources other than their usual ones. But there is nothing extraordinary about this practice; it is hardly limited to the single set of "dramatic" ceremonies which de Boor describes. It is truly surprising that de Boor, who, unlike Hardison, actually handled hundreds of medieval liturgical books, could so facilely accept the notion of "the paraliturgical," a notion which, as I have already suggested, has so little precedent in medieval liturgical practice but which has nonetheless played a decisive but misleading role in medieval drama scholarship.

Obviously it is not possible to summarize in any detail the findings of de Boor's inquiries into the textual history of the *Quem quaeritis* within the scope of the present essay. There is a great deal to be learned from de Boor's close scrutiny of a large number of individual textual examples. Yet in the end his unthinking acceptance of literary paradigms and his surprising adoption of the notion of the paraliturgical led de Boor to what seem to me some fundamental errors, even in the relative "factual" domain which he explores. In briefly indicating why I feel that this is the case, I shall draw heavily from an essay by Michael Norton, who, after spending extensive time in Europe scrutinizing hundreds of manuscripts containing the *Quem quaeritis* dialogue, is presently engaged in providing a series of studies which I believe will finally provide a basis for solid further exploration of the textual history of the Latin music drama for Easter, one in which, for the first time, musical notation will be taken as seriously as the verbal text.[26] Norton's work shows little theoretical awareness, however, and my use of his results in order to provide a critique of de Boor's work should not be attributed to him.

The attempt to arrange the examples of the *Quem quaeritis* in textually determined categories has a long and complicated history which, significantly, has never taken the musical setting of the text into account at all. For our purposes we need only consider the work of Carl Lange, who in 1887 arranged all of the texts known to him into three "stages" of dramatic development: the first contained only the encounter between the Marys and the angel at the tomb; the second included this scene but added on to it the race of Peter and John to the sepulchre; the third included the Magdalena scenes and the appearance of the risen Jesus. We can immediately notice the evolutionary presuppositions of this scheme, in which we move from a first stage "simple" presentation to a "complex" third stage. More significantly, this account of the textual differences among the various manuscripts is entirely based on the supposition that these texts are dramas which gradually accumulate additional "scenes." But a close examination of the evidence will not support such a view. The very notion of a "scene" is, of course, utterly foreign to the Latin music drama as we know it from the texts which survive; Lange's importation of this notion is a good example of the way that these texts were constituted as drama by the very methods that were used to study them.

The notion of "scene" is also responsible for a pervasive error in Lange's hypotheses concerning the textual history for the Easter *Quem quaeritis* texts. In allowing a scene-dominated scheme to determine the textual-historical categories of the tradition which he studied, Lange obscured the fundamental fact that the text of the dialogue and its settings differ greatly among themselves within the "first stage," an observation which sharply challenges his claim that these texts should be grouped together in order to establish a textual history. It also obscures the fact that the most obvious differences between the "stage one" and the "stage two" *Visitatio* is not the addition of a scene but a new form of the *Quem quaeritis* dialogue whose words and melody cannot be derived from "first stage" texts and, further, that the "stage three" *Visitatio* ceremonies have many verbal and musical affinities to both the "first" and the "second stage" versions of the *Quem quaeritis*. Lange was not unaware of these facts, but he considered them less important than the division of the texts into scenes. Thus the unexamined claim that these texts were dramas, combined with a faith in developmental teleology, hopelessly confused their textual history long before Manley, Chambers, and Young authorized an evolutionary understanding of them. Like Young, Lange knew that there were grave difficulties with the arrangement he proposed, but it seemed "natural" to him to think of a growing drama. Perhaps it was Young's dissatisfaction with the incongruities between this arrangement and the "facts" attested to by the surviving manuscripts that led him to proclaim that writing a textual history of the *Visitatio* was an impossible enterprise. However that may be, it is important to note that, while implicitly renouncing Lange's claims for a textual history, Young took over Lange's scheme and further authorized it by adding a new "pre-dramatic" and "purely liturgical stage" to it and claiming that, were all the evidence available, the development of the music drama would generally follow that pattern.

With this necessary background in mind, we can turn to de Boor's book itself. Simply stated, de Boor's book can be seen as an attempt to bypass Young's notions about the way the *Visitatio* developed, in the process correcting Lange's work on the basis of a closer observation of minute textual details. De Boor explicitly rejects an evolutionary approach to the material and claims also that the basis of his system of categorization is liturgical rather than dramatic. More significantly, he focuses on individual words and lines and their variants rather than on large "scenes." Just as significantly, he takes seriously the geographical location from which each manuscript containing the *Quem quaeritis* dialogue originated, an essential consideration in any attempt to reconstruct a textual history, yet one that was virtually ignored by all of de Boor's predecessors, including both Young and Hardison.

Without at all considering the way that de Boor arrives at them, I shall state just a few of the most important of his findings. It is impossible, he argues, on the basis of our present knowledge of the textual history to find or reconstruct the original *Quem quaeritis* trope, but the preponderance of evidence points to northern Italy as the place of its origin. De Boor distinguishes between two major textual traditions of the Type I *Visitatio*. One is derived from Italy, Germany, Switzerland, and Spain. The other comes from France, Lotharingia, and the territories under Lotharingian ecclesiastical supervision. The examples of the *Quem quaeritis* trope from St. Gall and St. Martial, generally thought to be the two earliest surviving exemplars of the trope, respectively represent these two different traditions. The *Visitatio* in the *Regularis Concordia* is an unusual conflation of the French and Lotharingian forms. The second type of the *Visitatio* has, according to de Boor, a wholly different rationale from the first type; it is an "entirely new form of liturgical poetry" which is governed by a tendency toward realism and biblical rather than liturgical models. The Type III *Visitatio* advances these tendencies even further, creating yet another "poetic type" which sets the events of salvation history squarely in human history and which much more directly than its predecessors depicts and evokes human emotions.

There can be no doubt that de Boor's scheme is much more attractive than Lange's and that it respects more faithfully the actual state of the surviving texts. Yet while de Boor's work is illuminating and rewarding in its observation of details of individual texts, in the end it only succeeds in shuffling around Lange's findings. We emerge from de Boor's conclusion with the same three categories of *Visitatio* texts, even though the differences within each of the stages are for the first time clearly marked. Significantly, these categories represent now not stages of a developing dramatic tradition but distinct "poetic" types. And because these creations are claimed to be essentially "poetic," serious consideration apparently need not be given to the melodies. These only support the spirit of liturgical poetry which has given rise to these creations. Indeed, the individual exemplars of these creations can, de Boor hints, be subject to the kinds of close reading widely practiced in the 1950s and 1960s in literary circles.

It is by no means my intention to dismiss de Boor's work. Certainly it is possible to see the various "stages" of the *Visitatio* as somehow related to different currents of piety and spirituality. Indeed this is an area of future exploration that seems potentially very fruitful. And close readings of individual texts are bound to teach us a good deal about them. Yet it must be said that, like every other heuristic construction, de Boor's work was the product of his presuppositions, which in this case were predominantly literary. A textual history such as Michael Norton is writing, or which Susan Rankin has shown us in miniature in her study of 'Mary Magdalene in the *Visitatio Sepulchri* Ceremonies',[27] both of which concentrate equally on the details of verbal expression and musical notation, will however bring us closer to an understanding of these texts in ways that we more usually consider textual-historical. But it will not, let it be stressed, bring us closer to the "naked truth" about these offices, for it, like every other cultural and interpretative structure, will be the product of its presuppositions. There is no escape from the hermeneutical circle.

III

The late 1960s and early 1970s saw a comparatively large number of publications on the subject of the Latin music drama, but the place of honor must surely be given to Walther Lipphardt's *Lateinische Osterfeiern und Osterspiele*. In a promised seven volumes Lipphardt proposed to edit all of the Easter *Feiern* and *Spiele*. Happily the first six volumes of the collection appeared prior to Lipphardt's death, and these include all the verbal texts Lipphardt had planned to publish. His seventh volume was to include elaborate indices, extensive bibliographies, and a glossary. Although Lipphardt is rumored to have finished the work, it has never appeared. Nonetheless we have good reason to be grateful for what he has given us for the study of the Latin music drama. The number of texts which Lipphardt's books make available has more than doubled those which had previously been in print. But Lipphardt's contribution goes far beyond increasing the numbers of texts that are readily available. Lipphardt on the whole follows de Boor's classification of the texts, but he arranged his texts within these categories by the geographical location from which each text comes. This new arrangement encourages us to see these texts in a new light, one in which we can see how a given text was altered in the same location across several centuries. Surprisingly, no study of the music drama known to me consistently follows this approach, one which would seem to be so potentially fruitful that we can only hope that future work will follow up on some of its possibilities. Even the most casual attempt to work on a geographical basis will produce a view of the *Quem quaeritis* texts which is bound to be strikingly different from the one which takes chronology, itself often determined on the sole and dubious criterion of the age of a manuscript, as its point of departure.

Despite its many assets, Lipphardt's work has its own set of serious problems. As scholars continue to scrutinize his printed versions with an eye for the various details which we expect to be correct in such a once-in-a-century undertaking, it is becoming apparent that Lipphardt's work was sometimes done in haste and often, unfortunately, carelessly. The evidence is growing that Lipphardt did not actually reexamine and reedit many of the texts which he printed. There are very many errors of minor and some of major proportions. A complete list of errata and corrections is greatly to be desired, but given the scope of Lipphardt's endeavor, it is likely to be very long in coming. Moreover, the problems raised by Lipphardt's books reach well beyond the kinds of errors which, even had he been an extraordinarily meticulous scholar, could hardly have been entirely avoided. Though Lipphardt was the author of a number of musicological studies and editions, his opus magnum is concerned only with the verbal text of the Easter offices and plays. Musical text was omitted, Lipphardt explains, because his publisher insisted that it would have been prohibitively expensive to print it. One cannot but be astonished by this situation. Many factors must have lead to this decision and probably Lipphardt's reluctant acquiescence to it. But the result is that what will surely be, if only by default, the "definitive" edition of the greater part of the Latin music drama repertory for several generations is wholly deceptive and inadequate. Once again the impression is given that these texts are literary and that they are musical in only a secondary way. It would, of course, make no sense to publish only the melodies to the *Quem quaeritis* dialogue; indeed, no one would ever think of doing such a foolish thing. Yet the appearance of an edition of the *Quem quaeritis* dialogues which takes into account only their verbal texts is almost as foolish, even though it is true that many exemplars lack written melodies in the manuscripts in which they were preserved – a situation which does not suggest that they were ever performed as merely verbal text, as Hardison has, wholly without historical foundation, on occasion suggested.

Lipphardt has published the texts of the *Quem quaeritis* and other pieces closely related to it, but naturally he has excerpted them out of medieval liturgical manuscripts which contain much else besides these texts. This practice was inevitable if he was to publish seven rather than seven hundred volumes, and in any case it follows the procedures of Young, Hardison, and de Boor in disregarding the immediate and more distant surrounding contexts in the manuscripts in which these pieces are preserved. But it is important to notice the theoretical presuppositions of this practice, one which, as we have seen, was frequently and openly stated by these scholars: the claim that these texts are plays or pieces of liturgical poetry which have their own history and which have no direct connection with the non-dramatic or non-poetic pieces found elsewhere in the manuscripts from which they are excerpted. Even when Hardison and de Boor argue that a given piece is "liturgical" and not "dramatic," they fail to consider its liturgical context by refusing to look beyond its immediate context to give careful attention to the details of the specific liturgical manuscript from which it was taken.

This practice of judicious excision is universally followed in all music drama scholarship, yet it seems authorized only by the assumptions about drama which these scholars and other students of the subject have allowed to determine their modus operandi. Save for a few exceptions, nothing in the medieval books which are the source of these "dramas" justifies this kind of excision. This practice of omission has prevented an even superficial consideration of the larger context of these "dramatic offices" from taking place; it is largely responsible for the fact that generations of students have become convinced that these texts belong in the same ontological category as Shakespeare's tragedies and Ibsen's realistic plays. Had students been forced to encounter the *Quem quaeritis* texts surrounded by the contexts in which they are preserved, the history of the scholarship might have taken a course unrecognizable to its present practitioners. What is more, such excisions have cut off these texts from their historical and material contexts and made them into objects of a *Geistesgeschichte* which seriously obfuscates their places in the daily routine of monasteries, cathedrals, and parish churches. These excisions have also authorized claims concerning the uniqueness of the *Quem quaeritis* texts which are, at the least, open to serious question. Clearly these are matters of such major concern that they cannot be discussed in any detail here. But precisely because they are matters of such import, a few words concerning this issue seem imperative.

It has been a persistent theme of this essay that we can never know "things" in themselves and that they become known to us only in terms of the models and paradigms which, in a very real way, construct them. Even attempts to study materials historically are the products of our own models of the past. History, R. G. Collingwood once said, "is nothing but the re-enactment of past thought in the historian's mind."[28] The past is past and can only be recovered by our actively involving ourselves and our understanding of our world in its recovery. Since the rediscovery of the Latin music drama in the nineteenth century, these texts have been looked on as dramas and construed and interpreted using models which have arisen in the modern experience and in a context foreign to their original "Sitz im Leben." Though the aesthetic object and the aesthetic experience are inventions of the eighteenth century, the Latin music drama, to name here the problematic term which has been in use throughout this essay, has been viewed as either the unaesthetic beginnings of an aesthetic phenomenon or as the potential source of aesthetic pleasure. There is ultimately nothing that can be said against such an understanding of these texts since all readings of historically distant materials are dependent on paradigms which are foreign to them. Understanding the *Quem quaeritis* texts in this way certainly helps us to make sense of our intuitive response to them, fashioned as it is by our own twentieth-century experiences.

However, if we must acknowledge that there is nothing "wrong" with placing these texts in dramatic paradigms which are historically foreign to them, we must also forcefully assert that there is no necessary connection between the *Quem quaeritis* texts and the aesthetic, literary, and dramatic paradigms which have been used to interpret them for more than a century. As we have seen, every major study of the last two decades has argued that we should see them – or at least some of them – as "liturgical" phenomena, though in the end every scholar mentioned here has fallen back on literary models and offered at least the "best" of the texts which he discusses as works of "literature" or, what is unfortunately for most of these researchers virtually the same thing, "drama." Perhaps the time has come to take seriously the ritual nature of these texts and, taking models of ritual which prevail in contemporary anthropology and the other social sciences, to inquire about their ritual (as opposed to their "literary" or "aesthetic") function.

It hardly needs to be said that "ritual" is as problematic as it is a key term in these disciplines and that the social sciences possess no single agreed upon definition of it. Yet there are common characteristics ascribed to rituals by even the highly diverse models in use in these sciences. Rituals, whether they be a solemn celebration of the Eucharist in the tenth century or a Fourth of July parade in rural America, are communal activities which have as their function the creation and confirmation of communal values, not theological "truths." Indeed, to the degree that "reality" is a social construct, it is possible to argue that rituals, more than any other element of a social environment, create and reinforce that reality. The excision of the texts of the Latin music drama from their context in medieval liturgical books has fundamentally obscured their communal nature and transformed them into the "autonomous" objects validated by romantic and post-romantic aesthetics. But to see these texts in the breadth of their "original" context is to see them in an entirely different light. Here they must be linked not only with other texts in the specific books from which they are taken but with all the other books with which that book is itself linked in the daily round of cultic observance in a specific church or religious house. The use of office or mass books which contain the texts for liturgical celebration implies the use of *rituales* and other books which record the liturgical actions that accompanied the performance of these verbal and musical texts. Furthermore, these books often imply the use of still other books, which frequently bear the designation of "customaries" and which describe how the daily practice of prayer in the chapel was to be integrated with other rituals more closely tied to the round of daily life in a monastery, cathedral, or parish church.

To see the *Quem quaeritis* texts in such a perspective is to see how they functioned within a much larger social domain than we usually ascribe to them. It is to see them as fundamentally social texts rather than as aesthetically autonomous "plays." It is also to expose their ideological function, by which I mean the way they served the socially useful purpose of making sense of experience and of repeatedly incorporating individuals into the social body in its local manifestation. The pursuing of such a model in the study of the "medieval Latin drama" is a task which I greatly hope will characterize at least some scholarly activity in the future. I can here only suggest what seem to be some of its advantages over the older "aesthetic" model:

1. It will relate our reflections on these texts to a concrete material reality, in contrast to the intellectualizing and spiritualizing tendencies of previous scholarship. In the process these texts will be shown to play an important role in the total life of

specific medieval communities. The present "literary" model assigns them at best a peripheral and necessarily secondary role in the totality of lived experience as it was understood and interpreted in the Middle Ages.

2. It will strongly call into question the presently made claims for the uniqueness of these texts in relationship to other liturgical texts. The *Quem quaeritis* texts have striking similarities with many other texts and other practices in medieval communities, and recognizing these similarities – similarities which have been utterly obscured by the way they have been transformed into "drama" – will enable us to construct typologies in which they can be included and which in turn will have new heuristic value. The claimed peculiarity of the *Quem quaeritis* texts among all liturgical texts is clearly related to the modern aesthetic model's demand for uniqueness; for that very reason it should stand under suspicion.

3. It will make apparent the untenability of claiming an ontological center for these texts, a claim which ascribes to them the same "nature" and function across different historical periods, times, and places of performance. Even though the *Visitatio Sepulchri* is found in only a few different textual locations in medieval service books, it would be a serious mistake to say that it served the same function in all the diverse communities which performed it. One of the abiding contributions of structuralism, whatever its other drawbacks, was its insistence that meaning is always the product of contexts rather than metaphysically endowed "natures." The "same thing" placed in a different context will not, indeed cannot, "mean the same thing." Thus, even if we possess texts of the *Quem quaeritis* which are verbally and musically identical (and what constitutes "the identical" in liturgical manuscripts is a question that deserves far more consideration that it has been given), we cannot assume that they served the save function or meant the same thing. We must recognize, in fact, that even the "same" text, performed in the same community, would acquire different meanings every year, though in most instances these fluctuations in meaning are probably forever lost even to our reconstruction of them. But there are alterations in context which are available to our scrutiny. If we consider only monastic usage, for example, we need to take into account the variations in the annual cursus of liturgical practice and daily life which would suggest different nuances in the understanding of our texts. On a more macrocosmic level, it is easy to see that once these original monastic practices passed over to cathedral and parish usages they inevitably acquired entirely different "meanings" and functions.

If future scholarship should center its concern on the "Sitz im Leben" of our texts, in the broadest sense of that term, it will surely open up dimensions which even such recent interpreters as Young, Hardison, and De Boor seem not to have imagined. But in order to do so, it will need to restore the texts to the contexts from which earlier scholarship has separated them. And it will need to renounce the idealist notion of fixity of meaning. Seen from this perspective, Lipphardt's in many ways magnificent editions are a mixed blessing, for they will prevent several generations of future scholars from being motivated to view the *Quem quaeritis* texts in their manuscript context. These texts will remain, then, the provenance solely of "drama" and dramatic studies.

IV

Such remarks seem to take us far from a review of scholarship. They can, however, conveniently lead us to a consideration of the last major text to be discussed here, Johann Drumbl's *Quem Quaeritis: Teatro sacro dell'alto medioevo*. Drumbl's book is a difficult one, with an argument so complex and dependent upon minute textual details that it cannot with justice be summarized here. I shall limit myself to a concern with what is clearly Drumbl's chief interest, the classical problem of the "origins" of the medieval drama.

First a few preliminary observations are in order. Like the other studies considered here, indeed much more than those studies, Drumbl insists that his book is more an investigation in liturgiology than in literary studies. He rightly insists that we must learn all that we can about the context of a manuscript which contains a *Quem quaeritis* text; we need to supplement office books with customaries, for example. In following out this program Drumbl is able to make a few tentative steps toward moving beyond the consideration of a trope or *Visitatio* text itself to consider its place in monastic life.

Secondly, though Drumbl's conclusions about the origin of the *Quem quaeritis* are markedly different from de Boor's, he accepts de Boor's *Textgeschichte* as a safe and general guide to the manuscript history of the texts associated with the dramatic rites of Easter. This means that his work has many of the same limitations that appear in de Boor's study. Drumbl takes as his point of departure de Boor's own starting point, the notion that since the *Quem quaeritis* texts are not "mandatory" pieces of the liturgy found everywhere in medieval Europe they may be regarded as only paraliturgical. Though it must be admitted that Drumbl arrives at some fruitful insights by making this assumption, the same caveat sounded in the discussion of de Boor's book must be repeated here: the dichotomy between "official liturgy" and the "paraliturgical" does not seem supported by the medieval books under discussion. Perhaps more significantly, Drumbl follows de Boor's most questionable practice: his utter failure to take the musical text into account, even though such a procedure allows important differences among texts to remain hidden, indeed unknown. A few works of musicological scholarship are cited in Drumbl's book, but like other literary scholars Drumbl does not, for example, hesitate to offer all manner of hypotheses about the *Regularis Concordia* text of the *Visitatio* without so much as consulting Alejandro Planchart's *The Repertory of Tropes at Winchester*.[29] It must be insisted here again that every study of the *Quem quaeritis* offices which does not take the musical text into serious account is at best suspect. One cannot but wonder when literary scholars will finally come to understand this.

We turn now to Drumbl's hypothesis concerning the origin of the *Visitatio*. In his *Textgeschichte* de Boor had tentatively opted for an Italian origin of the trope, primarily on the basis of a large number of early surviving examples from Italy. Drumbl submits these Italian texts to intense scrutiny and argues that each represents a local monastery's or church's revision of a text that it had inherited from elsewhere. Each Italian example, he claims, represents an accommodation of a local liturgy to a piece that came from outside of its traditions and whose adaptations cause tensions within the local practice. Thus Drumbl hypothesizes that the *Quem quaeritis* trope must have had its origins somewhere outside of Italy. This view causes him to examine in detail two of the earliest non-Italian documents among which, not surprisingly, the *Regularis Concordia Visitatio* text is the focus of interest.

The *Regularis* is, of course, a monastic *consuetudino* that was created in the service of the tenth-century Benedictine reforms in England; its sources, as the document itself makes clear, are practices both in Ghent and in Fleury. If we ask which of these two locations is likely to have provided the English with their famous and now oldest surviving text of the *Visitatio*, Ghent seems on first consideration a more likely candidate. Like de Boor, Drumbl draws on Dom Kassius Hallinger's study of Gorze-Cluny to supply data from monastic history crucial to his argument.[30] The Benedictine house at Ghent accepted in 937 the Lotharingian reform of Gorze. The liturgical tradition associated with this reform includes the performance of the *Quem quaeritis* as a dialogue at the end of Matins. On the other hand, we have no evidence of a *Quem quaeritis* ceremony of any kind at Fleury before the thirteenth century, when it is attested to in a customary. Though the manuscript in which it is preserved is, relatively speaking, a late one, its version of the *Quem quaeritis* dialogue is judged by Drumbl to be "primitive" because it contains nothing more than five simple lines of dialogue.

These observations bring us to the heart of Drumbl's claim: against a more commonsense assumption that Ghent gave the English Benedictines their *Visitatio*, Drumbl insists that the ceremony came to England from Fleury. Richard Donovan made a somewhat similar suggestion more than a decade ago,[31] but Drumbl, whose work reveals only a spotty knowledge of Anglo-American scholarship, seems unaware of it. Donovan offered his not wholly convincing argument tentatively, on the basis of certain textual similarities which the *Visitatio* text in the so-called Fleury Playbook uniquely shares with the English *Regularis* text. In sharp contrast, Drumbl offers us the boldest sort of conjecture. To understand that conjecture even in the oversimplified and summarized form in which it is offered in this review, the reader needs further information about Fleury and why it had not earlier been seriously claimed as the *Heimat* of the *Quem quaeritis* text.

Fleury underwent monastic reform in 930 under Odo of Cluny. As is widely known, Cluniac houses were never sympathetic to the practice of troping or the production of similar liturgical embellishments; as best as we can tell, *Quem quaeritis* texts were never performed in Cluniac houses. This very fact, which seems utterly subversive to any claim that the Benedictine abbey at Fleury was the place where the *Quem quaeritis* text was authored, paradoxically allows Drumbl to offer his tour de force suggestion. He rightly observes that, though in some areas of life Fleury bore the lasting marks of its reform under Cluniac auspices, its customary is totally independent of Cluny, at least as concerns "liturgical practices," and this fact suggests to Drumbl that the house retained its earlier, pre-Cluniac ritual. Yet the *Quem quaeritis* cannot, for a number of reasons, be much older that 930. Drumbl therefore suggests that the dialogue was written, perhaps by Odo himself, around 930 at Fleury and that it passed from there to England and to Italy. He offers additional support for this claim by pointing out that in the Fleury customary the *Quem quaeritis* serves a definite and recognizable liturgical function: it is to be sung at procession after terce and before mass on Easter. In this it differs from its Italian counterparts where, in Drumbl's view, we can see that an alien element has been fitted into an already pre-existing liturgy. In summary then, according to Drumbl the *Quem quaeritis* dialogue originated as a processional song (not as a trope) and as an original piece of liturgical "poetry" written at Fleury about 930 while the monastery was under the direction of Odo.

I recognize that this summary has been tedious and has occupied a disproportionately large amount of space within the scope of this essay, but it is impossible to discuss Drumbl's work without giving some sense of his exceedingly complicated argument. If anything, I have oversimplified it, though not, I hope, so much as to do a major injustice to it. In fact, I must beg the reader's indulgence for one more paragraph of summary which is necessary before we can assess Drumbl's contribution to the present state of medieval drama studies. Having discovered, at least to his own satisfaction, the original *Quem quaeritis* piece, Drumbl goes on to ask why the new ceremony was composed for the precise moment in the liturgical cursus in which we encounter it at Fleury. The reason is to be found, if I understand Drumbl correctly, in a reform of the Easter procession in France in the ninth century, a reform which limited the route of the procession to the interior of the church, whereas earlier it had encircled the entire complex of monastic buildings. This new processional practice, Drumbl claims, created a need for a new ceremony, one which could be constructed on the pattern of other processional and stational chants in use in Fleury. These pieces often contained a dialogue shared by two cantors. Odo, or someone under his direction, thus composed the *Quem quaeritis* chant in order to fill an "open space" in the Easter cursus. But when this piece of liturgical poetry passed over to other, non-French, communities, which had not experienced the reform of the Easter procession and hence did not require a piece in order to fill in a newly vacant moment in the cursus, they changed the text and inserted it, often with some difficulty, into their pre-existing communal rites. This explains, in Drumbl's view, why the *Quem quaeritis* text survives in three different forms: as processional piece, as trope to the Easter Introit, and as a dramatic ceremony performed before the singing of the *Te Deum* at Easter matins.

These claims merit far closer scrutiny than they can be given here; I will limit myself first to a few historical observations and then briefly consider the tacit theoretical conceptions which motivate Drumbl's endeavours. It must be recognized that some of the claims which Drumbl puts forth are the sheerest and, as far as I can see, unmerited conjecture. Père Anselme Davril, editor of the Fleury volume in the *Corpus Consuetudinum Monasticarum*,[32] has written with commendable monkish restraint on Drumbl's hypothesis of a reform of the Easter procession in ninth-century Fleury, "This is a reform of which I have no knowledge".[33] Yet in a recent review article on Drumbl's book, Davril shows himself surprisingly sympathetic to the case which Drumbl puts forward, though with an argument which alters and complicates Drumbl's claims even further. Davril notes similarities between the verbal text of the *Quem quaeritis* procession and antiphons used in the procession to the baptismal font during Easter Vespers. He conjectures that since there were no fonts in monastic churches, monastic communities moved these antiphons to the Easter morning procession after Terce, and in this environment the *Quem quaeritis* material was expanded and made appropriate to its new context.[34] This argument has some affinities with the view expressed by Hardison in 1966.[35] Davril offers further evidence, of the most general and unpersuasive nature, that Odo could well have been the author of the *Quem quaeritis* dialogue. But in a further complication, he argues that the *Regularis Concordia* did not come directly from Fleury (which in his view, as it is in Drumbl's, is its ultimate source) but from the abbey of St. Pierre of Ghent, which had undergone a Lotharingian type of reform. But, Davril claims, this abbey had undergone this reform under the influence of Fleury. Thus it is possible that Odo's new ceremony passed from Fleury to Ghent, where it took the form of the *Visitatio Sepulchri* rather than a processional piece, the form which it had at Fleury. In this new form it was carried to England to be incorporated into the now famous book which offers it to us as the oldest surviving example of the *Visitatio Sepulchri*.

Drumbl's hypotheses are not convincing, and Davril's complicating revision of them makes them even less so. In the first place the notion that a liturgical piece has a single definite place in the liturgy for which it was originally intended contradicts the evidence of surviving medieval books. If one reads through the whole of the office and the mass for paschaltide in a group of related books from any given community, it becomes apparent that the liturgy consists of frequently repeated elements which are placed in ever different contexts. The musical and verbal texts of a Psalm antiphon are often reused in a processional piece, and vice versa, and the same verbal text can sometimes reappear again in a respond or a gradual. Indeed, one could make a case for characterizing the experience of the liturgy as one marked by a constant recycling of familiar elements which acquire ever new contexts and therefore ever new meanings. It is true, of course, that new elements were frequently composed for the liturgy in Frankish territories in the ninth and tenth centuries; the *Quem quaeritis* was obviously one of them. But the notion that it filled some specific need and occupied its own proper place in the liturgical cursus in such a way that all other placements of it are to be seen as deviations from that norm seems very far removed from the practice of the medieval liturgy as we know it from surviving liturgical books. It is, significantly, much closer to modern notions of poetic and musical compositions.

There is yet another, related factor that Drumbl's argument overlooks. It is certainly true that the *Quem quaeritis* is preserved in tenth- and eleventh-century sources in a number of different positions in the liturgy. But as David A. Bjork has shown, the division between those which situate the chant before the Mass and those which incorporate it into Matins is neither haphazard, as Drumbl suggests, nor chronological, as Hardison supposed. It is geographical.[36] As a general rule to which there are, of course, exceptions, the dialogue was sung at Mass in southern France, in Catalonia, in Italy, and in a few East Frankish locales such as St. Gall, Rheinau, Heidenheim, and Minden. It was sung at Matins across northern Europe, in England, northern France, the Rhineland, and in most of the East Frankish territory. It is possible, of course, to integrate this observation into Drumbl's scheme, but it certainly calls into question the claim that monastic houses included the new composition in their observances because they found it attractive but were presented with the difficulty of finding a place for it since its creation was unmotivated by the historical situations of their communities.

We now pass to examine briefly Drumbl's tacit theoretical assumptions and their relationship to the larger scope of medieval drama scholarship. Of all the authors scrutinized in the present essay, Drumbl is the one who superficially appears aware of current developments in theory, though his perspective is entirely that of a conservative Germanist; at least the names of Walter Benjamin and Peter Szondi are very occasionally evoked. But the presence of these names is deceiving, for in many ways Drumbl's work returns us to the presuppositions which governed the study of the Latin music drama from its beginnings until the appearance of Hardison's book. Drumbl is no evolutionist; he rejects the old teleological model which Hardison called into question. But like Hardison, and Young, and indeed like Lange and Milchsack[37] in the nineteenth century, Drumbl is deeply committed to a quest for origins; he wishes to show us how the *Quem quaeritis*, and ultimately the entire modern drama, got its start. Such a quest for origins has, rightly in my view, been radically called into question in the last two decades. The now widely known critique of such an enterprise prompts us to consider some fundamental questions about Drumbl's work and similar studies by others.

In the first place, one must question why the point of origins has been granted such a privileged position in the study of our subject. Is there something which we will know when we discover the origins of the music drama which we could not know otherwise? It seems natural to assert that there is, but that "natural" response cannot really hold up to rigorous scrutiny. If indeed Drumbl were correct, and we could identify Odo as the "author" of the first *Quem quaeritis* ceremony and recognize in the supposed repression of an earlier processional practice the office's original "Sitz im Leben," that fact would not fundamentally change our study of the subsequent history of the music drama. Drumbl's discovery would illuminate the use of the piece at a moment in Fleury's history, and if we could place that information in a broader human scheme, it would be useful indeed. But discovering the source of the *Regularis Concordia Visitatio* in no way helps us to understand the function of that text in that community.

But obviously the remarkably learned scholars who have carried on the study of the music drama for the last century have thought otherwise. Why did they do so? Because, it seems to me, they shared with their contemporaries a belief in what I have termed "the ontological fallacy." They believed, and so apparently does Drumbl, that the being of a thing is fixed and permanent and that any usage which violates an object's pristine stage must be regarded as creating a distortion or a deviation. This is not the place to argue philosophy; Plato is more attractive to most of us than many of us would care to admit. But it seems to me that in the human sciences it is use that is significant and that use is defined by an ever-shifting series of contexts, only some of which are intellectual or spiritual. Meaning, to repeat a claim made more than once in this essay, is never fixed or permanent. Even if it is true that change proceeded at a much slower pace in the early Middle Ages than it does today (and how could we ever test the validity of such a claim?), it remains the case that a monk who observed or participated in the *Visitatio* at, say, Winchester, annually for a period of twenty years, would perceive and understand that ceremony differently on each of its twenty performances. And his varying perceptions would be related to, but not identical with, the shifting perceptions of his confreres. And certainly a monk in tenth-century England would view the *Visitatio* differently from a lay man or woman visiting a monastic church in the twelfth-century in order to observe a performance of a "dramatic office"; such a lay person's perceptions and understandings would, in turn, differ radically from his counterpart in a sixteenth-century German parish church in which vernacular plays were performed.

Cultural objects like the *Quem quaeritis* are made by humans to reflect and interpret their concrete socio-economic-cultural situations, and since "human nature" can be defined only by its changeability and by its actual processes of change, so also the objects made and used by humans are constantly changing. In doing so they are not losing their "true" or "original" essence, they are neither declining nor improving, and they are certainly not developing in a determined pattern impressed upon them at their moment of origin. They are merely changing, and in the process of this changing they are both reflecting and creating the ever-changing nature of human beings. That is the reason why any quest for ontological origins and any claims for teleological development will fail to withstand historical scrutiny. If this is so in general, it is especially so for the group of ceremonies which we have traditionally labeled the "liturgical drama."

But there is yet another reason why historical quests for origins such as we see in Drumbl's work are futile. Even if Drumbl's arguments were correct, he would not have discovered the "origin" of the *Quem quaeritis* in its primal purity. If we agreed today that Odo of Cluny were the author of the dialogue, tomorrow we would begin to investigate the "sources" of Odo's creation. We would consider, for example, the ways that the Cluniac tradition makes its appearance in the work, the possible patristic echoes, the ways that the processional customs inscribed in this new Easter procession are related to other customs in the peculiar form of Benedictine life that was practiced in tenth-century Fleury. I mention these topics not because I do not think that they would be useful subjects for investigation; on the contrary, I believe that these are useful issues for further inquiry, quite apart from whether or not Odo is the "author" of the *Quem quaeritis* dialogue. But an investigation of these topics in the hope of finally arriving at the beginnings of something is at least as futile as trying to write a comprehensive "Forschungsbericht" on any given topic.

These remarks bring my essay full circle, to the words and ideas of my introduction. I recognize that I have not completely met the assignment for this collection of essays, for rather than attempting to survey everything that has been written on the music drama I have chosen to examine a handful of works and to look at the presuppositions which underlie them. If I have been critical of the scholars whose work is described here, it is not because I do not admire their achievements. If I have omitted significant works by others – and I certainly have – it is not because I am unaware of them or because I do not think that they represent worthy scholarship. But I must insist that far more important than the detailed investigations of individual scholars is the direction that scholarship as a whole takes, its self reflection, its sense of its purpose. Unfortunately, except for the reflection on the evolutionary model of historical investigation that Hardison's book set into motion, such reflection has been painfully absent from the study of the Latin music drama. And even more unfortunate – and here I realise that I am raising an issue far more controversial than the question of whether Odo of Cluny wrote the first *Quem quaeritis* dialogue – is the lack of any indication that students in our field are even aware of the theoretical and political revolutions that have played such a crucial role in academic life in the past two decades.

As students of the music drama, the crucial question for our future is, what do we want to know? We can, if we wish, try to delude ourselves and claim that all we want to know is how the modern drama "really" began, but our knowing of anything cannot be disengaged from our own interests. We know only that which the models we live under and which we consciously or unconsciously employ make available as knowledge. Our predecessors in the study of the music drama construed and hence constituted these texts as dramas and as works of literature. We can, but need not, follow in their tracks. I would suggest that a more fruitful line to pursue in our studies would be marked by questions about the epistemological and ideological functions of the music drama and about its semiotic systems. I would choose to investigate how these practices were grounded in both material and mental existence and subsequently how, in conjunction with other producers of theoretical and practical knowledge, they enabled humans to construct their world in such a way that experience seemed meaningful for them. Whatever the pitfalls that await us as we pursue these questions, we can be certain that such lines of inquiry will move our subject, if not to the centre of things, at least from the periphery where it remains bogged down by historicist discourse. Investigating the medieval dramatic ceremonies from this perspective will genuinely restore history to our inquiry and our inquiry to history. It will give our subject a relevance it has not possessed, for in asking questions about the formation and transformation of meaning, it will confront us with our own meaning-formation processes and our own being-in-history.

Notes

1. C. Clifford Flanigan, "The Roman Rite and the Origins of the Liturgical Drama," *University of Toronto Quarterly* 43 (1974), pp. 263-84.
2. Rene Wellek and Austin Warren, *Theory of Literature*, New York, 1977 [3rd ed.]
3. Cfr. Jonathan Culler, *Structuralist Poetics: Structuralism, Linguistics, and the Study of Literature*, Ithaca, 1975.
4. Walther Lipphardt [ed.], *Lateinische Osterfeiern und Osterspiele*, Berlin, 1975-81 [*Ausgaben Deutscher Literatur, Reihe Drama*, 5], 6 vols.
5. O. B. Hardison, *Christian Rite and Christian Drama in the Middle Ages: Essays in the Origin and Early History of Modern Drama*, Baltimore, 1965.
6. Helmut de Boor, *Die Textgeschichte der lateinischen Osterfeiern*, Tübingen, 1967 [*Hermea, Germanistische Forschungen*, n.s. 22].
7. Johann Drumbl, *Quem quaeritis: Teatro Sacro dell'alto Medioevo*, Rome, 1981.
8. Cfr. Fletcher Collins Jr., *Medieval Church Music dramas: A Repertory of Complete Plays*, Charlottesville, 1976, and Idem, *The Production of Medieval Church Music dramas*, Charlottesville, 1972.

9. C. Clifford Flanigan, "The Liturgical Drama and Its Tradition: A Review of Scholarship, 1965-1975," *Research Opportunities in Renaissance Drama* 13 (1975), pp. 81-102; 14 (1976), pp. 109-36.

10. Diane Dolan, *Le drame liturgique de Pâques en Normandie et en Angleterre au moyen âge*, Paris, 1975 [Publications de l'Université de Poitiers, Lettres et Sciences Humaines, 16].

11. Cfr. Blandine-Dominique Berger, *Le drame liturgique de Pâques. Liturgie et Théâtre*, Paris, 1976 [*Théologie Historique*, 37].

12. Among those "hands": C. Clifford Flanigan, "The Fleury Playbook, the Traditions of Medieval Latin Drama, and Modern Scholarship" in Thomas P. Campbell and Clifford Davidson [eds.], *The Fleury Playbook: Essays and Studies*, Kalamazoo, 1985, pp. 1-25.

13. William L. Smoldon, *The Music of the Medieval Church Dramas*, Cynthia Bourgeault [ed.], London, 1980.

14. Cfr. William L. Smoldon, 'The Melodies of Music in Medieval Church-Drama and Their Significance', *Comparative Drama* 2 (1968), pp. 185-209, esp. pp. 187 ff.; rpt. with extensive revisions in Jerome Taylor and Alan H. Nelson [eds.], *Medieval English Drama: Essays Critical and Contextual*, Chicago, 1972, pp. 64-80.

15. Karl Young, *The Drama of the Medieval Church*, Oxford, 1933, 2 vols.

16. Jean-René Hesbert [ed.], *Corpus Antiphonarium Officii*, Rome, 1963-70 [*Rerum Ecclesiasticorum Documenta*, Series Maior, Fontes 7-11], 4 vols.

17. Cfr. E. K. Chambers, *The Mediaeval Stage*, London, 1903, 2 vols.

18. Cfr. Harden Craig, *English Religious Drama of the Middle Ages*, London, 1955.

19. See C. Clifford Flanigan, "The Liturgical Context of the *Quem quaeritis* Trope," *Comparative Drama* 8 (1974), pp. 13-44.

20. Ritva Jonsson et al.[ed.], *Corpus Troporum*, Stockholm, 1975-2011 [*Studia Latina Stockholmiensia*], 11 vols to date.

21. Thomas S. Kuhn, *The Structure of Scientific Revolutions*, Chicago, 1970 [International Encyclopaedia of Unified Science], 2nd ed.

22. Carl Lange, *Die lateinische Osterfeier: Untersuchungen über den Ursprung und die Entwicklung der liturgisch-dramatische Auferstehungsfeier mit Zugrundelegung eines umfangreichen, neuaufgefundenen Quellenmaterials*, München, 1887.

23. De Boor, *Textgeschichte*, p. 5.

24. *Ibidem*, p. 9.

25. Cfr. Bernard Beckerman, *Dynamics of Drama: Theory and Method of Analysis*, New York, 1970 and Keir Elam, *The Semiotics of Theatre and Drama*, New York, 1980.

26. Michael Norton, "Of 'Stages' and 'Types' in *Visitatio Sepulchri*", *Comparative Drama* 21 (1987), pp. 34-61, 127-48.

27. Susan Rankin, "Mary Magdalene in the *Visitatio Sepulchri* Ceremonies," *Early Music History* 1 (1981), pp. 227-55.

28. R. G. Collingwood, *The Idea of History*, New York, 1956, p. 228.

29. Alejandro Enrique Planchart, *The Repertory of Tropes at Winchester*, Princeton, 1977, 2 vols.

30. Kassius Hallinger, *Gorze-Kluny: Studien zu den monastischen Lebensformen und Gegensatzen im Hochmittelalter*, Rome, 1950-51 [*Studia Anselma*, 22-23], 2 vols.

31. Richard B. Donovan, "Two Celebrated Centers of Medieval Liturgical Drama: Fleury and Ripol," in E. Catherine Dunn, Titiana Fotitch and Bernard Peebles [eds.], *The Medieval Drama and Its Claudelian Revival*, Washington, 1970, pp. 41-51.

32. Anselme Davril [ed.], *Consuetudines Floriacenses saeculi tertii decimi*, Sieburg [*Corpus Consuetudinum Monasticarum*, 9], 1976.

33. Anselme Davril [ed.], *The Monastic Ritual of Fleury: Orléans, Bibliothèque municipale, Ms 123 (101)*, London-Wolfeboro, 1990, p. 69.

34. Cfr. Anselme Davril, "Johann Drumbl and the Origin of the *Quem quaeritis*: A Review Article," *Comparative Drama* 20 (1986), pp. 65-75.

35. O. B. Hardison, "Gregorian Easter Vespers and Early Liturgical Drama," in Dunn, Fotitch and Peebles [eds.], *Medieval Drama and Claudelian Revival*, pp. 27-40.

36. David A. Bjork, "On the Dissemination of *Quem quaeritis* and the *Visitatio sepulchri* and the Chronology of Their Early Sources," *Comparative Drama* 14 (1980), pp. 46-69.

37. Gustav Milchsack, *Die Oster- und Passionspiele: Literarhistorische Untersuchungen über den Ursprung und die Entwicklung derselben bis zum siebzehnten Jahrhundert, vornehmlich in Deutschland nebst dem erstmaligen diplomatischen Abdruck des Künzelsauer Fronleichnamsspiels*, Wolffenbüttel, 1880.

Books of Hours and the Construction of Reality in the Fifteenth Century
C. Clifford Flanigan[*]

*T*he topic of the relationships between clerical and "popular," or non-clerical, culture is an important and persistent one in medieval studies. Yet surprisingly, it has seldom been given the systematic consideration that it demands. That a variety of "cultures" – if that is the correct term – existed side by side in the medieval period is obvious. Yet when this phenomenon has been remarked upon, it has almost always been either from the perspective of post-medieval values and modern (but decidedly not post-modern) epistemological claims. Thus, for example, Renaissance and Reformation scholars admired certain aspects of medieval culture, but on the basis of their own value systems judged other of its features as crude and marveled at what seemed to them the hodge-podge of the medieval period. Not surprisingly, nineteenth and twentieth-century scholars have tended to deal with this mixture from the perspective of crass historicism and evolutionism. Here bicultural phenomena are viewed as the product of incomplete historical development, so that the "popular" – which at least until recently has been viewed by these students with much of the same repugnance which our Renaissance humanists and Reformation divines felt for it – is seen either as historical vestige or as proof of a so-called "cultural underlay" which demonstrates that civilization had spread only a thin veneer over earlier pagan barbarism. These views are obviously wholly inadequate, above all for their intellectual chauvinism. Those who wonder how the so-called sublime and the ridiculous could co-exist in the same text or same practice overlook the fact that most peoples, especially those who live in the late twentieth century, simultaneously inhabit different words with multiple value systems and fail to even realize that they do so until a social scientist points this out.

There is an even more fundamental problem with these ways of dealing with the manner in which medieval texts or practices simultaneously participated in different or even opposing cultural values. They do not allow us to move from historical observation to historical interpretation; they do not enable us to speak of the significance of multiculturalism for the medieval period or for our reading of it; in short, they do

---

[*] Reproduced by permission of estate of C. Clifford Flanigan. Paper read at the 24th International Congress on Medieval Studies, Kalamazoo, May 5, 1989.

not allow us to make sense of it. This is so, I believe, because most discourse on our subject does not consciously evoke explicit models of interpretation and is therefore doomed to remain a prisoner of its own implicit and often unexamined assumptions. Where hermeneutical paradigms are evoked to discuss this phenomenon, they are usually narrow and highly disciplinary in scope and lack a broad connection to the prevailing paradigms of the theory and practice of the human sciences as a whole. Thus, for example, stylistic traces of different "cultures" in the same text is explained in literary studies by reference to the figure of irony or by the ideological construct of *sermo humilis*. Whatever the validity of such claims, they tell us little about the world which produced this biculturalism. It is the purpose of this essay to suggest – and certainly no more than a suggestion can be made here – one way in which these deficiencies might be overcome, using late medieval Books of Hours as an exemplary case.

Books of Hours readily offer us a base for constructing our model. By Books of Hours I mean prayer books produced in the fourteenth to sixteenth centuries which typically contained as their centerpiece the little hours of the Blessed Virgin Mary along with a calendar indicating, among other things, geographically local liturgical observances, four Gospel lessons, the Penitential Psalms, various litanies, suffrages, meditations, and prayers, especially two widely employed prayers to the Virgin, the *Obsecro te* and the *O intemerata*. Such Books of Hours were perhaps the most widely read texts of the later Middle Ages. In the fifteenth century they represented almost certainly the most frequently printed book in Europe. We know of at least twenty-seven editions of Books of Hours from English printers in the fifteenth century, including four from Caxton. Félix Soleil lists sixty-five editions of Books of Hours printed between 1487 and 1498,[1] and Paul Lacombe's catalogue describes some 500 continentally printed Books of Hours in the fifteenth and sixteenth centuries.[2] It is no wonder, then, that Delaissé has designated them as the best sellers of their age.[3]

Despite their popularity, Books of Hours have been studied almost exclusively by art historians, and for that reason most of us tend to know only of the deluxe editions which have been made available to us as facsimiles, books such as the *Visconti Hours*, the *Rohan Hours*, the *Hours of Etienne Chevalier*, the *Hours of Catharine of Cleves*, Jean duc de Berry's *Très Riches Heures*, and the *Grandes Heures* of Anne of Brittany. But just as important, if not more so, are the less elaborate Books of Hours which made up the bulk of those used in the Middle Ages. Most of these are no longer extant, but we know of their existence from innumerable contemporary references, household accounts, and wills. Indeed according to Jo Ann Moran, the most bequeathed book of the later Middle Ages was the Book of Hours.[4] All of this evidence points to the use of Books of Hours by the laity; in fact, it is clear that Books of Hours were never intended for clerical use.

This observation brings us to the first of the many paradoxes and cultural contradictions in which Books of Hours are situated. Though they were produced for and used by the laity, Books of Hours are undoubtedly primarily the products of clerical and even monastic culture. The heart of every Books of Hours is the hours of the Virgin, a devotion which in form and content is nothing but an abbreviated version of the fuller breviary office of the Virgin. This is certainly also true for the Hours of the

Cross and the Hours of the Holy Spirit which are sometimes contained in Books of Hours. Similarly the numerous prayers, unique to each individual exemplar the way that the quasi-liturgical texts are not, are mostly based on forms of monastic prayer and meditation invented in the eleventh century by such figures as Anselm of Canterbury and John of Fécamp. The Penitential Psalms also have their origins in monastic practice, though by the high Middle Ages their recital, like that of the office, was imposed on secular as well as regular clergy. Perhaps the most striking clerical feature of Books of Hours is their latinity. Especially toward the end of the fifteenth century, vernacular Books of Hours made their appearance, but they were always in a distinct minority; the vast numbers of Books of Hours were written in Latin, the language of the clergy, even though they were intended for lay use.

On this basis, one might be tempted to say that Books of Hours were clerical in their production but lay in their consumption. But even a cursory study of a few surviving books makes such an assertion impossible to maintain. Wherever we look in these books of admittedly clerical matter we find the marks of a more popular – though by no means low-class – culture. Most striking are the ways that lay life enters into the book beside the clerical texts. This is perhaps most readily seen in the deluxe illustrated editions. The *Hours of Mary of Burgundy*, for example, contains a portrait of its owner in prayer before the Madonna.[5] In the *Savoy Hours*, commissioned by Blanche of Burgundy, there are twenty-five pictures of Blanche portrayed in various pious poses.[6] Incidentally, this book includes a number of other attempts to mark it as a book for a particular lay woman. It includes a "Prayer for Myself," and a number of the other prayers use feminine pronouns in places where elsewhere one finds the masculine. Even the less elaborate Books of Hours were often personalized in a number of ways: owners wrote their names into them, kept elaborate family histories in them, wrote remarks in the vernacular in the margins, painted their coats of arms, wrote, presumably in their own hands, an account of how they came to possess the book, and added personal prayers in the same way that today one writes recipes into a favorite cookbook. In the *Rouen Book of Hours* the man and the woman who owned the book had themselves depicted in the lower margin of one of the pages, kneeling before a painting of Virgin. The couple is dressed in clothing that can be dated from 1500, though the book seems to have been produced at least two decades earlier. In fact, these depictions of lay figures seem to be painted over earlier similar figures, and Roger Wieck has therefore suggested that these figures were most likely the second-generation owners of this manuscript and that the new owners had their portraits painted over those of the original owners. Actually similar alterations of coats of arms or mottoes by later owners occur frequently in Books of Hours. I have seen at least one book in which a later owner crossed out prayers which were apparently not to his theological taste. Thus both in their production and in their reception Books of Hours were usually marked as products of lay culture.

To open an exemplar and to see in a single glance both Latin liturgical text and ostentatious marks of lay culture is to have capsulized in cogent form the multi-culturality of Books of Hours. Indeed, wherever one turns in Books of Hours one is confronted with cultural duality. Consider, for example, the calendar, the first item that appears in virtually every Book of Hours. It indicates first of all the local liturgical observance for the place in which the book was to be used, indicating minor as well as major holy days. But the calendars contain all sorts of other useful information as well. An elaborate and sometimes color-coded system allowed users to calculate the days on which Sundays fall in any given year, as well as the date of Easter. Usually certain days of the month are marked as *dies mali*, days unlucky for any undertaking, especially for blood letting. Sometimes there is also a second series of unlucky days indicated, this one marked by the letter "e" for *dies aegypti*. Here is an example of the way that what we narrowly term "popular culture" makes its way into these "clerical" books. Indeed, as Claire Sponsler has pointed out, it would not be inappropriate to think of Books of Hours, especially the later ones, as something similar to modern almanacs, since they contain both in their calendars and elsewhere a great deal of useful information for organizing months and days.[7] Depictions of the zodiac usually accompany the calendar sections in illustrated Books of Hours. In the most deluxe of Books of Hours the calendar section is also accompanied by a series of paintings of the so-called labors of the month which seem to have nothing to do with the ecclesiastical year or with any other aspect of their clerical content. Thus, for example, the illustrations in a Book of Hours, produced probably in Paris around 1430, contains the following illustrations of the months:[8]

January – Janus feasting
February – Keeping warm
March – Pruning
April – Picking flowering branches
May – Hawking
June – Mowing
July – Reaping
August – Threshing
September – Treading grapes
October – Sowing
November – Thrashing for acorns
December – Slaughtering a pig

Such a list once again confronts us with the questions about the juxtaposition of clerical and lay – and even popular – culture in Books of Hours, for here the liturgical calendar is illustrated by wholly secular content, indeed even by paintings which include depictions of peasant life. Though this situation is commonly remarked upon, to the best of my knowledge no one has probed very deeply the significance of this amalgamation. In order to do so we must consider questions concerning the use made of these books, and we must do so at two different levels. At the first level we must ask what we know from the books themselves and other medieval documents about what medieval people did with these books. Here there is a fair amount of surviving information.

Clearly many, though not all, Books of Hours were used regularly and frequently as prayer books. Illustrations within these very books often record their devotional use, since various characters in these visualizations, including the owners of the texts and the Virgin herself, are depicted devoutly reading their Books of Hours. Numerous medieval records also document this use. Some laymen, among them Henry VI of England, if his chroniclers are to be believed, attempted to say the various hours at the appropriate times throughout the day (rising in the middle of the night for saying matins, reciting lauds at dawn, etc.), a practice that often was not followed even by monks in monasteries, let alone by secular clergy. Books of Hours often contained devotional material to used during the mass, such as a prayer to be said at the Elevation, and there is a good deal of evidence that they were often used this way. One bizarre example that comes down to us recounts how one Arthur Chapman was arraigned in 1570 for brawling in church, that is for reading too loudly from his Hours.

But to recount such "facts" about the consumption of these texts can in no way satisfactorily answer the question about the mixture of clerical and non-clerical culture which we are pursuing here. Such a question is an interpretive one and as such can only be considered in light of the implicit or explicit theoretical assumptions which we bring to it. And because the interpretive question arises out of our historical situation rather than the historical situations of medieval people, no medieval account can address it. These observations bring me to the third part of my title, "the construction of medieval reality". By this term I mean to evoke a form of theoretical sociology which stems from German phenomenology and which is concerned with the ways in which individuals and groups perceive – which is to say, structure – their worlds. The term evokes the well-known study on *The Social Construction of Reality* published by Peter Berger and Thomas Luckmann in the 1960s,[9] but I am using it here also to designate work on reality construction by such older researchers as Alfred Schutz[10] and George Herbert Mead,[11] and more recent scholars, above all Michel Foucault and Clifford Geertz. My model proceeds from the observation that the species *homo sapiens* is marked by an insatiable need for meaning since it lacks the instincts other animals possess. Yet the very diversity of cultures which we observe geographically and historically points to the fact that culture is not something given to humans biologically, even though we do seem to have a biological need for culture. Therefore humans construct what has not been provided for them in their biological constitution. They construct worlds in their socio-cultural and psychological formations. Thus "reality" is not something that is given to us, it is something that we necessarily create in order to manage in the midst of the constant flux of diverse and conflicting experience. Human beings live in the midst of extreme diversity, but they require a means of unifying things, of "making sense" in order to survive. "Reality" is what they construct in order to do so.

Of course reality is not something that individuals make. As structuralists like to emphasize, we are born into structures, or to use the term evoked here, realities, and though these realities are quite fragile, we can never escape from them to that "reality" of which philosophers and theologians dream. In fact, because experience is diverse, we are usually deeply enmeshed in several different realities, and this situation requires that we as individuals and as members of collectives reinforce and reconstruct an overarching and unifying reality. Such a reality remains real, in the sense of its having subjective plausibility, only as it is confirmed and reconfirmed by individuals in relation to social others. What is required is that our constructed reality appear to us not as it is, that is, as a fiction, but as something given, something that appears to have the quality of objective facticity.

All human activity is involved in reality construction. At one pole, as Irving Goffman has emphasized, is our day-to-day interaction with each other.[12] As that interaction is governed by social stratification and other mores, we create and recreate meaning, and this very act of recreation causes these meanings to become reabsorbed into our consciousness and regarded as objectively true. Our reality is reconstructed and reconfirmed. At the other end of the continuum of devices for reality construction are elaborate socially shared symbolic structures such as rituals. Religion is the ultimate legitimizing institution since it claims to interpret the order of society in terms of an all-embracing sacred order of the universe. Here the human is transcended by a superhuman reality and human history is placed within a sacred notion of time. Kinship relationships are said to reflect divine relationships and marginal and anomic experiences such as sickness and death are interpreted as events in a larger cosmic history, and as such are endowed with a supposedly ultimate significance. This latter point is of particular importance since such events significantly threaten our reality constructions and require special efforts in order for them to be integrated into the process of world construction.

From this rather cursory venture in theoretical sociology let us now return to our medieval users of Books of Hours. Romanticizing fantasies aside, there is no reason to suppose that experience was simpler or more unified for late medieval people than it is for us. What we perceive as the conflict of clerical and nonclerical, even popular, cultures is one expression of this diversity. At times this conflict became apparent, when representatives of the learned and clerical culture attacked popular practice. But often the contradictions were not apparent, realized only upon a reflection that was at best undertaken by a few. Nevertheless the potentiality for reality conflicts increased as city dwellers, who were the majority of users of Books of Hours, grew in number, rose in the social scale, and increasingly acquired the technologies to dominate culture which had earlier lain exclusively in the hands of the clergy. Indeed it has been argued that these city dwellers, in contrast to the clergy and to the old aristocracy, possessed no ideology of their own by which they could make sense of things. Under these circumstances it is not surprising that a number of institutions arose which enabled such city dwellers, as well as the clergy and the aristocracy who were becoming increasingly dependent upon them, to make sense of things and put the new socio-historical situation in meaningful perspectives. One of these devices was the great urban drama, which was typically based on the mythology guarded by clerical interests but which depicted that mythology in nonclerical and highly contemporary terms. The Book of Hours was another such device.

To cast one's eyes over its pages was to experience – and hence to construct – a world of meaning. Within this world the Latin monastic office and the life of nonclerical individuals recorded in a family history seem to fit together. The solemn days of the church year stood apparently irenically next to unlucky days along with depictions of aristocratic pleasures and peasant labor in a fictionalized countryside. What is more, activities which had once been open only to clergy now appeared – even to those whose knowledge of Latin was small or even nonexistent – to be open to laity since they could now say a version of the office and acquire its temporal and eternal benefits. Moreover, though this cannot be discussed here, Books of Hours also addressed those anomic and world-threatening situations to which I alluded above, especially in the text and possible illustrations of the Office of the Dead, which was included in virtually every Books of Hours. These books also often contained special prayers for sicknesses and for childbirth, and for other important but frequently threatening situations in life, including on occasion even tooth pulling. Thus for a laity increasingly acquiring literacy, Books of Hours became a useful tool for world construction. Though they were intended for private consumption, they offered a vast created world in which shared public myths and values were integrated with individual concerns.

In conclusion then, the function of Books of Hours, whether they were used for the actual practice of prayer, or were merely objects to be admired or even, as was also often the case, employed as text books of elementary education, was to make sense, to construct and reconstruct reality, to serve one of the most fundamental human needs. To say this of Books of Hours is only to say the embarrassingly obvious, but it is also to say what, as far as I can tell, has never been explicitly said in studies devoted to them. And to say this is to say why problems in the study of medieval culture, such as the relationship between clerical and popular culture which we are considering here, can only make sense to us when they are pursued equally in light of both past history and contemporary theory.

Notes

1. See Félix Soleil, *Les heures gothiques et la littérature pieuse aux XVe et XVIe siècles*, Rouen, 1882.
2. See Paul Lacombe, *Livres d'heures imprimés au XVe et au XVIe siècle conservés dans les bibliothèques publiques de Paris: Catalogue*, Paris, 1907 [repr. Nieuwkoop, 1963].
3. See L. M. J. Delaissé, James Marrow and John de Wit, *Illuminated Manuscripts*, London, 1977, pp. 13-20.
4. Jo Ann Hoeppner Moran, *The Growth of English Schooling, 1340-1548: Learning, Literacy, and Laicization in Pre-Reformation York Diocese*, Princeton, 1985, p. 198.
5. *The Hours of Mary of Burgundy: Codex Vindobonensis 1857, Vienna*; commentary by Eric Inglis, London, 1995. Originally published as *Das Stundenbuch der Maria von Burgund*; Kommentar Franz Unterkircher [*Glanzlichter der Buchkunst*, 3], Graz, 1993.
6. *Les Heures de Savoie: Facsimiles of 52 Pages from the Hours Executed for Blanche of Burgundy, Being all that is Known to Survive of a Famous 14th-Cent. Ms. which was Burnt at Turin in 1904*; with a preface by H. Y. Thompson, London, 1910.
7. See Claire Sponsler, "Devoted Bodies: Books of Hours and the Self-Consuming Subject," in Idem, *Drama and Resistance: Bodies, Goods, and Theatricality in Late Medieval England*, Minneapolis, 1997, pp. 104-35.
8. The manuscript referred to here is Walters Art Gallery, Baltimore, shelf code Ms W 285. It is described in Roger S. Wieck, *The Book of Hours in Medieval Art and Life*, London, p. 47.
9. Peter L. Berger and Thomas Luckmann, *The Social Construction of Reality: A Treatise in the Sociology of Knowledge*, Garden City, NY, 1966.
10. Alfred Schutz, *Der sinnhafte Aufbau der sozialen Welt: Eine Einleitung in die verstehende Soziologie*, Wien, 1932.
11. George Herbert Mead, *Mind, Self and Society from the Standpoint of a Social Behaviorist*; [intr.] Charles W. Morris, Chicago, [1934].

12. Irving Gofman, J. Ronnie Davis and John F. Morrall, *The Concept of Education as an Investment: Final Report*, [Washington], 1971.

Praying the Life of Christ: Late Medieval Devotion in the Light of Ideological Critique

C. Clifford Flanigan[*]

The study of medieval devotion has made enormous advances in the last two decades, but in many ways we are just at the beginnings of any serious study of late medieval prayer, particularly prayer in the vernacular. Thousands of prayer texts remain to be edited, for example. But of even greater importance, it appears that we have few models which can guide us in our hermeneutical encounter with these texts. In fact, for all of the prominence of devotional literature in recent research, there has been little explicit interpretation. For the most part scholars have been content to take these prayers on their own terms as pious evocations of the divine. But surely these texts deserve more serious treatment than is afforded by such an approach. Since it is we who wish to understand these texts, then we need to interrogate them on our terms and seek to understand them as having a functional rather than ontological basis. If we fail to do this, the study of medieval prayer will forever be caught in a positivist rut whose only exit will be determined by whether or not we as investigators do or do not hold certain religious convictions. Clearly such a state of things, which prevails in few other areas of medieval studies, is unacceptable. Furthermore, viewing medieval prayers in a positivist or naïvely "religious" posture needlessly privileges medieval sacred texts in a way that the human sciences do not do when dealing with the religious texts of other cultures.

The essay that follows is a first and very preliminary attempt to develop a paradigm which may be able to transcend the present impasse in medieval prayer studies. It seeks to understand prayer as a cultural phenomenon, one which has broad social ramifications. My concern will be not so much with the ideological content of prayer texts as with the mechanisms by which they accomplish their social functions. My original intention was to look at a group of vernacular prayers which are related to specific episodes of the life of Jesus. But because life is short – and the time allotted to presentations at Kalamazoo even shorter – I have elected to examine a single devotional text in order to develop a possible paradigm for understanding prayers as ideological

---

[*] Reproduced by permission of estate of C. Clifford Flanigan. Paper read at the 25th International Congress on Medieval Studies, Kalamazoo, May 13, 1990.

structures. The text I have chosen, Ludolph of Saxony's *Life of Christ*, was probably originally written for consumption by monks, but, like so many other monastic and quasi-monastic documents of the later Middle Ages, it found a ready audience among secular clergy and the laity. A very large number of manuscripts survive from the fifteenth and early sixteenth centuries, and the book was one of the most printed of all texts in the period of incunabula, going through at least eighty-eight editions from the time of its first printing at Cologne in 1472. Within a century and a half of its first appearance it was translated into Dutch, German, French, Spanish, Catalan, and Portuguese; strangely, no English translation has ever appeared. In more recent times it has received relatively little study, however. This relative lack of attention is not surprising when we consider the enormous length of Ludolph's book. The 1878 edition by L. M. Rigollot occupies four folio volumes and more than two thousand pages.[1]

In some ways Ludolph's *Life of Christ* is closely related to many better-known late medieval devotional works, above all the Pseudo-Bonaventuran *Meditations on the Life of Christ*, from which it borrows freely. Indeed Ludolph's work seems to have been influenced by all of the major works of devotional literature which proceeded it. In fact, it is its willingness to incorporate major sections not only of other devotional works, but of well-known patristic and medieval theological works which sets off this *Life of Christ* from most of the devotional books which preceded and followed it – and which provides it with its enormous length. But there are other distinctive markers of Ludolph's book as well. Each section provides a prolonged retelling of one or more episodes in the canonical gospels. Surprisingly, Ludolph eliminates from his account almost all apocryphal material. But this non-traditional stance is balanced by Ludolph's attempt to include massive amounts of traditional theology, some of which has, until it falls into Ludolph's hands, only the most incidental relationship to the narrative to which it is connected. It is difficult to suggest in a few words the way that the episodes in the book are constructed, but briefly we may say that each includes:

1. A citation of the appropriate gospel text, often treated word for word with extensively amplified explications of its "literal" meaning.

2. Explanation of the historical, legal, geographic, and similar materials cogent to understanding the text.

3. Moral and/or mystical interpretations of the pericope. These might involve interpreting the characters and their actions, or explaining etymologies, place symbolism and "deeper" meanings of events, people, and objects.

4. A discussion of the relationship between the gospel event discussed and the practice and experience of the liturgy.

5. A prayer, which, as we shall see, has a very intimate textual relationship with the biblical pericope discussed and with Ludolph's explanation of it.

This description can in no way suggest the texture of Ludolph's work since within each section there is a tightly interwoven and massive number of patristic references and quotations. Indeed, what is most cogent in this regard is to realize that canonical interpretation is so smoothly interwoven into the account of the biblical story that the distinction between narrative and its interpretation is almost entirely obfuscated.

Significantly, then, though not surprisingly, the *Vita Christi* which Ludolph offers us, despite its claim to cut away all that is apocryphal, is the ecclesiastical establishment's interpretation of that life and of the way that life was thought to be related to each reader's everyday experience.

As an example of Ludolph's technique, let us briefly consider his account of the presentation of Jesus in the Temple, an account which occupies sixteen folio pages in the Rigollot edition. Here is the beginning of Ludolph's description of the event:

> With the arrival of the fortieth day, when, according to the Law, "the days of her," that is, Mary's, "purification were fulfilled," she went out of the stable with Joseph and the child in order to fulfill the Law. There was nothing to be purged in her, because she had conceived without sin. In Circumcision, it is true, a boy was purged of the original sin he had contracted from his parents; and indeed, in Purification, a mother was purged of sin because she had conceived in passion: but nothing of these things was true for this boy or his mother. And "they carried" the boy, who had been previously circumsized, from Bethlehem "to Jerusalem," "so that" according to the Law "they might present"; i.e., offer, or present as an offering, "him to the Lord" in the Temple, "and so that they might give an offering," "a pair of pigeons or two young turtle-doves" for him.[2]

There is nothing here that is surprising or new. On first consideration the amplification seems only to make clear what is already "in" the biblical text. But no account is ever ideologically neutral, and that is certainly the case here. The exceptional character of Jesus' circumcision only points to what the text takes for granted, that conception inevitably entails sinfulness, that passion is evil, that proper conduct involves a submissive relationship to existing ecclesiastical structures of power. Indeed, as the account continues, the twofold theme of chastity as a model for life on the one hand, and the proper relationship to authoritarian structures on the other, forms the focus of Ludolph's supposedly simple "retelling" of Luke's story. These concerns in turn lead to a lengthy discussion of various aspects of the purification offering, both in terms of Jewish practices and moral lessons; here again chastity and obedience to authority are emphasized. There follows a discussion of the typological relationship between Mary and the ark of the covenant described in the Pentateuch. Mary contains the law, she submitted herself to the Law, and so Christ blossomed within her. Because of her chastity and her obedience, Mary's body never suffered corruption, just as, according to Ludolph, the Israelite's ark never perished. Because Mary "shone brightly with virtues internally and externally,"[3] she is an exemplary character to be imitated, a figure prefigured also by the candelabrum in the Temple. Thus all history is made to testify to the cultural values of sexual abstinence and submission to higher authority which Ludolph sees inscribed in the Presentation account. These connections lead "naturally" to a consideration of the liturgical celebration of Candlemas which commemorates the biblical event under discussion. This feast, it is said, points to the "Christian" (a term which Ludolph assumes to be synonymous with his own cultural formation) superiority to the old Jewish way. Thus Ludolph evokes a culturally sanctioned anti-semitism in order to call into question the correctness of other cultural formations. Then, following a long passage on the Old Testament typology of candles and lights, Christ is compared to the prophet Samuel and Mary is likened to Hannah, his mother. Ludolph insists that these are connections which are to be remembered when the reader participates in the Candlemas liturgy. In this way he provides yet another way in which his understanding of the pericope could be enforced in the reader.

One might think that no further interpretation could be teased out of the short gospel account under discussion, but Ludolph has pages yet to go. There ensues a consideration of the pigeons and turtledoves designated by Luke as sacrificial animals. Two new medieval cultural themes are introduced here: the necessity of willingly yielding a sacrifice of self, and the "value" of poverty. These thoughts bring Ludolph back to Luke's account. Simeon is said to mean "obedience." As the one privileged to hold the Christ child in his arms, Simeon is presented as a type of spiritual perfection since he has spent his entire life in prayer waiting (but not acting). This claim is followed by a long exposition of the *Nunc Dimittis* in which this liturgical song is offered as the key to the entire life of Christ, with its themes appearing in interwoven fashion to make a unity of the ministry and passion accounts which follow. These remarks by no means exhaust the treatment of this single gospel event in the *Vita Christi*, for Ludolph goes on for several more pages to allegorize Simeon, Anna, Mary (again), and Joseph and to explain how each is an exemplary figure who, it is implied, should be imitated. This concern leads to a long praise of holy women and their exemplary conduct. And finally the Church itself is praised and set against all of its deceitful sons and daughters for whom it has done so much and who all-too-frequently return so little to her.

There is more – much more! – in Ludolph's treatment of the Circumcision. But enough has been said here to indicate how this text operates. Everywhere patterns of conduct and systems of values are offered, not as theological or moral abstractions as such, but as meanings indelibly inscribed in the "simple" biblical account of Jesus' life. In this account all difference and disunity is excised. Every detail seems inextricably and necessarily connected to every other. The Bible and the Fathers and contemporary practice fall together to seem so "natural," so compelling, so matter of fact, that no reader could avoid coming to the conclusion – or rather having that "conclusion" reinforced – that the world and its values are just as Ludolph – or better, Luke – says they are. Of course, anyone at all familiar with medieval devotional texts will see nothing unusual here. One might with justice say that everything that I have described "goes without saying." But going without saying is precisely the point here, for the expectedness and naturalness of this ideological mix has kept readers both medieval and modern from realizing how Ludolph's text, and others like it, function as a tool of the various established and establishment ideologies of the late Middle Ages. Ludolph's *Vita* simultaneously offers both the dominant myth of the culture and privileged interpretations of it. Then by placing readers in the midst of this web of connoted and suggested values, making everything that is cultural seem natural, it reinforces the culture's prevailing norms and the structures of power connected with them in such a way that readers are enabled to construct imaginatively a world of values, to make sense of things, and thus to stave off the inhuman and unbearable contingency of a world without meaning. Or, to put it in Charles Conway's more conservative vocabulary, the chapters in Ludolph's book "are in modern terms devices for quick and easy retrieval of theological information, each person, event, name or object acting as a kind of tag or code which provides the meditator with reference points by means of which he may not only learn the essence of the whole gospel, but also learn a method of envisioning the universe in a pattern harmonious with the Gospel."[4]

But Ludolph is not content with merely presenting the Christian myth in this manner. He also seeks to facilitate its acceptance by devices which encourage his text's being appropriated in ritual-like manner. Rituals, it will be remembered, are cultural enactments performed in groups which promote a culture's central ideological values. Frequently they do so by seeming to roll back the barriers of time and space and making worshipers feel present in the sacred time and space in which a myth was believed to have first occurred. Since meditation and prayer are private actions, we would not normally consider them rituals. But employing and perhaps strengthening a device found elsewhere in meditative texts, Ludolph insists that readers should imagine the events he describes as occurring before their very eyes. In the Prologue (*Prœmium*) to his book Ludolph exhorts his readers that "although many of these things are told as in the past, you should meditate on all of them as if they were in the present; because without doubt you will taste a greater pleasantness from this. Therefore, read about what was done as if it were being done. Place before your eyes past actions as if they were present, and thus to a great extent you will taste things as more savoury and delightful."[5] He enjoins his readers: "be present at his [Christ's] Nativity and Circumcision like a good fosterparent with Joseph. Go with the Magi to Bethlehem and worship with them the infant king. Assist with his parents to take him and present him at the temple ... Be present at his death with his Blessed Mother and John ... Seek him resurrected with Mary Magdalene ... Worship him ascending into heaven ... Sit with the Apostles in their room."[6]

There is yet another ritual-like device by which Ludolph's readers are to appropriate the work, and this device finally brings us to the subject of this essay. Each gospel pericope in this book concludes with a brief prayer. Not surprisingly, these prayers explicitly pick up on and repeat the themes and vocabulary from the account which precedes them. By these means, the reader and her life experiences are inserted into Ludolph's mythical retelling and, should this procedure be successful, bent and shaped by the ideological structures found there. In the prayer attached to the Purification account (*Vita* 1:86), for example, Jesus is implored to do away with all impurity in the worshiper (a reference both to the Circumcision and the Purification). In the prayer connected with the flight into Egypt and the slaying of the Innocents, the prayer asks to be able to imitate the pattern of Christ's life "even if death is necessary."[7] But most striking are the prayers in which the prayer is actually construed as a participant in the divine action just recounted. Thus the account of the healing of a leper in Matthew 8 concludes with this prayer: "Lord, if you will, you can make me clean; stretch forth your gracious hand and touch the interior and exterior of this leper now praying to you. Be merciful to me ... cure the disease of this sinner."[8] Similarly the story of the cure of the demoniac (Mark 1) has the reader pray, "Lord Jesus Christ, take away and cast out the unclean spirit in me, who disturbs me by unclean desires."[9] The prayer attached to the story of the woman healed of a hemorrhage begins: "Lord Jesus Christ, heal my bloody soul with the touch of your grace."[10] And to add just one more example out of literally scores of similar occurrences, after reading of Jesus' calming a storm while he and his disciples are in a boat, the reader is instructed to pray: "Lord Jesus Christ, rebuke the winds and waves of the allurements of temptations; come and walk on the billows of my heart to ensure a great calm."[11] In all of these examples Ludolph continues the technique he used in the narrative sections in which biblical vocabulary and the details of the biblical episodes are expanded and seamlessly tied to systems of late medieval cultural values. But what is different here is that the reader, by his very act of reading or reciting the prayer provided, is explicitly made a participant in the sacred myth and is made to beseech the divine in the place of a character in the biblical myth. In this way the ideologizing of the reader is affectively – and effectively – made more potent and compelling.

I have dwelt so long on Ludolph's *Vita*, which is much more than a prayer book, because I believe it fully and explicitly illustrates what is partially and implicitly true for other prayers which do not come to us tied to a narrative. In the examples discussed here, we can see that prayers are heavily laden ideological devices which presuppose the validating myths of the society from which they come, as well as the established and sanctioned interpretations of those myths. But all medieval prayers are deeply embedded in these myths and interpretations. Though they may urge an unalloyed pouring forth from the individual's heart, they nonetheless can only say what has already been said by the culture of which they are a part. Though late medieval prayers in particular may seem uniquely private and personal, their function is to construct an individual in a socially approved way, to inculcate and endlessly reaffirm the systems of valuation, and therefore the systems of power, that are operative in that culture. This is not to say, of course, that social structure is a wholly closed system and that we must view medieval prayer only as a crude Marxist machine which simply and endlessly replicates the established social and economic structures. Societies are always in flux, the tendencies inscribed within them, and in prayers, are more changeable than the present essay has suggested. And, moreover, prayers, like other cultural institutions, could be and often were sites of negotiation between individuals and their societies. But such negotiations always take place within the larger framework of what is possible within a given culture at a specific historical moment. And most importantly of all, prayers are always and unavoidably agents of a socializing process. Certainly this acute dictum is not the last word on prayer studies. But if we are ever to demystify medieval prayers as something more than pious expressions which may or may not mean something to us today depending on whether or not we hold certain religions convictions, if we are ever to understand the hidden but powerful roles that they played in the lives of medieval men and women and the various communities which they inhabited, then this axiom will provide a useful and perhaps even necessary point of departure.

Notes

1. Ludolphus de Saxonia, *Vita Jesu Christi*, L. M. Rigollot [ed.], Paris, 1878, 4 vols. Selected English translations are from Charles Abbot Conway, Jr., *The "Vita Christi" of Ludolph of Saxony and Late Medieval Devotion: A Descriptive Analysis*, Salzburg, 1976 [*Analecta Cartusiana*, 34]. Biblical citations are italicized in the Latin text and are placed in quotes in the English translation.

2. Conway, Jr., *Vita Christi*, p. 27. "Et, adveniente autem quadragesima die, *postquam, secundum Legem Moysi, impleti sunt dies purgationis ejus*, Mariae scilicet, exiit ipsa de stabulo cum Joseph et Puero, ut Legem impleret, in qua nihil purgandum erat, quia sine peccato conceperat. In circumcisione quidem purgabatur puer ab originali, quod a parentibus contraxerat; in purgatione vero purgabatur mater a peccato, quia in libidine conceperat; sed nihil horum in hoc Puero vel in Matre erat. Et *tulerunt illum*, puerum Jesu prius circumcisum de Bethlehem, *in Jesualem, ut* secundum Legem, *sisterent*; id est, offerent, seu offerendo praesentarent, *eum Domino* in templo, *et ut darent* pro eo *hostiam*, scilicet *par turturum, aut duos pullos columbarum*." (Ludolphus, *Vita Jesu Christi*, Rigollot [ed.], vol. I, p. 98.)

3. "Maria intus et foris virtutibus resplendebat" (*Ibidem*, vol. I, p. 99).

4. Conway, *Vita Christi*, p. 36.

5. *Ibidem*, p. 124. "Et ideo quamvis multa ex his tamquam in praeterito facta narrantur, tu tamen omnia tamquam in praesentia fierent, mediteris: quia ex hoc majorem sine dubio suavitatem gustabis. Lege ergo quae facta sunt tamquam fiant; pone ante oculos gesta praeterita tamquam praesentia, et sic magis sapida senties et jucunda" (Ludolphus, *Vita Jesu Christi*, Rigollot [ed.], vol. I, p. 7).

6. Conway, *Vita Christi*, p. 126-7. "Adesto ejus nativitate, et circumcisioni, quasi bonus nutritius, cum Joseph. Sic vade cum Magis in Bethlehem, et adora cum eis parvulum regem. Adjuva cum parentibus portare puerum et praesentare in templum ... Adesto morienti, cum beata matre ejus et Joanne ... Quaere resurgentem, cum Maria Magdalena ... Admirare in coelum ascendentem ... Sede cum Apostolis in conclavi ... " (Ludolphus, *Vita Jesu Christi*, Rigollot [ed.], vol. I, p. 3).

7. "... ac etiam mortem, si oportet" (*Ibidem*, vol. I, p. 122).

8. "Domine Jesu Christe ... Si vis, potes me mundare; extende manum gratiae et pietatis; tange interiora et exteriora leprosi te invocantis; miserere mihi poenitenti, et impera morbo peccati" (*Ibidem*, vol. I, p. 348). For a complete translation into English of the prayers, see *Praying the Life of Christ: First English Translation of the Prayers Concluding the 181 Chapters of the* Vita Christi *of Ludolphus the Carthusian*, [transl.] Sister Mary Immaculate Bodenstadt, Salzburg, 1973 [*Analecta Cartusiana*, 15].

9. "Domine Jesu Christe, remove et ejice spiritum immundum a me ... qui per immunda nos agitat" (Ludolphus, *Vita Jesu Christi*, Rigollot [ed.], vol. I, p. 360).

10. "Domine Jesu Christe ... sana tactu gratiae animam meam sanguinolentam" (*Ibidem*, vol. II, p. 32).

11. "Domine Jesu Christe ... dignare in naviculam pectoris mei ascendere, et superbiae ventositatem, ac vitiorum insurgentium procellas sedare" (*Ibidem*, vol.II, p. 190).

Private Prayer and the Paschal Cycle:
A Low-German *Gebetbuch* in Cultural Perspective
C. Clifford Flanigan[*]

The study of prayer, as text and practice, is one of the most neglected areas of inquiry in the whole of contemporary medieval studies. There are a number of reasons for this shameful neglect. In the first place, although hundreds of manuscripts still survive from throughout Europe which contain individual prayer texts and collections of prayers, most of these manuscripts have never been edited and are therefore generally unavailable to all but scholars who at considerable expense and with a great deal of determination seek them out. Not surprisingly, then, there are few tools which can aid us in our study of medieval prayer; indeed there are few indices that can guide us to the so-called primary sources. This lack of concern with prayer has, of course, its own underlying cause. Even to most initiates, the subject of prayer seems lacking in interest. Surprisingly, this paucity of interest in prayer is not limited to medieval studies. The *Encyclopedia of Religion* reports that among all the genres of religious texts from the world over, prayer is perhaps the one most produced and the one least likely to be studied.[1]

Underlying and even promoting this neglect of prayer in serious academic query, especially in our own house of medieval studies, is, I think, a lack of a methodological paradigm which could govern such investigations. Deprived of it, we tend to think of prayers either as the quaint product of a passed age of faith, or to equate them with our own pious practices. But even if either of those assumptions could be justified – and I do not think that they can be – they could not enable us to raise questions about the function of prayer for individuals and communities in the medieval past, in short to ask what was prayer for, and to ask that question not as if we were seeking an answer in terms of the intentionality of the prayers, but in terms of our own scholarly endeavours to understand the past not on its own terms – for that is impossible – but on ours.

---

[*] Reproduced by permission of estate of C. Clifford Flanigan. Paper delivered at the 26th International Congress on Medieval Studies, Western Michigan University, May 9, 1991.

To raise the question of medieval prayer from this perspective is, of course, to place it squarely into the arena constructed by recent theoretical approaches of the "human sciences," where the question becomes: how does prayer relate to other characteristically human activities which have to do with creating meaning, with interpreting life experiences and making them bearable? Inextricably connected with such questions are ones that have to do with power relationships and the way that various groups promote their own ideological vision of things, by which I mean only a set of root metaphors which seem in some way to provide a means of unifying the diversity of experience. Recent writers like Foucault, Bourdieu, and de Certeau have suggested that there are several prime social devices by which human beings create and recreate themselves as human beings living in definite historical and social formations. Foremost among these are, on the one hand, such obviously socially self-reflexive forms as myths and rituals, which manifest and evince to a culture its own values with a special force of persuasiveness in order to establish and perpetuate those values, and so make the cultural seem natural and therefore "right." On the other hand, practices constitute meaning and value by the mere fact that they offer themselves as neutral techniques and thus are lived unquestioningly, rather than reflected upon. They derive their authority from the sheer fact that they are done by everyone in the community that one inhabits.

If we attempt to situate medieval prayer between myth and ritual on the one hand and cultural practice on the other, a number of interesting perspectives emerge. There is a strong argument to be made for prayer as apparently unreflexive practice. Indeed a number of writers from the later Middle Ages stress this point, that prayer is not something one thinks about but which one does; if one is to achieve the benefits of prayer, one must simply do it and do it regularly, not reflect upon it theoretically. Indeed it has been suggested more than once that the emergence of the texts of private devotion, which we usually think of when we speak of medieval prayer, represents a reaction against the elaborate ritual of the later Middle Ages. In most cultural theory, ritual is an efficacious communal enactment of the understanding of self and world that prevails in a given society. Certainly this describes the medieval eucharistic liturgy – and, perhaps, to a lesser degree the divine office – as it evolved in late antiquity and the early Middle Ages. However, for a number of reasons this ritual became alienated from the population of Christendom at large. Its language was inaccessible for all but the learned. It was gradually transformed from a rite in which all participated into one enacted only by clergy. The locus of the sacred, thought in late antiquity to reside in the total action of the rite, became increasingly localized until the thirteenth century, when it was identified with the consecrated elements effected by clergy in moments of awesome silence rather than communal participation. Indeed, in many places walls were literally built between clergy enacting the rite and others who, having been earlier reduced to spectators, were now not even granted that privilege. To speak of the high and late medieval liturgy in this way is to caricature it rather then to characterize it. Yet this caricature can, within the necessarily short compass of this paper, stand for a rather standard line of argumentation to be found in histories of the church and spirituality, which rightly claim that by the high Middle Ages much of the power which the liturgy earlier possessed, as a phenomenology of rites might lead us to expect, had been lost. The religious impulse, then, according to this model, sought new forms and outlets, and these led to the great proliferation of devotional literature and the newer forms of mysticism which appear in the later Middle Ages. These new forms seem to stand in marked opposition to the official ritual, both theoretically and pragmatically. Ritual is a communal phenomenon, whereas the focus of these new practices is personal and private. Furthermore, ritual inevitably has built within it a hierarchical structure that stands in a complex relationship to the hierarchies of the prevailing social order, while private devotions seem immediate and seek for the experience of an unmediated relationship with the divine.

One would be hard pressed to deny the at least partial validity of such claims. Yet if one surveys the history and practice of so-called private prayer in the later Middle Ages, one can hardly miss the manner in which it often – though certainly not always – seeks to ally itself with the communal forms of myth and ritual. In a paper presented at the 25th International Congress on Medieval Studies, Western Michigan University (1990) I attempted to show how certain forms of medieval prayer persistently evoked elements of the Christian mythology in order to insert the individual prayer into the mythological order, make her or him a participant in this mythology, and thus allow an appropriation of the sacred which is believed to be inscribed in myth.[2]

This prayer book is Manuscript 528 in the diocesan library at Trier, a small (15 x 11 cm) parchment codex of 242 leaves written in fifteenth-century minuscles by five hands. Though not profusely illustrated, the book does contain several great initials in gold, many small initials, and a number of illustrations beautifully executed. The book contains texts written in both Latin and in a low German dialect from around the city of Lüneburg. This manuscript was edited and published in 1960 by the Swedish scholar Axel Mante under the title *Ein niederdeutsches Gebetbuch aus der zweiten Hälfte des XIV. Jahrhunderts.*[3] Mante's interests were primarily philological, but he did provide a commentary with some historical and liturgical information.

Mante's designation of this text as a prayer book is an interesting one since the few scholars who have worked with the text have been at a loss as to how to designate it generically, some opting for "breviary" and others for "devotional manual." The difficulty of properly designating the text stems, of course, from its very diverse contents. On the one hand there is a large amount of Latin liturgical material. There are incipits and whole pieces of the ordinary of both the office and the eucharistic celebration. There are also Latin hymns, both those that usually are found in the Easter liturgy and others which seem to lack "official" ties to the rite. These hymns are often accompanied by neumes, as if intended for communal celebration. There are also occasional excerpts from the writings of the Fathers read at Matins in the Easter season. In fact, it is clear that this book is intended to govern the liturgical celebration of the paschal season, from Holy Saturday through to Ascension, with addition of the days from Ascension to Corpus Christi. But the book by no means contains all of the liturgy that one would expect, nor is it primarily a Latin document. There are many pious poems and verses in the vernacular, and many vernacular hymns, some of which are also neumed. In addition, and preeminently, there are hundreds of personal prayers written in Low German in a highly affective style characteristic of the piety of the period. There are also frequently dialogues between Christ and the soul, which are marked by this same style. Indeed, the German vocabulary significantly reflects the diction of the mystical writers of northern Germany. Drawing on standard dictions of mystical language, Mante lists about forty frequently used words which are employed in our book in senses peculiar to this tradition.[4] Many of the prayers evidence the quasi-erotic language associated with the so-called *Brautmystik* tradition. Indeed, God is frequently addressed as a "Bridegroom." Here is a brief sample of this usage in the book:

> O leue here!
> Wanne wultu komen unde wult mi vrowen?
> Wanne schal ik di sen?
> Ik en kan nicht lengher beyden.
> See, ik opene di min herte vnde mine sele, to entfanghende dine almechticheyt!
> Kum, alderhogheste koningh!
> Kum, alder-leueste broder!
> Kum, alder-truweste vrunt vnde alder-eddelste seghe-uechter!
> Lat mi di sen vnde diner vroliken bruken!
> O leue here!
> Kum to mi … (p. 101)

[O, my dear Lord! When will You come to me and when will You make me rejoice? When shall I see You? I can no longer endure without You. Behold, I open to You my heart and my soul, that I might receive You, in all of Your power! Come, O exalted king! Come, dearest brother! Come, dearest and truest friend and dearest and noblest conqueror. Let me see You and delight in You. Dear Lord! Come to me ...]

Obviously this mixture of liturgical and non-liturgical elements, of Latin and Low German, has raised basic questions about the intended users of this book. It is clear that the book was made for and, in all likelihood, by women; the prayer is instructed to use feminine descriptions of herself repeatedly in words such as "denst-maghet" and "sunderinne." But the diversity of materials has puzzled the few scholars who have pondered it. The account of the liturgical cursus is so complete that is seems clear that a rigorous life of a nun living under a Benedictine dispensation is presupposed. Yet the book provides liturgical aids at such an elementary level, seeming at times to anticipate a reader with no knowledge of Latin, that some have wondered whether the book really could be intended for a woman whose whole life, year after year, was marked by the mass and hours in Latin. Some have suggested the book was intended for a layperson, perhaps one of those who visited the convent for an extended retreat. Such a claim is based on no firm evidence, but it does have in support the fact that a manuscript closely related to the one discussed here seems to have been owned by a laywoman, at least for part of its history. Another related book, presently in Gotha, offers a prayer for the owner's husband, one Hinrick Tobinck, who was *Bürgermeister* of Lüneburg around 1480. But if our book really were intended for a laywoman – something that I think is extremely unlikely – it would be a prime example of the impracticality of attempting to offer monastic practices as a form of lay devotion.

I do not wish to enter further into the question here, but I do want to examine the nature of the relationship between liturgy and prayer which is at the heart of this discussion. At times, our book offers the simplest of liturgical paraphrases. For example, it repeatedly explains what the word *vigilia* means. In giving the Latin text of the preface in the Easter vigil – which after all begins the same way the daily eucharistic preface begins – such phrases as "Dominus vobiscum" and "Sursum corda" are translated word for word (p. 26). Similarly, the *Exultet* is paraphrased line for line (pp. 13-8). Antiphons are frequently quoted and translated. Similarly basic liturgical information is given, such as the fact that at the vigil mass, "the beginning part of the mass is not sung; the mass begins with the *Kyrie*";[5] or later, "the *Offertory* and the *Agnus Dei* are not sung."[6] Such details belong to any liturgical book, but here they are joined with various kinds of interpretations, some simple, some more elaborate. The use of the organ in the *Gloria in excelsis* at the vigil mass is explained by saying that at this moment in the heavenly Church year the angel choirs again take up their instruments and rejoice in the return of the risen Christ to heaven. Or, to take another example, after indicating that the content of the first lesson at the vigil is the Genesis account of creation, the following interpretation is given in German:

> Wente alse got do rouwede des souden daghes van alle sineme werke, dat he do vullenbrocht hadde, also rowede he nv an deme graue van alleme arbeyde siner bitteren martere vnde alle siner hilghen werke, de he louelken heft vullenbrocht an der hopene vnde bergheringhe siner vroliken vpstandinghe. (p. 18)
>
> [Just as God rested on the seventh day from all His works, which He had completed, thus Christ now rests in the grave from all His suffering of the bitter pains and from all His holy works He has lovingly completed, hoping and awaiting the celebration of His joyous resurrection.]

This explanation is certainly faithful to a traditional understanding of this reading, but one would not expect to find it in liturgical books themselves.

Indeed, one of the most surprising features of this book, which mainly consists of prayers and devotional material characteristic of the "new devotion" of the later Middle Ages, is the way that much earlier interpretations of liturgical rites are retained. The Introit for the first mass of Easter day, which begins *Resurrexi et adhuc tecum sum*, is glossed at some length according to the understanding of this piece – and the Psalm from which it is taken – which prevailed in monastic circles of the ninth century (p. 60 ff.). There, and here, it is understood as a dialogue between the newly resurrected and ascended Jesus and his Father, who now sits with Him at His right hand. One might not expect such a traditional reading of the piece, one which emphasizes so strongly the power of ritual reactualization, in a semi-popular book of the fourteenth century. Perhaps even more interesting is the way that traditional monastic interpretations of liturgical pieces are joined to the vocabulary and spirit of the new piety. For example, the angelic pronouncement in the Easter Gospel, that "He goes before you into Galilee" ['Seet, he wel iuk vore-ghan in Galileam!'] is explained thus: "Galilee means to 'pass over'" ["'Galylea' wert bedutet 'en ouer-ghan'" (pp. 32-3)]. Gregory the Great, the author of the lessons read at Matins on this occasion, is given credit for this insight, though in fact it is a patristic commonplace. But notice how, as this explanation continues, we move from the world of the Fathers and early medieval monasticism to the devotion of the later Middle Ages:

> Vnse loser heft warliken ouerghan van deme dode to deme leuende vnde heft vs voreghan to deme ouersten vader-lande.
>
> Dar scholle we ene seen an der ere siner almechticheyt.
>
> Wan dar vpgheyt dat nye morghen-rot der ewighen vroude, dat nenen auent hebben schal, so scholle we vs vullenkomelken an eme vrowen.
>
> Dar schollet vse oghen seen den konigh der ere an siner cyrheyt vnde schol-let ghe-sadet werden van siner schouwinghe, vnse oren schollet ver-vullet wer-den mit deme enghelschen schalle, vnde vse herte schal beret werden van der lustliken leue godes.
>
> So schal dar werden en sunnauent van deme sunnauende, dar we ane rouwen schollet mit gode an deme brut-bedde des hemmelschen rikes vnde schollet beghan desse alder-leflikesten hochtyt der hemmelschen schallinghe mit aller hemmelschen ridder-schop ewelken sunder ende. (p. 33)
>
> [Our redeemer has truly passed over from death to life, and has gone before us and passed over to our fatherland. There we shall behold Him in the glory of His almighty power. When arises the new dawn of eternal joy, that shall have no dusk, then we shall be perfected in rejoicing in Him. There our eyes shall see the king of glory perfected in His splendour, and we shall be sated in beholding Him. Our ears shall be filled with the angelic sound, and our hearts shall be given the joyful love of God. Thus it shall be a Sunday of all Sundays, when we shall recline with God on the bridal bed of the heavenly kingdom, and we shall begin the most beloved and jubilant wedding feast with the heavenly knighthood, eternally, without an end.]

I have thus far made it sound as if our manuscript is essentially an explanation of the liturgy. Nothing could be further from the truth. A large majority of its pages are occupied with prayers that begin "O dear Jesus," and similar such addresses. Yet these pieces seem always firmly anchored to the liturgy. Space will permit only one additional example. Our text repeatedly promotes a devotion to the Easter sepulcher, which is, without question, here a physical place used in the paschal rites. On holy Saturday the grave is first visited for the rites of the exaltation of the cross.[7] Then, during Compline, this site is formally visited again, apparently as part of a processional to church, since it is followed by directions for making a "station."[8] The book does not provide full information about the rites at this second visitation, though it is clear that the Harrowing of Hell is commemorated, almost certainly with the antiphon *Cum rex gloria Christus infernum debellaturus intraret*,[9] with its reference to the standard account of this myth in the Gospel of Nicodemus. Yet the book directs that this liturgical moment should be marked by its user by the reading of a dialogue between Adam and Christ in which, apparently, the sister is to insert herself into the role of Adam. Here is a brief excerpt:

[SOULS:]
Cum, alder-gnedegheste here, vnde help vns, verlornen luden!
Ver-barme dik ouer vs, iammerghen lude, de ewelken ver-domet sin!
DE LOSER:
O min creature, o min schippinghe!
Ik hebbe di dar nicht to schapen, dat du in desse plaghe vnde in desse not scholdest komen.
Ik hadde di beret dat paradis vnde nicht de helle, de wunne vnde nicht den iammer, de vroude vnde nicht dat wenent, dat leuent vnde nicht den dot.
ADAM:
Seet de hant, de mi scapen heft!
Seet den loser, de vs ghe-loset heft mit sineme duren blude!
DE LOSER:
Adam, wor hefstu mi to ghe-brocht vnde mi darto ghe-dwunghen, dat ik van deme stole der almechticheyt in dessen kerkener ghekomen bin?
Ik hebbe an der krubben leghen vnde bin wassen alse en minsche vnde hebbe wenet vnde hebbe slapen vnde waket vnde hungher vnde dorst gheleden. (pp. 42-3)

[*Souls*: Come, all gracious Lord, and help us, lost people. Have mercy on us, miserable people, condemned eternally. *Savior*: O My creatures, o works of My own hands. I have not created you so that you should come into this lamentable distress. I had intended you for Paradise, not for hell, for joy and not for sorrow, for happiness and not for pain, for life and not for death. *Adam*: Behold the hand that made me. Behold the Savior who has redeemed us with his precious blood. *Savior*: Adam, what have you done that has compelled me to leave my throne on high and to come into this dark prison? I have lain in a crib and have been washed and tended as a man, and have cried and slept and wakened and suffered hunger and thirst.]

The dialogue goes on at some length in this manner and then breaks into a poem in which the Savior ecstatically welcomes back all lost souls into his love and promises an inner tie between them and him that will last forever. This poem in turn gives way to a number of meditations and prayers which celebrate and explore "the unspeakable joy" ['vnsprokelken vroude'[10]] of the bond that unites the soul of the sinner to its Bridegroom.

Space will not permit me to share with you any more excerpts either from the visit to the tomb or from other places within the text where liturgical commemoration, hymns, poems, sayings, dialogues, and devotional prayers are mixed together in this truly lovely book. And there is, alas, even less space for a theoretical consideration which the study of this book demands. Permit me, instead, by way of conclusion, to make a few relatively obvious remarks about the relationship between liturgy and devotion in this manuscript, remarks which I can hope will be further elaborated on some later occasion. The author of MS Trier 528 certainly saw no dichotomy between early and traditional forms of monastic liturgical worship and the later forms of personal and private prayer and devotion. On the contrary, one way of reading this manuscript is as a very strong reading of the inherited liturgy, one which appropriates the past for its own understanding of the present. For surely the claim of this book is that the devotional meditations and prayers which it provides are precisely what the liturgy means. To perform the established rites and at the same time to read or contemplate the Harrowing of Hell in terms of affective piety is to insist that this later affective reading is one with the liturgy, no matter how much the history of spirituality, as we know it, might question such a claim. Thus our texts illustrate one of the most fundamental tenets in the study of religion: rites are fundamentally conservative institutions which tend to endure over centuries. But if rites are stable, their interpretation is not. Each generation can only appropriate those rituals by misreading them, by asserting that, rather than reflecting the ideology and world orientation of the past eras from which they come, they reflect the ideology and practice of the present moment. And this is, I think, a fundamental principle which marks not only the production and reception of MS Trier 528 but of many prayer books of the later Middle Ages. Books of Hours intended for laity, for example, make a similar move, asserting that the forms of life inscribed between their covers are to be equated with the meaning of the traditional monastic piety, even though for our own historical perspective such a case could never be maintained. Such a claim returns us to some of the concerns with which this essay began and which, it seem to me, must become axiomatic if prayer studies are ever to realize their potential. For the function of prayer is to map experience, to bring together a diversity of perhaps conflicting elements and make them "make sense." And this is, I think, the ultimate appeal of MS Trier 528 for us or, I should perhaps say more modestly, for me. For in a striking and moving way, we can see in it a hermeneutic model for one caught between the practice of a traditional monastic life and a new way of relating to the divine, which is to say in the famous phrase of Paul Tillich, to things of "ultimate concern."

Notes

1. "Prayer," in *The Encyclopedia of Religion*, Mircea Eliade *et al.* [eds.], 16 vols., New York, 1987, vol. XI, p. 489.
2. See "Praying the Life of Christ" in this volume, pp. 65-72.
3. Axel Mante [ed.], *Ein niederdeutsches Gebetbuch aus der zweiten Hälfte des XIV. Jahrhunderts*, Lund-Kopenhagen, 1960.
4. *Ibidem*, pp. cxxvii-cxxxiii.
5. "De anbeghin der missen wert nicht ghe-sunghen, mer de misse werr begunt mit deme *Kyrien*," *Ibidem*, p. 30.
6. 'Dat *Offertorium* vnde *Agnus Dei* wer nichte sunghen', *Ibidem*, p. 33.
7. *Ibidem*, pp. 2-3.
8. *Ibidem*, p. 52.
9. *Ibidem*, p. 51.
10. *Ibidem*, p. 44.

The Conflict of Ideology in Late Medieval Urban Drama

C. Clifford Flanigan[*]

*I*deology is regarded by some as a threatening word, and so I will begin with a quotation from a researcher whose credentials as a conservative scholar of medieval dramatic texts are beyond reproach, Professor Hansjürgen Linke, universally recognized dean of medieval German drama scholars, who in a recent article has offered a summary statement about the nature and function of medieval urban drama. Medieval drama, he tells, is a practice

> realised only in its performance, which is to say, in the interaction of performers and audience. ... [This is so because] the theater of the Middle Ages is a place of social communication between clerics and laity, as well as between all the social strata of an urban society. Here there is no performance provided by professional actors – for such did not yet exist – before a passive and anonymous public. Rather religiously, politically, and socially engaged members of a primarily or wholly lay community acted before equally engaged members of that not totally homogeneous community: Christian to Christian, city citizen to city citizen, holiday celebrant to holiday celebrant.[1]

Linke's characterization of these plays as forms of communication between social classes provides an excellent starting point for understanding their function within late medieval life, a starting point far superior to those offered by conventional literary analysis. Yet it leaves unanswered a number of basic questions. It does not make clear the content of the messages signed back and forth between engaged performers and engaged audience members. Secondly, though Linke admits that the community engaged in the semiological practice of play performance is "not totally homogeneous," he paints what may well be a too irenic picture of relations between classes and people in medieval towns. Ideological criticism seeks to fill such lacuna.

---

[*] Reproduced by permission of estate of C. Clifford Flanigan. Paper read at the 1st Annual Medieval Symposium, Indiana University, April 9, 1988.

"Ideology" is a term which covers a multitude of different and even opposing interpretive strategies. All contemporary discussion of ideology takes its point of departure from the development and use of that term in Marxist discourse where, not surprisingly, it is applied to a number of different phenomena. In the later Marx, ideology has to do with the relationship between inverted consciousness – that is, a consciousness which is unable to understand how things "really" are – and a reality which is itself inverted in terms of genuine human values. Ideology has to do with the way that things appear to alienated humans, in contrast to the way that they would see them if they could see with unbiased eyes. Thus ideology is equated with illusion, false consciousness, unreality, upside-down reality. It is contrasted to science, which is defined as objective knowledge about the world. I mention this classical Marxian notion of ideology because it is emphatically not the one which I wish to evoke in this essay. Though fully accepting the function of ideology as mystification and agreeing that ideology is partially – though not wholly, in my view – connected with class struggle, I suggest that the notion of ideology found in such twentieth-century "revisionist" Marxist thinkers as Antonio Gramsci and Louis Althusser will afford more useful hermeneutical tools for interpreting the praxis that is medieval drama. For Gramsci, ideology is socially pervasive; far from being only undesirable, it is necessary and unavoidable since humans cannot act without an orientation to the social world they inhabit and without specific rules of conduct. Althusser further developed this notion of the inescapability of ideology, distinguishing between general ideology, the function of which is to create social cohesion, and particular ideologies, which seek to secure the domination of a class. Thus for Althusser ideology is "a representation of the imaginary relationships of individuals to their real conditions of existence."[2] It interpellates individuals and constitutes them as subjects who accept their role within the system of production relations.

Eventually I want to suggest how such notions of ideology provide a model from which we can view late medieval plays and their place in urban life. But first I would briefly like to contrast such an ideological approach with the three major paradigms for medieval drama in the last century. The first of these we might term "historicist." According to it, medieval drama was "pretty sorry stuff," a highly inappropriate mixture of religious instruction with primitive and often offensive folk practices. These practices were thought to be included in the plays either because it was necessary to hold their audiences' limited attention or because, it was claimed, medieval people lacked sufficient refinement to write or appreciate serious drama. Medieval plays were thus conceived as simplistic, unsophisticated first steps on an evolutionary line of development which led to better things. For our concerns it is important to notice how in this model the plays were thought to be lacking in unity and the way that this lack of unity was attributed to *Urdummheit*.

It was precisely this claim of lack of unity which the next paradigm employed to study the medieval vernacular drama vigorously denied. Beginning in the late 1950s and inspired by already waning "new critical" practices in use in other areas of literary study in the United States and Britain (continental medieval drama scholarship continued to remain positivistically oriented) this view of medieval plays hotly contended for their "aesthetic unity." Inventive but extremely forced readings of plays were produced which purported to show that, for example, the Mak episode in the *Secunda pastorum* play in the Wakefield cycle was an analogue of the "salvation history" which makes its appearance in the end. The aim of this critical practice was homogenizing, and often the sublime unity of the medieval world was said to be mirrored in these unified texts and contrasted with the nasty world of difference and conflict which is part of the twentieth-century experience. Happily this way of construing medieval drama is finally waning, but no doubt next year at Kalamazoo, some poor soul will excitedly show us once again how, if only we understand some aspect of medieval theology, we will see the aesthetic beauties of play X. The mention of theology is important here, because medieval religion appears in this model as unified, disinterested, something that "everybody believed" and something that was good for everybody in exactly the same way.

Beginning in the 1970s a few continental critics began to call this view of medieval drama into question. One of the most important of these is Rainer Warning, who in a number of articles and in his book *Funktion und Struktur* argues against the assumptions of Anglo-Saxon medieval drama scholarship.[3] Warning takes issue with the fundamental claim of most traditional scholarship (in Hardison's work, for example) which locates the birth and development of the drama of the Middle Ages in a gradual emancipation of plays from ecclesiastical ritual. He sees the relationship between the church's liturgy and the religious drama instead as "a rivalry of two institutions which the church ultimately settled in its own favor after several centuries of toleration."[4] From its origins in liturgical allegoresis – that, in any case, is Warning's opinion – to its suppression by the church in the sixteenth century, the dramatic elaboration of liturgical practice and Christian dogma was marked by ideological clashes and uncertain liberations and restrictions. The data which Warning employs to support this claim are hardly new: items such as the unseemly deception of Mary Magdalen by the resurrected Jesus in the *Hortulus* scenes in both Latin and vernacular plays (especially the sexual and obscene connotations that the scene acquires in certain German plays), the pervasive presence of the scatological, the merchant scenes in Easter plays, and the delight in cruelty elaborated at astonishing lengths in passion plays from all over Europe. Warning insists that the usual claims about incarnational or Anselmic theology or passion mysticism cannot diminish the opposition between many of the "offensive" features of the medieval drama and official church teaching. Indeed, he argues, the Church was finally able to come to terms with such "offensive" elements only by banning these liturgical elaborations and dramatic performances altogether.

This bald summary does no justice to the intricate argument and the proliferation of evidence that is offered in Warning's book. What is most significant for the purposes of the present study is that Warning has stated in a scholarly fashion what every unschooled reader and viewer of these plays has grasped as their most surprising feature and what nearly every recent medievalist has vigorously attempted to deny: their sense of the "other," their counter-religious and counter-social function, their evocation and celebration of the demonic world, even if that world is ultimately contained by the ideologies of the then prevailing religious and social establishment. As Warning puts it, such a view "forbids us from unquestioningly equating the institutional function of these plays with their official self-conception. Rather we must take into account the possibility that the popularity of these plays was based less on their manifest function of moral instruction than on a latent aggressive function diverted into drama."[5] For Warning, then, medieval plays are fragmented between conflicting ideologies, one of which is termed "religious," the other "anti-religious." Thus Warning returns us to some of the fundamental claims of the earliest generations of interpreters of medieval plays. Not surprisingly then, his explanation for the dichotomies which he finds in the plays is the same which motivated Robert Stumpfl's pro-Nazi studies of the 1930s: that the plays manifest a reassertion of the "pagan" or pre-Christian layers of society which Christianity had sought to repress.

As I have already indicated, I believe that Warning's work needs to be taken with the utmost seriousness, yet at the same time I must argue that some of its conclusions are extremely questionable. There is no reason, as far as I can see, for attributing the anti-ecclesiastical element in medieval plays to the "pre-Christian." Warning's explanation conceives difference only in terms of diachronic origins in which one era does not completely succeed another. I would argue that conflicts in value inevitably exist in any society and that such conflicts are of synchronic or structural origin. What is more, Warning seems to overlook completely the *locus* in which these plays were produced. If the argument could be made for the continuation of oppositional pre-Christian beliefs, one would expect to find those beliefs in the countryside – that, after all, is what the world "pagan" means. But medieval drama is a decidedly urban phenomenon, and any study which seeks to situate the plays ideologically must take its point of departure from this fact.

In a superficial sense, of course, it has always been recognized that most medieval vernacular drama was produced in urban centers, usually under the official auspices of a city government. But only recently has the specifically urban character of the drama been explored. The section of *The "Revels" History of Drama in English* devoted to the great cycles of biblical drama is entitled "Religious drama and civic ceremonial,"[6] though its scant discussion of the urban setting of these plays is overwhelmed by a more standard literary appreciation. Berndt Neumann has described the German drama as a pervasive urban phenomenon.[7] Drawing on his work with records of performance, Neumann argues that German vernacular play production is nearly always tied to life in German cities and that these connections are complex and deeply rooted. Indeed, Neumann goes so far as to claim that every city in German-speaking territories fostered drama in some form in the late Middle Ages. More cogently for our concerns, in a broad survey which takes its point of departure from the Marian plays sponsored by the goldsmiths of Paris, Elie Konigson has argued that in France, at least, miracle plays – and one supposes, mystery plays as well – express a peculiarly bourgeois dialect of the medieval Christian religion.[8] For Konigson, central to any concern with the plays is a recognition of the ideology of the particular social groups which organized and patronized these performances. Thus medieval dramas are seen as devices through which the urban dwellers of the fourteenth and fifteenth centuries enacted and thus created a place for themselves in a broader scheme of things which had earlier failed to recognize their peculiar form of life.

The most detailed study of the ideology of medieval urban drama written so far is by the late Jean-Charles Payen.[9] Building on the claims of scholars like Erich Köhler, who argued that in the Middle Ages different narrative and lyric genres were cultivated by different classes, Payen insists that the vernacular drama is solely an urban affair, not only because it is attested almost exclusively in this physical environment, but also because only cities had the space, the skills of those needed to construct the spectacle, and an administrative organization that could arrange for the elaborate preparations requisite for such performances. Yet, argues Payen, the bourgeoisie – in the literal sense of that term – had no articulated class consciousness or a traditional "literary" form for expressing its solidarity. Under the auspices of urban power structures, plays were produced that cannibalized the narrative works associated with other classes: *chanson de geste, exemplum, pastourelle, congé* – all served as sources for plays written for urban presentation. The plays that issue from these sources carry with them, of course, some of their "original" ideological baggage but, claims Payen, they become transformed by their urban environment into quasi-bourgeois practices.

A similar transformation takes place with the great *mystères*, which contain the material of clerical culture, and indeed were often written by clerics, but which nonetheless bear the marks of urban lay interests. Thus medieval vernacular drama becomes for Payen "an ideological crossroads" that unintentionally parodies royal and aristocratic values from a bourgeois perspective and yet confirms the ideological positions inscribed in the plays' sources. The urban performances draw upon the latent desires of their audiences, but at the same time they restrain those desires by asserting that they lead to divine damnation. Thus the vernacular plays can be characterized as "un art de masse, qui est utilisé au service d'un conformisme latent."[10] Medieval urban drama is among other things a projection of the problems and issues that beset the community that produced the plays, but it presents those problems and their solutions from the perspective of a bourgeois conformity that, to a certain degree, has been determined – or overdetermined – by the ideological perspectives of other classes. Thus Payen seems to suggest that the plays are a product of the bourgeoisie's inability to escape an ideology that was not of its own making and may even have hindered the realization of its own interests.

For the present, at least, Payen's essay must be the point of departure for any future thinking about the ideology of medieval urban drama. Yet it is flawed, I think, in its use of history and in its theoretical conceptualization. In the first place, any reading of late medieval social history shows that class boundaries were considerably more fluid than Payen's model seems to posit. Such studies have also shown that the bourgeoisie was by no means a unified class. Towns tended to have an old patriarchate whose self-understanding sometimes tended toward that of the nobility and was in any case markedly different from what we might term lower middle class craftsmen and workers. These historical observations point to deficiencies in Payen's theoretical models, which appear to be Marxist in a rather crass sense of that term. For Payen, ideology is class consciousness and it is false consciousness. It is the product and the agent of class struggle. And religion here is conceived simply as the ideology of the clerical class, one which, as a ruling class, it used to dominate urban dwellers. It seems much more convincing, with Gramsci and, from a slightly different perspective, with mainline social scientists, to view religion as a means by which various and even opposing classes validate their understanding of themselves, their mores, and their place in the world. In the medieval drama, various class interests are projected onto a mythological plain, thereby supposedly acquiring a timelessness and a divine authorisation. Entirely missing, and greatly needed by Payen's views, is a sense of the necessity of ideology as that which enables humans to make sense of life and thus to act. Said otherwise, Althusser's distinction between general ideology and specific ideology is ignored.

Equally distressing is the understanding of language which is implied by Payen's model. Language, verbal and otherwise, is regarded as a tool which induces people to believe in models which contradict their own self interest. Language is, of course, that, but it is certainly not only that. Since the relationship between sign and signifier is always arbitrary, and utterances are doomed to defer signing the intentions of their makers, communication is at best always only partially successful. Even those ideological strategies which seek for totalization can never be wholly successful. What I am suggesting, then, is that ideology is a use of language which employs strategies of exclusion in order to provide straightforward answers to fundamental questions. But language does not function as ideology wishes; the other, the opposite, which ideology seeks to exclude in an act of communication, is never utterly excludable. In fact, I want to make the apparently paradoxical argument that even those portions of a medieval urban drama which are most overtly ideological in the negative sense of that term can be read – by medieval audiences and by contemporary critics – as utopian.

Obviously I do not have the space to demonstrate these claims in detail here. Instead, I will conclude by briefly suggesting what the shape of an ideologically aware reading of a medieval play might include. For my example, I will use the best-known of all medieval plays, the *Second Shepherds' Play* from the Wakefield cycle. In order to make clear how such a reading differs from the kinds of readings still found in anthologies and possibly even in journals, I will contrast it with a typical "new critical" reading of the play which, not surprisingly, is marked by an astonishing ideologically inspired blindness to ideological difference.

Briefly stated, in 1975 I characterized the *Secunda Pastorum* thus: "This play comes at a place in the cycle in which its audience was expecting a traditional Christmas play and was therefore eager to see Mary, Joseph and the infant Jesus. The playwright has constructed a drama which persistently frustrates that expectation until the closing lines. This apparently deliberate frustration had a devotional purpose. Rather than allow the audience to see the expected scene without religious reflection, the playwright chose to portray the fallen world in need of redemption and to do so in English time and space in order to bring his audience members to an understanding of the theological need for salvation in terms which they would recognize because they were drawn from their own experiences. The progression of the play is one, then, in which the viewer's expectations of seeing a creche are frustrated until the viewer comes to understand the "true" – actually I was not so naïve to use that word even in 1975 – meaning of Christmas. Thus the playwright first presents us with fifteenth-century English shepherds suffering from abuses of nature (cold, rain, etc.), of culture (domestic problems), and of political exploitation. The play then goes on to the Mak episode in which we see how poor people exploit each other, but also, since Mak figurally represents an anti-Christ figure, we see the devil at work in a world desperately in need of redemption. Finally, in the last few pages of this long play, the audience experiences the long-desired Christmas scene, only now with a much fuller experiential understanding of its significance."

Obviously, this reading was produced under a compulsion to find a unity in the play. What I missed, first of all, is that if the play actually proceeds in the manner which I have just described, it serves an oppressively ideological purpose. Its message is this: yes, it is true that the world is a bad place, that social institutions are oppressive, that shepherds (significantly, Wakefield is the smallest and the most rural of the centers from which surviving English "cycles" survive) suffer substantial exploitation at the hands of the nobility, the upper middle class, and of people enclosing lands, it is true that conditions are so poor that one shepherd is set against another and each robs the other, but one should not complain about such things because they are not the products of social institutions, but of the Fall. The only answer to these despicable conditions is Jesus. The salvation which he offers makes the temporary sufferings in this world seem as nothing. Here, then, is an overt example of the use of mythology to justify and validate social oppression. In Payen's terms, we can see it as an example of the way that the ruling classes used drama for its ideological purposes.

Simplistic as this summary seems, I think that it provides the basis for an ideologically aware reading of the text. But I do not think that such a reading can stop at that point. If the play does indeed have such an ideologically manipulative structure, it does not necessarily follow that it was successful in achieving its supposed ideological ends. Or better said, the ideological reading which I have offered is only one of many possible ideological readings. Thus one could argue that if the play represents attempts to silence the interests of those outside the ruling class, it fails to achieve its purpose since exploitation is presented as exploitation. Indeed, if the text is read straightforwardly as an attempt at ideological exploitation by the ruling classes, one will have difficulty in accounting for the fun made of theological Latin, of pretentious fancy dress, and the like. Or, to take a slightly different tack, the reconciliation that takes places between Mak and the shepherds before the announcement of Jesus' birth points to an alternative solution to social problems than the one offered by the Christmas story. Even more tellingly, the concluding Nativity scene can be read in more than one way. Interpretations which privilege a "clerical" reading frequently employ iconography to diminish the humble and rustic setting of the Nativity and of the gifts which the shepherds present to the baby Jesus. But such readings cannot be compelled, either by the playwright or by so-called historical critics of the present who want to insist on a "correct" and "medieval" reading. Thus the "solution" to the problems raised by the earlier part of the drama can be said to be found not in the claims of clerics or noblemen but in a Jesus who is of the class of the shepherds who suffer. This is an excellent example of how an ideological reading will need to take account of the slipperiness of all signifiers. It may be – though we can never know – that the intention of the Nativity scene is to authorize the practices of the ruling classes, but since language always defers and differs, that scene can be read as having an opposite effect. Indeed, one could seriously claim that the scene which from one perspective is ideologically restraining serves a utopian function for the segments of society whom it seeks to repress since it imagines and thus seeks to bring into existence a solution grounded in the lower classes who are suffering the problems presented in the play. Here is an example of how "religion" cannot be said to favour a clerical class or any class in the play. It might be better to view religion as the means by which every group – and let us remember that individuals are never members of a single group – seeks to validate and authorize its interests.

What I have offered here is nothing more than the crudest suggestion of how an ideological analysis of medieval urban drama might proceed. Much more work needs to be done even to lay the foundation for this endeavour. But a few things seem already clear. In the first place, genuinely dialectical reading must be practiced in such a way that unity is not privileged over lack of unity. Secondly, most thoughtful paradigms of ideological analysis have been developed within Marxist criticism, and these paradigms must be our point of departure. Yet Marxist practice is not sufficient, for in privileging production, it seeks to erase acts of reading in the service of arriving at some truth about the text. This is, of course, quintessentially paradoxical since ideological analysis should above all make us suspicious of all truth claims. What is required is an ideologically aware practice that, proceeding from a recognition of the arbitrariness and uncontrollability of language, privileges readers of the past and present rather than producers of ideological discourses. But most importantly, we must recognize that in the practice of the human sciences in the late twentieth century, we cannot shunt the ideological to the margins of our discourse. The goals of our disciplines have shifted, and our concern must now rest not on the supposed beauty of supposedly unified documents but with how humans in various times and places strove to make sense of things in the flux of experiences, which is to how they strove to be human beings.

Notes

1. "… die sich erst in der Aufführung – und das heisst: in der Interaktion von Darstellenden und Zuschauenden – verwirklicht. … [D]enn das Theater des Mittelalters ist ein Ort sozialer Kommunikation sowohl von Klerus und Laien als auch aller sozialen Schichten einer Stadtgesellschaft untereinander. Hier agieren ja nicht Berufsschauspieler, die es noch gar nicht gab, vor einem passiven und anonymen Publikum, sondern religiös, politisch oder gesellig engagierte Angehörige einer überwiegend oder ganz laikalen Gemeinschaft für ebenso engagierte Mitglieder der gleichen, wenn auch in sich nicht notwendig homogenen Gemeinschaft: Christ-gläubige für Christgläubige, Stadtbürger für Stadtbürger, Fastnachtfeiernde für Fastnachtfeiernde" (Hansjürgen Linke, "Drama und Theater des Mittlealters als Feld interdisziplinärer Forschung," *Euphorion* 79 (1985), pp. 55-6.

2. Louis Althusser, *Lenin and Philosophy, and Other Essays*, [transl.] Ben Brewster, [London], 1971, p. 153.

3. Rainer Warning, *Funktion und Struktur: Die Ambivalenzen des geistlichen Spiels*, München, 1974 [*Theorie und Geschichte der Literatur und der Schönen Künste*, 35].

4. Rainer Warning, "On the Alterity of Medieval Religious Drama," [transl.]. Marshall Brown, *New Literary History* 10 (1979), pp. 265-92, quoted on p. 267.

5. *Ibidem*, p. 267.

6. David Mills, "Religious drama and civic ceremonial," in A. C. Cawley *et al.*, *The "Revels" History of Drama in English*, London & New York, 1983, pp. 152-206.

7. Berndt Neumann, "Geistliches Schauspiel als Paradigma stadtbürgerlicher Literatur im ausgehenden Mittelalter," in George Stötzel [ed.], *Germanistik: Forschungsstand und Perspektiven. Vorträge des Deutschen Germanistentages 1984*, vol. II: *Ältere deutsche Literatur, neuere deutsche Literatur*, Berlin-New York, 1985, pp. 123-35.

8. Elie Konigson, "Religious Drama and Urban Society," in James Redmond [ed.], *Drama and Society*, Cambridge, 1979, pp. 23-36.

9. Jean-Charles Payen, "Théâtre médiéval et culture urbaine," *Revue d'histoire du théâtre* 35 (1983), pp. 233-50.

10. *Ibidem*, p. 242.

Localizing the *Visitatio Sepulchri*: Towards a New Orientation of Medieval Drama Studies

C. Clifford Flanigan[*]

The history of the history of the *Visitatio Sepulchri* has yet to be written, and it is vital that it eventually be so if we are ever to understand where we are in our interpretation of it, and how we got there. But even at the present state of our knowledge, certain things seem clear and significant. The most important of these is that the *Visitatio Sepulchri* as we know it is an invention of the late eighteenth century. In making such a claim I obviously do not mean that there are no medieval texts of the *Visitatio* – we have all seen hundreds of examples in Young's and Lipphardt's editions – but that the *Visitatio* that we know, the protodrama of the modern West, or at least the immediate precursor of that drama, first made its appearance, like so many other medieval phenomena, in the early Romantic period. Somewhere around the end of the eighteenth century, thanks to antiquarians and students of the then emerging textual practice termed "literature," the *Visitatio Sepulchri* became the first of a long line of dramatic/literary texts, which is to say, texts which, despite their so-called "religious" quality, were thought of as "essentially" possessed of Kantian universality and disinterestedness. This particular conceptualizing of the *Visitatio Sepulchri* has largely determined, at least until recently, most discourse about it. Thus scholarship has been persistently interested in distinguishing "liturgy" from "drama" because the prevailing discourse about "art" includes the one and excludes the other. Furthermore, because many readers have experienced significant difficulty in processing the *Visitatio* as "art," the prevailing modes of explication have proposed a dubious myth of origins according to which the *Visitatio*'s "core" is viewed as "genuinely dramatic" from its beginning, but in a way which allows students to see the later forms which "developed out of" the *Visitatio* as more fully "dramatic." O. B. Hardison's *Christian Rite and Christian Drama* is widely thought to have exorcized at least some of these notions, but an examination of most subsequent research on the *Quem quaeritis* dialogue, including Hardison's own work, will readily make clear how much scholarship is still operating under Romantic and Kantian paradigms about "art" and "literature."

---

[*] Reproduced by permission of estate of C. Clifford Flanigan. Paper read at the 23rd International Congress on Medieval Studies, Kalamazoo, May 7, 1988.

It is no part of my purpose here to discredit this view of the *Visitatio* as "wrong" and to offer a substitution which is "right." It seems evident to me that there is no knowledge without prejudice, no interpretation without presupposition. Yet seen in the light of more recent frameworks and under the aegis of the contemporary demystification of the discourses about art and literature, this view cannot but strike one as distorting. A first-hand acquaintance with the physical monuments in which the *Visitatio Sepulchri* texts have been preserved certainly makes such a view seem unlikely. Indeed, even when the discourses about art and drama were at their height, this view could be maintained only by the persistent, though unintentional, efforts of editors to obscure the nature of these channels of transmission. Texts of the *Visitatio Sepulchri* and of other medieval Latin "dramas" are seldom read even by experts in their "original" manuscript form. Rather, they are typically encountered in modern editions which completely wrench them from their contexts. But with a few exceptions, *Visitatio* texts are preserved in manuscripts which have, by anyone's standards, no interest in drama. Our earliest *Visitatio Sepulchri* text comes from the *Regularis Concordia*, a monastic customary, as do a number of other examples. Most exemplars are contained in liturgical books. No one has ever claimed that the majority of writings in these books is "art" or "drama," yet editors have regularly removed *Visitatio* texts from them and then claimed that they should be read in the light of these discursive practices. Nothing in the manuscripts justifies this practice of making the *Visitatio Sepulchri* an independent text. In the *Regularis Concordia*, for example, there is no tag which sets the *Visitatio* text off from the words which surround it. In fact, *Visitatio Sepulchri* texts usually have no title at all, and when they are in any way set off from the words which immediately precede and follow them, it is by such points of reference as "de die Paschae" or "ad visitandum sepulchrum" which merely follow standard scribal practices which enable something to be found in a manuscript which has neither table of contents or index. Nothing, then, justifies, wrenching a *Visitatio Sepulchri* text from its local textual environment and granting it the universally significant status of protodrama – nothing, that is, but the discursive practice which we call "literature."

Another way of describing the transformation that takes place in modern scholarship when the *Visitatio Sepulchri* text is transferred from manuscript to edition is to say that the medieval practice is deprived of its local context. Our editions of the *Visitatio* seek to obliterate essential distinctions in the manuscript traditions. In the first place, they make no attempt to sort out manuscripts of parochial and diocesan provenance from those in monastic use. Secondly, the earlier editors – and here, at least Lipphardt's work represents a major advance – largely obscured the local character of *Visitatio* texts. Almost no one has ever asked what a performance of the *Visitatio* was for a specific community at a definite moment in time, or inquired as to whether its enactment at Canterbury on a given Easter morning had the same significance as its enactment at, say, Bamberg, on the same Easter morning. And most striking of all, I cannot think of a single attempt to relate the *Visitatio Sepulchri* to the material existence of a given community or to scrutinize it for its ideological content. *Visitatio* texts have thus been deprived of their local character and indeed of their very *locus* in material history by a scholarship that has been wholly concerned with construing them as universal if somewhat undeveloped examples of the "natural" universal practice of drama, a practice which has to do with "art" and possibly "religion" rather than with a local practice arising out of and addressing both the material and intellectual coordinates of a specific human community at a given moment of its history. Thus it has come about that rather than trying to locate the *Visitatio* within an historical matrix, medieval scholarship has imagined that monastic communities invented and performed the *Visitatio* because, like their later counterparts, they enjoyed edifying plays.

It is time to stop universalizing the *Visitatio Sepulchri* in this way and to begin to ask what and how its practice signified for its local participants. Obviously, in such a study the character of the books in which the visitation rite is preserved must be an important issue. Here one needs to be concerned with such issues, thus far absent from medieval drama studies, as manuscript genres, relevant intra- and inter-textual relationships, and the ties between texts and sets of texts to the socio-politico-economic entities to which they were related as well as to theological and intellectual formations and their local manifestations. Let me here stress the first of these concerns, manuscript genres. *Visitatio Sepulchri* texts are primarily preserved in liturgical books and in customaries. The function of such books is to preserve and ensure common practices within a specific and often locally defined community. They are oriented towards performance and indicate what must be done at a given time and place. Psalters, lectionaries, hymnals, processionals, and other liturgical books need to be used together with customaries if we wish to know the details of a specific form of monastic life and local liturgical practice. Most importantly, we need to explore the relationship between the *Visitatio* and its immediate textual contexts. The results of such inquiries would, of course, vary from exemplar to exemplar, and from manuscript genre to manuscript genre. I will limit myself to a few remarks about the customary in which the oldest of all surviving *Visitatio* texts is found, the *Regularis Concordia*.

Like most monastic customaries, much of the material in the *Regularis* is specifically liturgical, but in addition to providing information about ritual practices, it details the rules and customs of monastic discipline in a definite place, in this instance in all tenth-century English Benedictine houses (though there is reason to doubt that, even under the monastic reforms of which the *Regularis* is the product, English monastic life was ever so uniform). The preface to the *Regularis* explains how the Synodical Council which established the practices detailed in the customary did so lest [the monks] "should all, which God forbid, prefer to act according to their own devices and thus wretchedly lose the most excellent fruit of holy obedience."[1] A modern reader cannot be but amazed at the detail of regularity imposed on the lives of monks in this text. For example a bell is to be rung before Terce, and at this sign "the brethren shall go and put their day shoes on." None should "presume to do this before the bell is heard, nor fail to do so then without permission."[2] Similarly night shoes are to be exchanged for day shoes after vespers and at no other time. It is likewise demanded that each member of the community must wash his feet at a specified time on Saturday afternoon, and to use only his own basin for doing so. Times for daily hand washing are detailed. Detailed schedules are provided for every major activity of every day, varying only between weekdays and Sundays and holidays on one hand, and the division between the summer and winter calendars specified in the Benedictine Rule on the other. Even times for providing for the "corpoream naturae necessitatem"[3] are specified: upon awakening, but only if certain prayers and Psalms are first said privately, or during the short period between Nocturns and before Lauds.

The *Regularis* provides for an effective enforcement of this detailed plan for living. No privacy is to be afforded any monk. Members of the community are seldom allowed to leave the watchful gaze of the group and are specifically prohibited from roaming around the monastic property without being under scrutiny. "Not even on the excuse of some spiritual matter," the *Regularis* warns, "shall any monk presume to take with him a young boy alone for any private purpose but, as the Rule commands, let the children always remain under the care of their master. Nor shall the master himself be allowed to be in company with a boy without a third person as witness."[4] In the Rule, monks are encouraged to accuse each other of faults publicly in Chapter, and an accused monk is never to deny that he is guilty, whether or not he is so. Furthermore the *Regularis* provides for a special officer named the *circa* who is to walk around the cloister to look for lazy brothers. If he finds one, "he should by no means keep silence about the matter at the Chapter on the following day." The *circa* is to go around the cloister after Compline, and if he finds there codices or garments "he shall take them away and show them at the next day's Chapter." The *circa* is to be given a lantern so that "he may look about him in the night hours, when it is proper so to do; and when the lessons are read at Nocturns, at the third or fourth lesson, as seems good to him, he shall go about the choir; and if he finds a brother drowsy with sleep he shall put the lantern before him and return to his place. Whereupon this brother, shaking off sleep, shall do penance on his knees and, taking up the lantern, shall himself go round the choir, and if he finds another overcome by the disorder of sleep, he shall do to him as was done to himself and so return to his own place."[5]

There is nothing in all of this that makes the *Regularis Concordia* an unusual customary. If anything it is less restrained and less detailed than some later continental examples. The question before us concerns the appearance of the *Visitatio Sepulchri* in the midst of this kind of discourse, where it appears, as we have already seen, as part of an extremely elaborate series of Easter celebrations. To attempt to answer this question requires us first to consider the function of a monastic customary. Historically speaking, we can take its claims on face value: these documents both record and create a form of monastic life which in turn has as its purpose the cultivation of the monastic spirit and the inculcation of ascetic goals. The *Visitatio* must then have been perceived as a practice which, like the others specified in the *Regularis*, fostered these goals. To make even such a general claim is to advance our understanding of the function of the *Visitatio* beyond what could even have been guessed on the basis of the extracted texts found in scholarly editions and textbooks. But perhaps it will be more illuminating to move momentarily to a broader generalization that might assist us in our quest to understand the more specific function of the *Visitatio Sepulchri* within monastic customaries.

Much contemporary philosophy and social science insists that the primary task which besets every human being is to make sense of things, to reduce the flux and meaninglessness of raw experience to sense and meaning, in short, to construct reality. To function, such constructions have typically been made to appear as independent of their makers, as given, as ordered by some force outside of the human. In order for the illusion of order to be maintained, its structuring principles need to be reaffirmed repeatedly every day; by means of these devices, life is made to seem meaningful. Of course, each of us does not really construct her own reality. We are born into social systems which we internalize and possess as our own, and our daily contacts with others who more or less share that social system serve to confirm the meaningfulness of the world, at least until we begin to examine it in a theoretical or reflexive way.

Significantly, many social sciences employ the terminology of drama in order to characterize the way that the constructed social world is reinforced in us and in our society. Individuals are thought of as actors in a great social drama: they are said to have roles to play in that drama, roles which are determined by such factors as their socio-economic class status, familial position, age group, and the like, as well, perhaps, as their own idiosyncratic inclinations. Frequently this drama is said to be "scripted," that is, individual roles and actions are largely determined by the overall cultural systems which produce them and of which they are a part. The goal of the study of any culture, whether it be one of the present or one which belongs to past history, is to understand as much as possible about its underlying systems. In most cultural systems, scripts are of course not written documents but the expectations and reactions of others in society which serve to enforce in negative and positive ways our own conduct. But in the case of monastic customaries, we are provided with scripts for living in a more literal sense, for here we actually have a written script which encodes practices by which individuals are constituted as members of a community. Of course, like written plays, this script is nothing until it is performed, and in its actual performance, it will still be the expectations and reactions of others in the community which will concretely determine behavior.

What are the implications of these observations for the study of the *Visitatio Sepulchri*? Most obviously, within the context of texts like the *Regularis Concordia*, it functions as a scripted social drama, rather than as an "aesthetic" drama. Its function is to provide roles for imitation, roles which by their very enactment have as their purpose the reinforcement of a particular construction of reality. In this regard the *Visitatio* is indeed no different from any of the other prescribed actions in customaries. We can see this clearly when we observe the use of the word "imitatio" in the *Visitatio* in the *Regularis*. Scholars who have wished to contend for what I have termed an aesthetic understanding of the *Visitatio* have frequently pointed to the use of this word in the *Visitatio* text as a justification for their views. The text reads thus: "Aguntur enim haec ad imitationem angeli sedentis in monumento, atque mulierum cum aromatibus uenientium ut ungerent corpus Ihesu."[6] But the peculiarly dramatic (in the narrower sense of that term) force of this imitation is significantly reduced if we compare this usage with other places in the *Regularis Concordia* where "imitatio" occurs. The first occurrence comes in the preface, where the writer claims that "we shall set forth plainly in writing those customs of the Holy Rule which have been constantly and everywhere observed both by the aforesaid Benedict and by his holy followers and imitators."[7] Here, as frequently in monastic and hagiographical documents, imitation is a moral process in which benefits are to be derived by imitating predecessors and seniors (which is precisely how, according to many social theoreticians, we learn to act in culturally, socially acceptable ways). The same sense occurs in a line which exhorts monks to begin each day with a blessing because "we are bound by monastic custom and the imitation of the fathers."[8] Here we see imitation function in the same way. Closer to the *Visitatio* practice, and yet utterly in conformity with this same sense of imitation, is a passage which recommends performing the deposition and elevation of the cross because "certain religious men" have instituted this practice "worthy to be imitated."[9] Clearly then, in the *Regularis Concordia* the *Visitatio Sepulchri* is one of innumerable practices to be imitated in order to cultivate and reinforce the roles which the customary assigns to those who would play a part in its own version of the drama of the monastic life. It is not motivated by a desire to create or put on a play, or by a desire to teach religious truths. Even if Hardison were correct – which seems highly unlikely – that the *Regularis* version of the *Visitatio* had its origins in secular Easter practices, this would have nothing to do with its function within the community envisioned by the customary. Seen in the context of that document, the *Visitatio Sepulchri* has nothing to do with the beginnings of modern drama, and one could only think otherwise by arbitrarily removing it from that context. That, of course, is exactly what every editor and every interpreter concerned with the text has done.

It would be interesting and worthwhile to consider at greater length the various demands of the *Regularis*. But enough has been suggested for our purposes, and I therefore wish to point to only one additional aspect of this text: its political interest. Though the *Regularis* is clearly a miscellany of various continental monastic practices, it ascribes its creation to the action of "Edgar the glorious, by the grace of Christ illustrious King of the English and of the other peoples dwelling within the bounds of the island of Britain," who "began carefully and earnestly to consider by what holy and deserving works it could be made to burn with the brilliance and ardour of perfection."[10] As "Pastorum Pastor," the King "saw to it wisely that his Queen, Aelfthrith, should be the protectress and fearless guardian of the communities of nuns; so that he himself helping the men and his consort helping the women there should be no cause for any breath of scandal."[11] Elections of abbots and abbesses are to be carried out "with the consent and advice of the King,"[12] and the monks are forbidden to consult any other secular person concerning this matter. In order to stress to the community the importance of the monarch, after each of the canonical hours, including Nocturns, a Psalm and Collect are to be recited for the King and another Psalm and Collect for the Queen. The morrow mass is said each day for the King. In this way the importance and power of the monarch are the subject of constant reminders at several different times during each day of the community's life. Monastic and regal concerns are inextricably tied together.

Much more could be learned by studying the *Visitatio* ceremony within the context of the monastic practice. And equally informative would be a consideration of the "same" text in diocesan usage, where the script of reality construction would necessarily change rather drastically. And much, much more needs to be said about the socio-economic and political determination of these practices than can be said here. But for now I must move to an immediate though necessarily provisional conclusion. Since its construction as protodrama in the discursive practice generally termed "literature," the *Visitatio Sepulchri* has been treated in universalizing terms; its significance has been achieved at the expense of depriving it of its specifically local character. One of the most striking features of this practice which still dominates almost all talk about the *Visitatio* is that it has led nowhere. It has produced no extended interpretations of this form, and it has been unable to explain why this practice should have had such singular importance; it has repeatedly engendered the wildest kinds of speculation while it has ignored a far richer textual context than has usually survived for medieval texts. The only real utility of viewing the *Visitatio* in these aesthetic terms emerges when we are performing the text, and rightly so, for no twentieth-century person can possibly appropriate the *Visitatio* the way that a tenth-century monk did. But for all of that, it is time to take a new look at the *Visitatio*, a look which is not grounded in literary or dramatic studies but in the study of local practice and, perhaps, in those semiological disciplines which are concerned with the ways that human beings create and transmit meanings in endless acts of reality construction, deconstruction, and reconstruction. I dare to hope, in fact, that this apparent retreat from Kantian universals to localized particulars will open the *Visitatio Sepulchri* to convincing interpretations for the first time since the Middle Ages.

Notes

1. Dom Thomas Symons [ed.], *Regularis Concordia: Anglicae Nationis Monarchorum Sanctimonialiumque – The Monastic Agreement of the Monks and Nuns of the English Nation*, London [etc.], 1953, p. 4.
2. *Ibidem*, pp. 15-6.
3. *Ibidem*, p. 11.
4. *Ibidem*, p. 8.
5. *Ibidem*, p. 56.
6. *Ibidem*, p. 50. The English translation of this passage reads: "Now these things are done in imitation of the angel seated on the tomb and of the women coming with perfumes to anoint the body of Jesus."
7. *Ibidem*, pp. 8-9.
8. *Ibidem*, p. 11.
9. *Ibidem*, p. 44.
10. *Ibidem*, p. 1.
11. *Ibidem*, p. 2.
12. *Ibidem*, p. 6.

From Popular Performance Genre to Literary Play and Back Again: The Literary Appropriation of Medieval Vernacular Drama
C. Clifford Flanigan[*]

There is no single manner in which the so-called "dramatic texts" of the Middle Ages became texts of "medieval drama" which we study today. My preliminary research into this process suggests that widely different strategies were employed for the conferring of literary status on these texts, and many of these strategies are more prominent in one area of Europe than in another. In Italy, for example, attempts were made to link them with the traditions of Roman drama, while in German-speaking territories, nationalist perspectives contributed more heavily to this process than they did elsewhere in Europe. But it was in England that eighteenth- and nineteenth-century students of literature experienced the most compelling need to establish medieval plays as part of a literary system. The reason for this situation seems obvious. English scholars of the eighteenth and nineteenth centuries despised medieval "dramatic" texts as much as their continental counterparts. Yet, unlike those counterparts, English scholars had to deal with the Shakespearian stage, which seemed to them to have some connection with earlier performance practices. Thus as Shakespeare was incorporated into the literary system, though initially it was rather into the pre-modern literary system which antedates the paradigm shift to which this essay gives its primary attention, it was increasingly felt necessary to somehow incorporate medieval "dramatic" practices into the literary canon. Because these English practices are particularly revealing about the ways that these texts were transformed into medieval "drama" and hence into medieval "literature," the remainder of this essay will be devoted to the invention of medieval drama in England, though ultimately I hope to treat this topic from a pan-European perspective.

The process by which those texts which were subsequently termed "medieval dramas" disappeared from the European consciousness in the later sixteenth and early seventeenth centuries requires more research than has been afforded it, especially for the Continent. That is of little concern for the present study, however. What is im-

---

[*] Reproduced by permission of estate of C. Clifford Flanigan. Paper read at the 2nd Annual Medieval Symposium, Indiana University, March 30, 1989.

portant for us is the fact that the survival of whatever remains to us from medieval performing traditions is due entirely to antiquarians, not men of letters. Critical editions of these texts did not generally appear until well in the nineteenth century. A representative statement of the relative ignorance about these plays, even on the part of a diligent researcher, along with an expression of a typical value judgment about them, can be seen in Robert Dodsley's study *A Select Collection of Old Plays*, published in London in 1744: "This period [the late Middle Ages, C.C.F.] one might call the Dead Sleep of the Muses."[1] And further on:

> I should have been glad to be more particular; but where Materials are not to be had, the Building must be deficient. And to say the Truth, a more particular Knowledge of these Things, any farther than as it serves to shew the Turn and Genius of our Ancestors, and the progressive Refinement of our Language, was so little worth preserving, that the Loss of it is scarce to be regretted.[2]

Fifty years later, scholars knew a great deal more about medieval performance texts, yet the value judgment expressed by Dodsley remained, even though the context in which it was asserted altered radically as the ideological system which we now term literature began to assert itself. Among the components of this system is the well-known Kantian demand for aesthetic disinterestedness according to which texts possessing "literary" value were said to be free of didactic and propagandistic concerns. (That such a demand was merely a mystification which enabled literary texts to be the vehicle for middle-class ideology goes without saying.) Similarly it was asserted that literary texts were marked by a creative organic unity which allowed the universal to be made manifest in their particular details. Thirdly, literary works were said to be the product of genius; indeed it could be argued that this Enlightenment and Romantic concern with genius was the stimulus for the creation of the discourse about authorship which has dominated the practice of literary studies down to the present moment. There were, of course, other components that went into the invention of literature, but I mention these chief points, so frequently rehearsed in the histories, because they stand in such striking contrast to the ways that medieval dramatic texts were perceived by late eighteenth- and nineteenth-century writers. For them, and perhaps for us as well, medieval plays seemed lacking in "organic unity," and they were regarded as highly didactic. Furthermore, since they were widely viewed as the product of dark age Popery, they seemed devoid of that universality which was regarded as the *sine qua non* of "genuine art." And yet, unlikely candidates though they were, medieval plays were gradually admitted into literary histories along with texts regarded as infinitely more sublime.

How could such a transformation come about? Primarily through the agency of nationalism and the discourse about national literature which was often joined to notions of the aesthetic and the literary. The same middle class ideology which underlies these latter discourses produced, of course, the idea of the national state, at least as we understand it today. Built into the union of the discourses about nationalism and the discourses about art is a fundamental contradiction which has not, I think, received adequate attention. "Literature" is a highly elitist notion, one which was used to authorize the manner of living of the bourgeois who were gaining ascendancy in the eighteenth century. But notions of national literature frequently evoked notions of "Das Volk," a concept which supposedly expressed the spirit of an entire nation. At the moment of its creation national literature frequently reached out to forms of popular culture and made them part of a national "literary" heritage. Yet such monuments of culture were alien to elitist claims which gave rise to the institution of literature. To the eighteenth-century man of sensibility, medieval drama seemed anything but refined, as we can see from a remark in Charles Gildon's "Essay on the Art, Rise, and Progress of the Stage, in Greece, Rome, and England," published by Gildon as a supplement to Nicholas Rowe's 1710 edition of the works of Shakespeare and subsequently incorporated into Pope's *Shakespeare* in 1725: "In England Plays began at the very bottom of the People, and mounted by degrees to the state we now see them in, the yet imperfect Diversion of Ladies, and Men of the first Quality."[3]

The means by which was achieved the reconciliation of the opposites of medieval drama, as a crude and popular form on the one hand, and the elitist system of literature on the other, was the writing of histories of national literature, a genre which was to dominate literary practice for the nineteenth and much of the present century. Indeed, the term literary history was, according to Michael Batts, first used in 1777 by the Swiss scholar Leonhard Meister in his notes on the history of the German language and German "Nationalliteratur."[4] Literary histories could be general, recounting the whole expression of a people in writing, or more specialized and devoted, for example, to drama. Especially in England, attempts to write the latter provide telling insights into the ways that our so-called dramatic texts were misread into the developing literary system. Typical is Adolphus William Ward's *A History of English Dramatic Literature to the Death of Queen Anne*, first published in 1875.[5] Ward's whole work is concerned with "the organic connexion [sic] between our dramatic literature and its proper vehicle of presentment – the national theatre."[6] For Ward, then, the history of English drama is closely tied to "the general progress of our national life and history, of which in its turn that literature has formed so measurable a part."[7] In fact the word "English" appears in virtually every paragraph of the Ward's first volume, often being repeated several times. Yet in contrast to most later writers about the English stage, Ward gives his discussion an international context. Even here, however, his treatment is decidedly chauvinistic. He argues that a large portion of European drama had its origins in minstrelsy and that minstrels were on the whole rather a low class lot. Yet he assures his readers that if certain dramatic practices evolved from minstrelsy, English drama is the product of a "higher class of minstrels."[8]

In other ways too, the superiority of English drama was asserted as a means of enabling admittedly crude texts into the canon of national literature. In John Addington Symonds's *Shakespere's Predecessors in the English Drama*, published in 1884, the tendency of English drama to include the whole history of the world into one cycle of plays (in contrast to the Continental practice of single subject plays) is said to mark the greatest striving for the universal in this particular and crude form. Symonds also seeks to endow medieval biblical "plays" with Kantian universality by arguing that despite its offensive qualities, medieval English Christianity "was not, as it now might be, a thing apart from life, reserved for pious contemplation. It gave artistic shape to all reflections upon life; presented human destinies in their widest scope and their most striking details; incorporated medieval science, ethics, history, cosmography, and politics; bringing abstractions vividly before the eyes and ears of folk who could not read."[9] The last few words of this quotation point to what no honest literary history could hide, even as it attempted to transform medieval texts into modern literary ones: that medieval vernacular drama was, for the most part, a popular, not an elitist practice.

Yet since the texts of medieval "plays" were increasingly being discovered in Symonds's time, if not necessarily published, makers of national literary histories had somehow to accommodate them within their schemes. One of most frequently employed methods for doing so was an appeal to growth and evolution so that these texts were seen as the humble beginnings of greater things. Thus Symonds could explain that "Art, like Nature, takes no sudden leaps, *nihil agit per saltum*; and the connection between the Miracles and Shakespere's Drama is unbroken, though the aesthetic interval between them seems almost infinite."[10] Thus, "[i]n spite of their colossal rudeness, they [miracle plays, C.C.F] are clearly no primitive works of art, but the final outcome of a slowly developed evolution."[11] And yet the maker of a history of literature had in the same breath to admit that regrettable lack of refinement in these texts: "Language in the Miracles barely clothes the ideas which were meant to be conveyed by figured forms; meagerly supplies the motives necessary for the proper presentation of an action. Clumsy phrases, quaint literalism, tedious homilies clog the dramatic evolution. As in the case of medieval sculpture, so here the most spontaneous and natural effects are grotesque."[12]

One frequent means of recuperating the early drama and lending it dignity was by means of comparing it with classical Greek plays. Thus James Wright, whose *Historia Histrionica: An Historical Account of the English Stage*, published in 1699, was one of the earliest studies based on some actual knowledge of medieval practice, claimed that "plays in England had a beginning much like those of Greece, the Monologues and Pageants drawn from place to place on wheels, answer exactly to the cart of Thespis."[13] Similarly Bishop Thomas Percy, in his famous *Reliques of Ancient English Poetry*, published in Dublin in 1765, said of *Everyman* that it is "not without some rude attempts to excite terror and pity … [I]n this old simple drama the fable is conducted upon the strictest model of the Greek tragedy."[14]

Yet even such claims were contradicted by counterclaims inscribed in the same arguments. One of the chief assumptions which marks most eighteenth- and nineteenth-century literary discourse is the belief that all genuine (which is to say, "literary") drama must be either comic or tragedy. Yet there was a widespread recognition that particularly the biblical drama could not be coerced into such forms. Thus Ward's long *History of English Dramatic Literature* begins with a discussion of medieval plays under the rubric "The Origins of Drama." The next chapter proceeds to describe "the Beginning of the English Regular Drama," by which Ward means drama that can readily be categorized as comedy or tragedy, or perhaps comic-tragedy. Yet earlier Percy has insisted, "I have now before me two [moralities] that were printed early in the reign of Henry VIII, in which I think one may plainly discover the seeds of Tragedy and Comedy."[15] In this connection it is worth recalling the thesis of Alan Knight's study of *Aspects of Genre in Late Medieval French Drama*, where he demonstrates that part of the reason that medieval plays occupy such a problematic place in French literary history is that critics have persistently tried to force them into the classically authorized genres of comedy or tragedy, genres which Knight argues are irrelevant to the generic traditions of medieval texts.[16]

I have thus far argued that the need to create a totalizing national literary history forced classically and romantically oriented critics to invent strategies of inclusion to appropriate medieval performance texts. Such acts of recuperation were undertaken, I believe, under the influence of the supposed Aristotelian claim that all "literature" consists of three basic modes: narrative, lyric, and drama. Since these texts were clearly neither of the first two items on this list, they necessarily had to be included in the last category. But in order to include the medieval "plays" into the literary canon in this way, significant strategies of exclusion had also to be employed. For medieval "drama" clearly has affinities with such performance practices as royal entries, folk games, and musical performances. Since it would be much more difficult to claim that these popular and nonverbal forms of action belong to the elitist, universal, and verbal "art" of drama, they found little notice in most national literary histories and other texts which contributed toward the invention of medieval drama as a literary practice.

But there were some significant exceptions to these practices, ones which aligned the supposed plays with some of the other performance practices I have just mentioned. Perhaps most telling in this regard is William Hone's influential *Ancient Mysteries Described*, which first appeared in 1823.[17] Hone (1780-1842) was, among many other things, an antiquarian and was especially interested in folk manners and customs, having written the then well-known *Everyday Book*, which traced numerous nineteenth-century social practices to ancient folk customs. He produced his study of the drama out of theological rather than literary motivations. In the first place, he wrote to demonstrate the pervasive influence of the apocryphal New Testament writings on the plays, a point which others, apparently offended by such scenes as the physical testing of the Mary's virginity "on stage," had sought to deny. But more fundamentally, Hone viewed the miracle plays as an abortive attempt to subvert the Wyclif Bible, as a weapon in the war of ideas finally won by the Reformation. Though viewing the plays in this way continues the charges of ignorance and Popery that were frequently raised in the England of his time, the manner in which Hone developed this claim implicitly offered an understanding of the plays which significantly differed from attempts to see in them a primitive literature. For Hone, the plays are social actions which have practical and ideological purposes rather than aesthetic ones. The full title of Hone's book indicates something not only of its extraordinarily broad scope but of the company in which Hone sets these texts: *Ancient Mysteries Described, Especially the English Miracle Plays Founded on Apocryphal New Testament Story, Extant Among the Published Manuscripts of the British Museum; Including Notices of Ecclesiastical Shows, the Festivals of Fools and Asses– The English Boy-Bishop– The Descent into Hell– The Lord Mayor's Show– The Guildhall Giants– Christmas Carols, etc.*

Others before and after Hone had made occasional references to some of these practices. Perhaps the best-known example is E. K. Chambers's *The Mediaeval Stage*, published in 1903.[18] Here much is made of "folk drama," various practices of miming, dancing and singing, as well as of popular forms of most agricultural rituals. A lesser known example of setting the medieval "plays" into the context of non-literary performance practices is Joseph S. Tunison's intriguing study, *Dramatic Traditions of the Dark Ages*, which appeared four years after the publication of Chambers's work.[19] Here, in the service of an unusual argument for the influence of Byzantine culture on medieval European drama, we encounter numerous and extended references to hymn singing, miming societies, and ritual dancing, along with more "literary" practices such as the twelfth-century *commedia*. This attempt to deal with the great variety of medieval performance practices in a wholly non-literary manner quickly passed into obscurity. Indeed, what is most salient for the present argument is that by the beginning of the twentieth century, almost all studies of the "medieval drama" excluded texts that could not be more or less readily assimilated into the literary system. From the perspective of the present moment in history, this exclusionary strategy is greatly to be regretted, since it expunged a method of rescuing medieval performance practices from the relentless domination of national literature and pointed to these texts as texts of social action, a perspective that is only now beginning to be pursued.

Space will not permit us to continue to trace out the continuing literary appropriation of medieval dramatic texts in our own century. Let it only be noted that the New Criticism and related formalisms undertook in the nineteen-fifties to complete what had been started in the eighteenth century. The result was a plethora of ever more unlikely readings which purported to "prove" the unity of a text or the "artistry" of its conception. Similarly these anonymous texts were coerced into systems of authorship by the invention of such designations as "the Wakefield Master" and "the York Realist." Such tactics have by now, it appears, played themselves out, and we seem poised on the verge of interpreting these texts in terms of paradigms derived from anthropology and sociology rather than from Kantian aesthetics. It seems likely that the so-called medieval drama is about to be liberated from literature and set in a broader context of the human sciences where it can be viewed as a pragmatic practice performed in specific socio-economic contexts for purposes of ideological indoctrination and reality construction. It is by now no doubt obvious that the present writer greatly prefers such a reading of these texts. Yet it is by no means the conclusion of this essay that the medieval drama is about to be rescued from the misreading process which has plagued it for centuries by readings that are more correct or appropriate. What the invention and history of the "medieval drama" as a literary institution teaches us is that all reading, including the form which we most cherish, is strong invention rather than weak explication and that therefore all reading is unavoidably and inextricably misreading. In terms of our topic, every construction is a reconstruction, and every reconstruction contains within it the seeds of its own deconstruction. It is perhaps rather late in the day to assert such a claim. But what I hope has become clear from this work in progress is that because of its especially problematic status as "literary text," the so-called medieval drama has much to tell us about the invention of literature and, perhaps, our potential deliverance from it.

Notes

1. Robert Dodsley [ed.], *A Select Collection of Old Plays*, 12 vols., London, 1744, vol. I, p. xiii.
2. *Ibidem*, p. xv.
3. Charles Gildon, "An Essay on the Art, Rise, and Progress of the Stage, in Greece, Rome, and England," in *The Works of William Shakespear*, [ed.] Alexander Pope, 6 vols., with a supplementary seventh volume edited by [George] Sewell, London, 1725, p. li.
4. Michael S. Batts, *A History of Histories of German Literature, 1835-1914*, Montreal, 1993, p. 83. According to Batts, Meister created the term "Nationalliteratur" at a time when the term "deutsche Literaturgeschichte" was beginning to replace the more standard "Geschichte der deutschen Literatur." [Note from the editor: I have not been able to substantiate Professor Flanigan's statement to the effect that it was Meister who first used the term "Literaturgeschichte"]
5. Adolphus William Ward, *A History of English Dramatic Literature to the Death of Queen Anne*, revised edition, 3 vols., London, 1899.
6. *Ibidem*, vol. I, p. 1.
7. *Ibidem*, vol. I, p. 3.
8. *Ibidem*, vol. I, p. 24.
9. John Addington Symonds, *Shakespere's Predecessors in the English Drama*, London, 1884, pp. 99-100.
10. *Ibidem*, p. 94.
11. *Ibidem*, p. 105.
12. *Ibidem*, p. 117.
13. James Wright, *Historia Histrionica: An Historical Account of the English Stage*, repr. in Dodsley [ed.], *Select Collection*, vol. I, p. clxvi.
14. Thomas Percy, "On the Origin of the English Stage, etc.," in Henry B. Wheatley [ed.], *Reliques of Ancient English Poetry*, New York, 1966 [repr. of the 1886 edition], 3 vols., vol. I, p. 104.
15. *Ibidem*, p. 435.
16. Alan Knight, *Aspects of Genre in Late Medieval French Drama*, Manchester, 1983.
17. William Hone, *Ancient Mysteries Described*, London, 1823.
18. E. K. Chambers, *The Mediaeval Stage*, 2 vols., Oxford, 1903.
19. Joseph S. Tunison, *Dramatic Traditions of the Dark Ages*, Chicago and London, 1907.

Amalarius of Metz
and the Ideology of Liturgical Semiotics
*C. Clifford Flanigan**

*E*ver since the work of Emile Durkheim, anthropologists and students of religion have insisted that rituals and ceremonies are privileged semiotic spaces in which a culture states, shapes, modifies, subverts, or obfuscates its values and social structures. Thus though rituals often seem to the outsider to have no pragmatic purpose, they represent a major, indeed for many cultures, the major work performed by it and for it. From "the native's point of view" – and I deliberately use that term to evoke Clifford Geertz's problematizing of it – rituals are the works by which the gods allow a society to continue or prosper, while from the point of view of contemporary anthropologists they communicate and reinforce understandings of self and society from one generation to the next. Medieval Christian professional practitioners of religion would likely agree with this assessment. Though monasticism, for example, may have begun as a liturgically neutral or even anti-ritual and anti-clerical movement, it soon became centered around the performance of the *opus dei*, God's work, that is, the daily cursus of mass, long nocturnal vigils, and a diurnal round of seven occasions for psalms and prayer. Indeed in the *Regula Benedicti* the *opus dei* is the prime work for every monk, second even to the labor of the hands which is one of the characteristics of Benedict's Rule. Similarly, as the monastic ideal came to dominate the conception of what constitutes appropriate work for secular clergy, ritual work occupied the preeminent and privileged place.

Yet as in other aspects of life, this liturgical work demanded and produced liturgical play, by which I mean the work of interpretation. It has long been a commonplace in liturgical history that the basic shape of the Christian rites was set early in Christian antiquity and certainly by the time of the establishment of the Church under Constantine and his immediate successors. Yet sustained and systematic explanations of these rites are never found among the writings of the Fathers. Ritual interpretation before the early Middle Ages is always occasional and incidental, and mostly found in

---

*   Reproduced by permission of estate of C. Clifford Flanigan. Paper read at the 5th Annual Medieval Symposium, Indiana University, April 4, 1992.

sermons, especially for catechumens, and in letters which address specific cultic issues. Beginning in the eighth century, however, attempts at liturgical commentary appear, haltingly at first, and then, more elaborately and systematically.

The key figure in this new development is Amalarius (*c.*780-850), Bishop of Metz in the second quarter of the ninth century. Amalarius was the first Christian scholar to produce sustained and systematic studies of the liturgy, the most important of which was the *Liber officialis*.[1] Amalarius is to all subsequent liturgical interpretation what Freud is to Freudianism or Marx to Marxism; drawing on and refashioning a number of predecessors, he set the parameters of all subsequent interpretation of the Christian liturgy up to the Reformation and often beyond. Despite his significance, Amalarius has received little attention; indeed, he has virtually been discussed in English language studies only in connection with the so-called liturgical drama, and then his work has, I would argue, been greatly misunderstood and misappropriated.

Amalarius saw his ritual hermeneutics as both innovative and traditional. In the Preface to the *Liber officialis* he explains that the meaning of the ritual over which he presided was unclear to him – quite an admission for one of the most educated and prominent clergy of the Carolingian Empire. Trying to understand the liturgy, he said, was like sitting in a dark crypt, until one day a ray of light hit him. That ray of light, he said, came from Augustine's *De doctrina christiana*.

Amalarius defends his cultic hermeneutics to Louis the Pious thus:

> I was greatly desirous to know what the earlier writers who established our rites had in mind. But it is very difficult for me to be certain that I have actually explained what they intended. Yet there is one thing that has aided me, so that things which I have written ought not to seem to your religious sensibilities to depart from the way of caritas. I am in fact defended by Augustine's *De doctrina christiana* from those who wish to seize me, as if I had written something dangerous, because I may have suggested something other than what were the intentions of the authors of our liturgy. In the first book of *De doctrina* Augustine says, "Whoever finds a lesson useful to the building of caritas, even though he has not said what the author may be shown to have intended in that place, has not been deceived, nor is he lying in any way.[2]

This passage sounds many of the keynotes of Amalarius' writings. Note the way that Amalarius seeks to legitimize his mode of liturgical interpretation by invoking an Augustinian methodology. Indeed, Amalarius' difficulties with understanding the liturgy closely parallel Augustine's difficulties with interpreting the Bible. Both Augustine and Amalarius sought historical explanations for the texts which puzzled them, but both also felt the need for some other hermeneutical method for those occasions when their historical research failed them. Beyond these parallels and the obvious prestige which the work of the bishop of Hippo had for Carolingian scholars, there was an even more basic reason for Amalarius' evocation of the *De doctrina*. Augustine was the only one of the Fathers to articulate a semiotic theory. Indeed, Augustine was the only writer in all Graeco-Roman antiquity who developed a multifaceted and consciously developed philosophy of the sign. Key here, as Amalarius recognized, is the famous beginning of the *De doctrina* where Augustine tells us:

> All doctrine concerns either things or signs, but things are learned by signs. Strictly speaking, I have here called a "thing" that which is not used to signify something else … There are signs whose whole use is in signifying, like words, for no one uses words except for the purpose of signifying something. From this may be understood what we call signs: they are things used to signify something. Thus every sign is also a thing, but not every thing is also a sign. (I.2)[3]

For Augustine, signs exist for the sole purpose of 'bringing forth and transferring to the other mind the action of the mind of the person who makes the sign' (II.2). Ambiguous signs are more pleasurable and more didactically effective than transparent ones (II.6). In order to read aright, Augustine argues, we require various kinds of linguistic, historical, and geographical knowledge, and this knowledge should be put to use to understand what he calls 'literal signs' (II.10ff.). Yet for Augustine there are signs which remain mysterious even after we have diligently researched a text, and these require a different hermeneutic in which the reader is guided by what Augustine takes to be the key to ultimate meaning, love for God and for our fellow men.

Amalarius' liturgical exegesis is firmly based on the interpretive program articulated in the *De doctrina*. He conceives of the liturgy as a group of divergent texts, written by various authors from disparate historical periods, with definite meanings in mind. The purpose of ritual is thus to teach doctrinal, moral, historical, or even scientific truths. According to Amalarius, patristic authors wrote liturgical texts and prescribed liturgical actions with definite meanings in mind, and therefore it is the interpreter's task to discover that meaning for every bow, every kiss, every cultic movement. If he could not discover such meanings, Amalarius invented allegorical ones in a manner which he believed was consistent with the program outlined in the *De doctrina*.

But things are not quite so simple; in many ways Amalarius' liturgical hermeneutic significantly differs from the way that Augustine interpreted cultic signs. Although it is perhaps not always overtly expressed in the *De doctrina*, Augustine's semiotic theory was conditioned by its Neoplatonic heritage. In the *De magistro*, for example, Augustine argues both that nothing can be taught without signs (an epistemological assumption with which Amalarius' works are in fundamental agreement) and yet, paradoxically, that nothing can be taught with signs, since all knowledge is in some sense innate (a claim which seems far from the Amalarian undertaking).[4] Underlying these seemingly contradictory claims is the Neoplatonic belief that the determining characteristic of a sign is that it awakens our minds to some higher reality by a process of participation. Thus although Augustine recognizes that language is based on conventional associations, he also claims that signs ultimately function by participating in, or at least pointing to, the originals or archetypes of that which they signify.

Of course, for Augustine not all signs are equally charged with the "reality" of their "originals"; however, there are signs which are so grounded in their archetypes that they directly connect their perceiver – or better, participant – with those archetypes. This class of signs is designated *sacramenta*. Augustine's *sacramenta* cannot be identified with those observances that high medieval theology would later identify as "sacraments." Rather, for Augustine they are imitative cultic actions that are filled with the ontic reality to which they point. A quotation from a letter written to Bishop Boniface will economically illustrate Augustine's notion of *sacramenta*:

> When we speak of the approach of Easter, it is usual for us to say that the Lord's Passion is tomorrow or the next day, although He suffered many years ago, and the Passion itself happened once and for all. It is usual also for us to say of Easter Sunday: "Today the Lord has risen," although many years have gone by since his resurrection. No one would be so foolish as to accuse us of lying when we speak thus, knowing that we name those days in memory of the events that happened on similar days, and that, when the day is mentioned, not itself but one like it in the passage of the year is meant. The *sacramentum* of the feast causes us to speak as though a particular thing were happening on this day when in point of fact it really happened a long time ago. Was not Christ offered in his person only once, yet *in sacramento* he is offered for mankind not only on every Easter Sunday but every day? If *sacramenta* had no resemblance to the things which they represent, they would not be *sacramenta*; … The Apostle said of baptism, "We are buried together with Christ by baptism into his death." He does not say we symbolize his burial, but says plainly, "We are buried with Him." He did not wish the *sacramentum* of so great an event to be known by any other name than that of the event itself.[5]

Such claims are frequently found in the Augustinian corpus. F. van der Meer has summed up Augustine's notion of *sacramentum* thus:

> [*Sacramenta*] are something more than mere memories of the baptism and last supper of our Lord, for they cause one of the facts in the process of our salvation to be re-enacted in the faithful. They continually place before us and actualize that fact. Nor are they simply "mystical signs that proclaim the sufferings and resurrection of Our Lord which now belong to the past." What they do is this: they cause the historic event in this process of salvation to be actually present as a means of the individual salvation of every one of us and "insinuate the spiritual gift" which the divine power makes effective by means of them.[6]

Such claims lead us to the heart of Augustine's cultic semiotics and to the fundamental divide between them and Amalarius' appropriation of Augustine. In short, we can say that for Augustine cultic signs belong in a particular semiotic category. Though other signs may be arbitrary or ontologically related in some indefinite way to their *signata*, cultic signs function just as modern anthropologists and historians of religion have led us to expect. They are peculiarly efficacious signs, which both sign and constitute. Cultic signs, on Augustine's account, are unlike other signs in that they are performatives which effect by their very act of signing. Their realm of action is emotional experience rather than the intellect. For Amalarius, on the other hand, cultic signs are puzzles which must be interpreted intellectually. Their function is didactic, to teach new facts and remind viewers of facts which they already know. Consider, for example, his explanation of the offertory of the mass in the *Liber officialis*.

Here Amalarius explains that in the liturgy we encounter signs functioning didactically at several different levels: "Primo ad memoriam reducenda est oblatio legalis, ac deinde Christi, postremo nostra";[7] thus the rite is related conceptually, but not, in Augustine's sense, sacramentally, to the Old Testament, the New Testament, and to the lives of ninth-century worshipers. The dual offering of bread and wine in the mass is explained by the biblical reports that in the tabernacle erected by the Israelites there were two altars. These two altars were used for two different kinds of sacrifices, and this fact immediately suggests to Amalarius an ethical interpretation of the rite: "Quia duae sunt nostrae obligationes: una est per mortificationem carnis, altera in oblatione bonorum operum."[8] The fact that the Levites, at the order of David, provided music for temple worship is said to explain the ninth-century choir's singing of the offertory chant.[9]

Amalarius' practice thus may at first glance seem Augustinian, but it leads to a number of highly un-Augustinian conclusions. In Augustine's writings, Old Testament and even pagan sacrifices are frequently said to be sacramenta because they prefigure the sacramenta of the Christian dispensation and thus partake in their ontic reality. Amalarius does not completely contradict this view but offers a related one which has an entirely different basis. Christian practices are often explained by him as didactic imitations of Old Testament rites; because the Hebrews did these things, Amalarius asserts, the ninth-century Church does likewise. The reason ninth-century clergy perform these actions is to teach worshipers facts about the ancient Israelites. Here we encounter a kind of reverse typology, wholly intellectual in its conception, which would have struck many patristic writers as peculiar to say the least.[10]

How could Amalarius create such innovations while at the same time insisting that he was only a faithful disciple of Augustine? What Amalarius has done is to authorize his new liturgical hermeneutic by ignoring the way that Augustine explained cultic signs and by instead appropriating techniques of Augustine's biblical exegesis to explain the liturgy. For Augustine cultic signs point to the archetype in sacred history which is their source and in which, on his account, they participate. They are not fundamentally polysemous (though, to be sure, there are a few places in the Augustinian corpus where he allows for a secondary semiosis in some liturgical signs). But for Amalarius liturgical signs are always polysemous, setting off theoretically endless chains of significations. Liturgical texts, like biblical texts, are treated on several different levels – historical, ethical, and even scientific. The offertory interpretations to which I have just alluded, for example, are manifold, but they belong only to the first level. This same ceremony is said to have other equally significant levels, including

New Testament history. From this perspective, the offertory is said to "point to Jesus' Palm Sunday entrance into Jerusalem." This strange linkage is justified by the greeting "Dominus vobiscum" exchanged between celebrant and people at the beginning of the offertory. Amalarius finds in this brief exchange an echo of the greeting which the first-century crowds gave Jesus.[11]

Nor is this all. Since patristic techniques of biblical interpretation are here applied to cultic acts, we are not surprised to learn that these ritual acts have moral meanings. The gifts on the altar are said to figure the sacrifice which the congregation is about to make "in which the elements are offered for sins, for the kingdom, for the sacrifice the worshipers are about to make, for the Church, for the Jews, for the prayers that we make and for those who offer the sacrifice."[12] Furthermore, Amalarius continues, the altar itself "symbolizes all kinds of just men, who are living among us now, who repeatedly offer their flesh to be crucified daily with their sins and concupiscences, and as a living offering to God. Thus the oblations signify our good thoughts and good works."[13]

This last sentence points to another fundamental difference between the way that Augustine understands cultic signs and the way that Amalarius does so. Here the spectators – I believe this is the correct word – of cultic signs see themselves signified in the ecclesiastical architecture and in the actions of the clergy. But Augustine's notion of cultic signs is rooted in a far more pervasive sense of community and community action. For Augustine, the great *sacramenta* of baptism and Eucharist are bound to communal actions; indeed, the sign not only effects the ontological reality to which it points, but through it the community constitutes and renews itself as a community. The water of baptism not only signs the death of Christ, it not only makes present the death of Christ, but it also incorporates the entire community into that death and makes it "sharers with Christ". Similarly in the Eucharist, Augustine explains, "Christ the Lord has in this sign made an image of ourselves, for he desired that we should all belong to him in common, and in his meal he has sanctified our peace and unity."[14] Indeed, for Augustine the community does not merely see the sign, but the community performs it and in this way is said to make visible what it is – the collective, communal body of Christ.

Significantly, there is not even a hint of this kind of talk in Amalarius' writings. For him, and those who followed him, the laity does not perform signs which make its hidden quality qua community visible. On the contrary, only the clergy perform and they do so not in order to create or constitute a community but to teach that community truths. Indeed Amalarian cultic semiotics presupposes and fosters a fundamental and hierarchical structure. Diachronically, this hierarchy is marked on the one hand by the "authors" of the rites who encoded their intentions into signs and by clerical interpreters on the other whose task it is to recover whatever was in the minds of authoritative senders of the sign. Synchronically, the hierarchy is expressed by the division between laity and clergy. It is clergy's function to convey information by means of liturgical words and gestures to a lay audience envisioned as passive recipients of it. In fact, the Amalarian explanation of the liturgy is so extensive and detailed, and at times so idiosyncratic, that only learned clergy could possible understand it, and then only if they consulted Amalarius' book or one like it.

As many contemporary theorists insist, no act of interpretation is ideologically pure or free from the exercise of power, and this is certainly true for Amalarius' work on the *opus dei*. In it we have a prime instance of a powerful discourse which, in sharp distinction to Augustine's cultic semiotics, constitutes clergy as privileged by rank and learning over the vast majority of the ritual audience. Indeed, this discourse joins with several others of the period to constitute laity not as participants but as spectators. Thus Amalarius contributes to the notion of liturgy as theater, though in a way quite different from that suggested by O. B. Hardison and his epigones.

To summarize in conclusion: the burden of this paper is that Amalarius' allegorizing interpretations helped enable the complete clerical appropriation of the *opus dei*, and thus the sense of lay liturgical alienation and subsequent alternative forms of lay piety. Yet interpretive work, no matter how serious, cannot escape playfulness. If the effect, intentional or otherwise, of Amalarian practice is to privilege clergy, it also opened the liturgy to a wide variety of alternative interpretations, some of which could be quite subversive. Let me conclude with a trivial but telling example of what becomes possible once the patristic connection between cultic act and archetype was replaced by a seemingly arbitrary allegorical practice. Though Amalarius does not himself suggest the connection, medieval commentators frequently explained the lavabo in the mass ceremony as being related to Pilate's washing his hands and protesting his innocence even while sentencing Jesus to death. In fact, this interpretation of the liturgical act has prevailed in popular belief until the present day, though learned commentators have repeatedly railed against it. And with reason, for having the celebrant stand for Pilate is a horrendous example of how, on either an Augustinian or modern anthropological account, ritual is supposed to operate. Such an interpretation inserts clergy into the "wrong" role in the drama of salvation. It also, of course, opens up a delightfully Derridean way of reading liturgy, one strikingly ideologically different from anything Amalarius could have envisioned. But the tracing out of such subversive possibilities must await a future occasion.

Addendum[15]

Mary Carruthers's recently published and astonishingly learned book purports to be a work about memory in the Middle Ages, and while it is certainly that, any reader who peruses its dense but richly rewarding chapters soon learns that it is about much more as well. Or rather we should say that Professor Carruthers has shown us how understanding memory in a medieval manner is an indispensable key to the understanding of many aspects of medieval elite culture, especially those which directly relate to text production and reception. Given the extraordinary scope of this book, it is perhaps surprising that little attention is given in it to the medieval liturgy. Ritual is, as anthropologists have reminded us for the past century, central to a culture's own self-understanding and to our own interpretation of a different and perhaps alien culture. Certainly most of the elites whose work is described in *The Book of Memory* spent hours of virtually every day of their lives engaged in ritual practices. Yet, and perhaps understandably, Professor Carruthers has left us with nothing more than the tantalizing assertion that "*memoria* was thought of as the praxis of liturgical and devotional prayer.... Thus, while there are virtually no medieval treatises *de memoria* much before the twelfth century, there are a number of writings on prayer, meditation, and the study of Scripture, which employ some basic features of practical memory-work that we find also in antiquity…."[16]

Yet the very notions which Professor Carruthers describes are applicable to areas of liturgical study which extend well beyond those devotional practices which she seems to have in mind. In this paper, building on some of the aspects of medieval remembering which I have learned from Professor Carruthers, I want to discuss how memory as a hermeneutic practice deeply affected the interpretation and ultimately the production of ritual habitus, praxis, and lexis of the Western liturgy. In the interests of time I shall focus on only one aspect of one writer, Amalarius of Metz.

Even to glance at practically any page in the three-volume edition of Amalarius' opus prepared by J. M. Hanssens is to see how central a role memory plays in his understanding of the liturgy. Words such as *memoria, recordor* and the like are found everywhere. Again and again we are told that the function of some liturgical word or gesture is that it *reducat ad memoriam* an historical, doctrinal, or in some cases even a scientific truth. In the *Liber officialis*, for example, Amalarius asserts that the antiphon of the mass introit recalls the exaltation of Christ and that 'therefore the cantors intone the Psalm verse which follows it, *ut ad memoriam reducant Christi novissimam humiliationem*'.[17] When the celebrant kisses the altar, he does so, on Amalarius' account, in *memoriam primi adventus Christi*,[18] having that event on his mind and bringing it into the memories of his congregation by his highly visible act.

Amalarius' appropriation of the ancient and medieval theory and practice of memory is as clearly and repeatedly spelled out throughout his works. For example, in a long passage in the *Liber officialis* in which Amalarius offers an interpretation of the responsory and verse which follow the reading of the epistle, he enumerates the characteristics of proclaimers of God's truths, urging his readers to compare these characteristics to different aspects of cows. By thus exhorting us to see these preachers as cattle, he follows the techniques for remembering by visual association described in Carruthers's book. Then he goes on to explain:

> Just as letters are written so that things can be brought back into memory which have been erased by forgetfulness, and just as in a similar way we remember by picturing those things which can be commended to the memory, so it is that the responsory exhorts the preacher how he should carry out the teaching which he proclaimed in the lectern: in the first place because of the sweetness with which it was proclaimed (sung), he should create many imitators of it. Secondly his proclamations should move the hearts of many to compunction and tears. And finally, lest he should exalt himself higher than he ought because of his proclamation, the verse [following the responsory proper] is struck so that he himself might remember the reasons for his own judgment before God.[19]

One could hardly wish for a more succinct statement of the theories elaborated in Carruthers's *The Book of Memory*. Yet even this remark, which is by no means atypical, does not mark the extent to which the early medieval theory of memory underlies

Amalarius' writings. Carruthers points to the persistent way in which teachers taught their pupils to build houses of memory with many *loci* and to insert elements of an item to be remembered into these houses or cells. Within each cell, there might be another array of cells which would hold in memory elements associated with the item occupying the front door, so to speak, of the *locus*. Students were urged to remember the content of the cells by visualizing the layout of the house in memory. Though to my knowledge no one has ever noted it, an awareness of this tradition greatly enhances our understanding of the interpretation of the mass liturgy in Amalarius' first major study, the *Eclogae de ordine romano*.[20] Here the Eucharistic liturgy is said to commemorate the life of Christ in the following way:

> Introit: Recalls the prophets
> Kyrie: Signifies Zacharias and John the Baptist
> Gloria: Reminds us of the choir of angels singing to the shepherds
> Collect: Recalls Jesus in the Temple at age of twelve
> Epistle: Signifies John the Baptist's wilderness preaching
> Responsory: Expresses the eagerness of the Apostles who heard the call of Christ
> Alleluia: Reminds us of the joy which the Apostles had in Jesus' promises and miracles
> Gospel: Stands for Jesus' preaching
> Prayers up to *Nobis quoque peccatoribus*: Recalls Jesus in Gethsemane
> Rest of Canon: Signifies the time which Jesus spent in the grave
> Commixture: Stands for Jesus' resurrection
> Post Communion: Reminds us of Jesus' resurrection appearances[21]

When this scheme is brought into contact with the above quotations taken from Amalarius' more mature work on the liturgy, it is apparent that for Amalarius the early medieval Christian liturgy is essentially an act of memory. Its function is to recall historical, intellectual, doctrinal "truths," some of which were known to the congregation and hence were recalled by the words and gestures of the ministers of the mass, while others were perhaps taught for the first time by means of liturgical words and gestures. The mass here serves a wholly didactic function, as the extremely frequent repetition of such words as *demonstro*, *designo*, *ostendo*, *significo*, and *intelligo* in the Amalarian corpus testify. By such terms and conceptions Amalarius fundamentally set the parameters by which Christian ritual would be discussed by elites for the next thousand years.

But if the conception of ritual in Amalarius' writings seems forward looking in the hindsight of subsequent history, it is less certain that it represents the view of liturgy prevalent in earlier periods of the Christian era or even in Amalarius' own time. Amalarius' works were vigorously opposed in his lifetime, especially by Agobard and Florus, both from the diocese of Lyon, as scandalous and offensive expression of novelties which had never before been uttered. Indeed his works were condemned by the Synod of Quiercy in 838. If we look at this unfavorable reception only in terms of Amalarius' adherence to what Professor Carruthers has shown to be an almost universally accepted theory and practice of memory, it is hard to understand these negative judgments. Indeed, of all of Amalarius' twentieth-century commentators, only one, Adolf Kolping, in a little-read article published more than forty years ago, has taken them seriously and tried to understand them.[22] But it is worth noting that in all of his writings Amalarius himself expresses a certain anxiety about the novelty of his readings. In the Preface to the *Liber officialis* addressed to Louis the Pious, for example (see above), Amalarius explains that he has diligently marked all of his patristic quotations and professes his unquestioned loyalty to them. But elsewhere, where the Fathers seemed to Amalarius not to have spoken on the matters under discussion – and it is important to remember that no patristic writer ever felt the necessity of systematically explaining the liturgy – he owns, "I say what I think."

In connection with such a defense, Amalarius tellingly explains his motivation for developing such a memory-centered understanding of the liturgy, and it is hardly surprising that a Carolingian bishop would evoke Augustine in his own defense, as we have seen. The theoretical distinction between, on the one hand, signs with primarily intellectual and ethical content directed to the memory as an mental faculty and, on the other, of signs which re-present and constitute a sacred reality, is fundamental to our understanding of both the theory and the practice of the ancient and medieval Christian liturgy; yet students of the medieval rites have, almost without exception, overlooked or confounded it. There is good reason for their doing so since these two notions are in diverse ways intermingled in all discussions of the liturgy after Amalarius, and most commentators, like him, unreflectively mixed these two notions. Yet, I would suggest, if we are ever to pass from a positivist chronicling or naïve appreciation of medieval liturgical commentators to an engaged interpretation of them, we shall have to come to recognize that medieval liturgical practice and commentary can be profitably plotted on a theoretical grid on which these two notions of sign and memory are played off against each other. It is, for example, in the crucible of the opposition of these signifying practices that the so-called liturgical drama was born and developed, not, as Hardison and his followers would have us believe, in the wholesale taking over of Amalarius' notions of ritual signs and memory. The development of that theme, however, must necessarily be left for another occasion. The goal of the present essay will have been achieved if we can come to appreciate the paradoxical ways in which Amalarius appropriated his patristic heritage to create a discourse about ritual acts which has one its bases in the medieval theory of memory so ably chronicled by Professor Carruthers.

Notes

1. *Amalarii episcopi Opera liturgica omnia*, Ioanne Michaele [Jean Michel] Hanssens [ed.], 3 vols., Città del Vaticano, 1948-50 [*Studi e testi*, 138- 40], vol II, *Liber officialis*.

2. "Ardor mihi inerat ut scirem quid priores auctores haberent in corde, qui nostra officia statuerunt. Sed quia hoc difficillimum mihi est affirmare, ut identidem scripsissem quod illi meditabantur, unum tamen suffugium mihi est, si ea quae scripsi, videbuntur vestrae pietati a via caritatis non excedere. Ex libro Au gustini de Doctrina christiana defendar ab illis qui me voluerint capere, quasi periculose scripsissem, eo quod mentes auctorum officii nostri non praesentes haberem. Dicit memoratus doctor in libro memorato primo: 'Quisque vero talem inde

sententiam dixerit, ut huic aedificandae caritati sit utilis, nec tamen hoc dixerit quod ille quem legit eo loco sensisse probabitur, non perniciose fallitur nec omnino mentituur'" (*Liber officialis*, Praefatio, p. 20). The citation of Augustine is from *De doctrina christiana* (I.36).

3. Saint Augustine, *On Christian Doctrine*, [transl.] D. W. Robertson Jr., Indianapolis, 1958, pp. 8-9.

4. Saint Augustine, *De magistro*, in J.-P. Migne [ed.], *Patrologia Latina*, vol. XXXVIII, col. 1194-1220. For the first thesis to the effect that nothing can be taught without recourse to signs, see section 6; for the counterthesis leading to the conclusion that all truth is interior and innate, see section 33 sqq.

5. "Nempe saepe ita loquimur, ut pascha propinquante dicamus crastinam vel perendinam domini passionem, cum ille ante tam multos annos passus sit nec omnino nisi semel illa passio facta sit. Nempe ipso die dominico dicimus: 'Hodie dominus resurrexit,' cum, ex quo resurrexit, tot anni transierint. Cur nemo tam ineptus est, ut nos ita loquentes arguat esse mentitos, nisi quia istos dies secundum illorum, quibus haec gesta sunt, similitudinem nuncupamus, ut dicatur ipse dies, qui non est ipse sed revolutione temporis similis eius, et dicatur illo die fieri propter sacramenti celebrationem, quod non illo die sed iam olim factum est? Nonne semel immolatus est Christus in se ipso et tamen in sacramento non solum per omnes paschae sollemnitates sed omni die populis immolatur nec utique mentitur, qui interrogatus eum responderit immolari? Si enim sacramenta quandam similitudinem rerum earum, quarum sacramenta sunt, non haberent, omnino sacramenta non essent. … [D]e ipso baptismo apostolus: Consepulti, inquit, sumus Christo per baptismum in mortem; non ait: 'Sepulturam significavimus,' sed prorsus ait: Consepulti sumus, sacramentum ergo tantae rei non nisi eiusdem rei vocabulo nuncupavit." ([Aloisius] Goldbacher [ed.], *Saint Augustine, Epistulae*, 2 vols, Prague [etc.], 1895-98 [*Corpus Scriptorum Ecclesiasticorum Latinorum*, 34], vol. I, pp. 530-1.)

6. F. Van der Meer, *Augustine the Bishop: The Life and work of a Father of the Church*, [transl.] Brian Battershaw & G. R. Lamb, London, 1961, p. 308. Both citations are from Augustine's *Contra Faustum Manichaeum Libri Triginta Tres*.

7. Amalarius, *Liber officialis*, p. 311.

8. *Ibidem*, p. 312.

9. *Ibidem*, pp. 311-4.

10. On this point, see Adolf Kolping, 'Amalar von Metz und Florus von Lyon: Zeugen eines Wandels im liturgischen Mysterienverständnis in der Karolingerzeit', *Zeitschrift für katholische Theologie* 73 (1951), pp. 424-64, esp. 433ff.

11. *Liber officialis*, pp. 313-4.

12. *Ibidem*, p. 316: "In praesenti offico altare nostrum praefiguratur regno, prop sanctuario, pro Iuda, pro votis, pro spontaneis."

13. *Ibidem*: "Altare nostrum designat in praesenti generalem vitam iustorum, qui carnem suam crucifigere cotidie cum vitiiis et concupiscentiis, atque in hostiam viventem Deo offere solent. … [O]blationes quae eo offeruntur, eorum cogitationes et bona opera designant."

14. Augustine, Sermon 272, as quoted in Van der Meer, *Augustine the Bishop*, p. 284.

15. [Note from the editor: Professor Flanigan gave a second paper on Amalarius of Metz at the 27th International Congress on Medieval Studies, held in Kalamazoo, Michigan, in May of 1992. The title of this paper was "Liturgy as Book of Memory: The Ritual Interpretation of Amalarius

of Metz," and, as the title might indicate, it was given in a session organized around the recent publication of Mary Carruthers's *The Book of Memory: A Study of Memory in Medieval Culture*, Cambridge, 1990. I have integrated parts of the latter into the text of the earlier paper, given above; the addendum consists of other, more extended developments from the later paper.]

16. Carruthers, *Book of Memory*, p. 56.
17. Amalarius, *Liber officialis*, p. 280.
18. *Ibidem*, p, 281.
19. *Ibidem*, p. 299: "Ideo scribuntur litterae, ut per eas memoriae reddatur quod oblivione deletum est; simili modo ex pictura recordamur quod interius memoriae commendari potest. Ita et responsorio ammonetur praedicator quomodo doctrinam, quae praecessit in lectione, exerceat. Primo, ut dulcedine suae imitationis plurimos sibi asciscat; coniuncti corda multorum excitent ad conpuctionem et lacrimas; et ne se extollere debeat de opere praedicationis, pulsatur versu, quatiunus ad memoriam sibi reducat de propriis causis iudicandum ante Dominum."
20. *Eclogae de ordine romano*, in Hanssens [ed.], *Amalarii episcopi Opera liturgica omnia*, vol. III, pp. 225-65.
21. *Ibidem*, pp. 230-1.
22. See note 10 above.

Comparative Literature and the Shifting Paradigms of Literary Study

Claus Clüver and C. Clifford Flanigan[1]

*e*ver since Comparative Literature began to establish itself as an academic discipline, comparatists have accompanied its development and growth with statements attempting to define it and to justify its existence. Invariably, such efforts were directed at carving out a place for Comparative Literature within a field of scholarly activity whose own right to an autonomous existence was taken for granted, although as an institution literary study has never been an independent and self-contained entity. Contrary to the vision of some of the earliest Romantic champions of *Literaturwissenschaft* as an academic discipline, and for reasons to be considered shortly, its introduction into the university curriculum during the nineteenth century invariably occurred by establishing chairs for the study of the "national literature" of the respective countries as a counterpart to classical philology, followed by the creation of foreign language and literature departments.

This institutional structure has remained in place until today, and within the framework of that structure Comparative Literature has sought to find its place. Its intellectual roots extend into the distant past, but its institutional foundations as an autonomous academic discipline were laid about a century ago. It experienced its most rapid growth in the decades following World War II, and the period from the late 1950s to the early 1970s was marked by the broad establishment of Comparative Literature programs on the North American and, to a lesser degree, the European scene. Not surprisingly, this period also saw the production of a number of methodological book-length "Introductions" which sought to define and characterize the nature and practice of Comparative Literature.

The years that followed were times of institutional retrenchment. It would be an error to attribute this only to socioeconomic factors. The last two decades have seen enormous changes in the way literary study in particular and the humanities and even the social sciences in general are understood and practiced. These developments have opened up new perspectives for comparative literary study, but they have also created a demand for a thorough revision of the very concept covered by that label. Prompted by such considerations, the publisher of *Comparative Literature: Method and Perspec-*

tive, the first US-American introduction to the field, which Newton P. Stallknecht and Horst Frenz edited thirty years ago, requested us to put together a new volume. Rather than a revision of the earlier text, we attempted an entirely new examination of the disciplinary discourse and practice of comparative literary study in the light of contemporary literary theory.

Difficulties with contributions by other hands delayed the completion of the handbook. In the meantime, the growth of Cultural Studies raised profound questions about the status of literary studies that a final version of the introduction would have to address, besides requiring substantial support for the critical positions assumed by the authors. The completion of the project was postponed indefinitely by Professor Flanigan's untimely death in 1993. The present text would, in a slightly different form, have served as the volume's Introduction. [C. C.]

We have retained the established label "Comparative Literature" as part of our title to indicate our primary audience – students and colleagues working in the field that currently bears that label – and to place this new handbook in its most immediate tradition. But it must be stated at the outset that we find it difficult to use the customary designation without following it with a question mark, for the current status of our discipline makes our endeavor necessarily interrogatory and tentative. It is the persistent burden of this book that only by bracketing the term or placing the words "Comparative Literature" under erasure is it possible to discuss the concept at all.

One of the most striking aspects of all the "Introductions" to our field written between the 1950s and the early 1970s is the way in which so much that today seems problematic was then taken for granted. Above all, so self-evident did the "reality" of the institution of "literature" seem to earlier generations of "comparatists" that its existence is always assumed without discussion in the standard handbooks. Though many of the early practitioners of comparative literature thought of themselves as literary historians, almost without exception they failed to consider that literature was a disciplinary discourse that had emerged only in the West and only in the course of the nineteenth century. Not surprisingly, they further failed to see that talk about "literature" made sense only in the light of certain institutional practices, above all those of the academy and the socio-political and economic forces implicated in the creation and perpetuation of that institution. For them, "literature" apparently seemed a metaphysically validated category of human production. Questions about its ontological status and its connections to elitist systems of the distribution of power and to strategies of oppression within the cultures in which it had appeared were never raised in these handbooks – although they were searchingly examined elsewhere.

We shall return to these concerns, but for now it is important to focus on what was at the center of most of the early "Introductions" to Comparative Literature: attempts to define and justify its existence as one literary discipline among many. Invariably, such efforts were directed at determining its proper place within the larger field occupied by departments of "national literatures." Thus, the Stallknecht-Frenz compilation opened with a programmatic essay by Henry H. H. Remak which included a definition of our field that was to be widely cited:

> Comparative Literature is the study of literature beyond the confines of one particular country, and the study of the relationships between literature on the one hand and other areas of knowledge and belief, such as the arts (e.g., painting, sculpture, architecture, music), philosophy, history, the social sciences (e.g., politics, economics, sociology), the sciences, religion, etc., on the other. In brief, it is the comparison of one literature with another or others, and the comparison of literature with other spheres of human expression.[2]

When this definition was first published, it had for many a revolutionary ring. It was seen as a manifesto of the "American School" of Comparative Literature whose conflict with the "French School" had formed the center of a much discussed crisis of our field in the 1950s. The new breed of comparatists, especially in the United States, was buoyed by a pioneering spirit that carried them across frontiers: what gave them their momentum was a thrust toward interdisciplinarity, which made Comparative Literature appear to be at the cutting edge of humanistic studies in the 1960s. But, as we have already suggested, Remak's definition took for granted much of what subsequent developments have shown to be at best problematic. Not only Comparative Literature itself, but all the disciplines it proposed to "compare" were then seen as possessing their own properly defined or definable object of study: a distinct "area of knowledge and belief" or "sphere of human expression." And just as music or history were believed to be the objects of essentially separate and isolated disciplines, so was "literature." By receiving the task of examining the relations between clearly distinct disciplinary "objects" as well as between disciplinary practices, Comparative Literature was granted a unique place among the humanities: for it alone, comparison was its very *raison d'être*.

Remak's definition further implies that "literature" has a peculiar mode of being which sets it apart from the "objects" of all other disciplines. Unlike music or philosophy, "literature" is represented as an apparently divided object that naturally presents itself in the form of "national literatures." It is the real existence of national literatures that authorizes the theory and practice of Comparative Literature. Remak's reformulation of a basic assumption underlying its institutional beginnings was to be repeated and elaborated in the manuals which followed his seminal essay. The claim that the disciplinary practices of the study of national literatures are grounded on some natural order, and the need to situate our "comparative" practice in relation to them (further complicated by such concepts as "General Literature" and "World Literature"), have until very recently dominated the theoretical concerns of practically all the US-American and European writers of manuals and introductions to our discipline.

One need not be a specialist in contemporary literary theory to realize that in the 1990s it is no longer possible to think about Comparative Literature in such terms. All one has to do, for example, is to compare Remak's essay, which forms the logical first chapter of the Stallknecht-Frenz manual, with the opening chapter of Terry Eagleton's widely used *Literary Theory: An Introduction*. It is entitled: "What is Literature?" and is intended to raise a number of disconcerting questions. After rapidly reviewing some of the historically most influential replies given well into the 1960s, Eagleton insists that the only possible answer to the question formulated in the title must be offered in "functional" rather than "ontological" terms. Thus, for Eagleton "literature" is a status which readers confer upon texts; the term refers to a relationship, not to an object, or quality, that is already "there" in the world. Here Eagleton is sounding one of the most basic of all of the claims in the human sciences as they are practiced today: that language constructs objects rather than describing them. It is our use of the term "literary" which confers the status of "literature" upon objects. Yet since language is a social system of shared assumptions, the determination of literary qualities is not wholly arbitrary; students of literature, who are by definition members of established communities of scholars, do to a certain point agree on what is and is not "literature" and what are and are not appropriate ways to study it. Nonetheless, the concepts of "literature" in general and of "national literature," which in the earlier view constituted the root elements of our discipline and as such authorized the practice of Comparative Literature, must, in Eagleton's words, "be recognized as *construct[s]*, fashioned by a particular people for particular reasons at a certain time."[3]

Eagleton further elaborates the ramifications of such a view, a view which we would not cite if it were peculiar to his perspective. Having concluded that a broadly acceptable description of literature is "valued writing," he emphasizes: "There is no such thing as a literary work or tradition which is valuable *in itself*, regardless of what anyone might have said or come to say about it. 'Value' is a transitive term: it means whatever is valued by certain people in specific situations, according to particular criteria and in the light of given purposes."[4] Thus, notions of "the literary" and "national literatures" must be understood in light of past and present institutional practices. And, insists Eagleton, these practices, especially when they are based on implicit or explicit value judgments, "have a close relation to social ideologies. They refer in the end not simply to private taste, but to the assumptions by which certain social groups exercise and maintain power over others."[5]

Even this casual glance at what is only an introductory text in literary theory makes clear how far Comparative Literature must go in rethinking its *raison d'être* if it is to have a viable intellectual basis. This rethinking must begin with the recognition that, as traditionally theorized, Comparative Literature is rapidly becoming irrelevant. Startling as this claim may seem to some comparatists, it is hardly a new one. We were long ago warned about the obsolescence of our discipline. As early as 1969, in a discussion of the changing paradigms of *Literaturwissenschaft*, Hans Robert Jauss characterized Comparative Literature (as he perceived it) as being incapable of achieving "real progress."[6] Jauss's reasons for this attack are, if anything, more cogent today than when his article was written. Comparative Literature, he claimed, belongs to a paradigm of humanistic studies which had its origins in Romanticism. As a result of the discovery of the historical dimensions of styles and works, which (along with their likewise newly discovered aesthetic dimensions) were made the criterion for the study of artworks, literary studies were dominated by a quest for historical explanation. The concept it offered to unify literary phenomena was the idea of national individuality, "immediate to God" ("gottunmittelbar"), as Jauss has it. Inserting works into a series labeled "national literature" and seeing them function as manifestations of national character and destiny, the new literary history was used as an instrument in the struggle towards achieving national unification and in the rivalries among national states.

Thus one might say that although there were documents written in French or German since the early Middle Ages, objects of French or German literature were constituted by discourses about nationality and national literature which were institutionally based and had their beginnings only at the end of the eighteenth century. Whatever the *Chanson de Roland*, for example, might have been to aristocratic readers in the eleventh century, it became a work of French literature only when that status was conferred upon it in the early nineteenth century by the discursive practice which we term "literary" and only when it was inserted into the newly invented institution of French literary history (whose social and political purposes seem clear). Furthermore, at least in Jauss's eyes, such literary history became the model of all historiography, and literature itself was viewed as "the highest medium in which the nation could realize itself, from its quasi-mythic beginnings to the achievement of a national classicism."[7] A fascination with origins – it was widely believed that the nature of an object could be known by discovering its "beginnings"– was paralleled in literary scholarship by a neglect of contemporary creativity, by granting the past an authority which was thought to be lacking in the present. Some of the most obviously "Romantic" elements of this paradigm eventually gave way to Positivism, the belief that humanistic phenomena could be studied by the same methods and with the same "objectivity" that prevailed – or better, was believed to prevail – in the natural sciences. Yet the shift toward Positivism was only a change in emphasis. The advance from historical-critical to Positivist methods occurred within the safe boundaries of the established paradigm with its emphasis on the ontological status of national literatures. This premise was never seriously put in doubt by the question of whether, for example, literature could be seen as something other than the manifestation of national character. Even when a new formalism – in North America we know it best in its "New Critical" guise – came to dominate the scene, the reality of national literatures was hardly ever questioned. One might be inclined to think of René Wellek's and Austin Warren's influential *Literary Theory* (1949) as a notable exception, with its call for abolishing the segmentation of the field in favor of an integrated discipline of "Literary Studies" (conceived of in terms of Western academic traditions and a Western perspective);[8] but Wellek's argument did not proceed from challenging the existence of national literatures as such. Even though Comparative Literature offered itself as an alternative to literary studies confined to an individual literature, it was its sanctioning of the ontological status of these literatures that caused Jauss to view the discipline as firmly anchored in the old paradigm, helping to perpetuate ideas and ideologies which are no longer among the discursive practices by which the currently most influential thinkers (and many of our students) make sense of experience.

Today, there certainly exist more profound and circumspect interpretations of the history of literary studies than Jauss's polemical sketch. But compared with the positions assumed in the major handbooks and introductions to Comparative Literature, most of which appeared around the time Jauss published his article, his views manifest an awareness of crisis and immanent change that is sadly lacking in the critical orthodoxy of those texts. As late as 1977, with no less a polemical stance than

Jauss's, Hugo Dyserinck roundly denounced him for hitting wide off the mark in his attack against our discipline, "since the borderlines crossed by Comparative Literature in its multinational research are not the arbitrary invention of philologists, but factual realities which Comparative Literature, far from 'ideologizing,' simply takes into account."[9] In his book Dyserinck poses as the proselytizing representative of a pioneering discipline, yet his *Komparatistik: Eine Einführung*, meanwhile available in a second edition, justifies a view of Comparative Literature which is demonstrably at odds with contemporary critical theory.

Jauss has been criticized by other comparatists on different grounds: they have argued that his portrayal of our field was a caricature of past practices that had little to do with present orientations. And indeed it must be pointed out that in many respects the actual practice of Comparative Literature has frequently and for a long time been oblivious to the way in which the handbook definitions theorized the field. In assuming a supranational perspective, "comparative" studies have often simply disregarded questions of national origin in the intrinsic study of literary phenomena. Exhortations that it is the comparatist's business to study the literary traffic between nations or to compare what is Russian in a Russian text with what is French in a French one had been widely disregarded until recently, when such concerns resurfaced in various projects of recontextualization, without thereby resanctioning the concept of national literature. The practice of using the comparison of two national literatures in order to demonstrate the superiority of one over the other – once employed in some quarters as the ideological motivation for the institution of our discipline – has long fallen into disrepute. Many "comparative" studies have pursued objectives that made the texts' membership in specific national literatures all but irrelevant. But in other respects, their methods and approaches resembled the products of those scholars and teachers who have been trained and continue to function in departments of national literature.

While the still prevailing institutional structures perpetuate the untenable compartmentalization of literary studies and help shape our outlook on the objects of our discipline, the profound chasm that exists between literary scholarship as it is conceived by contemporary literary theory and as it is practiced by most critical and pedagogical institutions does not primarily result from an insistence on the reality of national literatures. Rather, it marks the shift in the prevailing paradigm that has been taking place not only in literary studies, but in all the human sciences. Slowly – but certainly – a new paradigm is coming to prevail, a paradigm which questions many of the fundamental assumptions and practices of the previous one, even the institution of literature itself. Any consideration of the present and future of Comparative Literature will of necessity have to consider the place of our discipline – if it has a place at all – within that new paradigm. It is the burden of this book to offer the tentative beginnings of such a consideration. In order to understand the radical adjustments which an honest confrontation between the authorized practice of Comparative Literature and the present state of literary theory necessitates, it may be useful to remind ourselves briefly of some of the basic assumptions informing the practice of literary studies in general and Comparative Literature in particular under the now weakening, though in many places still dominant, previous paradigm.

- That paradigm conceived of literary studies as a field separate from other scholarly endeavors, with its own object and methods.
- It considered literature as an identifiable and coherent body of texts whose distinguishing characteristic was their "literariness," frequently defined in terms of a special kind of language or a foregrounding of the "aesthetic" or, with Roman Jakobson, the "poetic function" of that language.[10]
- It conceived of the literary text as a unique, self-contained, and autonomous work that was a unified, organic whole. It assigned to the reader the role of realizing that unity and thus achieving the text's poetic closure. Interpretation sought to exclude conflict and difference, or to maintain them within the supposed confines of an overarching irony which, it was claimed, resolved them at some higher level.
- It frequently showed little interest in the production of literary texts and had an ambivalent attitude towards authors. With the New Criticism, it often denied an author the role of a guarantor of the text's meaning and spurned consideration of authorial intention, and yet it usually favored the study of "an author" and inserted the individual text in a series called an author's "work," and claimed that it was "natural" to do so. When it dealt with questions of a text's genesis, its preferred activity was the tracing of "influence."
- It made its primary objective the understanding of individual texts, whose meaning was seen as residing in the work. It was the reader's task to realize this meaning by intricate and sophisticated methods of interpretation. Literary theory was a lowly handmaiden to interpretation, which was thought of as the prime activity of literary study.
- It assumed the possibility and importance of objective value judgments. The "purposeful purposelessness" of the aesthetic object was met with a "disinterested interestedness." Signs of authorial *engagement* and of ideological commitment brought to the text by readers were valued negatively, and claims that literary texts and systems were sites for the exercise of coercive power were often explicitly set aside or met with the assertion that texts which made such claims were not authentically "literary."
- It affirmed the ontological reality of national distinctions and consequently subscribed to the concept of national (or, in a slightly improved terminology, "individual") literatures. Literary periods and genres were likewise frequently accorded an essential status.

The theory and practice of Comparative Literature at midcentury, and indeed well into the 1970s, were firmly grounded on these assumptions. They seemed so obviously true to its practitioners that they provided the shared framework within which disagreements took place. Thus theorized, Comparative Literature produced, and was the product of, its own institutional practices. It recommended itself for looking at literary texts from a supranational perspective, which was certainly an advancement over the exclusion from consideration, so often practiced in the institutionalized study of national literatures, of any texts not belonging to that specific literature. But Comparative Literature defined itself almost exclusively in terms of the existence of such national literatures. The careful staking out of territorial claims, of deciding what kinds of study did and did not fall within the comparatist's domain, remained one of its most pressing preoccupations.

Only in one respect did Comparative Literature begin to distinguish itself from the traditional philological disciplines. It was expressed in the second half of Henry Remak's definition which called for "the comparison of literature with other spheres of human expression."[11] This pointed the way toward a much broader kind of cross-disciplinary study which, apart from such concerns in the theorizing of Comparative Literature, was to become the foundation for much of what has since happened in critical theory in general. The new theory has come to constitute a new kind of interdisciplinarity, one which is not based on comparative approaches to individual disciplines, as Remak's definition still envisions it, but on a fusion of the concerns and approaches of a great many disciplines. What has made this fusion possible is the recognition of the arbitrariness of all disciplinary boundaries and a concomitant refusal to honor them. This changed conception of interdisciplinarity, coupled with an ever greater awareness of the inadequacies of the old paradigm, has paved the way for the shift toward a new, transdisciplinary practice within the confines of Comparative Literature.

Comparative Literature may have been slow in realizing the possibilities offered by the new transdisciplinarity, but the inadequacies of the old paradigm and of the procedures it authorized are nonetheless being felt in many ways. As usual, it was the course taken by "the arts" (themselves constituted by the discursive practices of the prevailing paradigm) that made painfully evident the limitations of conventional critical assumptions. Texts that offered themselves as literary were deliberately "open," asked to be operated by the reader as a kind of game, or were constructed by aleatoric, or chance, methods. The creation of multimedia and intermedia works was a refusal to remain within the traditional confinements of the individual arts, and an invitation to read these works according to the codes of numerous and different sign systems. Indeed, ever since the appearance of the Cubist collage the distinction between "art" and "non-art" and the definition of "artworks" as "aesthetic objects" had been increasingly put in doubt. How was one to deal with Conceptual Art on the assumptions of the old paradigm? What "intrinsic" methods of interpretation could be applied when there was no tangible work at all?

The erosion of the old assumptions was fostered by extra-literary and extra-artistic contexts as well. In the socio-political context, we witnessed the growing importance of non-Western and Third-World countries. The student movements of the 1960s resulted, among other things, in curricular reforms, in a weakening of traditional disciplines, in the growth, already referred to, of transdisciplinary teaching and research programs, and in the reform of institutions of higher education – changes that certainly had a series of other causes as well. Intellectually, there was the increased popularity of Marxism in Western Europe (one of the motivating factors of the student revolts) and the rise and growth of other ideologically motivated movements, among which Feminism has turned out to be the most significant in its implications and applications. Within literary studies, there emerged (and resurfaced) concerns excluded by the old paradigm, most importantly the perceived need to set literary texts into a larger context. This expressed need was accompanied by a growing desire for systematization, which was facilitated by such non-literary discourses as Structuralism.

These developments, and others similar to them, have fostered the gradual emergence of a new paradigm in the human sciences. It is still in formation but is nevertheless gradually being accepted by members of our disciplinary community. Though its adherents would hardly agree among themselves on all of its aspects, one of its most fundamental and widely shared claims is the denial of literariness as a metaphysical entity. Basic also is the conception of literary study as a systematic science: it reaches beyond the explication of individual texts. Under the new paradigm, theory is the chief concern, for it enables the pursuit of what is now perceived as the central goal, which is to give an account of "literary" systems in their entirety. Following in the heritage of Structuralism, this plan may give synchrony preference over diachrony; but the foregrounding of theoretical awareness as ideological awareness has increasingly led to a revaluation of diachronic and historical approaches as well. It has also resulted, as we have seen, in a reconsideration of the place of value judgments: all discourse (including "literary" and critical discourse) is recognized as ideological and implicated in relations of power. Conceptions of "nation" and "national literature" are thus seen as ideological constructs, and canonical conceptions of literary studies are likewise viewed as ideologically informed.

At the broadest level, both the very acceptance of a paradigm and the dissatisfactions that lead to a crisis and to paradigm shift are perceived as ultimately grounded in ideology. Literary concepts are altogether understood as the product of model building, as constructs employed by disciplinary communities to resolve the problems conceived of within the parameters and on the assumptions of the reigning paradigm. The ideological foundation of these models supports both diachronic conceptions (such as periodization) and synchronic conceptions (such as genres). Under the new paradigm, it is recognized that these models are not representations of some ascertainable external reality, but constructs produced by a will to knowledge that is inevitably a will to power as well. The realization that there is no escape from ideology (whereas the previous paradigm was founded on claims to objectivity and universality) has resulted in a motivation and willingness to make one's own ideological assumptions explicit. In scholarship produced under the new paradigm one frequently encounters an affirmation of a partisan ideological stance.

Primacy of place in models of "literary" communication is increasingly given to the reader. This development has a precedent in ancient and medieval textual practice, but it can be best understood as arising from a profound skepticism concerning the status of "texts" as well as of "authors" on metaphysical, epistemological, and moral grounds, a skepticism based in part on the assumptions of intellectual activities collectively labeled as "Deconstruction." We now understand that it is the reader who, in his or her encounter with the "work," ultimately creates the "text"; it is the reader who assigns it its meaning and certainly its status as a "literary" text. These assignments are not arbitrary but conditioned by the norms and values accepted by the "interpretive community" of which s/he is a member. They are also determined, and it could not be otherwise, by the unique characteristics of each psyche. Such a view obviously endorses a relativism that sees every cultural fact and all signifying systems and their products as related to, and determined by, specific socio-historic contexts. As we stated earlier, model building and the operation with models (including Thomas S. Kuhn's model of the structure of scientific revolutions[12] on which Jauss's notion of paradigm shift in literary studies is based) are likewise perceived as relativistic: we are perfectly (and often painfully) aware that the new paradigm will be replaced by another, and that neither can bring us closer to a "truth" that can be established by reference to texts existing independently of the paradigm that constructs them.

We have presented here only the sketchiest characterization of recent developments in literary studies. The construction of the new paradigm, which admittedly has not yet achieved truly paradigmatic status simply because it has not yet been accepted by the majority of our disciplinary community, has proceeded far enough for us to state confidently that some version of it will be accepted, and that this acceptance will have ramifications for the institutional study of "literature" that we briefly outline here:

- Our discipline will acknowledge that "literary studies" has no metaphysically definable subject matter. Thus, "literary" describes not a class of texts, but a way of regarding a verbal text.
- The distinction between "primary" and "secondary" texts is likely to become blurred; in particular, "literary" texts may be regarded as theoretical texts, theoretical texts as "literary."
- No special significance can be given to notions of "national literature" or "Comparative Literature." All dealings with any text are inherently "comparative," since texts can only be defined in relation to their "other," and in terms of conventional expectations of genre, theme, and similar concerns.
- All statements will be seen as contextual points of view, all claims as relative. There is no reason why texts cannot be inserted in series of works created strictly in one language or belonging to the same cultural or political unit; but these are clearly not the only units for contextual placement, nor can they claim an inherently weightier status than other units. And since verbal texts, and especially such texts that are regarded as "literary," are the products of a second-order sign system, there is no compelling reason to assign priority to linguistic considerations. The study of a text in its original language is not inherently better in all contexts than the study of a text that is a translation.
- Literary canons will be considered as ideological constructs and continually re-examined. No text can be considered as intrinsically more suitable for study than any other. In the West, critical attention will increasingly be paid to the predominance of Eurocentric views. Texts stemming from non-Western traditions and texts written in "minor" languages are likely to receive more emphasis in literary study.
- "Transdisciplinary" discourse will be a central concern; individual disciplines can no longer claim an autonomous status.

- Scholarly competence will remain a *conditio sine qua non*, but it will not be based on traditional disciplinary demarcations. There can be no ideal training for a future comparatist. Claims for the universal validity of "core curricula" may be authentically based on the need to learn the conventional "language" of our discipline, but they are always ideologically suspect.

These are some of the major premises of the emerging paradigm in literary studies or, more exactly, in the constellation of discourses that involve the study of verbal texts. Of course, there is not and need not be total agreement on all of these premises. Any attempt to set out legislative terms according to which the practice of Comparative Literature must operate in future would run counter to the new paradigm we have outlined, for that paradigm is based on the assumption that all knowledge and all practice are dependent only upon an implied and imperfect agreement among interested parties and that such parties will surely have other interests which conflict with the paradigm to which they give their partial consent. Indeed, what sets off our "Introduction" from earlier examples of this genre is above all the plurality of voices which, taken together, insist that there can be no "correct" definition of Comparative Literature and its practice because the discipline and its "objects" do not exist independently of our talk about them. Yet it is also evident that disciplines can only be practiced within the context of the communal interests that construct them. Disciplinary practices are necessarily arbitrary, but they cannot be wholly solipsistic; what makes a paradigm a paradigm is that it consists of a series of working assumptions which are in some sense shared by a community, in the present case a community of scholars and readers. Shared paradigmatic assumptions do not dispel the possibility of dissent: on the contrary, they provide the common framework within which disagreement can take place. It seems evident to us that the new paradigm we have sketched out is presently and (so it seems to us) inevitably being established by communal practice and tacit agreement within the "literary" community at large, and within the confines of Comparative Literature as well. That paradigm appears to offer no room, theoretically if not administratively, for the study of national literatures or for Comparative Literature as distinct and institutionally separate disciplines.

There is little doubt that the organization of the human sciences will ultimately take a rather different shape from the one that is transparently present today in most college and university catalogues, both in Europe and in the United States as well as in countries that have shaped their academic institutions after these models. While acknowledging this likelihood, however, our book does not offer detailed discussions of the shape to be taken by the practice of the human sciences under those changed conditions, if for no other reason than that the future organization of knowledge is still a matter of projects and speculations. What we offer as an introduction to Comparative Literature (like all examples of that genre, whether they display an awareness of it or not) is presented tentatively and *in via*. We have not made it our goal to map out a new form of broad disciplinary practice and then situate Comparative Literature within it. Rather, this book has been designed to examine traditional discourse about Comparative Literature, as it has developed in its short history, in the light of the as yet only partially knowable new paradigm of the theory and practice of the human sciences. In the first section of our book we look at the *topoi* or received commonplaces of Comparative Literature as they were articulated in the Stallknecht-Frenz book and other similar American and European introductory manuals.

If we are to approach the goal which this book has set itself, it is hardly sufficient, however, to examine and reform the conventional topics of our disciplinary discourse. Discursive practices always claim to be accounts of objects in the world, but such claims simply serve to conceal their own ideological premise – usually even from the very practitioners themselves. Disciplinary discourses like those of Comparative Literature are, among other things, strategies of exclusion. If we wish to understand their purposes, we must not only analyze what they explicitly affirm or deny, but also what they do not say and what they do not overtly consider. The second part of our book, therefore, deals with topics which have, for the most part, not belonged to the traditional concerns of Comparative Literature as a discipline: non-Western cultures, popular culture, and ways of thinking about texts which have either not been authorized at all or have been questioned and marginalized because they were not judged sufficiently "literary." The final part of our book contains essays on topics that do not belong, strictly speaking, exclusively to the present or future discursive practices of Comparative Literature but seem to us to have major consequences for these practices because they touch upon some of the most basic issues in contemporary literary theory. Here appear essays on the discourse of "Otherness" and on the transformation of interdisciplinary studies into a new kind of discourse that disregards conventional disciplinary boundaries altogether.

The following section was not intended to appear in the printed version of the book; it was attached to the text circulated to students and colleagues in order to indicate in brief compass our notions of how the traditional topics of Comparative Literature as well as some of the newer ones would need to be revised in light of the new paradigm of literary studies. [C. C.]

Literary Theory

Whenever there is a paradigm crisis, theoretical considerations will take center stage, as at the present time. Nothing more strikingly marks the present situation in the human sciences than the recognition that "literary theory," a form of discourse formerly considered a separate subdivision in the larger area of literary studies, has now become central; any talk of texts without implicit and usually explicit theoretical reflection now seems intellectually untenable. More fundamentally, the theory of verbal texts and their study has become part of a more general discourse of critical theory. Theory can be expected to overshadow all other forms of study for some time. Of course, the reading of individual texts will continue to play an important role in the institutional practice of Comparative Literature, but it will usually be carried on as part of a conscious theoretical discourse which aims to produce some form of systematic knowledge.

Reception Studies

With the shift of theoretical and critical attention away from the author and "the poem itself" to the reader, reception studies have begun to be redirected and simultaneously to assume greater significance. Questions of an author's literary fortune are no longer central. In the future, literary history is likely to be constructed in terms of the meanings assigned to texts by different readers and audiences, synchronically as well as diachronically, and in terms of the conditions that produced these changing meanings. The reception of individual texts will be studied in the context of the simultaneous reception of other texts, "literary" as well as non-literary, verbal as well as non-verbal, and with reference to the social and cultural codes and value systems (the prevailing ideology) on which the readers based their reception of these texts. An ideologically aware sociology of literature, grounded in a firm historical knowledge of the material conditions of text reception and consumption, including the economic conditions neglected by the earlier paradigm, seems destined to play an important role (see also "Literature and Society," below).

Influence Studies

In his *Einführung in die Vergleichende Literaturwissenschaft*, Ulrich Weisstein claimed that "influence must be regarded as virtually the key concept in Comparative Literature studies, since it posits the presence of two distinct and therefore comparable entities."[13] Such a statement points to the manner in which influence studies, when they went beyond mere "source hunting," have been concerned with text production, conceived of as an individual author's creative act, and thus with questions of originality, derivation, and deviation. Notwithstanding Harold Bloom's theses about the "anxiety of influence"[14] motivating change and innovation – theses which keep critical attention focused on the role of the author – studies in accordance with the new paradigm have subsumed the question of influence under the larger context of an "intertextuality" that comprises the whole network of relations connecting the individual text with countless other texts. No set of texts is thus inherently more comparable than any other set of texts. Influence studies will no longer be limited to instances in which a historical contact between two texts is documented.

Translation Studies

The importance of translation studies will increase as they shift their interest from evaluation of individual achievement to the concerns of reception studies. Rather than determining whether a translation has done justice to the original, such studies will assess it as an interpretive reading according to the expectations and values of the translator and his/her audience and will place it in the context of the reception of other texts by the same audience. Shifting standards of translation will be examined as indices of changing ideological value systems. The translation practices of specific communities or cultures will be studied for what they reveal about these ideologies. The ways in which expectations are formed by the receiving community's language and its usage will be of particular interest.

Genre Studies

The object of genre studies can no longer be conceived of as a universal system of norms. The genre of a work is no longer seen as an intrinsic quality but as a quality assigned by the expectations of its audiences. It is of crucial interest within the new paradigm to discern what enables a particular audience to read a work as an elegy, for example, and what accounts for genre shifts and consequently for inserting a work in a new generic context. Generic assignation profoundly affects a work's reception and plays a large part in determining its "literary" or "non-literary" status for a given audience. Restrictions to the study of "literary" genres have already begun to fall away through the inclusion in the investigation of genre formation and transformation of narrative genres in historiography and of various kinds of philosophical and legal discourse. The creation of intermedia and multimedia texts has expanded genre studies beyond the realm of verbal texts altogether.

Stoff, Theme, and Motif Studies

In recent years, new interest has arisen in what was once a flourishing branch of comparative studies before it became suspect as too positivistic in its tendency merely to collect and accumulate material facts. Transformed from *Stoffgeschichte* into *Stoffforschung*, in English reluctantly labeled "thematology," the study of motif, *Stoff*, and theme as elements of structure and meaning rather than merely of "content" has found new impetus through formalist and structuralist endeavors. *Stoff* has frequently come to be considered as a constellation of specific motifs to which different themes can become attached as it reappears in different texts and contexts, in various forms of development and transformation. These categories, and in particular "theme," may best be considered as culturally determined critical and hermeneutic constructs, useful in considering series of both "literary" and "non-literary" texts from a diachronic or a synchronic perspective. Ideological criticism in particular has found new uses for thematological considerations.

Periodization

Comparative Literature has been thought of as a historical discipline, even under the dispensation of the "American School" with its formalist orientation. Academic specialties are usually defined by historical periods, and curricula typically have strong historical orientations. The old handbooks already recognized the impossibility of granting historical periods an ontological status and often grudgingly admitted that they were nothing more than roughly shared mental constructs. Yet this recognition did not prevent the domination of historical periodization in our discipline. Under the emerging paradigm, history becomes only one way, and not necessarily the best way, of organizing the objects which we construct in studying them. The writing of all history, including literary history, is now seen as the production of fictional texts meeting the needs and expectations of the authors and the audiences of these texts. It seems clear that we will never be able to know *wie es eigentlich gewesen*, and that our reconstructions of the past, like all our fictions, are informed by our mental habits and our values. An awareness of these limitations in no way forecloses the likelihood that historical discourse will play an important role in our discipline, but it will be constrained by the recognition that difference is inscribed in every discourse and that therefore no closed and unified understanding of a period is possible or even desirable.

Imagology

The study of the images of other nations and their representatives has recently resurfaced as a major topic of Comparative Literature. To the degree that this concern is preoccupied with national images, it may be seen as a last vestige of the old paradigm. Despite this limitation, imagology rightly foregrounds valid concerns which previously were all but neglected in our field. The currently most pressing issues in the study of *l'étranger tel qu'on le voit* involve the relations of "Third-World literatures," especially the literatures of former Western colonies, to the literature of the former colonizers. Certainly this issue is central to the human sciences in the late twentieth century and merits even more consideration than it is presently receiving. In future discourse, however, such topics will necessarily be subsumed under the far more general concerns of ideological criticism. Seen in the light of the new concerns, imagology becomes a discourse about differences that includes images of women and minorities, topics largely neglected by the past paradigm with its pervasive masculine and Western bias.

Models of Interliterary Relations

With a few exceptions, traditional Comparative Literature studies have made little more than gestures to non-Western cultures and their textual systems. There are many reasons for this neglect, most of them ideological. But more fundamentally, the relationships between these cultures and their verbal sign systems simply will not submit to the models of the Western nationalist state which underlies the older paradigm. What is one to make, for example, of the relationship of the many "literatures," old and new, of the Indian subcontinent, all of which and none of which can make a claim to being nationally "Indian"? Or how shall we construct hermeneutic models dealing with the use of Chinese sign systems in Tibetan culture? As literary study increasingly moves toward serious and more widely based consideration of non-Western cultures, we shall be confronted with new models of relationships between semiotic systems which will challenge our Western essentialist assumptions about such relationships. For this reason alone, such studies must move from the periphery to a more central place; we must cease to regard them as exotic and special cases to be set against the Western norm. Specialists in these areas should not be expected to conform to our forms of discourse; instead, we must learn from theirs. Indeed, the models prevailing in such studies may well be applied to the study of Western sign systems, even though there has been no previous historical connection between these cultures and the Western ones that most of us study. On the pedagogical level, the privileging of Western texts and the values implicit in placing them at the center of our disciplinary consciousness will have to be profoundly reconsidered.

Literature and Popular Culture

Since "aesthetic" value judgments are exposed as ideological biases under the new paradigm, and the closing of the canon now becomes an activity which must always be deferred, what was formerly regarded as "culinary" literature is seen to have as much claim to attention as the supposed "classics." Such forms as detective stories, comic books, "Harlequin" romances, and rock lyrics are recognized as elements of verbal and social systems which can be profitably studied according to the usual modes of production and reception. Jauss's claim for *Rezeptionsästhetik* notwithstanding, texts which do not "estrange" – a strange notion which itself should not be privileged – will be afforded no less attention than those that do. The mass media, including such "non-literary" forms of production as the cinema, television, and the radio, will receive increased attention.

Interarts Studies

The inclusion in the domain of Comparative Literature of the interrelations of literature with the other "arts" was one of the pioneering acts in its thrust toward interdisciplinarity. The comparative study of the arts was in the past generally conceived as a tripartite study of the impact of literature and literary works on music and the visual arts, of the impact of these other arts on literature, and of the coexistence of literary and visual elements in such phenomena as emblematics and the *livre d'artiste*, and of literary and musical elements in the *Lied* and in opera. While still designating fertile areas of study, this conception has increasingly been realized as too restrictive. Comparison in the strict sense is moving away from consideration of individual works to an investigation of the signifying processes of different sign systems. Semiotic approaches have been found to provide a unifying basis for discussing such questions as representation and the constitution of "meaning" in the various arts. The study of forms and possibilities of intersemiotic transposition and the carry-over of structuring and signifying devices from one art to another will be complemented by the development of strategies needed to deal with intermedia and multimedia texts. This kind of study will become increasingly important as the boundaries that used to separate the arts from each other and from forms of communication traditionally considered to be "non-artistic" collapse. Multimedia mass-culture genres such as the music video, the comic strip, and all forms of advertising are beginning to receive as much attention or more than the opera, both from a semiotic point of view (interaction of various sign systems) and from the perspective of ideological criticism. The comparative study of isolated visual, musical, and verbal texts may ultimately be subsumed under a general study of texts, conceivably as a new kind of textual rhetoric.

Literature and Society

In the past, where this concern was cultivated at all, socioeconomic factors were conceived of as causes which influenced or determined literary production. The new model will retain this concern, though rejecting simplistic versions of it. It will refuse to privilege origins over reception, which now must be equally related to social factors, though one must not be viewed as the cause of the other. Indeed, it is possible to view societies and classes within them as imaginative constructs similar to fictional texts, and thus to grant them no greater claim to ontological reality than these. Seen from this perspective, "literary" theory may appear identical with social theory. Reading society and reading "literature" are exposed as similar activities.

Conclusion

What we have presented here is hardly news to anyone who has been following developments in critical theory over the past fifteen or twenty years. But for many practitioners of literary studies and for institutional structures, these developments have had little or no effect, except possibly for the adding of courses in literary theory to the curriculum. What is at stake, however, is not the addition of new courses or the deletion of older ones, but a radical reformation of the way texts are conceived of and taught. Resistance to recent developments continues to be strong. At the present time, national literature departments still dominate the humanities, and most carry on business as usual. Their situation is often worse than that of Comparative Literature programs; in the case of English departments in the United States, even the necessity to know a foreign language is often minimized. But whatever advantages Comparative Literature programs may have should not serve as the grounds for self-congratulation. Almost all teaching of Comparative Literature is predicated on "literariness" as the marker of a class of verbal texts and on the supposed ontological reality of national literatures. These conceptions are simply no longer tenable, and wishing otherwise will not make them so. We recognize, of course, that not everyone currently engaged in the practice of Comparative Literature will approve of all of our claims. Some will decry the accommodation to the new paradigm in the human sciences as "anti-humanistic," but there seems to be no choice except to proceed with the dismantling of beliefs and practices which have little place in the new orientation which is upon us. The only alternative is to continue until the obsolescence of literary studies and of Comparative Literature as we know them becomes so apparent that they disappear from the scene as irrelevant to the present circumstance. The conclusion to be drawn from the issues at hand is as ineluctable as it is difficult. The task ahead of us involves the demystification of the older concepts with which we have been operating, a thorough re-examination of our traditional fields of scholarly activity, and most likely the development of new fields. Redefining our practice in terms of the basic assumptions of the new paradigm with respect not only to our research, but also to our teaching, is a major challenge, and it will ultimately have to lead to institutional reforms that are unlikely to leave a place for national literature departments or for Comparative Literature programs; it remains to be seen if literary studies themselves will survive as a separate discipline.

Notes

1. This text was to serve as the introduction of a new handbook intended to replace Newton P. Stallknecht and Horst Frenz (eds.), *Comparative Literature: Method and Perspective*, Carbondale, 1971 [1961]. The version published here dates from 1987. Earlier versions were presented by the authors at the Annual Conference of the Southern Comparative Literature Association, Knoxville, Tennessee, 13-15 February 1986, and as "Stallknecht-Frenz Revisited: New Methods and Perspectives in Comparative Literary Study" at the 9th Triennial Meeting of the American Comparative Literature Association, Ann Arbor, Michigan, 20-22 March 1986.

It was subsequently used in the graduate introduction to literary studies taught annually in alternation by Clüver and Flanigan in Indiana University's Comparative Literature Department. A Portuguese version was presented by Professor Clüver at the Universidade de Lisboa, 19 May 1988, at the Instituto de Letras, Universidade Federal de Rio Grande do Sul, Porto Alegre, RGS, Brazil, 17 May 1993, and at the Universidade Estadual Paulista, São João do Rio Preto, SP, Brazil, 31 May 1993.

2. Henry H. H. Remak, "Comparative Literature: Its Definition and Function," in Stallknecht and Frenz (eds.), *Comparative Literature*, p. 1.

3. Terry Eagleton, *Literary Theory: An Introduction*, Oxford, 1983, p. 11.

4. Ibidem.

5. Ibidem, p. 16.

6. See Hans Robert Jauss, "Paradigmawechsel in der Literaturwissenschaft," *Linguistische Berichte* 1 (1969), nr. 3, pp. 44-56.

7. "Literatur wurde zum höchsten Medium, in dem das Nationale von seinen quasi-mythischen Anfängen bis zur Erfüllung einer nationalen Klassik zu sich selbst kommen konnte" (Jauss, "Paradigmawechsel," p. 48).

8. See René Wellek and Austin Warren, *Theory of Literature*, New York, 1963^3 [1949^1].

9. "... weil die Grenzen, die die Komparatistik beim Zusammenstellen ihres multinationalen Forschungsbereichs überschreitet, nicht etwa von willkürlich verfahrenden Philologen erfunden wurden, sondern einfach gegebene Realitäten sind, denen die Komparatistik – statt 'Ideologie' zu betreiben – nun einmal Rechnung trägt" (Hugo Dyserinck, *Komparatistik: Eine Einführung*, Bonn, 1981^2 [1977^1], p. 100).

10. See Roman Jakobson, "Linguistics and Poetics," in Thomas A. Sebeok (ed.), *Style in Language*, Cambridge, Mass., 1960, pp. 350-77. Rpt. in Roman Jakobson, *Selected Writings*, The Hague, 1962 – , vol. III, Stephen Rudy [ed.], *Poetry of Grammar and Grammar of Poetry*, pp. 18-51.

11. Remak, "Comparative Literature," p. 1.

12. See Thomas S. Kuhn, *The Structure of Scientific Revolutions*, Chicago, 1970^2 [*International Encyclopedia of Unified Science*, 2.2].

13. Ulrich Weisstein, *Einführung in die Vergleichende Literaturwissenschaft*, Stuttgart, 1968, translated into English as *Comparative Literature and Literary Theory: Survey and Introduction*, [transl.] William Riggan, Bloomington, IN, 1973. Quoted from this edition, p. 29.

14. See Harold Bloom, *The Anxiety of Influence: A Theory of Poetry*, New York, 1973.

Part III

Playing by the Book: Performance of Liturgical Drama at Klosterneuburg
Amelia J. Carr and Michael L. Norton

On the 21st of August, 1594, Father Oswald Ostner lamented from his prison cell in the Augustinian monastery at Klosterneuburg: "Here I sit in darkness, and I do not see the light of the sky; during all the days, that I am now held, I wait until my redemption comes."[1] The inscribed lamentation marked a self-pitying pause in Ostner's work, that of copying a text entitled *Ordinationes chori Neuburgensis* (Liturgical Order for Klosterneuburg). The text copied by Ostner has been identified as a sacristan's handbook, for it contains lengthy and detailed instructions for the behind-the-scenes activities necessary for the smooth performance of the liturgy. Ostner's scribal activity of 1594 produced the latest text we have of the *Visitatio Sepulchri* as it was performed at Klosterneuburg. The *Visitatio Sepulchri* had been a part of the Klosterneuburg liturgy since the early twelfth century, but was most likely suppressed in 1578 when Roman practice was imposed on the protesting Augustinian canons.[2] From the shadows of his cell, Ostner looked forward to the light of future freedom, but in copying this manuscript, he gazed backwards on a religious experience that had largely disappeared.

The circumstances that produced Ostner's text are peculiar; most liturgical manuscripts, so far as we know, were not products of jailhouse scriptoria or even forced penance. But the very existence of this manuscript should remind us that the function of a particular text may not be obvious at first glance, and that the evidence of the *Visitatio Sepulchri* may well be embedded into textual situations that demand interpretation. In our detailed study of the sepulchre ceremonies (*Depositio*, *Elevatio*, and *Visitatio Sepulchri*) at the Augustinian monastery at Klosterneuburg, near Vienna, Austria, we have been fortunate to explore an extensive medieval library that is largely intact. Klosterneuburg's collection has yielded forty-three manuscripts containing one or more of these Easter ceremonies, almost triple the number catalogued there by Lipphardt.[3] From this abundance of evidence, in this essay we focus on books and on the way in which books and that which is inscribed in them functioned within the dramatic rites of Easter. We will begin with the sacristan's handbook and the other books mentioned therein, evidence for the ceremonies as they were performed during the third quarter of the sixteenth century. We will also examine the evidence for performance found within other liturgical books, and close by touching upon the aesthetic of the books in performance.

The sacristan's handbook that provided the model for Ostner's text was put together in the 1570s and is preserved as Codex 1026a in the Klosterneuburg library.[4] This manuscript devotes seven folios to the monastery's activities stretching from Good Friday through Easter morning – too long to treat in full. A passage or two will illustrate the flavor of the text, for example, this one from the end of the *Elevatio* and the beginning of Easter Matins, sung at 10 pm:

> Finally, *Christ ist erstanden* is sung by the convent. The prior exits to pray in the sacristy. Meanwhile at Matins ring four lesser bells as it says in the Breviary. Formerly at Matins it was required to ring eight bells. Rectors will say Matins around the altar of St. Augustine. They should sing out of the big, heavy, white book.[5]

Clearly, these instructions depart from the formality of most liturgical manuscripts. The traditional rubrics for the Holy Week liturgy at Klosterneuburg typically indicate only who is speaking or singing, and give but brief instructions to the participants. Codex 1026a, on the other hand, gives expanded directions to a single person, one who seems to be in charge of bell ringing, items of clothing, and other liturgical accessories. However, one liturgical accessory is particularly evident: the performance of the liturgy requires the use of books, many books. The management of these books, books containing texts and books containing music, must be coordinated throughout the liturgical cursus.

Whether in the Mass, Divine Office, procession, or other rite, books were pervasive. Most were of good size, quarto or larger, to facilitate reading at the altar or from a lectern. As prominent accessories in the liturgy, and as books containing the most sacred words, these were often beautifully illustrated and handsomely bound. Such great books are always visible in illustrations of liturgy, as much as part of the service as the eucharistic utensils.

In performing the Divine Office, for example, the canons shared an antiphonary, a book containing texts and music for the office.[6] Serving many pairs of eyes, such a book was generally quite large, set on a stand that could swivel from side to side of the choir. The antiphonary described in our sacristan's handbook, now Codex 66 in the Klosterneuburg library, dates to the 1420s.[7] Its production was a major event, and the financial records concerning payment of artists and scribes are the best, in some cases the only, sources we have for the names and activities of the Vienna court school of illumination. Masters Nicholas and Michael headed the teams of artists; Master Johannes was the music scribe. Their product is today preserved as a set of four volumes, each containing approximately 300 folios and measuring 16 3/8" x 23" x 6."[8] Each tome is heavy enough that one person would have difficulty in moving it elegantly, and when we examined it at Klosterneuburg, the elderly librarian brought it in on a trolley. Codex 66 contains the music for the Easter services, including the *Visitatio Sepulchri*.

As is typical of the ritual, much of the Holy Week liturgy at Klosterneuburg was stational, that is, it was performed at various specified places outside of the usual choir area. It was vital that the officiants and the chorus have with them the necessary texts in each location. With the help of his handbook, the sacristan could anticipate what would be needed and supply the need as efficiently as possible. At numerous points in the text, he shows concern for how the books are to be placed.

The Good Friday services take place in front of the Holy Cross Altar that was isolated in the middle of the nave. But the chorus is instructed: "...to stand around the S. Anna altar and to use the Benedictionale and then to continue the service out of the breviary and the Benedictionale."[9]

The *Benedictionale*, known also as a *Rituale* or *Obsequiale*, contained the texts, music, and instructions for various rites peculiar to priests. Included were the sacraments of marriage, ordination, and extreme unction, as well as numerous blessings, hence the name. Also included were various ceremonies of Holy Week, including the procession on Palm Sunday, the Adoration of the Cross on Good Friday, and the various Sepulchre ceremonies (*Depositio, Elevatio,* and *Visitatio Sepulchri*). At Klosterneuburg, there are two *Benedictionales* that might have been used at this point in the service: Codices 628 and 629, in quarto, both copied during the first half of the fourteenth century.[10] Each is handsomely produced and bound.

With the singing of the *Populer Meus*, a portable Christ figure is to be brought out of the choir and carried around the church and cloister. As the subdeacon intoned the collect, the sacristan's handbook directs:

> ...two brothers at the high altar are to sing the incipit *Populer Meus*. It is in my book. As the deacon begins, two boys dressed in the superpellicim use the book that the organist is supposed to use, followed by four boys with torches and two brothers with the crucified in a red tunic arranged so that his breast is bare.[11]

This text intrigues us, for it may refer to the sacristan's book itself. Codex 1026A does, in fact, have the lengthy text and music of *the Populer Meus* in the back. But we can not even speculate about the organist's book. What we can observe, however, is that combining a procession and a lengthy hymn puts a strain on the available copies. Somebody standing apart from the rest of the chorus must intone the incipit and he requires the text and music. Books that are normally out of sight in the sacristy or at the organ are here pressed into use.

Prior to Matins on Easter Sunday, the canons perform the *Elevatio*, in which they must remove the Host from the Holy Sepulchre. This ceremony again utilizes the portable Christ figure, and probably takes place at the Holy Grave tableau constructed in the church's side aisle.[12] Again there is a procession. But this time, the action takes place in the open or en route, and the prior is carrying the eucharistic capsule in his hands. Two boys are instructed "to carry his Benedictionale in front of him out of which he can sing the Responses."[13]

Easter Matins are intoned at the altar of St. Augustine, the matutinal altar in the choir. At this point appear the instructions that were cited above: "Rectors will say Matins around the altar of St. Augustine. They should sing out of the big, heavy, white book."[14] For Matins, the sacristan also specifies use of the "lectionary that is normally in the infirmary."[15]

The traditional performance of the *Visitatio Sepulchri* begins with procession to the place of the sepulchre. While the chorus processes three Marys stand in the pulpit, singing "out of the book in quarto in which the *Popule Meus* is contained."[16] This book may be one of the several Benedictionales. The Marys and Angel are then instructed to follow the ceremony as found in other books. The Prior is instructed "to carry his personal Benedictionale out of which he reads for himself what he is to do at the sepulchre."[17] At the close of the ceremony, all return to the choir, where the service is continued out of the Breviary.

The sacristan's guidelines for the distribution of books during the *Visitatio Sepulchri* does resolve one mystery about the antiphonary. While it does contain the *Visitatio secpulchri* text, Codex 66 gets it wrong. After each line of the ceremony, the text scribe, followed by the music scribe, inserts *differenciae*, the formulas for connecting Psalms with their antiphon. These are clearly inappropriate here, and we must question why such a mistake was allowed to remain in a book produced with such care and at such great expense. The answer turns out to be quite simple. The antiphonary, too heavy to be moved, remained in the choir, while the *Visitatio Sepulchri* took place in the nave. The canons are singing from quarto volumes, easily carried. The errors in Codex 66 simply did not matter because this book is not used for the actual service.

Welcome as it is, the sacristan's handbook does not enlighten us thoroughly about the performance of the *Visitatio Sepulchri*, preoccupied as it is almost solely with the needs of the officiating priest. How the Marys move from the pulpit to the sepulchre is unclear, as is the Prior's role in the ceremony. The books for other singers are not mentioned. Additional surviving texts themselves provide other clues about the performance of the *Visitatio Sepulchri*.

Two codices, 1210 and 1211, copied in about the mid-fifteenth century, contain the music for the special observances of Holy Week.[18] These are quite small in format, each approximately 4" x 5 ½" in size. Codex 1210 remains unbound, while Codex 1211 is very simply stitched into a wooden binding. The purpose of these books is unclear. With their German rubrics, they appear out of place for liturgical use, and their small format makes them nearly impractical for communal performance. Yet each is so well-worn and dog-eared that it is tempting to speculate that they were rehearsal copies or even prompt texts for the sacristan or school master. The use of German in liturgical books is also associated with women religious, and thereby raises the question of what books were used in the women's ceremonies.[19]

Klosterneuburg, like most south-German Augustinian foundations, was a double house, with separate, but attached, facilities for men and women. Although sorting out women's usage creates many problems of its own, our most recent research indicates that some manuscripts formerly attributed to the canons of Klosterneuburg should be assigned actually to the canonnesses.[20] Two small quarto antiphonaries probably represent the women's practice: Codices 589 and 1018.[21] Codex 1018 was copied in the early fourteenth century, while Codex 589 was copied somewhat later, but before mid-century. Each contains a *Visitatio Sepulchri* which differs in a melodic detail from that employed by the canons and contains unique rubrics. Most notably, the Klosterneuburg women employ a distinctive notation, the use of Laon neumes on four lines with a distinctive four-line clef. These two antiphonaries show considerable evidence of use, including numerous wax drippings within the Easter section of Codex 589. The identification of these books and the context for their use may well be the most intriguing question raised by the Klosterneuburg manuscripts.

Codex 1022B, a *Benedictionale* copied around 1330, is a book destined for male use within the female cloister.[22] This book provides blessings and various ceremonies performed by the priest on behalf of the women and includes all three of the sepulchre ceremonies. However, music is provided only for the Angel and Apostles, the parts that would have been performed by the male officiants, emphasizing their roles as givers of the word. In the *Benedictionale*, only the text is given for the Marys and the chorus. This situation is reversed in an earlier antiphonary, Codex 1013, which, like the other women's Antiphonaries, also employs Laon neumes. Here, the *Visitatio* includes music for the women and only the text of the priest.[23] The separation of music in the liturgical books underlines the strict separation of male and female roles in the convent. Both books are small, reminding us that the number of women religious is more restricted than that of the men, and that the services of the women are not public, but private and cloistered.

At Klosterneuburg, we have dozens of manuscripts that provide evidence about the Easter liturgy. While students of the drama are long accustomed to synthesizing many texts into one performance, relatively unchanging and similarly affecting each person involved, our documentation is so rich that we can and should differentiate varieties of experience. The texts chronicle changes over time in the visual appearance of the *Visitatio Sepulchri*, as properties are added and the Holy Sepulchre setting itself is drastically remodeled. The manuscripts also document revisions in the melodies used, the first occurring in the 1330s and again in the 1420s. At Klosterneuburg, the differences between the men's and women's Easter ceremonies are great enough that we must finally come to consider them as distinct liturgies.

While the books describe the performance, they must also be recognized as objects within the performance. In the *Visitatio Sepulchri*, as throughout the liturgy, the books themselves are visible and become part of the aesthetic of worship. Indeed, the size and decoration of the books can be directly correlated to the tone and requirements of the individual ceremonies. Books to be carried must be carriable; books that are to be visible must be presentable, even splendid.

Because liturgical books are created to serve the needs of a particular clerical function, the distribution of texts also mirrors the hierarchies of the community. At Klosterneuburg, the parts in the dramatic liturgy tend to be distributed according to clerical function and liturgical station. A deacon is assigned the part of the angel, while priests, sometimes including the Prior himself, play the part of the Marys. Whatever mimetic qualities we may today perceive in the liturgical enactment (if we are to acknowledge them at all), we must acknowledge them to be subservient to the ritualistic images of the ceremony.

And yet, the small Codices 1210 and 1211 might confirm the notion that Holy Week ceremonies differed from normal liturgy. These small, unbound pamphlets may have been rehearsal texts for individual performers who have used them hard. The instructions in German also suggest that the performers might not be clerics, but students, or even women. The stational liturgy forces the chorus away from its music, and these specialized texts might also have served as prompts for ringers within the chorus. Easter liturgy seems to have required rehearsal, and perhaps the addition of special musicians. Although no viewer in the mid-sixteenth century would confuse the *Visitatio Sepulchri* with the well-developed theater of the stage, if these texts were deliberately designed to be unobtrusive, perhaps our dramatic liturgy means to emphasize spectacle in addition to participation.

Clifford Flanigan among other scholars has made us very familiar with the middle ground that the liturgical ceremony of the *Visitatio Sepulchri* occupies, at once spectacle and communal reenactment. The books themselves are evidence of these tensions. But there are also books that seem to be removed from the liturgy itself and dedicated to private devotion. What are we to make of Oswald Ostner sitting in his prison cell in 1594 copying the sacristan's handbook? It is useful here to review what we know about these unusual circumstances.

Oswald Ostner was born in nearby Gabelbach, and assumed the robe of a Klosterneuburg canon in 1581.[24] In 1590, Ostner was recommended for the post of Prior in the nearby Augustinian monastery of Herzogenburg when it was discovered that he was an illegitimate child and therefore ineligible for the job. Deeply depressed, he forged himself new credentials, taking on the identity of a dead, but legitimately born, priest. He was arrested in Augsburg, where he had found himself a parish post. During his imprisonment, he must have requested the manual labor of copying the Ordinationes of Klosterneuburg. The handbook reflected the usage of Ostner's youth, before the monastery was re-catholicized after a protestantizing interlude. Ostner's act of copying allowed a vicarious participation in those services, one that he hoped would redeem him. By re-producing the voice of the sacristan, he identifies himself with a humble lay servant, a posture of particular penance. Here he also clearly marks his affection for the pre-Tridentine offices. Indeed, Ostner's decision to flee to Augsburg was probably no accident, for a papal dispensation had permitted the diocese to continue the old rite.

Surely it is tempting to think of the sacristan in modern terms as a stage-manager, sound-effects man, costumer and properties manager, although these categories are clearly inappropriate. Nowhere is the separation between theater and liturgy more clearly and poignantly embodied than here. Reading and copying the liturgy alone in his cell removes Ostner as far from drama as possible, and the ideal community that Ostner experienced in the old liturgy is very near at hand. Ostner is playing by the book.

Notes

1. Vienna, Österreisches Nationalbibliothek Ms 15078, f. 98v, below in bottom margin: "Oswald Ostner can. reg. Clau Ecce in tenebris sideo et lume- celi non iudeo cunctis diebus quibus nunc timeor expecto donec. Veniat, redemptio mia. 1594, 21 Aug."

2. Floridus Röhrig, *Stift Klosterneuburg und seine Kunstschätze* (Neu-Ulm, 1984); Floridus-Röhrig, "Protestantismus und Gegenreformation im Stift Klosterneuburg und seinen Pfarren," *Jahrbuch des Stiftes Klosterneuburg,* NF 1 (1961), p. 135-47. Perceiving that the offices were performed either sporadically or not at all, Prior Kaspar Christiani (1578-1584) received permission on 25 Jul 1578 to get rid of the earlier Missals and Breviaries and use the Roman ones. New Breviaries were purchased on 18 Dec 1578 (p. 147).

3. Walther Lipphardt, ed., *Lateinische Osterfeiern und Osterspiele,* 9 vols. (Berlin: Walter De Gruyter, 1975-90); Amelia Carr and Michael Norton. "New Sources for the Visitatio Sepulchri at Klosterneuburg." *Early Drama, Art, and Music Review* 15. 2 (Spring, 1993), pp. 83-90.

4. Leo Schabes, *Alte Liturgische Gebräuche und Zeremonien an der Stiftskirche zu Klosterneuburg* (Klosterneuburg, 1930), p. 11-12. Schabes identifies two copies of the Ordinationes at Klosterneuburg. The first is numbered in the 18th-century catalogue as Codex 1026, and Schabes describes it as the "careful" (sorgfältig) private work of a canon. The second copy (which Schabes does not number, but might be Cod 1026a) has the date 1573 at the end; it contains so many grammatical and orthographic mistakes that Schabes identifies it as the work of a lay brother who functioned as Sacristan. Unfortunately, Codex 1026 can no longer be found at Klosterneuburg. The exact relationships between the original CCl 1026, CCl 1026a and Vienna 15078 are unclear. An addition to the entry for Cod 1026 in the handwritten catalogue of Klosterneuburg prepared by Maximilian Fischer in 1807 indicates that Ms 1026 was preserved at that time in the ONB in Vienna under the shelfmark lat. 15078. Fischer's original entry specifies both the name of its scribe and the date of its completion (1594 and 1599). These notices were carried forward in the handwritten catalogue prepared by Herman Pfeiffer and B. Çernik [n.d.]. Writing in 1930, Schabes uses the original Cod 1026 as the basis for his discussion. However, neither the date of completion (1573) nor the folio numbers of particular ceremonies correspond to those found in the Vienna manuscript. In this paper, we base our discussion on Cod 1026a. Codex 1026a is usually dated to 1576, based on the comments on p. 28b that the Annunciation fell on a Sunday in 1576. Since this article was first written, the authors have located Codex 1026 misshelved in the Klosterneuburg Archives.

5. Codex 1026a, p. 40a: "Tandem per conventum canitur Christ ist erstanden. Exuit prelatum orratum in sacrario. Interim ad Matutinas compulsantur quatuor campanis inferioris qua dicit Breviaris. Antiquam ad Matutinam pulsatur fiat pulsatum octis campanis. Matutinas rectores intonat coram altari S. Aug. Canit ex albo libro crasso alta."

6. Andrew Hughes, *Medieval Manuscripts for Mass and Office: A Guide to Their Organization and Terminology* (Toronto: University of Toronto Press, 1982). For Antiphonaries, see pp. 61-223.

7. Alois Haidinger, *Katalog der Handschriften des Augustiner Chorherrenstiftes Klosterneuburg,* Teil 1, Cod. 1-100 (Vienna: Verlag der Österreichischen Akademie der Wissenschaften, 1983), pp. 114-121; Alois Haidinger, "Studien zur Buchmalerei in Klosterneuburg und Wien vom späten 14. Jahrhundert bis um 1450," Unpubl. Doctoral Diss. (Vienna, 1980); Berthold Çernik, "Das Schrift- und Buchwesen im Stift Klosterneuburg während des 15. Jahrhunderts," *Jahrbuch des Stiftes Klosterneuburg* 5 (1913), pp. 99-176; and Kurt Holter, "Die Wiener Buchmalerei," in *Geschichte der bildenden Kunst in Wien* 2, *Die Gotik* (Vienna, 1955), p. 224. Çernik documents payments to "Johanni scriptori musici" twice in 1422-23 (lines 176 and 224). In Codex 66, there have been two systems of pagination, such that Lipphardt (LOO 599a) places

the *Visitatio* on ff 136a-139d, while Haidinger puts it at ff 134r-137r. The illuminator Michael is responsible for the Agony in the Garden (f. 102v) and the Crucifixion (f. 113v) while Nikolaus executed the Three Marys at the Sepulchre (f. 132r).

8. Haidinger suggests that the antiphonary's present division into four volumes occurred ca. 1450.
9. Codex 1026a, f. 37b: "Chorus stant iuxta aram s. Anna utitur benedictionali. Ceterii sequuntur in Brevario et benedictionali continentur."
10. For Codices 628 and 629, see the handwritten entries in the catalogue by Pfeiffer and Çernik. Haidinger, *Catalogue* I, p. 130, identifies a Hand B, working after 1330, in Codices 71, 629 and 1022B. Codex 629 measures 9 1/8" x 13" x 2 ¾". Codex 629 measures 9 1/8" x 13" x 2 ¾".
11. Codex 1026a, f. 38. "…incipiunt duo fratres circa sumum Altare decantant popule meus, Est in libro meum, decano, incipitur in ciissu de s. spiritu quos procedunt duo pueri induti suppliciis, utuntur libro quo organista uti solet, geistantes Aeundimes, cernos baculos, duo fratres editur sequuntur. Portant effigiem, vel unus si sufficit induta effig. Rubea tunic, Im Lagh und a Sog iz losst."
12. On the staging of the Sepulchre ceremony, see Schabes, pp. 115-152, and Hermann Pfeiffer, "Klosterneuburger Osterfeier und Osterspiel," *Jahrbuch des Stiftes Klosterneuburg* 1 (1908), pp. 1-56. The building of an elaborate sculpted tableau with changeable scenes is documented in the years 1498-99. See Floridus Röhrig, "Das kunstgeschichtliche Material aus den Klosterneuburger Rechnungsbüchern des 14. und 15. Jahrhunderts," *Jahrbuch des Stiftes Klosterneuburg*, NF v. 6 (1966), p. 140; and Floridus Röhrig, "Das kunstgeschichtliche Material aus den Klosterneuburger Rechnungsbüchern des 16. Jahrhunderts," *Jahrbuch des Stiftes Klosterneuburg*, NF v. 7 (1971), p. 138. An over-life sized wooden image of the dead Christ is preserved in the Stiftsmuseum and has also been identified as the "effigy" carried in these ceremonies. The style of this carving seems to be somewhat later, however, and may belong to another monument.
13. Codex 1026a, f. 40a: "duo portant benedictionales ante prelatum ex quo Responsus canitur."
14. Codex 1026a, f. 40b. See note 5 above.
15. Codex 1026a, f. 40b: "Ad has lectiones legendas utuntur homeliis dorcathby consistantibus in lectura refactorii infirm."
16. Codex 1026a, f. 40b: "…tres Mariae stant infra suggestum, habentes pixides in manibus canunt ex libro in quarto in quo populo meis continetur."
17. Codex 1026a, f. 40b: "prelato defertur suum benedictionale, ex quo legit qu. ibidem aguntur circa sepulchrum."
18. For information on Codices 1210, 1211, see the Pfeiffer and Çernik handwritten catalogue, n.p.
19. The *Charta Visitationis* of 1419 addressed the literacy of the canonnesses among other questions concerning the reform of Klosterneuburg. The reform statutes and the Rule are explicitly to be copied in the vulgar tongue for the nuns, and a brother from the Stift was to be appointed to preach and instruct the women likewise in the vulgar tongue. See Anton Schmidgruber, "Beitrage zur Geschichte Klosterneuburgs in der ersten Hälfte des 15. Jahrhunderts," Unpubl. doctoral dissertation (Vienna, 1951), pp. 45-56. German sermons preached to the canonness in 1490 by Canon Peter Eckel are also preserved as Codex 845. See David Bell, *What Nuns Read: Books and Libraries in Medieval English Nunneries* (Kalamazoo, MI: Cistercian Publications,

1985), esp. pp. 57-71, for a useful discussion of the various levels of literacy among English nuns; and Julia Bolton Holloway, "Crosses and Boxes: Latin and Vernacular," in *Equally in God's Image: Women in the Middle Ages* (New York: Peter Lang, 1990), pp. 58-87. It should be noted that, at Klosterneuburg, German is by no means exclusive to female usage. Among the rich resources of the library are numerous German texts that can be associated with lay brotherhoods, school instruction, parish preaching, and notably, communal singing. Klosterneuburg manuscripts provide the earliest evidence of the vernacular text *Christ ist erstanden* and are a rich source for early German hymnography. Vernacular chronicles are an important source for Austrian history.

20. The authors have now addressed this question in Michael Norton and Amelia Carr, "Liturgical Manuscripts, Liturgical Practice, and the Women of Klosterneuburg," *Traditio* 65 (2011), pp. 69-170. The women's manuscripts are identified by a series of interlocking traits including inscriptions (many German), female portraits, distinct placement for the *Dedicatio Ecclesia*, and a distinct version of the *Visitatio Sepulchri*.

21. For Codices 589 and 1018, see the catalogue by Pfeiffer and Černik, n.p.

22. Codex 1022B dates to ca. 1330 and measures 5 ¾" x 8 ½" x ½".

23. The nature and sources of Codex 1013 has generated much speculation. See Jacques Froger, "Introduction," in *Le manuscrit 807, Universitätsbibliothek Graz* (Berne, 1974).

24. Röhrig, "Protestantismus," pp. 164-65.

Framing Medieval Drama: The Franciscans and English Drama

Lawrence M. Clopper[†*]

$\mathcal{S}$ome years ago I wrote an essay on lay and clerical impact on the civic biblical plays in which I made the argument that we have no documentary evidence of clerical participation in these dramas until well into the sixteenth century.[1] I was puzzled at the time by this gap in the record and perhaps overeager in wanting to enhance the role of the laity in the production of drama: they not only paid for and performed in the cycles, but they had the materials at hand in the vernacular to write the plays. I remain puzzled by this clerical "absence," especially since perhaps most scholars simply assume that the authors of these texts are clerics and friars: Glynne Wyckham, for example, asserted this to be the case – but provided no footnote to the assertion.[2] I take the occasion of this paper to rethink the issue, especially with regard to the friars.

A case can be made that clerics were not involved in dramatic performances because there was a long-standing admonition that clerics not attend upon *ludi* and other festivities. From around the time of Lateran IV in papal and episcopal legislation the clergy are instructed to refrain from participation in unlicensed play, lay games, and other entertainments because they were indecorous and potentially contaminating.[3] We might recall that William Melton, a Franciscan friar and preacher, commended the York plays to the people as good in themselves and laudable but asked that the plays be separated from the Corpus Christi procession because of the feastings, drunkenness, clamors, gossipings and other wantonness that occurred in conjunction with the plays.[4] Melton's intervention seems motivated by the desire to separate clerical procession and ritual – as well as the bodies of the clerics – from *ludi* appropriate for lay education and piety even though and because these latter have impurities attendant upon them.

On the other hand, there is good reason to assume that friars might be involved in the drama given Francis's participation in the crèche at Greccio and his references to the brothers as *joculatores dei*. Moreover, the Franciscans in Italy were deeply involved

---

* This paper was presented at the Modern Language Association, Toronto, December 1997.

with the *laudesi*, and we know that wherever they went, the Franciscans adapted popular forms – lyric and romance – to promote lay spirituality.[5] So why not drama in England?

Before proceeding to this question, let us look more closely at the events at Greccio.[6] Was the crèche a fully staged dramatic representation of the Nativity? Thomas of Celano says that Francis wished to recall to memory the little Child who was born in Bethlehem and so set before everyone's bodily eyes the inconveniences of his infant needs, how he lay in a manger, how, with an ox and an ass standing by, he lay upon the hay where he had been placed.[7] When everything was prepared the friars and other people came. While the brothers sang, Francis stood before the manger, uttering sighs, overcome with love, and filled with a wonderful happiness. The mass was celebrated. Francis, clothed in the vestments of the deacon, sang the holy Gospel. Then he preached concerning the poor King and the little town of Bethlehem. The scene is not enacted; indeed, there is not even the ritual action that we see in liturgical *representationes*. Rather, a scenic icon is created in order to bring the event more vividly into the memory. This is a gospel reading, which the deacon normally provides, with a scenic device, and an exhortation – the preaching – which the deacon may also do. The event is a kind of popularization of a liturgical *representatio*.

Thus far, I have been trying to suggest that there is a certain decorum associated with clerical activities that might account for the clerical absence from our dramatic records. At the same time, I think that Franciscan mentality frames medieval biblical drama.

One obvious place to begin is with the gaze on the tormented body of Christ.[8] My text is the Towneley Crucifixion (23.233-95) when the raucous and noisy action of the torturers ceases with their successful raising of the cross at which point Christ says:

> I pray you pepyll that passe me by,
> That lede youre lyfe so lykandly,
> Heyfe vp youre hartys on hight!
> Behold if euer ye sagh body
> Buffet and bett thus blody,
> Or yit thus dulfully dight;
> In warld was neuer no wight
> That suffred half so sare.
> My mayn, my mode, my myght
> Is noght bot sorow to sight,
> And comforth none, bot care.
>
> My folk, what haue I done to the
> That thou all thus shall tormente me?
> Thy syn by I full sore.
> What haue I greuyd the, answere me,
> That thou thus nalys me to a tre,
> And all for thyn erroure?

> Where shall thou seke socoure?
> This mys how shall thou amende,
> When that thou thy saveoure
> Dryfes to this dyshonoure,
> And nalys thrugh feete and hende?[9]

Christ accosts the audience, not the torturers; he invites the spectators to meditate on his wounds and their sins. This lyric, which has liturgical and biblical sources, is not in the past but the present tense. The spectators now inflict this punishment on Christ.

The image of the battered body of Christ is at the center of Franciscan spirituality.[10] I do not mean to suggest that no one else reflects upon the crucified Christ; rather, I want to suggest that this image is crucial to the kind of affective piety promoted by the Franciscans. I think we can see the difference if we compare Cistercian and Franciscan uses of the body of Christ. Although Francis, as far as I know, indicates no indebtedness to St. Bernard, the community frequently borrowed ideas and materials from the Cistercian saint. Bernard of Clairvaux too focused on the body of Christ as *accessus* to God, but for him the body of Christ is the gateway to contemplation of the Godhead. It is the shared fleshliness that enables the transition to higher contemplation.[11] By contrast, the Franciscans center their contemplation on the body of Christ. One need only recall Bonaventure's *Itinerarium mentis in deum* which ends with its vision of the crucified seraph. Bonaventure also tells us that when Francis and his first companions settled at Rivo Torto, "they had not yet got any of the liturgical books, so that they could not chant the divine office. Christ's cross was their book and they studied it day and night."[12]

Even more revealing, at least about the early Franciscans, is the legislation that directed the ministers to remove all glass or other decoration from Franciscan churches.[13] Churches were to be permitted images of the Crucifixion with Mary, John, Francis and Anthony behind the altar but no other decoration or rich vessels. Some of the most dramatic and earliest of such images are the Cimabues in the altar area of the Basilica in Assisi.[14] From the then undecorated nave, one would be unable to see the Cimabue and its companion piece in the choir. Only the friars in the choir would be able to see them.

This kind of presentation of Christ is indebted to the meditative directions that we find in works like the Pseudo-Bonaventure's *Meditations on the Life of Christ* and its vast progeny.[15] Indeed, I think we could say that the cycle plays are part of that progeny. In the *Meditations* the reader or practitioner is invited to imagine the events in Christ's life, not just the events as they are described in the gospel but to fill in the gaps of that narrative with the kinds of realistic detail that must certainly have been a part of the scene. The writer instructs the Poor Clare to whom the work was originally addressed:

> I have the greater hope that if you wish to exercise yourself in these things by continued contemplation, your master will be this Lord Jesus of whom we are speaking. However, you must not believe that all

things said and done by Him on which we may meditate are known to us in writing. For the sake of greater impressiveness I shall tell them to you as they occurred or as they might have occurred according to the devout belief of the imagination and the varying interpretation of the mind. It is possible to contemplate, explain and understand the Holy Scriptures in as many ways as we consider necessary, in such a manner as not to contradict the truth of life and justice and not to oppose faith and morality. Thus when you find it said here, "This was said and done by the Lord Jesus," and by others of whom we read, if it cannot be demonstrated by the scriptures, you must consider it only as a requirement of devout contemplation. Take it as if I had said, "Suppose that this is what the Lord Jesus said and did." (Ragusa trans., pp. 4-5)

The gospels tell us that Christ was tortured and nailed to the cross, but they do not tell us that his body was stretched to match the pre-drilled holes or that the torturers were focused on what a good job they were doing. But this is what the Pseudo-Bonaventure offers to his readers:

Here pay diligent attention to the manner of the Crucifixion. Two ladders are set in place, one behind at the right arm, another at the left arm, which the evil-doers ascend holding nails and hammers. . . . (Ragusa trans., p. 334)

Figure 4: Christ Ascending the Cross, Painting, Rimini School, Venice, Gallerie dell'Accademia

After describing Christ's voluntary ascent on the cross – an iconography promoted by the Franciscans – the writer says:

> There are, however, those who believe that He was not crucified in this manner, but that the cross was laid on the ground and that they then raised it up and fixed it in the ground. If this suits you better, think how they take Him contemptuously, like the vilest wretch, and furiously cast Him onto the cross on the ground, taking his arms, violently extending them, and most cruelly fixing them to the cross. Similarly consider His feet, which they dragged down as violently as they could (p. 334).[16]

One can argue then that the affective piety of the Franciscans in some way frames the cycle plays, but one also must note that the success of the friars makes their piety less distinctively Franciscan. If these are images shared by persons of various status and calling, then they cease in some ways to be specifically Franciscan. The Franciscans are present but also absent.

One of the remarkable ways that the Franciscans are absent is that their insistence on the utter poverty of Christ is written out of these texts. If the Towneley Crucifixion were a Franciscan text, we might expect Christ's poverty to be stressed at this moment of crucifixion, for in Franciscan defenses, commentaries and polemical literature, one key text that pointed to Christ's utter poverty was the verse that Christ said to a man who asked to follow him: Christ said, "Foxes have holes, and birds of the air have nests; but the Son of man has nowhere to lay his head" (Matt 8:20; Luke 9:58). The Franciscans took this verse to mean that Christ had no dominium or possession of anything either individually or in common; moreover, they – as does Friar Nede in *Piers Plowman* – associated the verse with the Crucifixion, the moment at which Christ's absolute poverty was most evident.[17] The lyric in the Towneley Crucifixion cites the verse but with no reference to poverty:

> All creatoures that kynde may kest –
> Beestys, byrdys – all haue thay rest,
> When thay ar wo-begon;
> Bot Godys son, that shuld be best,
> Hase not whereapon his hede to rest
> Bot on his shuder-bone. (23.255-60).

The only residue of the Franciscan ideology may be the iconographical tradition – but only if Christ is shown with his head resting on his shoulder, something he presumably is not doing while he is speaking.[18]

The other scene toward which we might look to is the Nativity, but here I think we find only a decorative poverty.[19] The iconography of the scene – and very probably the set for the plays – shows a broken roof to suggest the poor dwelling in which Mary and Joseph came to rest – but the rich clothing of the holy parents counters the poverty of the locus. There is poverty of place, but not of persons.

We need not think too hard about why poverty is written out of these texts: the producers of the plays are the burgesses and artisans of the city. What is desired is not just the story of the bible but an extravagant representation of wealth and prestige. Poverty is not a part of the spectacle.

Having described the Franciscan presence in and absence from these texts, I would like to conclude with some tantalizing evidence in the *N-Town* manuscript of the very things I do not find in the northern cycle plays. However, before I move to this part of my analysis, let me say that I agree with Peter Meredith and others that the *N-Town* manuscript is a compilation, not the text of a cycle like those in the north.[20] In suggesting there might be a more direct kind of Franciscan influence in some of these plays, I am not claiming that the *N-Town* manuscript represents a Franciscan cycle.

Some of the *N-Town* plays bring poverty into the text. In the "Marriage of Joseph and Mary," Joseph, as he takes leave of Mary to go prepare a house for them, says that they "ar not ryche of werdly thyng" (10.413) and that "he þat is and evyr xal be / Of hefne and helle ryche kynge / In erth hath chosyn poverté, / And all ryches and welthis refusynge" (10.417-20).[21] It is the insistence on Christ's *choosing* poverty and the assertion that he refused *all* riches that is suggestive of Franciscan mentality.

There is a similar trace in Passion Play I when Christ enters Jerusalem. There we are told four Citizens greet Christ barefoot and barelegged, that is, they are scripted as images of friars who were to go barefoot and, interestingly, in the short garment of the rigorists. The two blind men that Christ cures are called Primus and Secundus Pauper Homo. One might argue that in the Middle Ages anyone who was blind or halt was likely also to be poor, but it is nonetheless striking that this text puts Pauper into the name whereas the northern cycles do not.[22] I might add that in this same play, Simon the Leper is said to be a poor man (26.511), and Simon's house, where the Last Supper is taken, is described as a poor house (27.71); consequently, the matter of poverty is brought before us at one of the crucial moments in Christ's life, the institution of the sacrament of the Eucharist. Later Cleophas and Luke report to the disciples that they met Christ as a "pore pylgrym" (38.49).

But the most dynamic evocation of the mendicant mystique occurs in the play of the "Woman Taken in Adultery." The play opens with Christ preaching repentance directly to the audience and thus the address is like his speech from the cross in Towneley. The scene shifts to the scribe and Pharisee who, concerned that they will lose their law, set about trying to trap Christ. The scribe, in referring to the threat, says of Christ: "þat stynkynge beggere is woundyr bolde!" (24.48). This striking characterization – the bold beggar – constructs Christ as the friar come to preach – not doctrine – but penance, as Francis and the early brothers were authorized to do.[23] The detail might seem negligible to us but was not to the friars, for they justified their calling as beggars on the argument that Christ was a beggar.[24] Their opponents rejected the argument; indeed, some were both distraught and outraged. Richard FitzRalph, the most vocal English antimendicant accuser before Wyclif, charged that the Franciscan's theory of *dominium* threatened the whole institution of the propertied church. Midway through his *Defensio curatorum* he turns from the shared faults of the mendicant orders to the specific ones of the Franciscans: "Y speke þe more largelich in þis mater aȝȝenus frere menours, for þei bigunne þe cause at Londoun and ȝaf occasioun to oþere freres of oþere ordres; for þei disputeþ more þan oþere of þe parfitnesse of þe gospel and telliþ þat hit stondiþ in [w]ilful beggerye."²⁵ He goes on to claim that he recently heard a friar preaching the condemned thesis on Christ's and Franciscan poverty in which the argument that Christ was a beggar plays an important role. The *N-Town* playwright, therefore, not only constructs Christ as the mendicant preacher but implies that the accusers who call Christ a "stykande beggere," that is FitzRalph, Wyclif, the secular clergy who are critics of friars, monks and others, are scribes and Pharisees.

In the *N-Town* texts there is fleeting evidence of a Franciscan presence that is not in the northern cycles. Perhaps there is more evidence to be found, but perhaps all that we can say at present is not that the Franciscans or other friars were the authors of these texts but that they were the writers behind the writers who produced them. What we can affirm is that Franciscan spirituality and meditative practice inform and encourage the writing out of scripts of Christ's life that are not entirely attested by the gospels.

Notes

1. "Lay and Clerical Impact on Civic Religious Drama and Ceremony," in *Contexts for Early English Drama*, ed. Marianne G. Briscoe and John C. Coldewey (Bloomington: Indiana University Press, 1989), pp. 102-36.

2. Glynne Wickham, *Early English Stages: 1300-1600*, 2 vols. (London: Routledge and Kegan Paul, 1959-72), I.124-28. The case that the Franciscans were involved has been argued by Craddock – and elaborated by Jeffrey and Sticca – however, their historical documentation is often flawed when it cannot be shown to be a bibliographical or historical ghost (see Clopper, "Lay and Clerical Impact," pp. 114-15). Laurence G. Craddock, "Franciscan Influences on Early English Drama," *Franciscan Studies* 10 (1950): 383-417; David Jeffrey, "Franciscan Spirituality and the Rise of Early English Drama," *Mosaic* 8 (1975): 17-46; and Sandro Sticca, "Drama and Spirituality in the Middle Ages," *Medievalia et Humanistica*, n.s., 4 (1973): 69-87. Jeffrey follows Craddock's format and argument except that he enlarges the section devoted to Franciscan spirituality and makes a case for the Franciscan auspices of *N-Town* and some of the morality plays. Sticca's essay provides no additional documentation; instead, he presents as fact Wickham's speculation that the friars and secular clergy were midwives to the drama.

3. Liturgical *representationes* like the *Herod* and the *Visitatio sepulchri*, of course, were excepted. Bernardo Bottone's gloss on Innocent III's *Cum decorem* is the key document; both are quoted in my essay, "*Miracula* and the *Tretise of Miraclis Pleyinge*," *Speculum* 65 (1990): 882. For an overview, see Marianne Briscoe, "Some Clerical Notions of Dramatic Decorum in Late Medieval England," *Comparative Drama* 19 (1985): 1-13. I discuss these matters in more detail in my book, *Drama, Play and Game: English Festive Culture in the Medieval and Early Modern Period* (Chicago: The University of Chicago Press, 2001), pp. 63-107.

4. *York,* ed. Alexandra F. Johnston and Margaret Rogerson, Records of Early English Drama, 2 vols. (Toronto: University of Toronto Press, 1979), 1.43.

5. Sandro Sticca, "Italy: Liturgy and Christocentric Spirituality," in *The Theatre of Medieval Europe: New Research in Early Drama,* ed. Eckehard Simon (Cambridge: Cambridge University Press, 1991), pp. 169-88; and David Jeffrey, *The Early English Lyric and Franciscan Spirituality* (Lincoln: University of Nebraska Press, 1975).

6. Giotto, The crèche at Greccio; Assisi, Upper Church. For a reproduction of this figure see: http://www.wga.hu/frames-e.html?/html/g/giotto/assisi/upper/legend/scenes_2/franc13.html

7. Thomas of Celano, *The First Life of St. Francis,* in *St. Francis of Assisi: Writings and Early Biographies,* ed. Marion A. Habig, 4th rev. edn. (Chicago: Franciscan Herald Press, 1983), pp. 299-302 (chp. 30, paragraphs 84-87).

8. Cimabue, Crucifix; Florence, Santa Croce. For a representation of this work see: http://www.wga.hu/support/viewer/z.html

9. *The Towneley Plays,* ed. Martin Stevens and A. C. Cawley, Early English Text Society, s. s. 13-14 (Oxford, 1994), 1.294-95. The lyrics on which this text is based come largely from Franciscan sources; see Rosemary Woolf, *English Religious Lyrics in the Middle Ages* (Oxford: Clarendon Press, 1968), pp. 40-45.

10. Anne Derbes, *Picturing the Passion in Late Medieval Italy: Narrative Painting, Franciscan Ideologies, and the Levant* (Cambridge: Cambridge University Press, 1996).

11. Etienne Gilson, *The Mystical Theology of Saint Bernard,* trans. A. H. C. Downes (London: Sheed and Ward, 1940), pp. 76-81.

12. *Legenda major* 4.3 (in Habig, pp. 654-55); 1 Celano 16.42 (p. 264); 17.45 (pp. 266-67); and 2 Celano 154.203 (pp. 524-25).

13. Constitutions of Narbonne, 1260, cap. 3.15, 3.18; also Paris, 1292, cap. 3.18. P. Michael Bihl, O.F.M., "Statuta generalia ordinis edita in capitulis generalibus celebratis Narbonne an. 1260, Assisii an. 1279 atque Pariis an. 1292," *Archivum Franciscanum Historicum* 34 (1941): 48, 51-52. This legislation dropped out of the Franciscan Constitutions in the early fourteenth century, at the time that the Conventuals succeeded in their fight with the various groups of rigorists and other opponents. However, as anyone who has ever been to Assisi knows, the injunctions against decoration were frequently ignored and Franciscan churches from early on were lavishly decorated.

14. Cimabue, Upper Church, Assisi. For a representation of this work see: http://www.museumsyndicate.com/item.php?item=30802

15. All citations are from *Meditations on the Life of Christ: An Illustrated Manuscript of the Fourteenth Century,* trans. Isa Ragusa and Rosalie B. Green (Princeton: Princeton University Press, 1961).

16. Gerard David, Christ Nailed to the Cross; London, National Gallery. For a representation of this work, see: http://www.nationalgallery.org.uk/paintings/gerard-david-christ-nailed-to-the-cross.

17. See the data and discussion in my *"Songes of Recehelesnesse": Langland and the Franciscans* (Ann Arbor: University of Michigan Press, 1997), pp. 53, 94.

18. Derbes's argument in *Picturing the Passion* is that a painter like Cimabue depicts the radical poverty of Christ by painting him as naked as possible and by having Christ lay his head on his shoulder to evoke the thesis that Christ had literally no where to lay his head, that he is without place.

19. Hugo van der Goes, Portinari Altarpiece; Florence, Uffizi Gallery. For a representation of this work, see: http://www.virtualuffizi.com/portinari-triptych.html.

20. "Manuscript, Scribe and Performance: Further Looks at the N. Town Manuscript," in *Regionalism in Late Medieval Manuscripts and Texts: Essays Celebrating the Publication of A Linguistic Atlas of Late Mediaeval England*, ed. Felicity Riddy (Cambridge: D. S. Brewer, 1991), pp. 109-28.

21. *The* N-Town *Play*, ed. Stephen Spector, Early English Text Society, s. s. 11-12 (Oxford, 1991).

22. In York they are called *Burgenses*, but there is also a character named *Pauper* with *Cecus*. There is no Entry in Towneley. In Chester there is *Caecus* and 1st and 2nd *Vicinus*.

23. Because Francis and most of the early brothers were laymen, the pope did not authorize them to preach; however, he did allow them to testify and exhort. See my "*Songes of Rechelesnesse*," pp. 41-42.

24. See my '*Songes of Rechelesnesse*', pp. 59-60, 63.

25. In John Trevisa, *Dialogus inter Militem et Clericum...*, ed. Aaron Jenkins Perry, Early English Text Society, o. s. 167 (London, 1925), p. 70. The edition reads "skilful" for my emendation, "wilful," the latter of which is used elsewhere in the text. "Wilful" means "voluntary, without necessity."

Leudast's *Passio* and Sacred Violence in Gregory of Tours
Thomas Goodmann

> "Only violence can put an end to violence, and that is why violence is self-propagating."
> – René Girard, *Violence and the Sacred*

> "… there were McCoys on the Hatfield side and Hatfields on the McCoy side."
> – Altina Waller, *Feud*

𝒞liff Flanigan was one of my finest and favorite teachers both inside and outside of the classroom during my years of graduate study at Indiana University. His infectious energy formed a real invitation to converse; he could move a group of students deftly from a general question such as "Did you like this?" to a reading of the *Aeneid* or of Nithard's life of Charlemagne that still makes useful sense as I look over old notes. He was demanding as a teacher in all the best senses, a good storyteller, too, who interrupted himself with laughter pouring out of him. The people of medieval studies seemed as important in Cliff's conversation as the books they wrote, and the books or phenomena they wrote about. Scholarship, reading, writing, studying – these were activities that were very lively in Cliff's way of talking, acts of being alive, rather than withdrawals from life. They seemed primary acts in his hands, and never distant from the joys he took in being with friends, in sharing music and meals. His reading lists were ambitious; we were behind from the beginning, and finished the reading in extra sessions over reading days in the Comparative Literature annex, with Cliff furnishing refreshments. No one seemed to mind the extra time. He wrote challenging assignments and gave exams that were (I mean this) enjoyable exercises. Cliff's teaching in all respects reminded you of the root sense of enthusiasm: if you weren't already converted, you were about to be.

When I took some courses with him, a fortunate interloper from the English Department, Cliff was in mid-course. Educated at Washington University, he held a great respect for the generation of scholars who had taught him, people such as Liselotte Dieckmann, and for the people she knew: Curtius and Auerbach writing in the circumstances of wartime. He knew their work well, and had read Eliade carefully too. When I first met him, the tides of theoretical engagements seeping into literature programs everywhere had caught his attention, and I saw him grow excited, as if he had rediscovered the things he loved to work on, music, and drama, and ritual, all over again, via cultural theory.

As a way to remember C. Clifford Flanigan, I would like to return to a text I first read with him, Gregory of Tours' *History of the Franks*, which ends with events for the year 591. I want to examine the ways, both historiographical and literary, that this text has been important and productive for its readers since it was first written and carefully reproduced.[1] And within the text, I want to focus on a particularly productive figure for the *Historiae*: this is Leudast, Count of Tours, whose rise, fall, and death by torture Gregory narrates. I will trace in my rereading, as a kind of homage, some of the steps I saw Cliff taking as he moved from readings in religion and literary history to those incorporating new understandings of textuality and the new anthropology. Cliff taught me to ask what a text makes time for, and in this light I want to interrogate the social order of violence in Gregory's text, to read this text, as Cliff suggests in his essay on Turner, Bakhtin, and drama, "as a form of social action rather than as a literary text …" (58). My intention is not to look back on the *Historiae* or on the work of its other readers with a sense that I know more than they do; rather, I return to this text and to its representations of violence to learn something that might be useful in our own struggles both with narrative and with social order. I will examine Gregory's use of Leudast and a number of uses of Gregory's *Historiae* while charting a series of mimetic successes and failures alleged against this text, or committed within it. To approach both the generative history of the *Historiae*, its thematic concern with violence, and the representative figure of Leudast within the text, I employ Girard's critique of *mimesis* and extend his idea of the scapegoat to look at what kind of work Gregory performs in this account.

One large context for the story is formed by the rivalries among the sons of Chlothar, who died in 561, and their wives and households: Charibert, Guntram, Sigibert, and Chilperic in the years 573 to 584 (Wood 89). Leudast's fortune as count changes according to who among these sons, and their sons, holds Tours. Like many parts of the *Historiae*, the episodes concerning Leudast are remarkable in their graphic detail, a major episode forming a long conclusion to Book Five.[2]

Gregory tells us that Leudast was born on an island off Poitou, the son of a slave. He served poorly in the household in which his father worked and one of his ears was slit as a punishment for his repeated attempts to escape. He flees to the household of King Charibert, where he enjoys the special favor of Queen Marcovefa, and from a position he gains as Master of the Stables he bribes Charibert to make him Count of Tours. When the king dies, Leudast makes the mistake of looking to Chilperic, but it is Sigibert who takes the city. When Sigibert is murdered in 575, Chilperic gains Tours, reinstating Leudast as count. Neither man is friendly to Gregory.

Gregory presents Leudast as a menace to social order who, chiefly among other outrages, plots with two clergymen of the bishop, a priest and a subdeacon (both named Riculf), to say that Gregory had slandered Queen Fredegund, wife to Chilperic, by alleging an affair between her and Bishop Bertram of Bordeaux. Leudast claims that torture of two other members of Gregory's clergy, archdeacon Plato and one Galienus, will produce the truth of these charges. Gregory is acquitted, in part at least because his brother bishops refuse the evidence of their inferior, and Leudast flees. Though Gregory, as he tells us, intervenes successfully against the death sentence, he could not prevent the subdeacon Riculf from being tortured to the extreme, at which point the subdeacon reveals the truth of the plot; I will return to the nature of this torture (which Gregory describes in some detail) and this truth. The slanders were supposed to effect Fredegund's deposition and the elevation of her stepson, Clovis, to the throne. Riculf the priest was to have been made bishop in Gregory's place; Riculf the subdeacon would have been archdeacon, and Leudast, dux. Clovis is murdered, however, possibly at Fredegund's instigation. Ian Wood speculates that, torture notwithstanding, this turn of events might cast doubt on the truth of subdeacon Riculf's confession (87).

Gregory reintroduces Leudast in Book Six, at a point when he asks the Bishop to be re-admitted to communion. His request is passed on with the support of the military to the King, who asks him to be patient so that he can appease the Queen who, Gregory suspects, will have him killed. But Leudast imprudently throws himself at her feet in the cathedral at Paris, begging forgiveness, and Fredegund has him thrown out. Waiting for an answer, believing all will be well, Leudast is shown to linger foolishly, shopping in the market, when he is inevitably arrested. Seriously wounded as he resists, the former count lives to undergo torture and medical care administered so that he may suffer a gruesome death "at the personal command of the Queen," who orders that he be laid out with a block of wood under his neck, and struck repeatedly on the throat with another piece of wood (363).

The account changes pace as Gregory expands several moments; it is filled with action, drama, dialogue, and graphic detail. We hear the words of Gregory, of Fredegund's letter, of the Queen herself, and of Chilperic. The only words we hear from Leudast, however, are spoken in vain, as he goes about shopping for jewelry, assuming he will be forgiven. We see him throwing himself first at Chilperic's feet, then at those of Fredegund, who "was furious, for she hated the sight of him. She burst into tears and thrust him aside" (362). These are not so much reported actions as dramatic scenes for which the text makes time, replete with gestures of emotion and of dramatic and/or violent action. I am not suggesting that Gregory has concocted Leudast's career of social disruption; nor am I simply urging sympathy for a figure identified as anti-social by one occupying the high place of episcopal power. The question I want to explore is one of social action: beyond reportage, what kind of work does this account of Leudast perform within Gregory's long text?

We might ask why the career of a relatively minor figure receives such expansive attention in Gregory. One response lies in Leudast's challenge to Gregory's episcopal authority, and another lies in the ways in which Leudast helps the writer to make sense of his world. Leudast is a productive and significant figure for the Bishop of

Tours, as well as for his readers of later centuries, someone seen as typifying the social disruptions of the era. As I examine some of the ways in which Leudast is useful for Gregory, and some of the ways in which both Leudast and Gregory have been useful to others eager to understand the sixth century, I am aware that I too am making use of Leudast and cannot altogether avoid complicity with the violence of the text. But I hope to show that studying such representation, and its reception in literary history and historiography, can lead to something other than recapitulation, to some revelation of the text not only as potential historical record but as a social act relevant to our own concerns with justice, class, and social identity.

Most previous attention to Gregory has been of two kinds: critical literary appraisal, or compliant and complicit historiography. One of Gregory's most admiring readers, Augustin Thierry, blended both responses out of Romantic impulse. Inspired by reading Chauteaubriand at school, Thierry published a history of the Norman conquest in 1825, and followed it with the *Récits des temps mérovingiens* in 1840. Filled with supposition, speculation, and psychological embellishment, the *Récits* present a sort of novelization of the *Historiae* in sympathy with the viewpoint of Gregory, his principal source for the period. Thierry follows Gregory's chronology, reweaving the sources into a series of episodes organized around individuals. It is this impulse to novelize that prompts him to explain Leudast's behavior by citing that "he completely forgot his origins and the old days of slavery and distress" (Thierry, trans. Jenkins 95).[3] Writing in the preface to a new edition in 1866, Thierry accounts for these very qualities in stating his intention to craft "un travail d'art en même temps que de science historique" (5). Leudast serves as an explanatory example of a great deal within the period; Leudast, that is, helps Thierry to make sense out of the past, however mediated by Gregory's text. Thierry concludes his remarkable renarration of episodes from Gregory, overflowing with his own additions, with great confidence in what Leudast's story reveals:

> So ended the adventurous existence of this sixth-century parvenu, the son of a Gallo-Roman serf who was raised through a stroke of royal favor to the same rank as the leaders of the conquerors of Gaul. If the name Leudast, barely mentioned even in the most voluminous of the histories of France, is little worthy of being rescued from oblivion, his life, which was closely interwoven with those of several famous persons, presents one of the most characteristic episodes of the general life of the period. Problems on which scholarly opinion has been much at variance are, so to speak, resolved of their own accord by the facts of this strange story. What could be the fortunes of a Gaul of servile condition under Frankish rule? How were the diocesan cities administered, placed as they were under the twofold authority of their counts and their bishops? What were the mutual relations between these two naturally hostile (or at least rival) powers? These are questions clearly answered by the mere retelling of the adventures of Leocadius's son. (Thierry, trans. Jenkins 151)

This summary encapsulates some of the key issues of social identity raised by Gregory himself. Thierry divides Leudast's obscure name, which stands in for his social origin – his true identity – from his life, which is constituted by a nexus of social relations made available to him by being raised out of his obscure and low origins "to the same rank as the leaders of the conquerors of Gaul." This formulation contains its own presuppositions: Leudast may have been raised to this rank, but this rank is not his true identity. What accounts for Leudast's behavior is his inherent failure to be anything but what he is already known to be by his birth; I return to this mimetic shortcoming below. Leudast must fail to be the same as those in power in order for the sense of the text to remain intact; at the same time, his story offers to Thierry a perfect metonym of the times, as it were. And Thierry's certainty in the answers provided by this story has been confirmed by the attention it has received, at least in passing, in literary and historiographical accounts of the period. With few exceptions, readers trust Gregory's account absolutely.

The most famous literary attention to Gregory (though not specifically to Leudast) is given in the well-known chapter on "Sicharius and Chramnesindus" in *Mimesis*, wherein Auerbach concludes that Gregory's style "reveals to us a first early trace of the reawakening apprehension of things and events …" and notes how words in Gregory "break out in a moment and change the moment into a scene" (*Mimesis* 87). The reader is led along in the critical analysis with which Auerbach opens his discussion of Gregory's narrative. He offers for example several negative evaluations of Gregory and of his Latin: "the amount of data requisite for the purpose confuses him. He has neither the energy to dispose of it … nor the foresight to recognize the difficulty and get around it …" (*Mimesis* 82). Or, again, he writes that "Gregory is not capable of arranging the occurrences themselves in an orderly fashion" in a story of local violence that an earlier Latin writer would not have treated at all (*Mimesis* 83). Auerbach would seem to criticize Gregory for failing to narrate things in a clear fashion, replete with each individual's motivation for action; this is to say that Gregory is incapable of imitating the Latin of Livy and of Julius Caesar. But of course Auerbach knows what more he wants to say as he notes repeatedly Gregory's talent for "visual directness" (84), "visually vivid narration" (85), and "visual vividness" (86). As well, he comments on the use of direct discourse: "Any story that he can, he thus makes into a scene" (87). The fall of the Roman Empire explains everything from dynastic feuds to Gregory's Latin: "He has many horrible things to relate; treason, violence, manslaughter are everyday occurrences; but the simple and practical vivacity with which he reports them prevents the formation of that oppressive atmosphere which we find in the late Roman writers and which even the Christian writers can hardly escape. When Gregory writes, the catastrophe has occurred, the Empire has fallen …" (*Mimesis* 94). Like Thierry, Auerbach seems to trust Gregory's text absolutely as a historical record, Latin style aside: "reading it, we almost smell the atmosphere of the first century of Frankish rule in Gaul" (*Mimesis* 90).

In *Literary Language and Its Public in Late Latin Antiquity and in the Middle Ages*, Auerbach revisits his earlier work on Gregory to explore the Bishop's detailed self-criticisms of his style at various places in his writings. While Gregory imagines the voices of his detractors – "you use accusatives for ablatives" – he yet adjures his readers, however learned, to let his text stand unchanged (103ff). In this revisitation Auerbach attributes to Gregory a signal achievement as an author. Both in Caesarius and in Pope Gregory Auerbach locates a common impulse to write from the vernacular, from the surrounding spoken language: "But it is in Gregory of Tours, the most individual of the sixth-century writers, that the drive to write in a colloquial style seems most intense …" (*Literary Language* 103). This style is the personal achievement of an individual author: "By the force of his personality Gregory developed a form of written Latin suitable for historiography, or more exactly, for the narration of concrete events; it was related to the language of the people, from which in all probability it was intuitively developed" (*Literary Language* 109). For Auerbach this style constitutes "a reawakening of the directly sensible" (*Mimesis* 94), a "reawakening sensory apprehension of things and events" (*Mimesis* 95). And the explanation for this reawakening lies in a cultural collapse, a decadence that infects the language, as well as in the collapse of high and low styles in the drama of the Passion that Auerbach has already explored (92 and *passim* in the second chapter of *Mimesis*). The referential nature of Gregory's language, its attachment to ordinary, empirical events that it communicates in sensory terms, however ill-chosen and poorly arranged and managed as narrative material, is the point of arrival in this stylistic analysis.

With some of the same attention to dramatic elements, but with none of Auerbach's assumptions about authorship, Joaquín Martínez-Pizarro argues in *The Rhetoric of the Scene* that early medieval Latin narrative does not derive from historiographical predecessors, but instead incorporates elements of oral narrative, including speeches, gestures, and objects. That is, he does not at all read Gregory as "the most individual of the sixth-century writers," as Auerbach does. Although Martínez-Pizarro, like Auerbach, sees in Gregory's style elements of the vernacular, widespread use of dialogue, and the tendency more to present dramatic scenes than to create an orderly narrative of events, he does not understand such writing as an individual achievement. The resultant style "is not a function of the individual manner of the author, but constitutes a basic narrative approach, a fundamental technique adopted by a great variety of narrators" (14). And the source of this style lies in oral narrative, so that reading it is not a matter of literary analysis. In any case – and, again, like Auerbach – Martínez-Pizarro sees little quality in Gregory's Latin *per se*, dismissing it as "clumsy, childish prose, in no way worthy of literary consideration as such" (14-15).

In writing both a continuation of and a challenge to Auerbach, he analyzes the scene of Leudast's final capture for its psychological touches and its stereotypical, rather than mimetic, potential. "A fool's death has a peculiar pathos," writes Martínez-Pizarro, "and it is Leudast's foolishness and vanity that are revealed by his irrelevant remark [in the scene of his capture] as much as by his carefree shopper's attitude; the words are both psychologically true and dramatically effective," if similar as well to those used elsewhere for other figures in the *Historiae* (100). Thus, the debate with Auerbach is a matter of stylistic origins: literary and particular to Gregory, a style of writing that incorporates the vernacular (if stylistically degenerate), as Auerbach would have it, or oral and typical (if also stylistically worthless), according to Martínez-Pizarro. But these terms overlap, particularly what Auerbach calls "vernacular" and what Martínez-Pizarro calls "oral," so that the two readers are not far apart from one another. One distinction is that for Martínez-Pizarro, the *mimesis* here is not one of actual events or of real individuals, but of a more general human nature.

Indeed, almost alone among literary and historiographical readers, Martínez-Pizarro approaches Gregory's account with some skepticism, and particularly with regard to the representation of violence: "When modern historians describe the Merovingians as extraordinarily explosive and unrestrained people, and their bloodfeuds as slumbering volcanoes that now and then become unexpectedly active, they could perhaps be making a psychology of what is primarily a style of presentation" (34).

Edward James's *The Franks* offers confirmation of Martínez-Pizarro's critical suggestion as it makes only a gesture of caution towards the source as the historian heartily vilifies Leudast, while exploring the very issues of names and of social identities raised by Augustin Thierry:

> When we meet what appear to be Frankish names in southern Gaul, can we assume they are Franks? There is Count Leudast, for instance, Count of Tours and opponent of Gregory of Tours, the very epitome of barbaric cruelty and oppression, who bears what seems to be a Frankish name. Gregory does not reveal his nationality, but he does say that he was born the son of a slave called Leucadius, who worked in the vineyards. If we can trust Gregory's account of the origins of a man he hated, Leudast was not an example of a Frank from north-east Gaul implanted in the south as part of the process of conquest and control. Yet he may have dressed as a Frank, and thought of himself as a Frank … (108)

James's speculation on Leudast's dress and self-understanding and his characterization of him as "the very epitome of barbaric cruelty and oppression" signal an empathy with Gregory's understanding of Leudast's presumption to the ruling class. And while the question of "nationality" – very different from its modern meaning, of course – is interesting in itself, the point, I would argue, is that Gregory has identified Leudast sufficiently for his purposes.

Likewise, in the *The Birth of France: Warriors, Bishops, and Long-Haired Kings*, Katharine Scherman exhibits an even more exuberant trust of the text, making a similar exemplary use of Leudast:

> Fredegund's regency was one of brutal efficiency. She had the approval of most of her aristocracy, and she kept it by dealing ferociously with the occasional mutinous seigneur. One Leudast, a vicious and degenerate count who may have deserved what he got, led a plot against her. One of his followers was captured, his hands were tied by his back by the queen's order, and he was hung thus from a tree for six hours. Then he was taken down and put on the rack with ropes and pulley, to be beaten with sticks and whips by anyone who passed by. Just before he died, incredibly still vocal, he confessed his part and gave the names of the other plotters. (198)

This retelling accepts and participates in Gregory's account without question. As Scherman uses it, this story is supposed to demonstrate Fredegund's ferocity; but in calling Leudast "vicious and degenerate" – based only, of course, on Gregory's account – and in accepting without question the truth exacted from the subdeacon Riculf, Scherman suggests that Fredegund enacts justice against Leudast. Like other readers, Scherman criticizes Gregory's composition while praising its vividness: "although it is naïve and nonanalytical, and often illogical and unstructured, it is full of zest. Above all it is genuine history. Its author neither embroiders nor fabricates, and he makes an effort to preserve chronological unity" (276).

I think there is more to be said, however, alongside matters of political and grammatical decadence, authorial and literary versus oral and typical origins of Gregory's style, and a generally unqualified acceptance of his account as historically accurate. The point is not whether these events occurred, or whether Leudast was a disruptive figure within his society; rather, what evidence does this account give of how one observer makes sense out of the world around him? How does the account of Leudast, as one example, constitute a form of action within that society?

"When Gregory writes, the catastrophe has occurred, the Empire has fallen," writes Auerbach, and so "the oppressive atmosphere" of the late Roman writers is dissipated (*Mimesis* 94). So much may be true – but there is still a great deal at stake in social order for Gregory, if in more local terms than for writers addressing the fate of an empire. And even while I share Martínez-Pizarro's doubts about the empirical truth at every point of the *Historiae Francorum*, I disagree with his assessment of the "self-effacing quality of the narrator ... most striking in the total absence of authorial moralizing" (34). Gregory's judgments are very plainly pronounced within the narrative, and his perception is apocalyptic. That is, in claiming not to be able to order (*narrare*) confusing events, he assumes that there is an order, both immediate and ultimate, within or behind these events, one that is not apprehensible to him because its time is not yet at hand. And that sense of an order nonetheless presses upon and organizes his understanding of Frankish history. James W. Earl has formulated apocalypticism with regard to Germanic society within *Beowulf* : "An apocalypse, of course, is a revelation, a revealing of something hidden. The idea of an apocalypse, then, depends upon a prior sense that something is hidden from us – something we know, insofar as we know it is hidden; and something we do not know, insofar as it is hidden from us" (362). What Auerbach both criticizes (but I think this is not altogether serious) and celebrates, Gregory's penchant for the sensory and sensational, reveals not Gregory's failure but his sense of things. Sensationalized violence forms the focus of his writing at many points; I suggest that these representations organize reality for him, and form the rationale of his narrative.

I have explored the readings of Thierry, Auerbach, Martínez-Pizarro, James, and Scherman in order to map the ground of Gregory's usage among subsequent writers as a variously reliable source for the times in which he lived, and to establish the *Historiae Francorum* and Leudast in particular as a productive means of constructing literary, religious, and political history. As I have said, I am not exploring here the historiographic accuracy of Gregory's text or its literary and mimetic value – not at least in Auerbach's Aristotelian sense of *mimesis*. The *mimeses* I want to examine in

Gregory's *Historiae* are not those of Auerbach's critique, which excludes desire in the manner of Plato and Aristotle, but of Girard's critique, which is based upon desire. He formulates the idea in *"To Double Business Bound"*: "If one individual imitates another when the latter appropriates some object, the result cannot fail to be rivalry or conflict" (*DBB* vii). Or again, in broader social terms: "If mimetic desire and rivalries are more or less normal human phenomena, how can societal orders keep back this force of disorder, or, if they are overwhelmed by it, how can a new order be reborn of such disorder? The very existence of human society becomes problematic" (*DBB* xii).

It remains to outline the mimetic desires and rivalries circulating within, and organizing, the *Historiae Francorum*. Gregory's text represents selected events with immediacy, using direct dialogue, gesture, and scenes of dramatic action, imitative of what we might agree are plausibly observable experiences. But there are other *mimeses* operating here. Even though Martínez-Pizarro would say that Gregory's style is not derived from earlier Latin historiography, by his own account the Bishop seeks to render his society in terms mimetic – that is, imitative – of his predecessor and model historians, terms which themselves present a mimetic crisis in three ways. First, Gregory intends to write in the same way as, but not the same as, Eusebius, Severus, and Jerome. His historiographical anxieties are apparent in the opening of Book Two:

> As I continue to follow the march of history I recount for you at one and the same time, and in the muddled and confused order in which these events occurred, the holy deeds of the Saints and the way in which whole races of people were butchered. It will not, I am sure, be held unreasonable of me if I describe the blessed lives of the Saints together with the disasters of the unfortunate: for it is the course of events which demands this and not my own fantasy as a writer ... Just as I have done myself, so Eusebius, Severus, and Jerome mingled together in their chronicles the wars waged by kings and the holy deeds of martyrs. I have composed my book in the same way ... (103)

While Gregory feels it necessary to explain the inadequacies of his narrative, at the same time he defends it by saying that its order is natural, is imitative of the events he relates, and is as well in accordance with the narrative practices of authoritative historians – even as he senses that his own book will not read in the same way as their books do.[4] There is an anxiety expressed here to imitate authoritative historians; yet no reader has argued that Gregory's book is anything like those of Eusebius, Severus, or Jerome. Gregory understands himself as an aspiring literate historian working within an established genre, even while his text may bear the influences of an emergent vernacular language and of an established style of oral narrative. That is, for any number of reasons too numerous to detail here, Gregory's anxieties and desires notwithstanding, the *Historiae* is a text unlike those of his model authors. This unlikeness constitutes the first mimetic crisis within the book, a matter of narrative and stylistic discord that cannot be resolved by its author, who has himself of course constructed these comparisons and the problems they invite for him.

The second crisis stands within the text as the Franks' failure to imitate the example of their predecessors; they are to be just what they are not. At the beginning of Book Five, Gregory asserts:

> The Franks ought, indeed, to have been warned by the sad fate of their earlier kings, who, through their inability ever to agree with each other, were killed by their enemies … If only you kings had occupied yourselves with wars like those in which your ancestors larded the ground with sweat, then the other races of the earth, filled with awe at the peace which you imposed, might have been subjected to your power! Just think of all that Clovis achieved, Clovis, the founder of your victorious country, who slaughtered those rulers who opposed him, conquered hostile peoples and captured their territories, thus bequeathing to you absolute and unquestioned dominion over them … But you what are you doing? What are you trying to do? You have everything you want … Only one thing is lacking: you cannot keep peace, and therefore you do not know the grace of God. Why do you all keep stealing from each other? Why do you always want something which someone else possesses? (253)

Here is the heart of the matter of *mimesis* in Girard's formulation: desire. Just as Gregory wants his book to be like those of his authoritative predecessors, he wants too for his contemporaries to live their lives like those of their predecessors he has read, or has learned about otherwise. The Franks do not fail to imitate Clovis, they fail – as they must do – to *be* Clovis, and have fallen into a cycle of endemic, competitive violence, the violence of the feud. In a period long after the migration into Gaul, where might the frontier of new conquests lie? "Other races" and "hostile peoples" are imagined, but not located.

The internally disruptive desire of which he accuses the Franks at the close of this passage is certainly in tune with and may even have contributed to one of the oldest saws in the pedagogy of early Germanic culture: violence directed outward was productive; when that violence turned inward it was destructive.[5] And yet such violence may not have been destructive in all of the ways that Gregory understands it to have been. Ian Wood argues that while several individual Merovingians were the objects of rebellion, there is no surviving evidence of anyone questioning the family's right to rule.

Equally Leudast's position in Tours was closely connected with changing royal control of the city. Numerous conflicts within the kingdom were therefore centered upon the royal court. Thus the civil wars, so decried by Gregory, actually held the kingdom together, because the struggles between members of the Merovingian family provided a focus around which other conflicts could cluster (100). Katharine Scherman also understands a basic stability to the Merovingian dynasty, regardless of violence directed at one another (201).

"Why do you always want something which someone else possesses?" Gregory asks. This question of a rival object suggests a third mimetic failure, represented in the text in Leudast's effort to imitate a social rank to which he is not born. His crime is one of presumptive *mimesis*, and it is continuous with his marginal relation to the social rank he fails to imitate, indeed, because he is not the same as that rank in Gregory's eyes. The object of rivalry, that is, between Gregory and Leudast is social place: the stability of social identity is what is at stake for Gregory. He needs to know who is who, even if (as Auerbach puts it) "the catastrophe has occurred, the Empire has fallen …" (*Mimesis* 94). We know nothing of Leudast beyond what Gregory tells us; his motivations are buried in his nature which, as represented to us, is equivalent to his low social origins. Even his name is problematic. As Edward James argues, Leudast "bears what appears to be a Frankish name. Gregory does not reveal his nationality …" (*The Franks* 108). He may have been of Germanic origin, or a Roman "of the less privileged classes, adopting the fashions of the ruling elite" (109). In any case, he is not to be thought of as socially respectable or acceptable by someone of Gallo-Roman heritage like Gregory.

Gregory's account of Leudast's career, while apparently quite full, conceals as much as it reveals. For instance, if Leudast was so obviously bad in service, why is it that Queen Marcovefa "received him with great kindness, promoted him and put him in charge of the finest horses in her stable"? The only answer given accords great power to Leudast, and no blame to those who favor him: "In consequence his conceit and arrogance became so great that he applied for the post of Master of the Stables" (Thorpe 314). How does he get this? We are not told; "quo accepto" is the next clause: "In this new appointment he looked down on and slighted everyone." When the Queen dies, Leudast's allegedly ill-gotten money allows him to bribe Charibert; but why doesn't Charibert see what Gregory knows? Now we are told: "Post haec, peccatis populi ingruentibus, comes Turonis destinatur"; "The sins of the people of Tours were immense, and Leudast was well chosen as count of the city." Leudast subsequently participates in pride, theft, and adultery, a metonym of the sins of the community: their sinfulness brings him upon them as just the leader they deserve. In Gregory's understanding (not at all self-effacing, as Martínez-Pizarro suggests) there is an order operating here, shaping events to suit its own purposes, looking ahead to a final re-ordering of things.

Within Gregory's narrative, then, Leudast's death may be understood to stand in for the sins of all. Leudast serves Gregory's narrative as an appropriate scapegoat to contain the violence the Bishop sees within his world. Of course the sacrifice here is literal, not symbolic, and it is performed by unnamed agents of royal law. As Girard argues in *Violence and the Sacred*: "As soon as the judicial system gains supremacy, its machinery disappears from sight. Like sacrifice, it conceals – even as it also reveals – its resemblance to vengeance … In the judicial system the violence does indeed fall on the 'right' victim …" (22). Leudast is socially marginal by his birth as a slave, and marked as well physically by his slit ear – "there was no possibility of concealing this mark on his body," says Gregory – and he is made to stand in for the sins of his fellow citizens, among whom he is not native. Within Gregory's account Leudast fits in broad lines at least Girard's description of the scapegoat: "outsiders of one type or another, the physically or otherwise handicapped …" (*Violent Origins* 87).

As Girard analyzes the issue in *The Scapegoat*: "Each time an oral or written testament mentions an act of violence that is directly or indirectly collective we question whether it includes the description of a social and cultural crisis, that is, a generalized loss of differences (the first stereotype), crimes that 'eliminate differences' (the second stereotype), and whether the identified authors of these crimes possess the marks that suggest a victim … (the third stereotype). The fourth stereotype is violence itself …" (24). Gregory's account of Leudast neatly suggests each of these stereotypes: his career poses a threat to categories of difference, even as the mark on his body keeps the scandal from being more than temporary, and his death contains the crisis. And even as Gregory states that he tried to warn Leudast in the end of the displeasure of the Queen towards him, he concludes the narrative of Leudast's brutal ordeal with words of his own approval, a form of participation: "Sicquae se perfidam agens vitam, iusta morte finivit"; "His life had been one long tale of perfidious talk: so that he met a fitting end" (Thorpe 363). In Gregory's terms, *perfidam* and *iusta*, we hear the authority and the objectivity of the law operating to silence one who would annihilate social distinctions.

Gregory's treatment of the priest Riculf is similar, including the same charges of low social status accompanied by presumption. In a strikingly plain statement, Gregory reveals the mechanics of social definition working themselves out: "The poor fool seems not to have realized that, apart from five, all the other bishops who held their appointment in the see of Tours were blood relations of my family" (321). The other Riculf, the subdeacon, whom Gregory says he could not save from the torture, "tunc" – on the brink of death – "aperuit veritatem et archana doli publice patefecit"; "then he revealed the truth and publicly confessed his secret plotting" (320-21). "Truth" in these words is both *a priori* and by nature hidden, secret; torture brings it out into public light, even as Leudast's *perfidia* are silenced by torture. And the bodies upon which these acts of violence are worked are containers of truth; Leudast's slit ear is the mark of truth upon him, showing outwardly his true social identity, despite his occupation of the rank of count.

In *Torture and Truth*, Page duBois traces "how the logic of our philosophical tradition [in ancient Greece], of some of our inherited beliefs about truth, leads almost inevitably to conceiving of the body of the other as the site from which truth can be produced, and to using violence if necessary to extract the truth" (6). Gregory's *Historiae Francorum* may be read productively from this point of view, including duBois's critical reading of Heidegger's meditation on Plato's *aleithea*: a conception of truth shaped by its privative prefix, yielding "that which is not forgotten," that which must be wrested from concealment, oblivion, darkness – wrested with effort, by violence.

In the relations of Sicharius and Chramnesindus, Auerbach also selected an episode of violence by which he could explore Gregory's representation of the world around him, but rereading Gregory in light of Clifford Flanigan's suggestions of a text as a social act, I see something other than Auerbach's characterization of the *Historiae* as a disordered, if new and vibrant kind of narrative of violence reflecting a disordered and violent society. I see, rather, something useful for Gregory (and historically recurrent) in the ways in which the text performs its representations of social disorder and of seemingly endemic violence. Indeed, his theme is war: "the wars waged by kings against hostile peoples, by martyrs against the heathen and by the Churches against heretics ..." (67), from Cain's role as "the first man to shed his brother's blood and to murder a member of his own family" down to his own day (70) to recount "the muddled and confused order in which these events occurred, the holy deeds of the Saints and the way in which whole races of people were butchered" (103), following the historiographic examples of "Eusebius, Severus, and Jerome [who] mingled together in their chronicles the wars waged by kings and the holy deeds of martyrs" (103). But within this defended disorder, an effort of social ordering is apparent, as I have said, in the apocalyptic sense underlying the whole effort.

Gregory's narrative is located within the double timeframe of mythic salvation history as it is co-extensive with human history. The whole work begins by looking forward to that imminent violence – "the end of the world coming nearer and nearer" (67) – that will make an end to all reprisals and revenges in the revelation of God's just and final war against the wicked. The problem of history for Gregory – mythic, scriptural, and local – is violence. The solution to history, both within history and at its apocalyptic margin, is also violence.[6]

As Girard argues in *Violence and the Sacred*, in a situation of mimetic crisis, whether sacrificial or judicial, "Only violence can put an end to violence, and that is why violence is self-propagating. Everyone wants to strike the last blow ..." (26). The graphic violence in Gregory's text – so much else is not told – displays mechanisms of moral truth and of divine justice, even while such representations both fetishize and conceal violence as a collective instrument of social organization, whose agents are customarily unidentified. Gregory's repeated denunciations of violence are undercut by his inclusion of scenes in which individuals are ritually excluded and eliminated by collective violence. In Judaic and in Christian apocalypticism, as James Earl writes with regard to *Beowulf*, the "ideal structures of experience are not revealed in an absent world, but in the immanent recurring structures of history; the transcendent world is revealed in history itself; God is revealed in the very fabric of our worldly experience" (364). So Gregory's account of Leudast, while it resolves the problem of its anti-social subject who poses a threat to social differences, paradoxically may be read for the ways it empowers him as an instrument of social order in the *History of the Franks*. Leudast, that is to say, is terribly useful to the Bishop's effort to make sense out of his world.

Revisiting Gregory has allowed me to recall some of the learning that Cliff Flanigan made possible. I learned much from him, and though I can hardly imitate him as a reader, a teacher, a writer, a host, or a recruiter for the International Congress on Medieval Studies at Kalamazoo, there is pleasure in the effort, and in remembering. I am still learning from him.

Notes

1. As Wallace-Hadrill remarks in *The Long-Haired Kings*, "The *Historia* is preserved to us in an altogether exceptional number of manuscripts, no less than four belonging to the seventh century" (51).

2. For the Latin text I have used the edition of Henri Omont and Gaston Collon (Paris, 1886-93), and have consulted as well both the earlier edition of J. P. Migne (Paris, 1836), published in the *Patrologiae Cursus Completus* (1844-1903), and the more recent edition of W. Arndt and Bruno

Krusch in the *Monumenta Germaniae Historica* series (Hanover, 1951-69). Translated passages appear here from *Gregory of Tours: The History of the Franks*, translated with an introduction by Lewis Thorpe (Harmondsworth, Middlesex, 1974), where the account of Leudast appears on pages 313-22 and pages 361-3. Thorpe discusses the later chapters as interpolations in his Introduction (26); Goffart (1989) has taken to task this time-worn assumption about the textual history of the *Historiae*.

3. Thierry would seem to borrow this gesture from Gregory, who makes a similar assessment of the priest Riculf, one of the alleged conspirators: "This man had been raised up from very humble beginnings by Bishop Eufronius and had been made archdeacon. When he was promoted to priesthood, he showed his true nature. He was always above himself, boasting and presumptuous" (Thorpe 321).

4. Scherman accounts for the level of local events narrated by citing the precedent chroniclers Gregory names: "Under the influence of Christian teaching fourth- and fifth-century chroniclers had inaugurated a fresh method of historical narrative which slotted local history into biblical history" (276). This influence explains Gregory's decision to begin his history with Adam and Eve, to be sure, but does not explain the selection and style and function of subsequent events, especially local and contemporary ones.

5. A familiar point of reference is the opening of *Beowulf*, where the Scylding dynasty is founded in conquest; later in the poem Hrothulf's displacement of his cousin Hrethric, son of King Hrothgar, is often cited as example of destructive internal rivalry. To say the least in literal terms, the "ins" and "outs" of social identity have not yet been usefully deconstructed in Anglo-Saxon studies.

6. J. M. Wallace-Hadrill also sees in Gregory an underlying belief in retributive violence: "Look through his writings for the view of Gregory of Tours on divine vengeance and it will be found that he visualizes it as nothing less than God's own feud in support of his servants, who can have no other kin … God's vengeance is of the same nature as that of any head of a family or warband. He strikes to kill, to avenge insult – to himself, to his children or to his property. The Frankish churchmen cannot in any other way see *ultio divina* in a society dominated by bloodfeud" (127).

Works Cited

Auerbach, Erich. *Literary Language and Its Public in Late Latin Antiquity and in the Middle Ages*. Trans. Ralph Mannheim. Bollingen Series, 74. New York: Bollingen Foundation, 1965.

—. *Mimesis: The Representation of Reality in Western Literature*. Trans. Willard R. Trask. Princeton: Princeton University Press, 1953.

duBois, Page. *Torture and Truth*. New York: Routledge, 1991.

Earl, James W. "Apocalypticism and Mourning in *Beowulf*." *Thought* 57.3 (1982): 362-70.

Flanigan, C. Clifford. "Liminality, Carnival, and Social Structure: The Case of Late Medieval Biblical Drama." In Kathleen M. Ashley, ed., *Victor Turner and the Construction of Cultural Criticism: Between Literature and Anthropology*. Bloomington: Indiana University Press, 1990.

Girard, René. "Generative Scapegoating." In Robert G. Hamerton-Kelly, ed., *Violent Origins: Walter Burkert, René Girard, and Jonathan Z. Smith on Ritual Killing and Cultural Formation*. Stanford: Stanford University Press, 1987, 73-105.

—. *The Scapegoat*. Trans. Yvonne Freccero. Baltimore: The Johns Hopkins University Press, 1986.

—. *"To Double Business Bound": Essays on Literature, Mimesis, and Anthropology*. Baltimore: The Johns Hopkins University Press, 1978.

—. *Violence and the Sacred*. Trans. Patrick Gregory. Baltimore: The Johns Hopkins University Press, 1977.

Goffart, Walter. *Rome's Fall and After*. Ronceverte, WV: The Hambledon Press, 1989.

Gregory of Tours. *The History of the Franks*. Trans. Lewis Thorpe. Harmondsworth: Penguin, 1974.

James, Edward. *The Franks*. Oxford: Blackwell, 1988.

Martínez-Pizarro, Joaquín Martínez. *A Rhetoric of the Scene: Dramatic Narrative in the Early Middle Ages*. Toronto: University of Toronto Press, 1989.

Omont, Henri and Gaston Collon, eds. *Grégoire de Tours, Histoire des Francs*. Paris, 1886-93.

Scherman, Katharine. *The Birth of France: Warriors, Bishops and Long-Haired Kings*. New York: Random House, 1987.

Thierry, Augustin. *Récits des temps mérovingiens*. Paris: Furne et Ce, Éditeurs, 1862.

—. *Tales of the Early Franks: Episodes from Merovingian History*. Trans. M. F. O. Jenkins. Tuscaloosa: University of Alabama, 1977.

Wallace-Hadrill, J. M. *The Long-Haired Kings*. Medieval Academy Reprints for Teaching, 11. Toronto: University of Toronto Press, 1982.

Waller, Altina. *Feud: Hatfields, McCoys, and Social Change in Appalachia, 1860-1900*. Fred W. Morrison Series in Southern Studies. Chapel Hill: The University of North Carolina Press, 1988.

Wood, Ian. *The Merovingian Kingdoms: 450-751*. London and New York: Routledge, 1993.

Imagining a Medieval Performance:
A Phenomenological Approach
Jesse Hurlbut

𝒯he study of performance is governed by an inherent dualism. On one hand, the enactment of the performance itself constitutes an ephemeral and unique event with strict spatial and temporal limitations. On the other hand, the documentation regarding the event – often in the form of a text – serves to record the experience and extend it beyond the limitations of the immediate performance. This document may be a script, composed prior to the enactment, prescribing roles, dialogue and actions to the performers. The text may also be a post-facto record that memorializes the performance as a historical phenomenon. While some scholarship examines the dramatic event proper, a large branch of performance studies focuses on the documentation and its relationship to the event. Notably, then, a great deal of successful research establishes its arguments and conclusions on the basis of an imagined reality closely drawn from texts, but completely isolated from the original live performance.

Whenever interpreting the textual record of a dramatic event, the reader typically engages in processes and strategies different from those used for reading other kinds of texts. One might compare, for example, the reader's different approaches to J. R. R. Tolkien's imaginative description of a hobbit in narrative fiction, and the didascalia at the beginning of Richard Wagner's *Das Rheingold*. In both texts, the reader is called upon to formulate a composite image based on the elements of the respective descriptions. Tolkien's novel allows readers to envision his fanciful protagonist in many different ways, limited only by the specific details included in the textual description. However, in Wagner's opening scene there is the added challenge of making the description conform to the parameters of a staged event. In fact, the opera begins with the image of water raging in and out to fill the stage. Rhine maidens swim below the surface of the water and sing to Alberich, who hops from rock to crag like a toad. Ultimately, the reader is led to wonder in either a historical mode: "How did they manage to do that on a stage?", or else in an anticipatory mode: "How might one accomplish such feats in an opera house?"

In an attempt to theorize this process of concretization associated with performable texts, Marvin Carlson invokes the models of Wolfgang Iser and Anne Ubersfeld. These theorists view texts as incomplete and the reader as "co-producer of the meaning of a text by creatively filling gaps."[1] For Carlson, applying such theory to performable texts is complicated by the inevitably confused roles of performance text. In other words, a reader concretizes the dramatic text in a different way from the performer of the same text. Both the reader and the performer are different still from the audience, who concretizes the performance in yet another way. Nevertheless, the more one is removed from the original event, the more restricted the options for concretization become. As Erika Fischer-Lichte summarizes, "the difficulties in analyzing a performance … hinge for the most part on the impossibility of preserving it as an artifact."[2] Thus, the historian is reduced to consulting the second- or third-hand documentation that stands in lieu of the artifact proper.

Not all performances are well documented, however. In the absence of eyewitness accounts or scripts, research into the nature of specific dramatic activities may benefit from other records not originally intended to serve the literary historian. Many texts survive, for example, in the financial archives of governing or sponsoring institutions. In some cases, these may provide enough clues to partially reconstruct a lost performance. However, extracting drama from financial ledgers requires a different approach from studying a theatrical script. For instance, dialogue and stage directions are generally not included in the accountant's registers. By contrast, the list of expenses associated with a performance may be particularly complete. In the end, however, a phenomenological reading process converts the incidental archival document into a kind of "drama text" from which the reader can concretize or imagine the original event. Such a process begins by tracking down clues and scraps of evidence, then stringing them together with informed assumptions and associations. To a certain extent, probing the archives for such material resembles the bit-by-bit reconstructive deciphering of an epistolary novel or of a piece of detective fiction. As important as archival records may be for scholars, they necessarily remain an inadequate representation of a given live event. No matter how thoroughly a text may represent its signified, there will always be substantial gaps to be filled by the reader or performer. In many instances, historical records are far from complete and countless dramatic events stand on the brink of oblivion unless research turns up some descriptive record, however fragmentary. In the absence of more complete accounts, it may be possible to postulate, on the basis of experience with analogous documentation and contexts, the potentialities of the historical event. Thus, whatever evidence for a dramatic incident can be established will stand in lieu of the performance itself and become subject to analysis for the purposes of reconstructing the original.

The lacunal nature of these archival resources compels the reader to interpret them on the basis of a combination of textual indications and the reader's own interpolations. The reconstructive nature of the endeavor resembles Iser's model for the reading process. Iser deals specifically with the interaction between text and reader. He describes text as a system of phenomenological processes and concludes:

there must be a place within this system for the person who is to perform the reconstituting. This place is marked by the gaps in the text – it consists in the blanks which the reader is to fill in.... Whenever the reader bridges the gap, communication begins.... Hence the structured blanks of the text stimulate the process of ideation to be performed by the reader on terms set by the text.[3]

As Iser points out, the interaction between the reader and the text is not governed by chance, for it remains specifically determined by the parameters of the document. Thus, in addition to filling gaps in the text, the reader must respond to the effects of sequent sentences on one another: "Every sentence contains a preview of the next and forms a kind of view finder for what is to come; and this in turn changes the 'preview' and so becomes a 'view finder' for what has been read."[4] For Iser, then, reading becomes a process that occurs over time, each sentence meeting or frustrating the readers' expectations and ever invoking a reevaluation of the mental "picture" generated by the text of fiction.

Finally, Iser points out that this concretization or image-building in the reading of fiction cannot be the same as the perception of everyday life, because the knowledge of real events prevents one from imagining them; it is impossible to creatively fill gaps that do not exist:

> [N]o author worth his salt will ever attempt to set the whole picture before his reader's eyes.... If one sees the mountain, then of course one can no longer imagine it, and so the act of picturing the mountain presupposes its absence. Similarly, with a literary text we can only picture things which are not there; the written part of the text gives us the knowledge, but it is the unwritten part that gives us the opportunity to picture things ...[5]

Even though Iser suggests here that the process of reading fiction cannot be applied to the perception of real events, the gaps in historical information created by the passage of time and by the absence of more complete records demand an inferential process similar to the way we read fiction. The main difference between the reconstruction of fiction and that of historical fact is that for the former, the arrangement of gaps is pre-determined by an author who has set out to generate a calculated reaction. Gaps in the historical archives more frequently result from happenstance.

For a practical application of this process to the study of historical drama, this article will examine, step by step, a reconstruction of the ceremonial entry of Charles, Count of Charolais, into Dijon in October 1461. Charles was the sole surviving legitimate son of Philip the Good, and in 1467 he would receive his deceased father's titles and become the duke of Burgundy. Ceremonial entries celebrated the arrival of high-ranking nobility into a city. The day's activities included the decoration of the streets and, notably, the presentation of mime characters on temporary stages along the procession route between the gates of the city and the residential palace or lodging.

To begin with, what does history report regarding the entry of Charles into Dijon? Herman Vander Linden has compiled, on the basis of archival research, enough information from the ducal expense accounts to trace a nearly complete itinerary of the travels of both Duke Philip and his son Charles. According to this itinerary, Charles – who spent most of his life roaming the northern Burgundian possessions in Flanders and Brabant – made a trip to Paris, and then traveled from Paris to Troyes and from Troyes to Dijon, arriving in the evening of Sunday, the 11th of October. The count remained in Dijon for one week, after which he toured the other major cities in Burgundy. By Christmas, he had already completed his visits to these areas and had returned to his father's lands in the north.[6] Not counting the few years immediately following his birth in Dijon, this was Charles's only visit to Burgundy and its capital before becoming duke. Charles returned to Dijon for his first entry as duke only in 1474, seven years after receiving the title and thirteen years after the entry under examination here.

His arrival in Dijon in 1461 was from the northwest, coming from Troyes. The gate through which he entered the city was no doubt Porte Guillaume, a remodeled portion of which is still standing today in downtown Dijon. He presumably followed the direct route (today's Rue de la Liberté) toward his father's palace in the center of town.

No contemporary descriptions of the count's ceremonial entry survive in chronicles or histories. The municipal archives in Dijon, however, contain a dossier labeled "Joyeuses entrées des ducs de Bourgogne à Dijon."[7] In this dossier of about one hundred detached folios, only nine very brief documents relate to this entry. None of these gives a description of the event. The longest, and the one which will be examined here, is a list of money spent by the city for the staged entertainments which were provided. This document is a narrow, ten-folio *cahier* or quire including almost ninety short paragraphs, or items. An edition of the complete text appears at the conclusion of this article. In order to explore Iser's process at work, these items are considered below in the order in which they appear in the document.

In the opening lines of the first paragraph, we read:

> Expenditures made by me, Guillaume Jomart, for the mysteries and plays (*mistieres et jeux*) which were produced in the city of Dijon for the joyful arrival of my lord of Charolais. In order to produce the said mysteries, seven stages of wood were made along the streets.[8]

In the final clauses of this introductory paragraph, we learn that our author, Guillaume Jomart, had been commissioned by the mayor and aldermen of the city to distribute municipal funds for this undertaking.[9] Although we come to this manuscript knowing very little about this entry – the fact that it occurred on a given date and that Charles entered through Porte Guillaume – this first paragraph informs us that there were dramatic presentations and that seven stages were built to accommodate them. On the basis of evidence from other entries, it can be safely suggested that there was one play for each stage, thus, seven plays. It is also probable that there were no speaking roles in these plays, as it is often explicitly stated in the accounts of other entries that the characters described any action through gestures and mime or with text written on panels (*escripteaulx*) attached to the stages.

The first several items in this document help establish a chronology of events both prior to and following the actual celebration. We learn that on the day after Jomart received his charge, Tuesday the 6th of October, the city paid sixteen carpenters and one cart driver a daily wage for loading and transporting some of the wood with which the scaffolds were built. This was apparently the beginning of the preparations for the entry. On Wednesday and Thursday, eighteen carpenters and six unskilled assistants (*menovriers*) continued to transport the wood that had been borrowed from various citizens, and they began working on the stages. On Friday, no mention is made of carting the wood, but the same number of workers devoted the day's labor to the stages. The eighteen carpenters and six helpers completed the platforms on Saturday the 10th by laying down the planks. The assistants also carried poles, and lances (*perches et lances*) to the stages. Nothing in the description reveals whether these last objects served structural or decorative purposes.

Sunday was the day of the entry celebration and goes unmentioned in the logs of this account. Following the entry, however, more municipal funds supported the dismantling of the stages and props. One item unexpectedly discloses a useful detail:

> four good citizens were paid for taking down the two giants and they untied and took down the poles and lances that were on the giants, and gathered the tapestry with which the stage of these giants was covered.[10]

This sudden and unqualified reference to "the two giants" demonstrates how knowledge affects our ability to imagine actual events. The immediate audience to Jomart's text did not have to imagine the giants because of first-hand experience. The medieval accountant assumed that his audience was already familiar with these and other various features of the entry. By contrast, once the collective memory of both the performance itself and the conventions associated with this performance type vanished, the brief mention of giants serves the modern investigator as a springboard for an abstract conceptualization. This casual comment in the record constitutes the first foothold in the reconstruction of the performance: there were two giants on a stage decorated with a tapestry. Although the poles and lances appear to have functioned as stage properties, their exact role remains unspecified. Meanwhile, this all-too-brief indication generates more questions than it resolves. Whom did the giants portray? Does the reference to lances indicate a joust or mock-battle? Were these characters located at the beginning, middle or end of the procession route? Giants are not a common feature of the entries, thus there is little corroborative evidence to supplement our understanding of these characters. Researchers familiar with the representation of giants in modern folk festivals (notably in northern France) may interpolate assumptions about the giants and their role in the dramatics of the political ceremony. To this point in the reading of this document, however, little more can be assumed.

To continue with Jomart's account, the dismantling of the stages took several days to complete. On Monday the 12th, eighteen carpenters and four assistants began taking apart the stages. On Tuesday, Wednesday, and Thursday, sixteen carpenters and six workers divided their time between disassembling the stages and carting the wood they had borrowed back to those who had made the generous donations. They apparently finished the job on Thursday.

The next few paragraphs from our document identify the services of specific individuals regarding the preparations. Four cart drivers received remuneration for the use of their large rigs to transport the wood, planks, poles, and lances. Two carpenters tallied up the damage to all the borrowed wood. Two municipal officers supervised the project and an archer spent six days helping to dispatch the planks for the stages.

Without preface or commentary, we learn in the next section that eight large wooden planks were purchased for depicting the City of Jericho. Another six pine boards were used to give titles (*escripteaulx*) to the plays and were attached to the stages. Other supplies purchased included nails to hang tapestries and drapes for several of the plays. Thick paper and bed sheets were purchased to cover (*housser*) the clubs of the giants and also to help make the City of Jericho. Without a better understanding of the original vocabulary, it is impossible to know whether these last materials were used to make slip-covers or if they were rather shredded to construct properties in *papier-mâché*. Three more wooden planks were purchased to depict the "six clercs desdits geans."[11]

Each of these details adds to the pool of information gathered about this event but gives only tantalizing hints about the dramatic activity that took place on these stages. Thomas le Noir, who sold the wood for Jericho, was also recompensed for three other planks which were "lost." Are we to understand from this word that the boards were misplaced, or were they damaged beyond repair, perhaps in the dramatization of when the walls came tumbling down? Why are there only six boards for the *escripteaulx* of seven stages? What was written on the planks? Who were the six clerks, what was their relationship to the giants, and why are they painted on boards rather than depicted by live performers?

The city also bought several *aulnes* of cloth for various costumes.[12] Eight *aulnes* of black and violet cotton clothed two characters named Jaquot Quenot and Maistre Pierre le Bossu. Seven *aulnes* of yellow and violet cloth became turbans (*bourrelés*) for the giants. Two fool's costumes required six *aulnes* of brown, yellow, and violet. More black and yellow cloth was added to the bill in order to finish the costumes of Jaquot Quenot and the giants.

This same budget paid for nails, ropes, pulleys, and hooks. One of these references reads: *for nails used to hang the drapes above the stage that was in front of the court.*[13] This minor note implies, almost accidentally, that one of the stages was built on the square in front of the ducal palace. This raises the question of the location of each of the other stages along the procession route. In a typical entry, there were stages or characters at both the city gates and the conclusion of the entry, in front of the palace or residence. Other performances took place along the route between these two points. The position and content of the plays potentially took on political significance.

In this case, the mayor himself took interest in the arrangements. Jomart records a reimbursement to the mayor for hosting a meeting to discuss the final plans for the plays. The meeting included dinner and a visit to each of the stage sites.

Each of the stages is mentioned by number in the next sequence of items. The organizers of each stage received a subvention which funded the costs for materials as well as a food allowance for participants. In itemizing the amounts allocated to each stage, other valuable information is revealed. For instance, the first stage was located just outside Porte Guillaume. On the second stage, there was a representation of the Tower of Jerusalem. The organizer of the fourth stage used city resources to pay for two masses at the Church of Notre Dame. This suggests that the organizers were associated with that parish and perhaps that their stage was located in front of the church.[14] This would have been a small digression for the count's cavalcade, but assumes that the last four stages were bunched together in a relatively small space. The sixth stage received nearly double the funding of the other stages. The brief annotation mentions only that the stage included a donkey. We learn in a later item that a giant meat pie was on the same stage with the donkey. The seventh stage, otherwise unqualified, received about half what the other stages received. This was probably the stage at the duke's palace, mentioned above.

In the following twenty-six items, individual citizens were reimbursed for wood they had lent and which had been either cut, damaged, or lost. Ten of these items specify that the borrowed wood had been mortised. While some of Guillaume Fromont's donated poles were lost, others were returned with holes drilled in them. Such descriptions, as imprecise as they may be, are of interest, even if they can only hint at the construction technique of the stages.

According to the document, some individuals received remuneration for special skills. Several people loaded and carried wood. One anonymous soul spent two days carting manure away from the chapel square near the ducal palace. Of particular interest is the employment of the various craftsmen or artists who provided stage props. We learn, for example, that Pierrenot Odin the wickerworker made four clubs and the turbans for the giants. Jehan Changenet, a painter, contributed in several areas. He drew the City of Jericho and nailed it together. He repainted and restored the two heads of the giants.[15] He also covered and painted the giants' clubs and depicted the mysterious six clerics of the giants. Changenet also designed ten new diadems and repainted and added gold to five others. Again, we do not know which characters wore these crowns, but the numbers alone help establish a sense of proportion for the drama. Finally, he painted seventeen *escripteaulx* for the stages, twelve on paper, and five on whitewashed pine boards.[16] With this many *escripteaulx* for seven stages, there would have been enough to put at least two on each stage.

Only at this point near the end of the document do we learn that one citizen, Hugues Millecot, was hired to dress the giants like Turks. The depiction of Turks in the civic celebrations following the Turkish invasion of Constantinople in 1453 necessarily served to remind the court of Duke Philip's intention to organize a Crusade. This clue may also serve to remind the reader of the elaborate entertainments at the Feast of the Pheasant, where the Duke formally announced his intention to mount a crusade. There too, a giant dressed as a Turk played an important role in the drama. With this additional information in mind, the reader is forced to reevaluate all previous assumptions about the giants.

In the last few items, two minor but colorful details surface regarding the plays. Four children at the nearby chapel wore hats with violets. Costumes were made for four other performers who shared the sixth stage with the donkey. The itemization of expenses draws simply to a close with no further explanation or description.

The document concludes with a statement by Jehan Rabustel, who verifies Jomart's description and calculations and certifies them to be accurate. The grand total of expenses adds up to 99 *francs* 10 *gros* and 3 *blancs*.[17] Given the carpenter's daily wage of 2 *gros* and the cost of 5 *blancs* for one *aulne* of black cloth, the proportionate value of certain expenses becomes more apparent. The cart driver's daily wage (with rental of his cart) was 8 *gros*. Thirteen of Denisot de Mastot's lances were lost and he was reimbursed at the rate of 6 *blancs* each for a total of 19 and one half *gros*. The mayor's dinner cost just over 21 *gros*. Five of the seven stages received between 2 and 3 *francs* (24-36 *gros*) as a municipal subvention. By far, the greatest single expense in this ledger is the payment of 6 *escuz d'or* (99 *gros*) to Jehan Changenet the painter.

In the end, the restoration of this triumphal entry remains extremely fragmentary. Nevertheless, the discovery of each new dramatic element in the terse language of the accountant increases our overall understanding of the event. Layer upon layer, each bit of information causes the previous ones to be reconsidered, while inviting revised preconceptions of all the forthcoming layers. Many large gaps remain, but several pieces may yet be uncovered. The present study is limited to Jomart's *cahier* – certainly the richest source of information available on this entry. Within the framework thus far established, additional clues individually provided by other documents will make more sense.

For example, a single folio in the Dijon archives signed on January 2, 1462, articulates additional expenses not calculated in the original report.[18] One of the three items in this document granted 8 *escuz* paid to Freminet le Masier, an armorer who had lent several suits of armor (*harnas a armer*) for the production of the plays. The armor was damaged and ruined, thus incurring the largest expense of the entire entry. In isolation, this detail reveals relatively little about the entertainments for Count Charles. But in the more complete context established here, one easily imagines the suits of armor put to good use in a mock battle of Jericho or a mini-crusade against giant Turks.

Interestingly enough, Jomart's job as tax collector and accountant consisted of unambiguously recording the municipal expenditures on this occasion. His document originally purported to elucidate every relevant detail without omission. Over time, however, the concerns of his audience have changed, thus transforming the very function of his document. The modern reader finds only skeletal remains upon which to base an understanding of the past. The appreciation of this once comprehensive document now heavily relies on the fruits of the imagination.

Notes

1. Marvin Carlson, *Theatre Semiotics: Signs of Life*, Bloomington, IN, 1990, p. 11.
2. Erika Fischer-Lichte, *The Semiotics of Theater*, [transl.] Jeremy Gaines & Doris L. Jones, Bloomington, IN, 1992, p. 172.
3. Wolfgang Iser, *The Act of Reading: A Theory of Aesthetic Response*, London, 1978, p. 169.
4. Wolfgang Iser, "The Reading Process: A Phenomenological Approach," in Jane P. Tompkins [ed.], *Reader-Response Criticism: From Formalism to Post-Structuralism*, Baltimore, 1980, p. 54.
5. Iser, "The Reading Process," pp. 57-8; see also Iser, *The Act of Reading*, p. 140.
6. Herman Vander Linden, *Itinéraires de Philippe le Bon, duc de Bourgogne (1419-1467) et de Charles, comte de Charolais (1433-1467)*, Bruxelles, 1940, pp. 432-6.
7. Archives Municipales de Dijon [= Arch. Mun. Dijon], I.6.
8. Idem, I.6, (cahier), fol. 1^r. Translations are my own.
9. The minutes of Jomart's meeting with the town council also survive in Arch. Mun. Dijon, I.6 (folio dated October 5, 1461). Specifically, Jomart was charged to collect a special tax from three parishes in order to fund the stages and plays (*misteres et personnages*) as well as a gift for the count.
10. Arch. Mun. Dijon, I.6, (cahier), fol. 2^r.
11. Idem, I.6, (cahier), fol. 5^r.
12. An *aulne* of cloth is roughly 1.20 meters.
13. Arch. Mun. Dijon, I.6, (cahier), fol. 5^r.
14. The fact that there were seven parishes in Dijon at this time invites one to speculate that each parish was responsible for one stage.
15. Because this was restoration work, we can assume that these heads had been used before, but we have no indication of what those occasions may have been. It is possible that the heads were remnants of the entertainments for the visit of Philip the Good in 1454. At that time, the city represented a three-headed Goliath and a giant Holofernes. See Arch. Mun. Dijon, I.6, folio dated December 13, 1454.
16. One wonders what happened to the sixth pine board purchased for the *escripteaulx* mentioned above.
17. The monetary system implemented in this document consists of the following units:
    1 *escuz d'or* = 66 *blancs*
    1 *franc* = 12 *gros* = 48 *blancs*
    1 *gros* = 4 *blancs*
    1 *blanc* = 3 *engroignes*
18. Arch. Mun. Dijon, I.6, folio dated January 2, 1461.

Appendix[*] Archives Municipales de Dijon, Dossier I.6, Cahier
20 octobre 1461

[f. 1^r] Despense faite par moy, Guillaume Jomart, pour les mistieres et jeux qui ont esté fais en la ville de Dijon pour la joyeuse venue de Monseigneur de Charolois. Pour faire lesquelz mistieres ont esté fais sept chaffaulx de bois du travers des rues. A laquelle despense faire j'ay esté commis par Messeigneurs les Maieur et Eschevins de la ville et Commune de Dijon comm'il appert par deliberation faite du ve jour d'octobre mil iiij c lxj.

Premierement
Pour seze journees de charpentiers qui le vj^e jour d'octobre ovrerent a chargier une portion du bois duquel l'on a fais les chaffaulx, chacune journee au pris de deux gros, pour ce **ij francs viij gros**

A Arnoul Bouguellet qui charria une portion dudit bois dés environ dix heures du matin dudit jour, pour ce **iiij gros**

[f. 1^v] A dix huit charpentiers qui le vij^e jour dudit mois chargerent une portion dudit bois en pluseurs lieux ou l'on l'avoit emprunté et firent une portion des chaffaulx, chacune journee au pris de deux gros, pour ce **iij francs**

A six menovriers qui cedit jour ont aidier a chargier et deschargier ledit bois **vj gros**

A dix huit charpentiers qui le viij^e jour dudit mois chargerent et deschargerent une portion dudit bois et ovrerent a faire lesdits chaffaulx, pour ce **iij francs**

A six menovriers qui cedit jour aidirent ausdits charpentiers, pour ce **vj gros**

A xviij charpentiers qui le ix^e jour dudit mois ovrerent a faire lesdits chaffaulx, chacune journee audit pris de deux gros, pour ce **iij francs**

A six menovriers qui cedit jour ovrerent avec lesdits charpentiers, pour ce **vj gros**

[fol 2^r] A dix huit charpentiers qui le xe jour dudit mois assovisserent de faire lesdits chaffaulx, pour ce **iij francs**

A six menovriers qui cedit jour aidirent ausdits charpentiers a asseoir les ays et pourter les perches et lances, pour ce **vj gros**

---

[*] This edition incorporates a minimum degree of intervention. Proper nouns have been capitalized, abbreviations have been expanded, *i* and *j* have been interchanged to reflect modern usage (except in roman numerals). Punctuation, elision, and occasional diacritics are intended to assist the modern reader. Folio numbers are indicated in square brackets.

A Thevenin Bidault, Thevenot Galois et deux aultres ovriers qui pour leurs peines d'avoir dessendus les deux geans et desloirent et dessenderent les perches et lances qui estoient sur lesdits geans et recullirent la tapisserie dont estoit couvert le chaffaulx d'iceulx geans, pour ce **vj gros**

A dix huit charpentiers qui le lundi xij^e dudit mois ovrerent a despecer lesdits chaffaulx chacune journee, au pris de deux gros, pour ce **iij francs**

A quatre menovriers qui cedit jour aidirent ausdits charpentiers, pour ce **iiij gros**

[f. 2^v] A seze charpentiers qui le mardi suigvent ovrerent a despecer lesdits chaffaulx a chargier et deschargier ledit boisés lieux ou l'on l'avoit prins, pour ce **ij francs viij gros**

A six menovriers qui cedit jour aidirent ausdis charpentiers, pour ce **vj gros**

A seze charpentiers qui le mercredi suigvent ovrerent comme dessus, pour ce **ij francs viij gros**

A six menovriers qui cedit jour aidirent ausdits charpentiers, pour ce **vj gros**

A seze charpentiers qui le juedi suigvent assovisserent de despecer et ramener ledit bois, pour ce **ij francs viij gros**

A six menovriers qui cedit jour aidirent ausdits charpentiers, pour ce **vj gros**

[f. 3^r] A Guiot Taillier pour huit journees faites de son harnois a trois chevaulx a mener et remener une portion du bois, ays, perches et lances dont l'on a fais lesdits chaffaulx, chacune journee au pris de huit gros, pour ce **v francs iiij gros**

A Arnoul Bouguellet pour trois journees de son harnois qui a mené et ramené une portion des ays, perches et lances pour lesdits chaffaulx, pour ce **xviij gros**

A Pierreaul de la Croix pour sept journees de son harnois a trois chevaulx qui a charrié, mené et remené une portion du bois desdits chaffaulx, chacune journee au pris qui dessus, pour ce **iiij francs viij gros**

A Joffroy Mairet pour quatre journees de son harnois a trois chevaulx qui a semblablement chargié, mené et remené une portion dudit bois, chacune journee au pris qui dessus, pour ce **ij francs viij gros**

[f. 3^v] A Guillemot Michelin et Jehan Lomme pour une journee qu'ilz ont vacqué a tauxer le bois et perches qui ont esté rompus, coppés, mortaisiés et gastés, pour ce **iiij gros**

A Jehan Paleffroy, Sergent de la maierie, pour huit journees par luy faites a estre avec les charpentiers et harnois, chacune journee au pris de six blans, pour ce **j franc**

A Girard Pauserot, Sergent, qui semblablement a vacqué cinq jours entiers comme ledit Jehan, pour ce **vij gros demi**

A Jehan Patin, Archier, pour six journees par luy faites a chargier, deschargier, mener, remener et marquer les ays qui ont esté mises sur lesdits chaffaulx, chacune journee au pris de deux gros, pour ce **j franc**

[f. 4ʳ] A Thomas le Noir pour huit grandes ays de sapin desquelles l'on a fait la cité de Jherico, pour ce **xvj gros**

Audit Thomas pour trois ais qui luy ont esté perdues, pour ce **ij gros**

A Maistre Nicolas le Bourguinon pour six aultres ais de sapin sur lesquelles l'on a fais les escripteaulx qui estoient devant lesdits chaffaulx, pour ce **vj gros**

Pour cinq linxeulx qui ont esté emploiés tant a housser les voles et massues des geans comme a faire ladite cité de Jherico, pour ce **x gros**

Pour cloux emploiés tant a faire ladite cité comme a tandre les tapisseries et draps sur pluseurs chaffaulx et en aultres ovraiges, pour ce **vj gros x engroingnes**

[f. 4ᵛ] Pour trois quahiers de gros papier a housser, pour ce **iij blancs**

Pour ung quahier d'aultre bon papier **ij blancs**

Pour huit aulnes de toille noire et violette pour faire les habis de Jaquot Quenot et Maistre Pierre le Bossu, pour ce **x gros**

Pour sept aulnes de toille violette et jaulne pour faire les bourrelés des deux geans pour ce **vij gros j blanc**

Pour une piece de vin despensé par les charpentiers en l'ostel Pierre Cornille en chargeant le bois et pour une aultre piece et ung pain pour ceulx qui dessendirent les deux geans, pour ce **xiij engroingnes**

Pour six aulnes de toille marron violette et jaulne pour faire deux habis de foulz **vj gros iij blancs**

Pour deux aulnes de toille noire baillee a Jaquot Quenot pour assovy son habit, pour ce **ij gros demi**

[f. 5ʳ] Pour trois aulnes de toille jaulne baillie a Pierrenot le vannier pour assovy les bourrelés des geans, pour ce **iij gros**

A Monsseigneur le Maire qu'il a despensé en pluseurs menues parties, tant pour le disné fait en son hostel a faire la conclusion des jeux come en visitant ou l'on feroit les chaffaulx, pour ce **xxj gros x engroingnes**

Pour trois ais de soul desquelles l'on a fait les clers des geans **ix blancs**

A Guiot Martenot pour huit journees de luy et de son varlet faite a faire la cité de Jherico et les six clers desdits geans, pour ce **xvj gros**

Pour cloux emploiés a tandre les draps dessus l'eschaffault estant devant la court **j blanc**

Pour despense faite par Colin Malart a tandre et mectre a point [f. 5ᵛ] le chaffault dehors la Porte Guillaume tant pour despense de bouche come en cloux et cordes, pour ce **ij francs xj gros**

Pour despense de bouche faite ou second chaffault par Pierre Angelin et Anthoine du Bois et pour les estouffes de la tour de Jherusalem en ce non comprins les vacations desdits Pierre et Anthoine, pour ce **xxviij gros x engroingnes**

Pour despense de bouche faite ou iijᵉ chaffault par messire Girard Poiret **xxv gros vij engroingnes**

Pour despense faite ou iiijᵉ chaffault par messire Jehan Jovy comprins deux messes qu'il a fait dire en son lieu a Nostre Dame **ij francs ix gros viij engroingnes**

Pour despense faite ou vᵉ chaffault par Jehan de Chalon et Ninceaul Bertin, pour ce **ij francs viij gros ij engroingnes**

[f. 6ʳ] Pour despense faite ou vjᵉ chaffault ou estoit l'asne **iiij francs j blanc**

Pour despense faite ou vijᵉ chaffault par messire Bauldot Villpenet, pour ce **xj gros viij engroingnes**

A Jehan de Garongne sairment pour xviij croichetz et xviij bernelles qu'il a faites et mises és pans de la cité de Jherico pour icelle assembler, pour ce **iiij gros demi**

Tauxe de bois gasté a faire lesdits chaffaulx faite par Guillemot Michelin et Jehan Lomme charpentiers A Hugues le Noiset pour bois qui a esté mortaisié et roingnié et és aucunes pieces a eu des espis, pour ce **iiij gros**

A Julien Bien Monte pour deux pieces de bois qui ont esté dommaigees, pour ce **j gros**

[f. 6ᵛ] A Jehan de Chenges pour son bois qui a esté dommaigié **ij gros**

A Nicolas Raillart pour semblable cause **ij gros demi**

Au Maire d'Auxonne pour pluseurs pieces de bois qui ont esté mortaisees **iiij gros demi**

A Jehan Pevisse pour semblable cause **vj blancs**

A Pierre Cornille pour une piece rompue et bois mortaisié **ij gros demi**

A Guillaume Chameron pour bois coppé et mortaisé **ij gros**

A Jehan Monnet pour pluseurs pieces de bois tres fort dommaigees **vj gros**

A Girard Gelenote pour bois mortaisié **vj blancs**

A Hugues Croichot pour bois mortaisié **iij gros**

[f. 7^r] A Humbert David pour une grosse piece de bois qui a esté mise en trois troux **ij gros**

A Pierre Aingueaul pour pluseurs pieces de bois qui ont esté tresfort mortaisees **vj gros**

Au Miroleur pour pluseurs pieces de bois qui ont esté mortaisees **iiij gros**

A Hugues de Longchamp pour semblables pieces de bois tresfort dommaigees, pour ce **iij gros**

A Estienne de Mastot pour pluseurs perches de thillot qui ont esté les unes perdues et les aultres roingniés et percees, pour ce **vj gros**

A Denisot de Mastot pour le dommaige que l'on luy a fait en pluseurs perches de thillot, pour ce **ij gros**

[f. 7^v] A luy pour treze lances qui ont esté perdues, chacune lance au pris de six blancs, pour ce **xix gros demi**

A luy pour ung boisseaul duquel l'on a fait le pasté qui estoit devant l'asne, pour ce **vj blancs**

A Guillaume Fromont pour le dommaige qu'il a eu en pluseurs perches de genesvre qui ont esté perdues et les autres pertusees, pour ce **vj blancs**

A Estienne Lespolot pour bois mortaisié et dommaigé **j gros**

A Jehan Changenet paintre pour ses peines et estouffes mises a faire et trassier la cité de Jherico, icelle cloer, assembler avec l'archier et paindre, pour avoir repaint et reffait les deux testes des geans, avoir fait oussees et paintes [f. 8^r] leurs deux massues et voles, avoir estaintes les pointes desdites massues, ensemblé les six clers de bois, pour avoir fait dix diadaimmes tout neuf et en avoir redoré et repaint cinq aultres, pour avoir fait xij escripteaulx de grosses lettres sur papier et cinq autres qui estoient escrips sur ais de sapin qui ont esté blanchies par dessus, et avoir pourtrait les six clerfz desdits geans, pour ce **vj escuz**

A Hugues Millecot pour les peines de luy et de ceulx qui ont aidié a habillir les deux geans en façon de turcqz et pour leurs despens fais en faisant lesdites vacations, pour ce **x gros**

A Denisot de Mastot pour quatre perches de thillot qui ont esté perdues, pour ce **ij gros demi**

[f. 8ᵛ] A luy pour seze polies qui ont esté perdues **iiij gros**

A Jehan Lourdellot cordier pour xij trais de charrue quatre pieces de corde lampere et une autre [?] et aultres deliés cordelles, pour ce **xiij gros**

A Jehan Colibet cordier pour lixes **iiij gros j engroingnes**

Pour quatre chappeaulx de violectes achectés pour les quatre enfans de la chappelle: **iiij gros**

A Pierrenot Odin, Vannier, pour ses peines d'avoir fait quatre massues pour les geans ensemble deux bourreletz, les avoir portés dés l'ostel Guillemot Chambellain jusques en l'ostel du Mireur, les avoir dressiés sur l'eschaffault et iceulx remis en pieces et les avoir repourtés en l'ostel dudit Mireur, pour ce **iiij francs**

[f. 9ʳ] Pour pluseurs ays que l'on avoit empruntees qui ont esté les unes perdues et les autres fandues et rompues, pour ce **vij gros demi**

A trois menovriers qui le samedi xᵉ jour d'octobre aidirent a pourter les perches, lances et autres choses neccessaires és chaffaulx, pour ce **iij gros**

Pour cloux achectés par Jehan Gueneaul et emploiés a tandre les draps sur les chaffaulx, pour ce **ij gros**

Au monde coustumé pour la façon de quatre habis de toille, tant de foul que aultres, pour le chaffault de l'asne, pour ce **ix gros demi**

Pour cloux achectés par Nicolas de Dempmartin pour tandre les draps et tapisserie sur lesdits chaffaulx, pour ce **j gros**

Pour deux journees d'ung harnois qui a charrié et mené hors de la [f. 9ᵛ] ville les bourbes et fumiers qui estoient en la place devant la chappelle, chacune journee au pris de six gros, pour ce **j franc**

Je, Jehan Rabustel, clerc procureur de la ville et commune de Dijon certiffie[§] a vous mes trés honnorés Seigneurs Messeigneurs les Maieur et Eschevins de ladite ville et commune que par vostre ordonnance et par deliberation sur ce faite és jours declarés en ce petit kaier et cy devant escrips j'ay, entre aultres charges que m'avés donnees pour le fait des misteres qui ont esté fais et joués a la joyeuse venue de nostre tresredoubté Seigneur Monseigneur de Charrolois et bien souvant en la presence de vous Monseigneur le Maire, esté present avec Guillaume Jomart qui a prins et fait provision de ovriers et matieres cy devant bien au long declareez chacune en l'article dont il fait mention iceulx assés au long visites et conteroles et tellement que jusques au samedi x^e jour de ce mois que je fus malade j'ay veu et sceu tout le contenu esdits articles estre [f. 10^r] vray dont la despense veue et cartulee monte a la somme de quatre vins dix neuf frans, dix gros, trois blans, laquelle despense ledit Guillaume a conduite et faite selon le contenu esdits articles. En tesmoing de ce, j'ay signé ceste presente certiffication escripte au darrein d'iceulx kaier et articles le xxe jour du mois d'octobre l'an mil quatre cens soixante et ung.   Rabustel

---

[§] D. cert certiffie a

The *Miracle of the Pregnant Abbess*: Refractions of the Virgin Birth

Eric T. Metzler

The *Miracle of the Pregnant Abbess* figures as one of many popular stories of the miracles performed by the Virgin Mary that found its way into a wide variety of genres, languages, and literary forms beginning in the twelfth century. Some of the story's earliest occurrences, for example, appear in collections of miracles of the Virgin such as William Adgar's *Le Gracial*, set in rhymed Anglo-Norman verse, and a Latin prose version, falsely attributed to an Austrian monk, Potho, whose influence was particularly widespread in German-speaking lands.[1] The miracle enjoyed popularity through the Middle Ages with many versions dating from the thirteenth, fourteenth, and fifteenth centuries. In some instances, the tale even circulated beyond the Middle Ages into early modernity. In addition to its lengthy history, the *Pregnant Abbess* enjoyed a wide geographical range, from Northern England to Austria and from Galicia to Ethiopia, occurring in Latin as well as several vernacular languages.[2] As the tale's broad dissemination might suggest, it was also set in several genres, including exempla, sermons, legends, miracle collections, lyric, long poems, encyclopedias, and dramatic productions.[3]

Because of the tremendous scope of historical, geographical, linguistic, generic, and formal aspects of *The Pregnant Abbess*, versions differ in detail and length, sometimes significantly. However, central to each is the initial sexual dalliance of the abbess, the conception of a male child, and the face-saving miracle wrought by the Virgin Mary, restoring the abbess to her virginal pre-maternal state. From this short description alone, one can imagine that the *Miracle of the Pregnant Abbess* offers a rich ground for various interpretive moves. Robert L. A. Clark, for example, studies the tale through a Turnerian lens, examining the liminality of the anti-structural miracle sequence which allows for the breakthrough of the holy. John Boswell, in his well-known study of child abandonment, uses the *Pregnant Abbess* briefly as part of his analysis of how literary works can inform the historian of social realities. Still others have studied the coeval Iberian versions by Alfonso X and Gonzalo de Berceo (cited in notes 1 and 2) using semiotic analysis, typological analogy, or feminist approaches as methodologies, arriving at interesting interpretive conclusions.[4] In this paper, however, I would like to investigate the way the tale links the abbess typologically to the Virgin Mary by refracting *the* Virgin Birth, that is, by projecting a similitude to Mary's mythical parturition of Jesus and locating it somewhere on the continuum between reflection and distortion. For while Mary's miraculous intervention propels the abbess into the symbolic economy of the Virgin Birth, conferring a singular grace on mother and child, it also restates the inseparable link between fallen sexuality and motherhood, whose signs must be entirely erased from the abbess's body prior to her spiritual rehabilitation.

The version of the *Pregnant Abbess* from the Lille processional plays (see synopsis in appendix) offers a special opportunity for scholars because we know a considerable amount about its performative context as well as its source, which the text itself designates as Vincent of Beauvais's *Speculum Historiale*.[5] Comparing the two versions, separated by some two hundred years, is of particular interest vis-à-vis the typological identifications between Mary and the abbess because the later version delineates and intensifies the connections, suggesting a conscious intent on the part of the playwright to fashion the abbess as a type of Mary.

First instituted in 1270 and continuing for over five hundred years, the annual Grand Procession of Lille honored a small statue of the Virgin Mary called Notre Dame de la Treille which had survived a church fire and become associated with several civic miracles. Dramatic presentations, mostly of biblical stories, were added to the procession during the fourteenth century and continued to be performed throughout the fifteenth century. The plays, seventy-two of which have been preserved in a luxury manuscript, enjoyed broad community support since so many civic groups had a hand in their production. The playwrights of the various dramas seem to have been clerks from the collegial church of St. Pierre in Lille, while the plays were performed by young men of various neighborhood associations, small club-like organizations associated with the various districts of the City of Lille. The Bishop of Fools, elected during the previous octave of Epiphany, organized the dramatic presentations, and prizes were underwritten jointly by the Duke of Burgundy and the City of Lille. Hence, the Lille plays enjoyed the support of both church and city, nobility and commonalty.[6]

The *Pregnant Abbess* figures as the only miracle play in the collection, an astonishing fact, considering the popularity and availability of Marian miracles by the fifteenth century. Situating the comparison of the playwright's dramatic representation to its source in the context of the play's performance and social milieu can help us understand – or at least to speculate – why the Lille playwright added elements which increase both the focus on the Virgin Mary and her connection to the audience. By fortifying the way the *Miracle of the Pregnant Abbess* reduplicates the Virgin Birth, the playwright is able to emphasize Mary's power as miracle worker and to honor her as the site of one of Christianity's premier miracles. The increased connection between both miraculous births thus underscores Mary's decidedly prominent position as paragon of Christian motherhood in the Lille play, for it shows how a woman can be virgin and mother at the same time. In addition, emphasizing Mary's salvific power tied in well with the Procession, which purported to celebrate that power, in this instance as located in the small statue.

Turning to the play itself and its source, let us begin by examining the details of the miracle sequence. In both Vincent's *Speculum* and in the Lille play, the abbess is delivered of her child after falling asleep (*obdormiuit*; *se endormi*), suggesting effortless childbirth.[7] In the Lille version, however, the playwright develops the birthing sequence a step further in terms of ease for the abbess. At the critical moment, when Mary performs the miracle, Vincent writes "*tunc duobus Angelis astantibus praecepit eam prolis onere, quo grauabatur, exonerare, & cuidam eremitae in vicino posito deferre*" [and then she told the two angels who were standing by to deliver her of the burden of her progeny which weighed her down and to bear it away to a certain hermit living nearby]. In the Lille version, however, the Prologue character narrates a much more detailed account:

> Et a tant
> la mere du roy tout puissant
> – et deux angeles qui resambloient
> deux jovencheaux aconpaignoient –
> a l'abbesse lors se apparu.
> Et conme orez en nostre ju,
> a son besoing le conforta;
> car sans doleur elle enffanta,
> et fu son honneur bien gardé. (ll. 563-71)

[At that moment the mother of the almighty king – and two angels who looked like young men accompanied her – appeared to the abbess. And as you will hear in our play, she comforted the abbess[8] in her hour of need; for she gave birth without feeling pain, and her honor was kept intact.]

While the Latin remains silent about the nature of the birth, the French version specifies that the abbess gives birth *painlessly* and that her honor is kept intact. The proximity of these ideas strongly suggests that the abbess's virginity is already restored *while* she is giving birth: like Mary, she is a virgin mother *in partu*.

In addition, in both versions it is discovered that the abbess is without any visible sign of pregnancy: "*nullumque in ea signum vteri praegnantis deprehendentes ...*" [(the angels), perceiving no sign on her of a pregnant womb]; "*la bonne religïeuse / est pure, chaste et vertueuse / et n'a point en son corps enffant*" (ll. 721-23) [this good abbess is pure and chaste and has not even a hint of a child in her body]. These statements indicate that the abbess's belly is demonstrably flat, and hence that her womb is empty. The Lille playwright, however, adds a matron to the cast and creates an exchange between her and the bishop's clerks, indicating a gynecological examination beyond the mere exterior inspection executed by the clerks in Vincent's version. In the play, therefore, postpartum virginity becomes verifiable fact, not just outward appearance. Thus, in both the Lille play and in Mary's Virgin Birth, both mothers retain their virginity *in partu* and *post partum*, and the lapserian punishment of pain is dissociated from childbirth.

The remarkable resemblance of the miracle Mary performs to the religious myth of Virgin Birth suggests a popular response to the age-old Christian curiosity about an event that was simultaneously necessary and impossible. On the one hand, Christianity demanded belief in the Virgin Birth as literal reality and not merely symbolic myth; on the other hand, conception requires sexual intercourse. Hence, Christian scholars from Justin Martyr in the second century onward have argued the details of the Virgin Birth, defending it logically and illogically – sometimes to the point of comedy – in order to justify its occurrence.[9] This keen interest over the centuries in the impossible necessity of Mary's unique parturition strongly suggests that Christians in general have continued to wonder just how Jesus could be born of a mother whose virginity was maintained before, during, and after birth.

As a cultural production in many forms, the *Miracle of the Pregnant Abbess* responds to this quandary of faith by projecting a similitude of Mary's parturition onto the abbess's. Here the audience sees a realized interpretive model of Mary's special case: the details of a birth where the mother remains miraculously physically virginal during and after parturition. Admittedly, this representation explains the problem tautologically: it returns a supernatural question (How could a woman give birth and keep her virginity?) with a supernatural answer (Mary works a miracle). Yet there is a crucial difference: the abbess is not a mythic figure of the past but a contemporary of the audience. Hence, the drama brings the impossible Virgin Birth into the here and now of the audience's world. It thematizes and realizes the Virgin Birth so that the audience may actually imagine how at least some aspects of the impossible but necessary might occur. In its realization of the Virgin Birth, the play also fashions the abbess, an ordinary woman, after the Virgin Mary, whose cult grew to tremendous popularity through the High and Late Middle Ages because of her status as paragon of chaste motherhood. She brought together the mutually exclusive categories of motherhood and virginity, the former embracing sexuality and fertility, the latter denying both. Mary seemed to project the extremely admirable image of the woman who could have the impossible all in the Christian spiritual economy: participation in the unique power to bring forth life and at the same time absolute sexual containment, on which the church placed the highest premium.[10]

In addition to the typological links between the abbess and her benefactress situated in the miracle sequence, the special status of both women's children links the women typologically. The miraculous parturition of the abbess's child serves to mark him as bestowed with grace, as when the bishop's clerk remarks, while looking at the child, "*Helas, le enfanchon, / il est de tresbelle fachon / et bien compossé par nature*" (ll. 861-63) [My what a handsome little baby; he is so well formed by nature]. In addition to his physical beauty, the child is graced with piety and righteousness, as we learn at the end of the play:

> Et chilz en son lieu succeda,
> ou de parolles et de vie
> le nom de la vierge Marie
> et sa glore tousjours prescha,
> magnifia et exaucha;

> car ainsy le porte le histoire.
> Samblablement il fist encoire
> d'autre grans fais, conme lisons
> par escript ou trouvé l'avons,
> mais nous en taisons maintenant.
> (ll. 896-905)

[The young man succeeded him in the bishopric, where in word and in deed he praised and exalted the name of the Virgin Mary; he also performed many other virtuous acts, as we read what we have found written, but we will pass them over in silence.]

Though the infant boy is not of course conferred with divinity, the text makes it clear that he has been smiled down upon by the heavens and that he naturally deserves to occupy a position of ecclesiastical power. The miracle worked on his birth by the Virgin Mary thus seems to allow him to partake in the miracle as well, gaining special holiness and grace from the event.

In one unique version of the *Pregnant Abbess*, found in the otherwise unknown Henmann of Bologna's *Viaticum narrationum*, the child's unique holiness is emphasized still more as the *Pregnant Abbess* miracle is conflated with a second miracle of Bonus, the abbess's adult child, who leads an extremely holy life and is favored by Mary. In a dream, Bishop Bonus sees the Virgin Mary splendidly arrayed, sitting on the altar along with the accouterments for mass "*quasi manibus angelorum facta*" [as if they were made by the hands of angels]. Bonus uses these special vessels and vestments as a token of the Virgin Mary's favor since it was she who delivered him as a baby from the abbess and has blessed him with holiness and grace. When Bonus dies, however, and his successor, who is not evil, only "multo minor in devocione et gracia" [less by far in devotion and grace], attempts to use the holy items, he comes to an immediate and unfortunate end: "*Qui statim ut preparamenta tetigit ad induendum, cadens exspiravit*" [Immediately as he touched the accouterments to put them on, he fell down and died]. Although Bonus is not divine as is Jesus, the conflation of the two miracles demonstrates particularly well that the abbess's progeny is bestowed with unique holiness and grace: just as Mary's unique birth marks Jesus as divine, the abbess's miraculous birth of Bonus confers him with special favor.[11]

Still, as tantalizing as it may be to see the abbess's delivery as a dramatic representation of the Virgin Birth, and as logical as it may seem to link the infant typologically to Jesus because of how both enter the world, these analogies are problematic. Although the abbess is restored with all the visible signs of virginity and the incriminating evidence borne away, the audience nevertheless knows that concupiscent and consummated human sexuality are undeniably present in this tale. Hence a refiguring of the Virgin Birth which may have satisfied curiosity and provoked awe and reverence at the divine miracle would be accompanied by winks and sideward glances at seeing the impossible depicted as the possible with the help of smoke and mirrors. This mixed message concerning the Virgin Birth, with its reverent refiguring and wry subversion, can be linked to the paradoxes of the Virgin Birth as it was argued about and systematically developed by theologians beginning in Late Antiquity.

Christologically, the Virgin Birth had to be both necessary and impossible. As orthodox Christianity was defining itself in the second century, Catholics stubbornly maintained a tenuous course between the Scylla of the Docetists and the Charybdis of the Arians. The Docetists asserted that Jesus was pure spirit, entirely divine and free of matter, while the Arians insisted that he was entirely human and only adopted by God to be the chosen son. Staunchly maintaining Jesus's nature as both entirely divine *and* human, the Catholics leaned on the Virgin Birth as the cornerstone of their orthodoxy. Because Jesus emerged from the womb of a woman like every other human being, he was entirely human, but because he was conceived by the Holy Spirit without the stain of sexual concupiscence, he was also entirely divine. Further, Jesus was marked as divine precisely because the Virgin Birth suspended the natural order. Hence, the entire cultic myth of Christianity and its soteriological premise, that the Almighty be incarnated into frail human flesh, depended on a birthing process which was by definition inimitable, unrepeatable, and completely other.[12] The *Miracle of the Pregnant Abbess*, therefore, in its very attempt to represent the Virgin Birth also subverts it by imitating the inimitable.

Nevertheless, the *Pregnant Abbess* struggles to represent the oxymoron of the Virgin Birth in Mary's footsteps, quite possibly in response to the tremendous popularity of the cult of the Virgin in the later Middle Ages. Much of Mary's popularity derived from her status as paragon of chaste Christian motherhood. As Dyan Elliott explains in *Spiritual Marriage*, Mary's special status did remind married women of their duty of absolute obedience to their husbands, thus helping to maintain the gendered expectations of married life. In a way that was far more threatening to the clergy, however, Mary's example encouraged sexually chaste female religious to picture themselves in a maternal role: "Cloistered female visionaries suckled and even bore the infant Jesus, while some religious communities developed elaborately staged Nativity rituals that were focused on the crèche."[13] Thus, while the imitation of Mary could on the one hand contribute to the control of women's spirituality and sexuality, it could also on the other hand subvert that control if it placed women in the unique position of fancying themselves as mothers *and* virgins, an act which allowed women to appropriate an exalted and powerful position unavailable to men. Needless to say, acts of imitating Mary which conferred this special status on women became symbolically dangerous and potentially uncontrollable to churchmen.

The clergy handled their anxiety about the possible social disruption of women fancying themselves as chaste wives or nuns as mothers by instructing that Mary's example was beyond imitation; she belonged in her own category, apart from humanity, even if she was paradoxically and necessarily entirely human. In order to keep women from attaching themselves to Mary, even symbolically, the clergy insisted that women devoted to Mary – whether married or celibate – were to *admire* but not to *imitate* her example; they were to keep their sexuality strictly categorized as either virgin and unavailable to men or married and sexually under men's control. Female celibates were not to fancy themselves as mothers; married women were not to model their marriages after the asexual marriage of Mary and Joseph where Mary retained her virginity throughout. This categorization and strict separation of female sexuality and fertility on the one hand and female chastity and spirituality on the other was one of the strategies men – both clergy and lay – used to control women.[14] When the clerical precept of *admiratio* not *imitatio* is taken into consideration, the fractured representation of the Virgin Birth in the *Miracle of the Pregnant Abbess* begins to fit logically into the context of medieval spirituality. The abbess's birthing experience, as we have seen, does appear to be quite similar to Mary's; still, Mary remains categorically different from the abbess, who engages sexually with a man and conceives such that after a while she cannot hide her pregnancy. She experiences food cravings and aversions:

> L'Abbesse
> Or ne say je vïande eslire
> qui soit a mon goust, meismement
> celles dont coustumierement
> je mengüe. Et pourtant vieng cha.
> Desormais avoir me fauldera
> auchunes vïandes nouvelles
> de aultre espesse, et furnir, que celles
> dont j'ay acoustumé de user. (ll. 316-23)

[Oh I can't find any food to my liking. Everything I usually eat is tasteless. (To the servant): Come here! From now on I'll have to have new foods, different from the things I'm accustomed to eating.]

Nor does the abbess's misdeed escape the notice of the nuns:

> La premiere religieuse
> Seur, ung petit cecy notez.
> Nostre abbesse enlaidist et gaige
> auchunes vïandes. Je gaige
> que elle est grosse, et je y ay pensé
> il y a plus de ung mois passé.
>
> La IIe religieuse
> Aussy ay je et principalment
> a son alure. (ll. 328-34)

[*The first nun*: Sister, have you noticed? Our abbess is losing her figure and she's started to crave certain foods. I'll bet she's pregnant. I've been suspecting it for over a month now. *The second nun*: I've suspected it too, but mainly from the way she walks.]

Because of the dramatic situation, we can just imagine the opportunity for the staging of hilarious antics played out by the embarrassed abbess, the petty nuns, and eventually the matron who examines the abbess. Yet, as interesting and integral as these aspects may be to this particular miracle, they clearly do not belong in any way to the Virgin Birth, but rather to the human realities of childbirth, which, as we all know, can only originate from the participation in human sexuality – at least in the Middle Ages.

This strange combination of the obvious results of sexuality and miraculous maintenance of virginity with its painless parturition strongly suggests still another facet of the Virgin Birth: Mary's redemption of Eve's disobedience in the Garden of Eden. As the episode in the Garden of Eden came to be interpreted by the church fathers, Adam's disobedience to YHWH's injunction against eating the forbidden fruit became a multi-layered means of explaining how evil came into a world ruled by a deity who claimed to be both entirely benevolent and omnipotent. Eve's disobedience, however, was interpreted narrowly and was inextricably tied to sexuality and the flesh:

> [T]he female sex was firmly placed on the side of the flesh. For as childbirth was woman's special function, and its pangs the special penalty decreed by God after the Fall, and as the child she bore in her womb was stained by sin from the moment of its conception, the evils of sex were particularly identified with the female. Woman was womb and womb was evil.[15]

Thus, motherhood in general and the conception of children in particular always carried with it symbolic linkage to Eve's disobedience, which propelled humanity into a state of fallenness. Every human being was begun with fallen sexual desire and every human being inherited that concupiscent desire as original sin.

The one exception to this endless cycle of fallen humanity was Mary, who, by the Virgin Birth, "conquered the post-Eden natural law that man and woman couple in lust to produce children. Chaste, she escaped the debt of Adam and Eve."[16] Mary conceived Jesus in strict obedience to the paternal God and this obedience translated directly to her sexual chastity, just as Eve's disobedience became synonymous with sexual desire and sexual activity. Mary was thus able to overturn the association of motherhood and childbirth with fallenness so that Jesus could be born fully human but without the stain of original sin. Once again, orthodox Christology rested firmly on the necessary but impossible Virgin Birth.[17]

Viewed from this perspective, the *Miracle of the Pregnant Abbess* as a whole becomes a typology of *Heilsgeschichte* specific to women. In the span of this relatively short drama, the abbess progresses through sin and salvation, beginning as a righteous woman, falling to perdition by her own free will, and depending on Mary for her rehabilitation. There are, of course, variances within this allegorical understanding of the miracle. For instance, the abbess's transgression does not bring with it a multi-generational curse as does the Fall narrative in Genesis 3. Further, and perhaps most important, Mary saves the abbess in an idiosyncratic and temporal way, whereas with *Heilsgeschichte* humanity is saved eschatologically. In other words, Mary's miracle does not dispense with the necessity of Christ.

Yet these obvious differences notwithstanding, the *Miracle of the Pregnant Abbess* reverberates with strong echoes of humanity's fall and redemption focused here on the abbess's sexuality, once again inextricably linking women's spirituality to their sexuality. Through pious entreaties, the abbess summons the Virgin Mary, who redeems her integrity entirely by delivering the child, returning the womb to its virginal state, and bearing away the incriminating evidence. In effect, Mary's miracle redeems the abbess entirely, returning her to her "prelapsarian" state. The abbess appears never to have engaged in sexual activity, conceived, given birth, or been a mother at all; she is saved in the erasure of all visible signs of sexuality and motherhood. Thus, the miracle symbolically links women's participation in the sexual to perdition and women's sexual continence to salvation.

The *Miracle of the Pregnant Abbess*, therefore, which seems so woman-friendly at first glance because it celebrates woman as both redeemer and redeemed turns out to be profoundly misogynist upon closer inspection. As Marina Warner points out, women have no chance in the Christian sexual economy to experience the full range of their humanity, including sexuality and motherhood, should they choose, and be holy too:

> But the very conditions that make the Virgin sublime are beyond the powers of women to fulfil unless they deny their sex. Accepting the Virgin as the ideal of purity implicitly demands rejecting the ordinary female condition as impure. Accepting virginity as an ideal entails contempt for sex and motherhood, with the result that far from remaining a privileged state undertaken by a few women of vocation, virginity and sexual chastity become a general condition of sinlessness applicable to both the married and the unmarried.[18]

The way the *Pregnant Abbess* advances the doctrinal party-line on women's sexuality may well explain the great popularity and wide dissemination of a tale which seems permissively to excuse the breaking of vows of chastity and the indulgence in wanton lust. Some scholars have even categorized *The Pregnant Abbess* as morally dubious.[19] Yet these reservations are but surface observations in a text which strikes still deeper chords of the orthodox Christian understanding of women, sin, and sexuality. The *Miracle of the Pregnant Abbess* redeems women but reminds us once again that women are essentially fallen creatures through their sexuality and can only be holy by denying their sex.

Appendix: Synopsis of *The Miracle of the Pregnant Abbess* from The Lille Processional Plays

A certain abbess, who administers her convent with an iron hand, and her male table waiter are one day tempted by the devil, responding to the wishes of three gossipy nuns in the abbess's charge. Assailed by lust, the table waiter and the abbess yield to their carnal desire and a child is conceived. Soon, the nuns, who resent the strict disciplines imposed by the abbess, notice their superior's food cravings and aversions, her changed gait, and the loss of her figure. Enthused with *schadenfreude*, the nuns decide to write a letter to the bishop, who, upon receiving it, is appalled at the abbess's transgression and decides to investigate. Meanwhile, distraught at her condition, the abbess retreats into her chapel, where she repents and beseeches the Blessed Virgin Mary for help. She falls into a deep sleep and the Virgin Mary appears with two angels. Mary, who cannot resist a sincere prayer, hastens to answer her plea and delivers the child painlessly in the abbess's sleep. Mary then seals the womb, restoring the abbess's virginity, and commands the angels to bear the child away to a hermit, where it will be raised for seven years. Meanwhile, the bishop and his entourage arrive at the convent. The bishop promptly orders a matron to examine the abbess; the matron soon declares that the abbess is chaste and has no child in her womb. The bishop is embarrassed by the news and begs the abbess's pardon and vows to punish the underling nuns by banishing them. The abbess, however, wishing to avoid punishing those who deserve no punishment, decides to confess her secret. The bishop forgives her entirely, without imposing any penance whatever, remarking that she must be especially loved and blessed by the glorious Queen of Heaven. Finally, the bishop sends for the baby and the hermit produces it, showing it to be "very handsome and well-made by nature." The play closes with an epilogue assuring the audience that the child was raised well first by the hermit and then by the bishop whose *cathedra* the child later fills after the bishop's death.

Notes

1. Adgar, "De l'abesse enceintee par la dame deliveree," Pierre Kunstmann [ed.], *Le Gracial*, Ottawa, 1982, pp. 319-25; T. F. Crane [ed.], *Liber de Miraculis Sanctae Dei Genitricis Mariae*, Ithaca, 1925, pp. 51-5.

2. Botho's *Liber* (cited above) is from Austria; from Northern England: John Small [ed.], *English Metrical Homilies from Manuscripts of the Fourteenth Century*, Edinburgh, 1862, pp. 164-71; from Galicia: Alfonso X, *Las Cantigas de Loor de Alfonso X el Sabio*, Luis Beltrán [ed.], Barcelona, 1990, pp. 217-21; and from Ethiopia: E. A. Wallis Budge [ed.], *One Hundred and Ten Miracles of our Lady Mary Translated from Ethiopic Manuscripts*, London, 1923, pp. 75-82.

3. The following citations represent the historical, geographic, linguistic, generic, and formal variety found in the various examples of *The Miracle of the Pregnant Abbess*. This list is by no means exhaustive, but provides a sampling of the variety I discuss in addition to the versions cited in notes 1-2: Mary M. Banks [ed.], *An Alphabet of Tales*, EETS orig. ser. no. 126, 127, London, 1904-5, rpt. in 1 vol., Millwood, N.J., 1972) p. XX; Alfons Hilka [ed.], *Beiträge zur lateinischen Erzählungsliteratur des Mittelalters. 3. Das Viaticum narrationum des Henmannus Bononiensis*, Berlin, 1935, pp. 73-75; Gonzalo de Berceo, *Los Milagros de Nuestra Señora*, Brian Dutton [ed.], London, 1971, pp. 159-76; Vincent of Beauvais, *Speculum Historiale* 7.86, *Speculum quadruplex, sive, Speculum maius*, Douai, 1624, rpt. Graz, 1964-65, 4:252; and "Le miracle de L'abbeesse grosse," *Miracles de Nostre Dame par personnages*, Gaston Paris and Ulysse Robert [eds.], Paris, 1876-83, 1:57-100.

4. Robert L. A. Clark, "The *Miracles de Nostre Dame par personnages* of the Cangé Manuscript and the Sociocultural Function of Confraternity Drama," Ph.D. diss., Indiana University, 1994; John Boswell, *The Kindness of Strangers: The Abandonment of Children in Western Europe from Late Antiquity to the Renaissance*, New York, 1988, pp. 371-73; Mari Carmen Barrado Belmar, "Estudio Semiotico Comparado de la *Cantiga 7* de Alfonso X, el Sabio y el *Milagro XXI* de Gonzalo de Berceo," *Literatura medieval: Actas do IV Congreso da Associaçao Hispánica de Literatura Medieval, Lisboa, 1-5 Outubro 1991*, Lisbon, 1993, pp. 355-59; M. Ana Diz, "Berceo y Alfonso: La historia de la abadesa encinta," *Bulletin of the Cantiguerros de Santa Maria* 5 (spring 1993): 85-96; Helen Boreland, "Typology in Berceo's *Milagros*: The *Judïezno* and the *Abadesa Preñada*," *Bulletin of Hispanic Studies* 60 (Jan. 1983): 15-29.

5. The play's heading reads: "De ung miracle de la glorieuse Vierge Marie / Quy est escript ou Miroir Historïal de Vincent"; Alan E. Knight [ed. and trans.], "De ung Miracle de la Glorieuse Vierge Marie," Cod. Guelf 9 Blankenburgensis, Herzog August Bibliothek, Wolfenbüttel, Germany.

6. By indicating the broad-ranging support of the Lille plays, I do not mean to paint an overly-idealized picture of the dramatic context. Nor do I mean to suggest that there were no subversive elements at work. City records from the period routinely mention bans on non-processional plays due to perceived or actual danger associated with the single young men who performed them. In addition, scholars have suggested that the competitions for the best play were a civic means of exerting control over potentially subversive acts. For extensive details on the performative context of the Lille plays, see Alan E. Knight, "Processional Theater in Lille in the Fifteenth Century," *Le Théâtre et la Cité dans l'Europe médiévale, Actes du Ve Colloque International de la Société Internationale pour l'Etude du Théâtre Médiéval (Perpignan, juillet 1986)*, Edelgard E. DuBruck and William C. McDonald [eds.], *Fifteenth-Century Studies* 13 (1988): 347-58; and Knight, "The Sponsorship of Drama in Lille," *Studies in Honor of Hans-Erich Keller: Medieval French and Occitan Literature and Romance Linguistics*, Rupert T. Pickens [ed.], Kalamazoo, Mich., 1993, pp. 275-85.

7. All Latin references to Vincent's version are from page 252 of the *Speculum Historiale* cited above. Translations are my own. French references to the Lille play are from an edited and translated manuscript generously given me by Alan E. Knight (see note 5). I am thankful to Alan Knight for the translations of the fifteenth-century French. It was through this manuscript translation that I first became interested in *The Miracle of the Pregnant Abbess* in a graduate course on medieval drama taught by C. Clifford Flanigan in the fall of 1991.

8. *Le* is frequently used for the feminine direct object pronoun in the Picard dialect.

9. For an overview of the Virgin Birth, see Marina Warner, *Alone of All Her Sex: The Myth and the Cult of the Virgin Mary*, New York, 1976, rpt. New York, 1983, pp. 34-49.

10. As Barbara Newman points out in her study of virginity and formation literature for nuns in the Middle Ages, female chastity and sanctity were inextricably linked in a way they were not for men. Newman writes: "The perception of virginity as the quintessence of female holiness had momentous consequences for the spiritual life, and advice on preserving this state dominates the women's literature of formation" (28). Barbara Newman, "Flaws in the Golden Bowl," *From Virile Woman to WomanChrist: Studies in Medieval Religion and Literature*, Philadelphia, 1995, pp. 19-45.

11. *Viaticum narrationum*, cited above in n. 3, p. 75; my translation.

12. Warner, *Alone of All Her Sex*, pp. 63-65.

13. Dyan Elliott, *Spiritual Marriage: Sexual Abstinence in Medieval Wedlock*, Princeton, 1993, p. 179.

14. I am indebted to the work of Dyan Elliott for helping me to see how imitating Mary could be both supportive and subversive to the controlling efforts of the male clerical hierarchy (Elliott, pp. 176-83).

15. Warner, *Alone of All Her Sex*, p. 57.

16. Warner, *Alone of All Her Sex*, p. 52.

17. Warner, *Alone of All Her Sex*, pp. 50-76.

18. Warner, *Alone of All Her Sex*, p. 77.
19. Eileen Power, for example, uses *The Pregnant Abbess* miracle to exemplify her statement that "Indeed the kind of people this divine and most imperious Lady brought into heaven must have given rise to endless difficulties, even in that many-mansioned realm." Eileen Power, introduction, *Miracles of the Blessed Virgin Mary*, by Johannes Herolt, London, 1928, p. xxvii.

Athens, Jerusalem, and Fray Luis de León
Ignacio Navarrete

In preparing this essay I have gone back over some of the material from the first course I took with C. Clifford Flanigan, in the fall of 1976, my first semester in graduate school, and then applied some of these principles to a research project of my own, the commentary to the Song of Songs by Luis de León.

"Traditions of Christian Literature" was in some ways an old-fashioned course; fall 1976 was before Flanigan's sabbatical in Cambridge, that turning point during which, among other things, he "discovered theory." Still, there were important books that were fundamental to his understanding of this topic, and I want to start by going over three of these. The first is Rudolf Bultmann's *Jesus Christ and Mythology*, which Flanigan recommended on the very first day of class. Bultmann was one of his favorite theologians, not least because, both raised as Lutherans, they shared a preference for Bach over Mozart. Bultmann was fundamental to the course in a number of ways. First, as a pioneering form critic, he had insisted that the gospels, however inspired they might be, could nonetheless be subjected to scholarly investigation of the archaeology of forms they contain. Such an investigation reveals them to be not documents through which we can arrive at any specific knowledge of the historical Jesus, but products of the early church, formulated out of preexisting material in response to its needs, particularly in the contexts of preaching and worship. Thus they are not historical documents in the most narrow sense, but products of history itself, through which we can see the evolving understandings about the meaning of Christ's life and death. Secondly, Bultmann insists on the mythological nature of the language used in the Gospels to describe Jesus. Bultmann wrote:

> We must ask whether the eschatological preaching and the mythological sayings as a whole contain a still deeper meaning which is concealed under the cover of mythology. If that is so, let us abandon the mythological conceptions precisely because we want to retain their deeper meaning. This method of interpretation of the New Testament which tries to recover the deeper meaning behind the mythological conceptions I call de-mythologizing.[1]

The gospels are thus written in a sort of meta-language, essentially figural, which must be recovered through the study of myth if we are to recuperate its meaning. To Flanigan, demythologizing Jesus began with undoing the process of exclusion that resulted in the creation of the New Testament canon, recognizing that the gospels themselves, outside the context of a faith community, are not privileged texts. Rather, they need to be studied genetically and generically, on a par with the enormous body of non-canonical early Christian literature from a number of different communities. What became early orthodox Christianity was not a single starting point, but some strands of Jewish/Christian thought that existed in competition with many others, including Palestinian Jewish and Gnostic ones; generically, the gospels are kerygmatic works, proclamations of a particular understanding of the "Jesus event." As a generic innovation they are one of the distinguishing features of early Christianity, but the canonical gospels must be investigated according to the procedures of form and redaction criticism (not to mention all other literary approaches), alongside with and in the same way as the non-canonical texts that history relegated to the category of *pseudepigrapha*.

This brings me to the second fundamental source, Ernst Robert Curtius's *European Literature and the Latin Middle Ages*. Curtius, we were told, with World War II bombs falling around him, had gone looking in the trash heaps of late antiquity, and found the foundations of Western culture. The fundamental lesson here was that there was no place for aestheticism in historical literary scholarship; the roots of medieval Christian writing lay as much in *pseudepigrapha* as in what became the canonical texts. Moreover, Curtius provided not just an ideal of scholarship, but a phenomenology of literature and an explanation for the continuity of literary transmission, through his study and exposition of the rhetorical system of topics. Literature is made out of other literature; topics, as Curtius defines them, "are intellectual themes, suitable for development and modification at the orator's pleasure." But with the decline of rhetoric as a forensic science, "it penetrated into all literary genres. Its elaborately developed system became the common denominator of literature in general. This is the most influential development in the history of antique rhetoric."[2] Curtius's analysis of topoi ranged from the most mundane formulae for closing a letter, to themes such as that of the *puer senex*, with its profound Jungian overtones. Indeed, Curtius admits that "in my book there will also be found things which I could not have seen without C. G. Jung,"[3] and this aspect of Curtius's thought made him all the more attractive to Flanigan.

In his own appropriation of Curtius, Flanigan combined aspects of topology with the practice of typology, as expounded in Auerbach's famous essay;[4] if Curtius offered a somewhat secularized analogy to *Formgeschichte*, Auerbach provided the complementary element of *Redaktionforschung*. The notion of rhetorical topics provides a clue to the typological transfer of images and patterns from the Old Testament to the New Testament and beyond. As an example we can look at how Flanigan applied these methods to the problem of Old Testament models for elements in the gospels and the *pseudepigrapha*. In particular the opening chapters of Luke pose a problem, for they are clearly woven out of a tissue of reminiscences from the Septuagint, including stories of the patriarchs, allusions to king David, and even lyrical material. Luke uses these to locate the story of Jesus's birth and infancy in a continuum with Jewish sacred scripture; but more to the point, they reflect the perception, in the early church, that there was such a continuity, that it was in fact to Jesus that those prophecies referred. Once again, the gospels document not the life of Jesus *per se* but the theological understanding of the early church; topological inquiry would show the basis of certain passages in Old Testament sources, and a typological reading reveals the perceived connection to Jewish scripture in the "Sitz im Leben" of the early church. Moreover, this combination of the topological and typological establishes images and patterns available to later authors as well. Even as the gospel narratives were taking their characteristic forms, parallel texts expanded them, so that the infancy material in Luke, for example, also served as a model for the Marian infancy narrative in the *Protevangelion* of James, and material from the Passion narratives was expanded and embroidered in the historically and theologically significant Acts of Pilate/Gospel of Nicodemus. The *pseudepigrapha* also provide a link between the gospel-writing period of the early church, and the lives of the martyrs which were the earliest forms of hagiography. In contrast to Hippolyte Delehaye's historical classification of the acts of the martyrs, Flanigan demythologized them, showing how stories about the death of Jesus become the model for the stories of the deaths of the martyrs, both in terms of specific details (topological analysis) and overall conception (typological analysis), revealing the thought-process of the early church. The martyrs were Christian heroes for their imitations of Jesus's death, and their stories an encouragement to others to do the same. Later still, the same patterns reappeared in ascetic literature; Athanasius's life of Anthony, for example, seeks to show that the saint in the desert also struggled with the devil, also died to this world, also lived the life of a martyr. By so doing he too lives out an imitation of Christ and becomes a model hero for his own time. And so the course went on, examining a succession of texts, each in its own way kerygmatic, and thus a window into the needs and understandings of a succession of Christian communities.

    According to Curtius, "the bases of Western thought are classical antiquity and Christianity."[5] A third aspect of the course was the connection between "pagan" and "Jewish/Christian" cultural products. Aspects of this relationship can be studied in New Testament texts and in the *pseudepigrapha*, particularly the Gnostic texts which fascinated Flanigan in a way I was never able to fathom, but it became a much greater issue with the classicizing of Christianity in the next few centuries. Curtius himself studies the place of grammar and rhetoric in Jerome, Augustine, and the other church fathers, but for this aspect of the course the fundamental work was Jean Leclercq's *The Love of Learning and the Desire for God*. Leclercq specifically reflects on the study of the classical authors in the lives of the monastic communities. Monks were responsible for the preservation of latinity, and for its subsequent diffusion during the Carolingian renaissance. Some monks read the classics only at the beginning of their studies, but others continued to do so throughout their entire lives; these texts were not studied as the surviving evidence of a dead culture, but to educate in whatever way they could, to help develop a taste for beauty and literary substance. "Ovid, Virgil, and Horace belonged to these men as personal property; they were not an alien possession to which to refer and quote with reverence and bibliographical references."[6] Wisdom was found in the ancients because the Christian already possessed it, and thus the ancient authors were, through their reception and appropriation, "made Christians."[7] Leclercq goes on to reflect,

> This fundamentally Christian culture avails itself, in the realm of expression as well as in the realm of the inner life, of antiquity's human experience. … The literary heritage of all of antiquity, secular and patristic, can be found in it, yet less under the form of imitation and reminiscences of ancient authors than in a certain resonance which discloses a familiarity acquired by long association, with their literary practices. … The purpose of liberal studies had been attained. The most dangerous author had been "converted," in the mind of the student of literature.[8]

Thus in spite of Tertullian's declaration, "What has Athens to do with Jerusalem?", echoed by Jerome's "What has Horace to do with the Psalter, Virgil with the evangelists, Cicero with the Apostles?",[9] classical culture was gradually absorbed, and subjected to the same hermeneutical filter as the Old Testament. To cite Leclercq once more, all that is salutary that can be found in reading and "scrutinising" the grammarians, poets, historians, and the writings of both Testaments, all must be referred to Christ in accordance with the advice of St. Paul: "Try everything, keep what is good."[10]

I have spent time going over these three books, not only because they were important to Cliff Flanigan in that course, but also because the study of rhetorical topics and the relationship between classical and Hebrew culture are relevant to a very different research project of my own. When St. Jerome described himself "shaving off and cutting away all in her [classical learning] that is dead whether this be idolatry, pleasure, error, or lust, I take her to myself clean and pure, and beget by her servants for the Lord of Sabaoth … my efforts promote the advantage of Christ's family,"[11] he represented the classics as a woman stripped of her enticements but nonetheless fertile, while reserving for himself the male role of lying with her, if only to increase God's family. Thus having his cake and eating it too, Jerome reveals the role of pleasure in the patristic appropriation of classical literature. The classics were not only used as models for attainment of an eloquent style and as sources of protosecular scientific information about plants, animals, etc., but also as exegetical, and hence, hermeneutic, tools. The use of rhetorical figures by early Christian writers presupposed a technique for decoding those figures that was also the basis for allegorical and typological interpretation; thus, for example, it is necessary to recognize figures of speech to rise above the superficial lewdness of St. Jerome's remarks, quoted above, and the same technique is applied to classical literature and to the Bible itself. Yet the perception of a conflict between "Athens" and "Jerusalem" was not limited to the early Christian period, but continued through the Renaissance, troubling no less a humanist than Petrarch himself.[12] In voicing these concerns, however, Petrarch self-consciously echoes Jerome, underscoring the distance between them and setting himself up as the renewer of Christian humanism. Yet while Athens, for Petrarch, continues to stand as a synecdoche for classical literature, Jerusalem has ceased to serve in the same capacity for Jewish culture, which as an entity in itself seems almost unknown for him as for many other Renaissance Christian writers; instead, Jerusalem the Jewish city has been typologically usurped by Jerusalem as a metonymy for salvation. With relatively few exceptions, the Bible for the Renaissance is either a Latin or a vernacular text, the Old Testament intelligible only through typology and allegory. What remains of this paper is devoted to one of the exceptions, Fray Luis de León's attempt to recover the literal, Hebrew meaning of the Song of Songs, through a philological, rhetorical, and performance-oriented analysis. We will touch on the first two of these approaches, and concentrate on the third.

Fray Luis was born c. 1527; his father was a lawyer and subsequently a judge, but his great-grandmother had been imprisoned for Judaizing in 1512. These facts are significant; the Spanish Inquisition was founded in 1478 to ensure that former Jews, converts to Christianity, were not continuing to practice Judaism in secret. Given the supposition that crypto-Judaism could be passed along for generations, all persons of Jewish descent were suspect, and were banned from certain offices including the priesthood; the fact that Fray Luis became a priest and that his father had been a judge shows how easily these strictures could be avoided through the construction of false genealogies, but the details about his great-grandmother show how these facts could still come back to haunt one.[13] He grew up near Madrid and in 1541 went to Salamanca where he joined the Augustinian order, making his final vows in 1544; he then studied at the universities of Salamanca and Alcalá de Hernares (where the polyglot Hebrew, Aramaic, Greek, and Latin Bible had been published), taking his higher degree in 1560 and thereafter teaching in Salamanca. His election to the St. Thomas Aquinas chair of theology inevitably led to conflict with the more conservative Dominican order, and subsequently to a charge of heresy and arrest by the Inquisition in 1572, followed by five years of prison. Among the charges were that Fray Luis preferred the Hebrew text of the Old Testament to the Vulgate, and that he disseminated a vernacular translation of the Song of Songs. After his acquittal and release Fray Luis returned to Salamanca, where he obtained the chair in Sacred Scripture in 1579. He was denounced again in 1582, but this time he was not imprisoned and was absolved two years later. In 1591 he was elected head of the Castilian province of the Augustinians, and he died later that year. In addition to his well-known original poetry, his writings in Spanish include commentaries and translations of the Song of Songs and the book of Job, a treatise on marriage, a dialogue on the names of Christ ("Prince of Peace," etc.), and translations of Pindar, Horace, and other classical writers. He also edited the first edition of the works of St. Theresa of Avila.

As E. Ann Matter has shown, the place of the Song of Songs in the biblical canon has always been problematic; the erotic nature of this text "presents a number of oddities which invite elaboration on a level 'beyond' (or at least 'away from') the apparent surface."[14] The Jewish interpretative tradition that read the book as an epithalamium between God and his chosen people,[15] was typologically transformed by Christian writers into an interpretation of the book as a love song between God and the church. Beginning with St. Bernard, a new interpretation (although one not without patristic antecedents) began to predominate, in which the poem is a love song expressing the desire between God and the individual human soul. Finally, many passages of the book were appropriated for use in the liturgy, particularly with reference to the Virgin Mary. Yet all of these were allegorical interpretations; as Matter puts it, "there is no 'nonallegorical' Latin tradition of Song of Songs commentary."[16] These medieval interpretations continued to hold sway into the Renaissance, when the introduction of printing gave the earlier interpretations an even wider audience, and even Jewish commentaries, after philological details, gave the book a spiritual reading.[17] Thus it was quite remarkable that in 1561-62, at the age of thirty-four, Fray Luis de León undertook a commentary based on the Hebrew text that largely set aside questions of allegorical interpretation in favour of a philological and literary explication of its literal meaning.[18]

Fray Luis's philological comments are fairly straightforward, even if sometimes critical of the officially-sanctioned Vulgate translation of the Bible. Thus, for example, in a gloss to chapter 7, line 4, "nasus tuus sicut turris Libani" ("your nose like a tower of Lebanon"[19]), he notes that the Hebrew word *aph* could mean face or nose. Similarly, for a phrase in chapter 7, line 1, rendered by St. Jerome as "filia principis," Fray Luis explains that the Hebrew word is not *melech* which is used for kings but *nadib*, which means generous, and which the Septuagint left untranslated. "And just as we in the Spanish language call a prince a prince, because in fact he is the principal one amongst us, as the word itself indicates, the Hebrews called him *nadib*, which is to say the noble one, because that is a virtue of the prince that should distinguish him amongst others." This quality of nobility, he goes on to say, is not merely an attribute, but also a description. "It is like saying that the gentle movement of her body conveyed the generosity and nobility of her heart; for that virtue, more than any other, can be discovered through the air and movement of the body."[20]

The difficulties presented by a literal understanding of the Hebrew text, however, are not limited to particular words. The images are also difficult to understand, and Fray Luis explains how the metaphors work. For example, for chapter 7, verse 2, "your navel is a finely wrought bowl never lacking drink, your belly like a heap of wheat fortified with lilies,"[21] he explains that the navel is round like a cup, filled with a finely proportioned mixture of wine and water because the belly is neither too soft nor too thin, and that the belly itself is like a wheat stack because these are also perfectly round. Yet Fray Luis is particularly interested in elucidating those images made obscure by the rustic nature of the comparisons, and because of the different canons of beauty in ancient Hebrew and Greco-Roman-based Renaissance culture. Thus, for example, several parts of the beloved's body are compared to goats and sheep, in metaphors that seems strange but are easily understood once they are placed in the context of a pastoral culture. The beloved's teeth can be compared to a flock of sheep (Song 4.2), for gentility in teeth consists in their being small, white, equal, and close together, all of which characteristics are made vivid by this comparison; an ugly mouth, he declares, is enough to make a woman ugly, and even with a beautiful face nothing is worse than bad teeth. Her breasts can be compared to twin kid goats, for,

> There can be nothing more beautiful nor more appropriate than to compare the beloved's breasts to small twin goats, which, in addition to their tenderness as kids, and their similarity as twins, and in addition to being pretty and pleasing, full of joy and happiness, have within them a *je ne*

sais quoi of mischievousness and grace, which steals the eyes of those who gaze on them, filling one with the wish to approach and to fondle them with one's hands. All these qualities are appropriate, and would thus be found in the breasts to which they are compared.[22]

In this gloss, which is typical, Fray Luis explains on a literary level how the conceit is a viable one, if we suspend prejudices and seek those points of similarity between the tenor and the vehicle. Implicit here is the assumption that the attractiveness is a constant, and that only the arbitrary metaphors used to express that attraction have changed.

This becomes clearest in those comparisons where cultural contrasts are most specific. For example, he considers the comparison of the beloved's hair to a flock of goats on the mountainside (Song 4.1):

What is marvelous here is the comparison, which seems gross and far from that purpose for which it was made. It would be more correct if he said it was like a skein of gold, or that it competed with the sun's rays in number and colour, as our poets are fond of saying.[23]

There follows an explanation of how the goats on the mountain have their hair brushed by trees and bushes whose resin also oils it, so that it shines. The problem then lies not at all with linguistic translation of the image, but with its cultural valorization, which now eludes the reader more accustomed to what "our poets" would say. Yet in providing his own Petrarchist topics of beauty (hair of gold, hair that competes with the sun) in place of the Hebrew ones, Fray Luis underscores the necessary cultural limitations of all imagery, and the arbitrary relationship of the metaphor / signifiers to the beauty signified. Fray Luis specifically compares the rhetorical procedure of the Song of Songs to that of Petrarch and his classical predecessors:

Those who wish to make something precious by praising it and declaring its qualities avoid using shallow, proper terms, but use the names of the things in which that quality they praise is most perfectly found. … as did that great Tuscan poet who, having to praise hair, called it gold, called lips kermes, teeth pearls, and eyes lights, fires, or stars; and this skill can be seen more in Sacred Scripture than in any other writing in this world.[24]

Civilizations, as systems of signification, come and go, and thus Solomon's images have been superseded. Yet Fray Luis is concerned with demonstrating that communication across systems is not impossible, for there is a common referent in the stability of the signifieds, and the ancient Hebrew hermeneutic is recoverable through poetry. Moreover, that arbitrariness of signifiers is in reality just another instance of the power of similarity, for literary genres and categories are themselves analogous. Thus Fray Luis describes the Song of Songs as a pastoral eclogue, where with rustic words and language, Solomon and his wife speak,[25] as if it were a poem by Virgil; even though the

Biblical poem exhibits features alien to Greco-Roman and Renaissance pastoral, the similarities enable him to use the latter term to approximate and explicate the genre of the older poem. In this way Athens and Jerusalem are reconciled: it is knowledge of classical literature that instructs the Renaissance reader in the understanding of metaphors and other rhetorical tropes, and that in turn enables an understanding of the Bible. Individual metaphors may be bound to a particular time and place, but the very process of metaphorization makes it possible for readers to appropriate and talk about the literature of another time and culture.

Still Fray Luis is left with the problem of the nature of the Song of Songs, what he describes as its breaches of decorum. Here again an analogy with classical literature helps him to resolve the issue, through a double theory of performance. The poems in the Song of Songs violate decorum not only because of their erotic imagery, but also because these images seem inappropriate in an exchange between King Solomon and his wife, the daughter of the king of Egypt:

> These things are said … in conformity with what most often occurs amongst shepherds and farmers who live in the countryside, whose qualities Solomon imitates in this Song; for as they spend most of their time in the fields, it is natural for those lads and lasses to harmonize their loves with the meadows and woods where they find themselves.[26]

Just as Roman poets, however, used shepherds in their pastoral poetry to convey profound sentiments, so too Solomon composed these poems as if he were a shepherd and not a king, and in keeping with the role of a shepherd, he used the rustic and erotic imagery that seems so out of place.

Yet the poems and their metaphors are also a performance in an even profounder way. Investigating the metaphors for God can be, as Thompson has argued, for Fray Luis "a form of contemplation."[27] In the Bible, however, the process is reversed, for that great repository of metaphors is not a human-built image of God, but rather the result of God speaking human language, and in the Bible the Holy Spirit shows himself to be a great performer:

> mimicking our language and imitating in it all the variety of our genius and emotions: he pretends to be happy and sad, he shows himself angry and shows himself repentant, he sometimes threatens and he sometimes vanquishes with a thousand tender remarks. There is no fancy nor quality so proper to us nor so alien to him, into which he does not transform himself.[28]

The Song thus presents particular difficulties, both because of the way it was composed, using metaphors that may have seemed appropriate in the time of King Solomon but which no longer do, but also because its subject matter, divine love, exceeds the capacities of human language and requires the use of that special, illogical rhetoric, unique to lovers. Almost forgotten is the allegorical interpretation, that the erotic attraction and its unique rhetoric serve a mythological purpose: beauty points to the beauty of the human soul, and Solomon's infatuation is the Holy Spirit's clever way of communicating God's fascination with and love for mankind.

Spain, during the Middle Ages, had a more profound exposure to Semitic cultures than did any other country in Europe, and conversely went further to suppress them. Fray Luis de León lived up to the humanist ideal of fluency in the three classical languages, but at a historical moment when a thoroughly assimilated latinity, represented equally by Virgil and the Vulgate, was less foreign than the language of the original Jerusalem. Fray Luis defamiliarizes scripture by trying to recover its original meaning, and seeking to uncover the Jewish roots of Christian culture. The key to the relationship is poetry, both in its mimetic function (as a representation of a stable reality), and in its performative function of the power to move the reader through striking rhetorical devices.

If I once studied with Flanigan, I have also gone in a number of different ways, as a hispanist, as a student of lyric poetry, and as someone more fundamentally interested in the Renaissance than in the Middle Ages. In this paper, I have tried to bring in all three of these interests, along with three of Flanigan's. When I was originally working on this paper as part of a larger project on metaphor and hermeneutics, I would automatically think, whenever I encountered something I did not understand, "I've got to ask Cliff what this means"; and on rarer occasions when I made a discovery I would mentally snap my fingers and say, "Wait 'til Cliff Flanigan hears about that!" He was an inspiration as a scholar and a teacher, a uniquely generous individual, and I miss him terribly.

Notes

1. Rudolf Karl Bultmann, *Jesus Christ and Mythology*, New York, 1958, p. 18.
2. Ernst Robert Curtius, *European Literature and the Latin Middle Ages*, Willard R. Trask [transl.], Princeton, 1973 [Bollingen Series, 36], p. 70.
3. Ibidem, p. ix.
4. Erich Auerbach, *Typologische Motive in der mittelalterlichen Literatur*, Krefeld, 1953 [Schriften und Vorträge des Petrarca-Instituts Köln, 2].
5. Curtius, *European Literature*, p. 596.
6. Jean Leclercq, *The Love of Learning and the Desire for God: A Study of Monastic Culture*, [transl.] Catherine Misrahi, NewYork, 1982, p. 119.
7. Ibidem.
8. Ibidem, pp. 141-3.
9. See J. N. D. Kelly, *Jerome: His Life, Writings, and Controversies*, London, 1975, p. 43.
10. Leclercq, *The Love of Learning*, p. 39.
11. Brenda Schildgen, "Petrarch's Defense of Secular Letters, the Latin Fathers, and Ancient Roman Rhetoric," *Rhetorica* 11 (1993), pp. 119-34, quoted at p. 125.
12. Ibidem, p. 126-34.

13. The requirement that office-holders prove the purity of their ancestry may be, ironically, a typological imitation of the post-exilic purging of the Jewish priesthood (See Américo Castro, *The Spaniards: An Introduction to Their History*, [transl.] Willard F. King and Selma Margaretten, Berkeley, 1971, pp. 65-71). For the Inquisition in general see Henry Kamen, *The Spanish Inquisition*, New York, 1968.

14. E. Ann Matter, *The Voice of My Beloved: The Song of Songs in Western Medieval Christianity*, Philadelphia, 1990, p. 49.

15. Ibidem, p. 51.

16. Ibidem, p. 4.

17. See Max Engammare, *Qu'il me baise des baisers de sa bouche: le Cantique des cantiques à la Renaissance, étude et bibliographie*, Geneva, 1993 [*Travaux d'Humanisme et Renaissance*, 277], pp. 39-44.

18. See Olegario García de la Fuente, "Traducciones y comentarios de Fray Luis de León al Cantar de los Cantares," *Analecta Malacitana* 14 (1991), pp. 71-85, for an overview of Fray Luis's writings on the Song of Songs, which include two translations and a Latin as well as the Spanish commentary, and for the traditional view that Fray Luis wrote the commentary for a nun, Isabel de Osorio, who requested it because, while familiar with its spiritual interpretations, she wanted to know its plain meaning. However, the humanist structure of the commentary suggests a wider intended audience than the private communication to a nun (See Victor García de la Concha, "Fray Luis de León: Exposición del Cantar de los Cantares," in Victor García de la Concha [ed.], *Fray Luis de León*, Salamanca, 1981 [*Academia Literaria Renacentista*, 1], pp. 171-92, esp. p. 171). The standard work on Fray Luis's knowledge of Hebrew remains Alexander Habib Arkin, *La influencia de la exegesis hebrea en los comentarios Bíblicos de Fray Luis de León*, Madrid, 1966.

19. See Matter, *The Voice of My Beloved*, pp. xxx-xxxi.

20. "Y como nosotros en la lengua española al príncipe le llamamos príncipe, porque de hecho es principal entre los demás, como lo suena la voz, entre los hebreos se llama *nadib*, que es decir el noble, éstas son propias virtudes del príncipe y en que se ha de señalar entre todos" (Fray Luis de León, *Cantar de los cantares de Salomón*, [ed.] José Manuel Blecua, Madrid, 1994 [*Biblioteca Románica Hispánica IV*, Textos 22], p. 218). "Como si dixese que en el gentil meneo de su cuerpo mostraba bien la generosidad y gallardía de su corazón; porque esta virtud, más que ninguna otra, se descubre en el movimiento y aire de todo el cuerpo" (Ibidem, p. 219).

21. See Matter, *The Voice of My Beloved*, p. xxxi.

22. "No se puede decir cosa más bella ni más a propósito que comparar las tetas hermosas de la Esposa a dos cabritos mellizos, los cuales, demás de la terneza que tienen por ser cabritos y de la igualdad por ser mellizos, y demás de ser cosa linda y apacible, llena de regocijo y alegría, tienen consigo un no sé qué de travesura y buen donaire, con que roban y llevan tras sí los ojos de los que los miran, poniéndolos afición de llegarse a ellos y de tratarlos entre las manos; que todas son cosas muy convenientes, y que se hallan así en los pechos hermosos a quien se comparan" (León, *Cantar de los cantares de Salomón*, p. 144).

23. "Lo que es de maravillas aquí es la comparación, que al parecer es grosera y muy apartada de aquello a que se hace. Fuera acertada si dijera ser como una madeja de oro, o que competía con los rayos del sol en muchedumbre y color, como suelen decir nuestros poetas" (Ibidem, p. 137).

24. "[L]os que mucho quieren encarecer una cosa alabándola, y declarando sus propiedades, dejan de decir los vocablos llanos y propios, y dicen los nombres de las cosas en que más perfectamente se halla aquella cualidad de lo que loan. … como lo hace aquel gran poeta toscano que, habiendo de loar los cabellos, los llama oro, a los labios, rosas o grana, a los dientes perlas, a los ojos luces, lumbres, o estrellas; el cual artificio se guarda en la Escritura Sagrada más que en otra del mundo" (Ibidem, p. 185).

25. Ibidem, pp. 57-8.

26. "Lo qual es dicho, … conforme a lo que mexor dice y asienta y suele acontecer más comúnmente a los pastores y labradores que viven en el campo, cuyas personas y propiedades imita Salomón en este Canto; a los quales, así como andan lo más del tiempo en el campo, así les es muy natural en el campo el concertar sus amores los zagales con las zagalas por las florestas y arboledas, donde se topan" (Ibidem, pp. 262-3).

27. Colin P. Thompson, *The Strife of Tongues: Fray Luis de León and the Golden Age of Spain*, Cambridge, 1988, p. 10.

28. "imitando en sy toda la variedad de nuestro ingenio y condiciones, haze del alegre y del triste, muestrase airado. y muestrase arrepentido: amenaza a vezes, y a vezes se venze con mill blanduras: no ay aficion ny qualidad tan propria a nosotros tan estraña a el que no se transforme" (León, *Cantar de los cantares de Salomón*, pp. 44-5).

Works Cited

Auerbach, Erich. *Typologische Motive in der mittelalterlichen Literatur*. Krefeld, Germany: 1953. Schriften und Vorträge des Petrarca-Instituts Köln 2.

Bultmann, Rudolf. *Jesus Christ and Mythology*. New York: 1958.

Castro, Américo. *The Spaniards: An Introduction to Their History*. Trans. Willard F. King and Selma Margaretten. Berkeley: 1971.

Curtius, Ernst Robert. *European Literature and the Latin Middle Ages*. Trans. Willard R. Trask. Princeton: 1973. Bollingen Series 36.

Engammare, Max. *Qu'il me baise des baisers de sa bouche: le cantique des cantiques à la Renaissance, étude et bibliographie*. Geneva: 1993. Travaux d'Humanisme et Renaissance 277.

García de la Concha, Victor. "Fray Luis de León: Exposición del Cantar de los Cantares." *Fray Luis de León*. Ed. Victor García de la Concha. Salamanca: 1981. 171-92. Academia Literaria Renacentista 1.

García de la Fuente, Olegario. "Traducciones y comentarios de Fray Luis de León al Cantar de los Cantares." *Analecta Malacitana* 14 (1991): 71-85.

Habib Arkin, Alexander. *La influencia de la exegesis hebrea en los comentarios Bíblicos de Fray Luis de León*. Madrid: 1966.

Kamen, Henry. *The Spanish Inquisition*. New York: 1968.

Kelly, J. N. D. *Jerome: His Life, Writings, and Controversies*. London: 1975.

Leclercq, Jean, O.S.B. *The Love of Learning and the Desire for God: A Study of Monastic Culture*. 3rd ed. Trans. Catherine Misrahi. New York: 1982.

León, Luis de, Fray. *Cantar de los cantares de Salomón*. Ed. José Manuel Blecua. Madrid: 1994. Biblioteca Románica Hispánica IV. Textos 22.

Matter, E. Ann. *The Voice of My Beloved: The Song of Songs in Western Medieval Christianity*. Philadelphia: 1990. Middle Ages Series.

Rivers, Elias. *Fray Luis de León: The Original Poems*. London: 1983. Critical Guides to Spanish Texts 35.

Schildgen, Brenda. "Petrarch's Defense of Secular Letters, the Latin Fathers, and Ancient Roman Rhetoric." *Rhetorica* 11.2 (Spring 1993): 119-34.

Thompson, Colin P. *The Strife of Tongues: Fray Luis de León and the Golden Age of Spain*. Cambridge, England: 1988.

Music, Dramatic Extroversion, and Contemplative Introspection: Hildegard of Bingen's *Ordo Virtutum*
Nils Holger Petersen[*]

*M*odern scholarship of the so-called medieval liturgical drama did not deal with Hildegard of Bingen's music dramatic text *Ordo Virtutum* until Peter Dronke around 1970 took up her poetry in general, and in particular the *Ordo Virtutum*, the *Play of the Virtues*. Among other reasons, Dronke was seeking a more open-ended and sensitive approach to medieval Latin poetry than found in most scholarship at the time; and in particular, he wanted to reconsider the influential and masterful, yet dogmatic work of Ernst Robert Curtius. Peter Dronke's *Poetic Individuality in the Middle Ages*, although not solely devoted to Hildegard, turned out to be, among other things, a new departure for a serious engagement with Hildegard's deeply original, in fact unprecedented music dramatic text in the general context of the Western literary and musical artistic production.[1] At a time when literary scholarship looked upon Hildegard with great suspicion, Dronke rather courageously redirected the reception of her writings whose fate it had often been – and to some extent still is – to be embraced either by separate religious groups interested in particular in her so-called mystical visions or, in recent times, by feminist circles drawn in particular to her image and possible role-model as a strong female who was able to stand up against church leaders. It has frequently been noted in the most recent scholarship that the *Ordo Virtutum* was not discussed in the classical treatments of the Latin music dramas of the Middle Ages by Karl Young, William Smoldon, and O. B. Hardison; in fact, even today Hildegard's play is discussed separately rather than in the general liturgical drama discourse.[2]

---

[*] Please note that this article has appeared in *Transfiguration: Nordic Journal of Religion and the Arts* (Museum Tusculanum Press: Copenhagen, 2009) pp. 95-112. We wish to thank Museum Tusculanum Press for granting us permission to publish the article as originally printed.
I want to thank Michael Klaper from the Musikwissenschaftliches Institut, Universität Erlangen-Nürnberg, for reading this manuscript and for a number of valuable suggestions and references. An earlier version of this paper was read at a Nordic symposium on mysticism and the arts, arranged by the Centre for Christianity and the Arts, University of Copenhagen, in collaboration with other Nordic universities, in Copenhagen, August 1998.

Although both images of Hildegard, as a "mystical" visionary prophetess and as a prefiguration of a feminist leader, can be supported by facts from Hildegard's life and production, such readings are anachronistically narrow. In the last decade, however, the enormous increase in Hildegard scholarship has brought well-balanced discussions of her biography and her extremely broad field of productivity, which included poetic writings and musical compositions as well as medical and other scientific writings, historical and theological treatises, autobiographical sketches, and a vast amount of letters. Hildegard in her long life (1098-1179) produced writings alongside her daily work as a leader of a growing monastic community, and at the same time, having been recognized as a prophetic figure by church authorities, she traveled as a preacher and healer, mainly in Germany.

Prominent among recent reconsiderations of Hildegard, Barbara Newman and Sabina Flanagan have emphasized that the so-called mystical side of Hildegard's literary – and visionary – output should be seen in a larger context, which modifies such an impression to a considerable extent.[3] This accords well with the literary observations of Peter Dronke and a few other literary and musicological scholars who have dealt with the *Ordo Virtutum* and with the observations I will make from yet another angle. Distancing herself from the notion of female mysticism, Barbara Newman points to very different sides of Hildegard:

> A church historian, looking at her activities rather than her gender, might see her as a leading proponent of the Gregorian reform and associated monastic reform movements. Staunchly papalist, unyielding in her defense of hierarchy, insistent on the purity as well as the dignity of priests, she opposed imperial encroachments on the Church and defended clerical privilege with all the intransigence of a Thomas Becket or an Anselm of Canterbury. The importance of her political stance has been obscured by concentration on her mysticism, although in this respect she anticipated later political visionaries like Catherine of Siena and Birgitta of Sweden. Her apocalyptic preaching – the only aspect of her work that remained widely influential in the next three centuries – was closely connected with her program for the reform of the Church.[4]

Characterizing Hildegard's writings, Barbara Newman compares them to Hugh of St. Victor, Rupert of Deutz, and Honorius of Regensburg, authors often classified as pre-scholastics, emphasizing that Hildegard's Biblical commentary, her moral and spiritual teaching, as well as her dogmatic instructions were, despite certain peculiarities of style, essentially of a conservative nature.[5] She does note an affinity to Hildegard's famous contemporary, Bernard of Clairvaux (c. 1090-1153), when discussing Hildegard's treatment of the virtue *caritas*, an important figure also in the *Ordo Virtutum*. Pointing to theological differences, she does at the same time warn against overestimating this influence.[6]

Gunilla Iversen has demonstrated the literary affinities with Bernard in Hildegard's vision of the Virtues and the penitent soul from the *Scivias*, Hildegard's first visionary literary work, in particular concerning the theme of *superbia* versus *humil-*

itas. Here Hildegard closely follows Bernard's emphasis on *humilitas* (as for instance in his *De gradibus humilitas et superbiae*), inspired, of course, by the famous chapter 7 in Benedict's *Rule* describing the Ladder of Humility, which highlights *humilitas* as the queen of the virtues.[7]

A preliminary version of the *Scivias* was scrutinized by papal authorities, including both Pope Eugenius III and Bernard of Clairvaux, in connection with the synod of Trier 1147-48.[8] Hildegard first made contact with Bernard of Clairvaux in 1147 in an attempt to seek advice – or simply to secure his support. The importance of Bernard's authority had become clear not the least after the condemnation of Abelard's teachings in 1140.

The *Scivias* was written down with the help of the monk Volmar some time between 1141 and 1151, a period of Hildegard's life culminating in the important move, in 1150, from Mount Disiboden to Mount Rupert, or Rupertsberg, near Bingen. The vision of the Virtues from the *Scivias* has been understood as either a preliminary stage or a condensation of the longer version with music which constitutes the *Ordo Virtutum*. Nothing in particular is known about the composition of the latter, which is preserved in one twelfth-century manuscript, the so-called *Riesencodex*, copied at Rupertsberg. According to recent investigations, the codex was probably started during Hildegard's lifetime but seems not to have been finished until after her death. The *Ordo Virtutum* seems to belong to the later part of the manuscript, together with a collection of Hildegard's liturgical songs, the so-called *symphonia armonie caelestium revelationum*, part of which are also found in an earlier important musico-poetic source written at Rupertsberg during Hildegard's time. The only other medieval manuscript, however, which contains the *Ordo Virtutum* is a much later copy of 1487.[9]

The close yet not straightforward relationship between the vision of the Virtues in the *Scivias* and the *Ordo Virtutum* has been discussed by Gunilla Iversen, who has argued that the differences may be clarified through the importance of Hildegard's connection with Bernard in 1147-48, when she may have been more likely to let herself be influenced by his writings – needing his support – and when the vision from *Scivias* may have been written down for the first time. The *Ordo Virtutum*, on the other hand, may reflect somewhat different intentions, presenting many more Virtues and emphasizing the Virtue of Virginity or Chastity, *castitas* (not mentioned in the *Scivias* version), almost as much as *humilitas*.[10] Margot Fassler, in her reading of the play, emphasizes how the *Ordo Virtutum* together with the *Scivias* forms part of an overall educational program for Hildegard's nuns, including poetry, music, and theological exposition.[11]

The action of the *Ordo Virtutum* concerns the fight of an individual *anima* (soul) to overcome the temptations of the World with the support of a number of Virtues, seventeen of which are named in all and have lines to sing. The Virtues fight for her in vain in the beginning, and *anima*, tempted and urged by the Devil, leaves them to enter the World. The Virtues then present themselves in a long "scene," and the soul finally comes back to them, repenting and asking for help. Now the Virtues, led by their queen *humilitas*, and the soul in collaboration fight the Devil and the latter is finally conquered and bound through the strength of the Virtues – not the least of these being *castitas*, who is identified in her lines towards the end as the Virgin Mary.

In his 1970 reading of the play Peter Dronke briefly characterized it in the following words: "The *Ordo Virtutum* is a morality-play by its theme, the fight for a soul, but its language often reaches out into mysticism."[12]

Morality plays, in the way this notion is usually employed, did not exist prior to the fourteenth century. As pointed out by Robert Potter, there are a number of fundamental differences between Hildegard's play, which may be characterized as "essentially a cloister drama," and, for example, the English moralities of the late Middle Ages. Potter refers mainly to the difference between the emphasis on a "lyrical celebration of Hildegard's monastic ideal" in the *Play of the Virtues* and the "dramatization of the uncertain pilgrimage of a human soul" in the moralities.[13] Similarly, the *Psychomachia* by Prudentius († c. 410) or the plays by Hrotsvitha of Gandersheim (tenth century) focus on the same basic theological theme. The genres of all these plays differ so much from Hildegard's, however, that comparisons do not seem very helpful except to emphasize the originality of the *Ordo Virtutum*. Moreover, Hildegard's play does not seem to have influenced other dramatic texts during the following centuries.

It seems more promising to read the *Ordo Virtutum* in its liturgical context. This has been done in various ways by different scholars.[14] In the following I will take up the more general relationship between what are usually referred to as dramatic and liturgical texts in the post-Carolingian centuries. As with so many other of the so-called dramatic texts of this period, Hildegard's *Ordo Virtutum* is attached to the liturgy already through its title, the word *ordo* being the term for a liturgical ceremony. Certain such "dramatic" texts, notably the famous *Visitatio Sepulchri* texts concerning the visit of the three Marys at Christ's grave on Easter morning, have been read as the beginning of the history of medieval (music-)drama, although, when read in the context of the liturgy, they do not stand out at all from other edifying ceremonies as found in many *consuetudines* of Benedictine monasteries and convents after the tenth-century revivals and in cathedral liturgical *ordines* and other manuscripts for liturgical use.[15] On the other hand, in the twelfth century, dramatic texts, as for instance large *Visitatio Sepulchri* ceremonies or plays, shepherd and magi ceremonies or plays, and St. Nicholas plays (as they are known from the twelfth-century collection of plays, the Fleury Playbook) have more or less strong relations to the liturgy but seem increasingly difficult to read solely as part of a liturgical celebration to which they were still somehow tied.[16] When is it possible to talk about a genre of "liturgical drama"? It almost seems to be a matter of choice. We can read texts such as the ones mentioned here both as liturgy and as drama for quite a period. In the first centuries of such dramatic texts, however, reading them as drama seems to be anachronistic in the sense that there are no signs in contemporary records of a consciousness of a concept of drama nor any kind of departure from a liturgical thinking. If, on the other hand, we decide to read the tenth- and eleventh-century texts in question as strictly liturgical and no more, we obscure a manifest continuity between them and the mentioned later texts.

The answer to this dilemma, as I see it, is to do both. We must recognize that anachronistic views may tell us something, in this case about a continuity which could obviously not have been perceived at the beginning of the period. Concerning Hildegard's dramatic text, the question arises how (or if) to read it in the context of this developing genre. Apart from the copying of the *Ordo Virtutum* in 1487, there are no records of connections between the play and liturgico-dramatic activities between the early manuscript from the 1180s and the modern and in recent years very vivid appropriation of the *Ordo Virtutum*.

Nothing is known about an original performance context for this play. This, of course, leaves room for speculation. Apart from the unlikely suggestion that the play was never performed, many of these suggestions seem reasonable: the play could have been written for and performed in connection with the dedication of the new convent at Rupertsberg in 1150[17] or, as Pamela Sheingorn has argued, it could have been performed as a preparation in connection with the Mass including the *ordo* for the consecration of a virgin, i.e., the ceremony for receiving new permanent members into the community. Sheingorn has demonstrated how well the play would fit in with the wording of this *ordo* as it is found in the Roman-Germanic Pontifical, the closest to an authoritative liturgical *ordo* in the post-Carolingian world, compiled in the mid-tenth century in Mainz, the archbishopric under which Hildegard lived all through her life. The episcopal blessing of the nun's garments and veil, with which she is invested during the ceremony, accompanied by three prayers over the garments and one over the veil, connects smoothly to Hildegard's play. The names of three of Hildegard's Virtues mentioned in the first of these prayers – *humilitas* (humility), *contemptus mundi* (contempt of the world), and *castitas* (chastity or virginity) – are strongly suggestive of an intimate connection between the ritual and the basic contents of the drama.[18] In the beginning of the play, when the soul, *anima infelix*, is tired of her struggle against the body and is about to give up, the Virtues try to help her, reminding her:

> Vide quid illud sit quo es induta, filia salvationis,
> et esto stabilis, et numquam cades.

[Behold what you are clothed in, daughter of salvation,
be firm and you will never fall].[19]

In the above-mentioned prayer, it is emphasized that the garments signify humility of the heart and contempt of the world (*haec indumenta humilitatem cordis et contemptum mundi significantia*), and the text also refers to them as the clothes of blessed chastity (*beatae castitatis habitum*). Sheingorn traces the metaphorical use of the vestments further in the play. However, it is not easy to see whether these literary and theological connections can say more than that Hildegard's play clearly belongs to the monastic context, a context in which such metaphors were readily understood and used. The suggestion makes sense but is in no way necessary in order to understand the play. In fact, the assumption of such a performance context does not change our understanding of the play.

Gunilla Iversen has analyzed the *Ordo Virtutum* in the context of a tragic and well recorded episode in Hildegard's life to which Barbara Newman and Julia Bolton Holloway have also pointed.[20] Iversen gives detailed comparisons of verbal texts from the *Ordo Virtutum* and the *Scivias* vision with texts from letters in which Hildegard comments the death of her favorite nun, Richardis of Stade, who had supported Hildegard during the writing of the *Scivias*. Shortly after the move to Rupertsberg, Richardis accepted to become abbess of the important abbey of Bassum against the will of Hildegard, who fought to keep her and, when unsuccessful, even to get her back. Hildegard wrote to family members, church authorities, and to the pope in order to retain Richardis. She (mis?)used her prophetic authority to claim that Richardis's acceptance was against the will of God and an example of worldly aspirations. In the end, Richardis died in Bassum shortly after (in 1152), and Hildegard apparently saw this as the intervention of God and the salvation of Richardis's soul. I will not go further into this highly revealing and complex story which has been convincingly and fruitfully analyzed as an important context for the play by Iversen but only mention that in particular the text of one letter of consolation from Hildegard to Richardis's brother, bishop Hartvig of Bremen, strongly suggests a connection between the incident and the *Ordo Virtutum*.[21]

Together, the mentioned contextual readings widen our appreciation of the text. Peter Dronke has pointed to the Biblical figural readings in the play, while Margot Fassler has noted how the liturgico-musical context for the songs of the *Ordo Virtutum* gives rise to symbolic meanings stemming from word-music associations.[22] Clearly, the biblically informed monastic world with its particular symbolic universe and its spiritual priorities creates the most necessary framework for an understanding of the play.

Hildegard's music is at the same time firmly rooted in medieval monophonic chant traditions and yet highly original.[23] Peter Dronke's characterization of the verbal language of the *Ordo Virtutum* can, with necessary modifications – musical exclamations instead of interjections, repetitions of certain key phrases in place of the adjectives – to a large degree be taken as a valid comment on the music too:

> It is a highly individual language, at times awkward and at times unclear; the adjectives can be repetitious and limited in range, the interjections excessive. It is the language not of a polished twelfth-century humanist but of someone whose unique powers of poetic vision confronted her more than once with the limits of poetic expression. At its finest, however, Hildegard's poetry faces these limits triumphantly, and achieves a visionary concentration and an evocative and associative richness that set it apart from nearly all other religious poetry of its age.[24]

Scholars have pointed to the uncommon use of modality in Hildegard's melodies (changing, or "modulating," within a textual unit), a usage editorially but tacitly changed in the Barth and Ritscher edition of the *Ordo Virtutum*, as Fabian Lochner has noted.[25] Lochner also observes that Hildegard uses the direct tritonus interval (F-B natural) at a point where it seems to be used consciously to create the highest possible tension in the drama – also tacitly changed in both existing musical editions. Lochner points out that this tritonus was written also in the late fifteenth-century manuscript of the play, which makes it less likely that the interval was due to scribal error. The unhappy soul decides at this point not to pursue her struggle for chastity. "I cannot wear to the end the garment in which I have been clothed," she has just said;[26] a bit later she continues:

> Deus creavit mundum: non facio illi iniuriam, sed volo uti illo!

[God created the world; I do no harm to him, but I wish to enjoy it].[27]

On the word *iniuriam*, which in the context of the play reveals the illusion of the unhappy soul, the melismatic melody on the syllable *in-*, according to Lochner's observation of the manuscript evidence, spans exactly a tritonus, the so-called *diabolus in musica*, an interval seemingly not used in the high Middle Ages. Lochner comments the passage in the following words:

> The tritonus F-B expresses all the offensiveness contained in the word *iniuriam* and makes this one of the most dramatic musical moments of the *Ordo*. By contrast the "emendation" of the Salzburg editors (which is not recorded in the apparatus) renders the passage trivial.[28]

In other words, also in her musical composition Hildegard went beyond what is usually considered to have been the traditional norms of her time. The musical text of her work seems to work at an aesthetic level of expressiveness similar to what Peter Dronke has pointed out concerning her poetry. This is true for the often mentioned characteristic intervalic structure of Hildegard's melodies, which exceeds the normal medieval monophonic idiom in her extensive *melismas*;[29] and in her use of large intervals, quite often featuring even two such intervals juxtaposed in the same direction, notably the leap of a fifth followed by a further leap of a fourth thus creating a rising octave.[30]

At an important point in the dramatic construction of the play, towards its conclusion after the binding of the Devil, a crucial answer is given to his former unanswered challenge that virginity amounts to a denial of nature: the virgin birth was not against nature but greater than nature, drawing mankind to itself.[31] After this, a further strengthening of the above-mentioned musically expressive juxtaposed intervals – even repeated twice within the same song – creates a musical high point in which two leaps of a fifth follow upon each other, thus creating the highly unusual rise of a none as the Virtues praise God for his miraculous act of salvation, *O deus, quis es tu* [God, who are you]. Thus the musical and the verbal text seem to reinforce each other, expressing the overall theologico-dramatic culmination of the play.

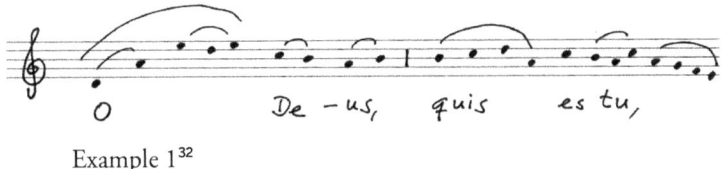

Example 1[32]

The *Ordo Virtutum* should be seen not only in the monastic and biblico-prophetic tradition, but also in the context of the earlier mentioned music dramatic tradition of the Latin liturgy. Hildegard's play, to be sure, conforms neither stylistically nor in terms of a precise relationship to a particular day of the annual cycle of celebrations to the contemporary tradition of the so-called Latin music dramas, but this does not mean that we should not be able to read it – and appreciate it – in this context.

Gunilla Iversen, among others, has pointed out how the very introduction to the play hints at the traditional use of question, answer, and announcement found in the early liturgico-dramatic texts, the *Quem quaeritis in sepulchro* dialogues preserved from the tenth century onwards; in the similarly formed dialogues for the shepherds' ceremonies from the tenth-eleventh centuries; and also in the introit antiphon for Ascension day.[33] The introductory verses of the *Play of the Virtues* form – as pointed out by Margot Fassler, who reads the play in the light of the tradition of the *Ordo Prophetarum*[34] – a Jesse Tree. The Patriarchs and Prophets are the roots and the Virtues live as branches on this tree, thus combining the idea of the Virtues with a traditional christological interpretation of Isaiah 11:1-2, about the branch which shall grow out of the roots of the stump of Jesse, and John 15:1-8, about the tree and its branches.

This introduction gives a theological framework for the understanding of the play and for the understanding of the roles of the Virtues. But, as already mentioned, in its form it is also reminiscent of the quintessential structure of the Latin music dramas, a practice which by the twelfth century was very well established all over central Europe. Further, the melody to the initial question in the *Ordo Virtutum* can be related to the first song, *Stella fulgore nimio rutilat*, of the traditional *Ordo Stellae*, the magi ceremony, which was well known at the time and with which Hildegard could have been familiar. For comparison I give the two melodies:

Example 2a: Who are these, who come like clouds?

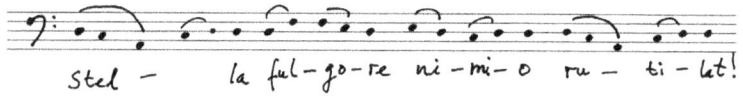

Example 2b: The star shines with great strength[35]

One should not talk of quotation here, but rather – as is typical for Hildegard's more intuitive approach – of a procedure of associative invocation, as Margot Fassler has pointed to, or maybe simply of an unconscious contextual reminiscence.[36] It may be enlightening to read the play with this in mind. What seems to be typical for the Latin music dramas from very early on is a structure which I have frequently discussed.[37] The so-called liturgical dramas seem to move back and forth between a liturgical celebrative mode, from which they take their point of departure, and an unfolding linear narrative (sometimes even laid out in a processional movement), which again leads back to – and reinforces – the celebration in songs of praise, announcements, prayers or the like, most often songs of praise as befitting the Easter and Christmas messages.

Such a structure can be found in Hildegard's play, which does not quote the established liturgy – as already noted, the style of Hildegard's poetry and music is much more individualistic than any of the other known Latin music dramas of her time – but still preserves the dichotomy of the two modes of liturgical action: celebration and narration (representation). The narrative must reinforce the celebration, which otherwise runs the risk of becoming an empty postulate. And the celebration must occur to make it clear that the narrative is not just a narrative but points to the meaning for the assembly of the congregation *hic et nunc*.

For Hildegard's convent – possibly including guests, of which there were many – the *Ordo Virtutum*, regardless of its unknown exact performance circumstances, would not just have been an entertainment. The form, intensity, and deeply theological mood of the play all make it clear that we are dealing with an essential ritual celebration, shaped in a very individualistic way but emphasizing the conventual meaning. The nuns of the convent would have had to be the performers of the Virtues and the soul. Thus the play would have been experienced – and no doubt meant – as a play, a ritual about themselves as well as the whole world, a play about the meaning of the conventual life of Hildegard's virgins.

In the understanding of the anthropologist Clifford Geertz, brought to my attention by C. Clifford Flanigan, rituals form the meeting point between the daily life and the theoretical concepts by which we understand the world: "in a ritual, the world as lived and the world as imagined … turns out to be the same world."[38] In this way, the *Ordo Virtutum* works as a ritual just as some *Visitatio Sepulchri* ceremonies may be said to have as their function to bring to life the underlying Christian mythology in an efficacious way for the congregation assembled to celebrate Easter.[39] The *Ordo Virtutum* actualizes the meaning of the conventual ideology of Hildegard and (doubtless) of the sisters of the convent as it confronts this ideology with the daily struggles of the women. Just as the more common types of Latin music dramas had recourse to liturgical antiphons, hymns, and, for instance, the *Te Deum*, the *Ordo Virtutum* has recourse to celebrative elements which may not have been part of actual daily celebrations but which had the same form and intention as these.

Thus the play starts in a celebrative mood (the Jesse Tree) before the inner conflict of the *anima felix* becomes evident and the first part of the action unfolds. When the action has come to its nadir, when *anima* has left the community of Virtues and the devil has posed a challenge which cannot easily be answered by the Virtues, the play turns away from the linear action or narrative and, in what seems to be a very Hildegardian way, a kind of celebrative dance (as Peter Dronke has suggested) takes place. The verbal and musical text constitutes a self-presentation of the Virtues, individual voices always being taken up by the whole group of Virtues. This, again, is not known as an established liturgical procedure, but certainly it must have been a manifestation of the convent and its self-understanding in a mood that seems to be very close, indeed, to the mood of the self-understanding of Hildegard's nuns, possessing a clear celebrative tone praising God for his gifts to the community.[40] Then the action is taken up again with the arrival of the repentant *anima*, the fight with the Devil, and the ultimate victory leading into songs of praise that end in a hymn-like song, the *In principio omnes creature viruerunt* [In the beginning all creatures grew and flourished], a hymn where Christ himself is speaking to God and to mankind, pointing to both the virgin birth and the redemption on the cross and concluding – certainly in a celebrative, liturgical mood – on words set to a highly melismatic melody. This melody is in turn related to the earlier mentioned culmination (the two consecutive leaps of a fifth), here, however, smoothened out a bit, but still recognizable as a reference to the mentioned melodic culmination:

> Ergo nunc, omnes homines,
> genua vestra ad patrem vestrum flectite,
> ut vobis manum suam porrigat.

[Therefore now, all men bend your knees to your Father, so that he may reach out his hand to you].

One may to a certain degree understand the contents of the totality of Hildegard's dramatic text as a ritualized celebration of the idea of the conventual life, but then one must also speak of an individualization of the rituals of the church as its immediate background. These two things go together, reinforcing – as my reading of Hildegard's drama in the context of the Latin music dramas of the liturgy seems to underline – the understanding of Hildegard as a woman of the Gregorian church reform of the eleventh century. The Gregorian reform in its own way may be said to have paved the way for a further sacralization of the priesthood as well as of pious monastic practices as a response to the process of individualization whereby lay people became able to share (earlier) pious ideals which had been the prerogative of monks and clerics.[41]

Notes

1. Peter Dronke, *Poetic Individuality in the Middle Ages: New Departures in Poetry, 1100-1150*, Oxford, 1970, pp. 150-92, gives a critical edition of the verbal text of the *Ordo Virtutum* on pp. 180-92. See also Peter Dronke, "The Composition of Hildegard of Bingen's *Symphonia*," *Sacris Erudiri* 19 (1969-70), pp. 381-93. Later works by Peter Dronke partly dealing with Hildegard include *Women Writers of the Middle Ages: A Critical Study of Texts from Perpetua († 203) to Marguerite Porete († 1310)*, Cambridge, 1984, pp. 144-201; and *Nine Medieval Latin Plays*, Cambridge, 1994, pp. 147-84, which contains Dronke's translation of the *Ordo Virtutum*. Ernst Robert Curtius, *Europäische Literatur und Lateinisches Mittelalter*, Bern, 1948, is often considered as the most influential scholarly work on medieval Latin literature in this century. For a recent critical assessment of Curtius's role in the history of this scholarship see Richard Utz, "'Cleansing' the Discipline: Ernst Robert Curtius and his Medievalist Turn," in Richard Utz and Tom Shippey [eds.], *Medievalism in the Modern World: Essays in Honor of Leslie J. Workman*, Turnhout, 1998, pp. 359-78.

2. Karl Young, *The Drama of the Medieval Church*, Oxford, 1933; O. B. Hardison, *Christian Rite and Christian Drama in the Middle Ages: Essays in the Origin and Early History of Modern Drama*, Baltimore, 1965; William L. Smoldon, *The Music of the Medieval Church Dramas*, Oxford, 1980. The lack of references to Hildegard's drama has been commented on by Pamela Sheingorn, "The Virtues of Hildegard's *Ordo Virtutum*; or, It Was a Woman's World," in Audrey Ekdahl Davidson [ed.], *The "Ordo Virtutum" of Hildegard of Bingen: Critical Studies*, Kalamazoo, 1992, pp. 43-62, esp. p. 44; and Robert Potter, "The *Ordo Virtutum*: Ancestor of the English Moralities?", in Davidson [ed.], *The "Ordo Virtutum" of Hildegard of Bingen*, pp. 31-41, esp. p. 31. Three fairly recent general introductions to medieval Latin (music) drama do not mention Hildegard's play either: Glynne Wickham, *The Medieval Theatre*, Cambridge, 1987[3]; Susan Rankin, "Liturgical Drama," in Richard Crocker and David Hiley [eds.], *The Early Middle Ages to 1300*, Oxford, 1989[2] [*The New Oxford History of Music*, 2], pp. 310-56; David Hiley, *Western Plainchant: A Handbook*, Oxford, 1993 (see the section on liturgical drama, pp. 250-73). On the other hand, in Audrey Ekdahl Davidson and Clifford Davidson, *Performing Medieval Music Drama*, Kalamazoo, 1998, the *Ordo Virtutum* is dealt with as a part of the liturgical drama tradition.

3. Barbara Newman, *Sister of Wisdom: St. Hildegard's Theology of the Feminine*, Berkeley, 1987 [1997[2]]. Also: Barbara Newman [ed.], *Voice of the Living Light: Hildegard of Bingen and Her World*, Berkeley, 1998; Sabina Flanagan, *Hildegard of Bingen, 1098-1179: A Visionary Life*, London, 1989 [1998[2]].

4. Newman, *Sister of Wisdom*, p. xx. Michael Klaper has drawn my attention to the similar view in Barbara Newman, "Seherin–Prophetin–Mystikerin: Hildegard von Bingen in der hagiographischen Tradition," in Edeltraud Forster et al. [eds.], *Hildegard von Bingen: Prophetin durch die Zeiten, zum 900. Geburtstag*, Freiburg, 1997, pp. 126-52.

5. Newman, *Sister of Wisdom*, pp. xx-xxi.

6. Idem, p. 77, particularly n. 90.

7. Gunilla Iversen, "*Ego Humilitas, Regina Virtutum*: Poetic Language and Literary Structure in Hildegard of Bingens Vision of the Virtues," in Davidson [ed.], *The "Ordo Virtutum" of Hildegard of Bingen*, pp. 79-110, esp. pp. 93-4. Here Iversen also points out that Bernard's *De gradibus* seems to have been known by the clergy of Cologne, who were closely related to Hildegard's convent at Rupertsberg. Compare also Margot Fassler's chapter, "Composer and Dramatist: Melodious Singing and the Freshness of Remorse," in Newman [ed.], *Voice of the Living Light*, pp. 149-75, here pp. 158-9. Hildegard's *Scivias* is edited in Adelgvndis Führkötter and Angela Carlevaris [eds.], *Hildegard's "Scivias," Corpvs Christianorvm XLIII and XLIII A*, Turnhout, 1978. The word *scivias* apparently was coined (or received) by Hildegard. It seems to have been constructed from *scio* and *vias* and may be understood as knowledge of God's ways. See Führkötter and Carlevaris [eds.], *Hildegard's "Scivias,"* pp. xiii-xiv.

8. Flanagan, *Hildegard of Bingen*, p. 5; Newman, *Sister of Wisdom*, pp. 8-9.

9. I thank Michael Klaper for valuable information about the new view on the Riesencodex (based among other things also on research by A. Derolez), also found in his comments to the facsimile edition of the musical parts of the Riesencodex which has recently appeared. Cf. Lorenz Welker [ed.], Hildegard von Bingen, *Lieder: Faksimile Riesencodex (Hs. 2) der Hessischen Landesbibliothek Wiesbaden, fol. 466-481^v; mit einem Kommentar von Michael Klaper*, Wiesbaden, 1998 [*Elementa Musicae*, 1]. Concerning the mentioned manuscripts see also Hildegard von Bingen,

Lieder [eds.], Pudentiana Barth and M. Immaculata Ritscher, Salzburg, 1969, pp. 317-23. Also Dronke, *Poetic Individuality*, p. 180; Audrey Ekdahl Davidson, "Another Manuscript of the *Ordo Virtutum* of Hildegard von Bingen," *Early Drama, Art, and Music Review* 13 (1991), pp. 36-41; and Audrey Ekdahl Davidson, "Music and Performance: Hildegard of Bingen's *Ordo Virtutum*," in Davidson [ed.], *The "Ordo Virtutum" of Hildegard of Bingen*, pp. 1-29, here pp. 23-5. The *Ordo Virtutum* is critically edited in Barth and Ritscher [eds.], *Hildegard von Bingen*, pp. 165-205; another recent (performance) edition is Audrey Ekdahl Davidson [ed.], *Hildegard von Bingen: "Ordo Virtutum,"* Kalamazoo, 1984, containing an English translation by Bruce Hozeski and Gunilla Iversen, to which I refer throughout this paper.

10. Iversen, "*Ego Humilitas, regina Virtutum*," pp. 96 and 104. Similarly, Gunilla Iversen, "*O Virginitas, in regali thalamo stas*, New Light on the *Ordo Virtutum*: Hildegard, Richardis, and the Order of the Virtues," *Early Drama, Art, and Music Review* 20 (1997), pp. 1-18, esp. p. 3.

11. Fassler, "Composer and Dramatist," pp. 168-75.

12. Dronke, *Poetic Individuality*, p. 178.

13. Potter, "The *Ordo Virtutum*," pp. 31-33 and 36. Compare also Robert Potter, "The Holy Spectacles of Hildegard of Bingen," *European Medieval Drama* 2 (1997), pp. 315-31.

14. Notably, Fassler, "Composer and Dramatist," and Sheingorn, "The Virtues of Hildegard's *Ordo Virtutum*."

15. As pointed out by C. Clifford Flanigan, "Medieval Liturgy and the Arts: *Visitatio Sepulchri* as Paradigm," in Eva Louise Lillie and Nils Holger Petersen [eds.], *Liturgy and the Arts in the Middle Ages: Studies in Honor of C. Clifford Flanigan*, Copenhagen, 1996, pp. 9-35, esp. p. 29.

16. An important contribution to this discussion is C. Clifford Flanigan, "The Fleury Playbook, the Traditions of Medieval Latin Drama, and Modern Scholarship," in Thomas P. Campbell and Clifford Davidson [eds.], *The Fleury Playbook: Essays and Studies*, Kalamazoo, 1985, pp. 1-25.

17. Potter, "The *Ordo Virtutum*," p. 39 and n. 19.

18. Sheingorn, "The Virtues of Hildegard's *Ordo Virtutum*," pp. 53-7. See also for the order for the consecration of virgins in the Roman-Germanic Pontifical, Cyrille Vogel and Reinhard Elze [eds.], *Le Pontifical Romanogermanique du dixième siècle*, Citta del Vaticano, 1963-72, vol. I, pp. 38-46. The episcopal prayer is found on p. 40.

19. Dronke, *Poetic Individuality*, p. 182; Davidson [ed.], *Hildegard von Bingen*, p. 5.

20. Iversen, "*O Virginitas, in regali thalamo stas*"; Newman, *Sister of Wisdom*, pp. 222-3; Julia Bolton Holloway, "The Monastic Context of Hildegard's *Ordo Virtutum*," in Davidson [ed.], The *"Ordo Virtutum" of Hildegard of Bingen*, pp. 63-77. Very recently also Gunilla Iversen, "Réaliser une vision. La dernière vision de Scivias et le drame *Ordo virtutum* de Hildegarde de Bingen," *Revue de Musicologie* 86 (2000), pp. 37-63, has appeared.

21. Iversen, "*O Virginitas, in regali thalamo stas*," esp. pp. 7-14. Iversen's article can be summarized to the effect that, although we shall "never fully know the mystery which lies behind the *Ordo Virtutum*" (p. 14), there seems to be a basis for assuming that after the tragic incident Hildegard arranged the vision from *Scivias* into a play on the basis of a vision of Richardis in the royal bedchamber (of God) which she related in the mentioned letter to Hartvig.

22. Fassler, "Composer and Dramatist," esp. pp. 161-2, where three ways of word and music interactions are outlined, and pp. 166-7 and pp. 171-2, where the author demonstrates the use of the traditional votive antiphon *Ave regina celorum* as a kind of model for the *O nobilissima*

viriditas from the *Scivias* and also for the *Gaudete o socii* from the *Ordo Virtutum*, sung by Victory as the Devil is bound near the end of the play – in both cases with a clearly significant meaning.

23. For descriptions of Hildegard's style, see Marianne Richert Pfau, "Music and Text in Hildegard's Antiphons," in Barbara Newman [ed.], *Saint Hildegard of Bingen, Symphonia: A Critical Edition of the Symphonia armonie celestium revelationem with introduction, translation and commentary*, Ithaca, 1988/1998, pp. 74-94; and Fassler, "Composer and Dramatist," esp. pp. 151-5 and 161.

24. Dronke, *Poetic Individuality*, pp. 178-9.

25. Fabian Lochner, "The Music for Hildegard of Bingen's *Ordo Virtutum*: Problems Solved and Unsolved," unpublished paper given at *Novus et antiquus, The Twenty-third Annual Interdisciplinary CAES Conference* (arranged by the Committee for the Advancement of Early Studies), Ball State University, Muncie, Indiana, USA. I am grateful to Fabian Lochner for letting me use his unpublished manuscript and for helpful discussions. See also Davidson [ed.], *The "Ordo Virtutum" of Hildegard of Bingen*, pp. 4-5. Cf. Margot Fassler's description of the meaningfulness of the departures and returns to the main pitch in a Hildegard song, in her "Composer and Dramatist", pp. 165-6, and, generally, Pfau, "Music and Text in Hildegard's Antiphons."

26. … *non possum perficere hoc quod sum induta*. See Davidson [ed.], *Hildegard von Bingen*, p. 6; Dronke, *Poetic Individuality*, p. 183.

27. Davidson [ed.], *Hildegard von Bingen*, pp. 6-7; Dronke, *Poetic Individuality*, p. 183.

28. Lochner, "The Music for Hildegard of Bingen's *Ordo Virtutum*," p. 4. The passage in question is found on fol. 479^r in the Riesencodex, and fol. 209^v in the late London manuscript. The normalized versions Barth and Ritscher [eds.], *Hildegard von Bingen*, p. 171; Davidson [ed.], *Hildegard von Bingen*, p. 7.

29. Cf. Fassler, "Composer and Dramatist," p. 154.

30. Davidson [ed.], *Hildegard von Bingen*, pp. 1, 3, 14, 18, 24, 27, 30, and 33; Barth and Ritscher [eds.], *Hildegard von Bingen* , pp. 165, 167, 180, 185, 192, 196, 198, and 201. See Pfau, "Music and Text in Hildegard's Antiphons," pp. 78 and 88; and also Joseph Schmidt-Görg, "Die Gesänge der heiligen Hildegard," in Barth and Ritscher [eds.], *Hildegard von Bingen*, pp. 9-16, esp. p. 11.

31. *Unum virum protuli, qui genus humanum / ad se congregat, contra te, per nativitatem suam*. See Dronke, *Poetic Individuality*, p. 191; Davidson [ed.], *Hildegard von Bingen*, p. 33; Barth and Ritscher [eds.], *Hildegard von Bingen*, p. 201. Concerning the understanding of this passage, which in Davidson's edition is taken to refer directly to the human nature of Christ, but which Dronke understands as referring to salvation through Christ, i.e., that the Virgin birth "gathered human nature towards itself," see Dronke, *Poetic Individuality*, p. 177.

32. Davidson [ed.], *Hildegard von Bingen*, p. 33; Barth and Ritscher [eds.], *Hildegard von Bingen*, pp. 201-2.

33. Iversen, "*Ego Humilitas, regina Virtutum*," pp. 95-6.

34. Fassler, "Composer and Dramatist," pp. 168-9. For general, recent information on the Prophet plays, see Rankin, "Liturgical Drama," pp. 348-9.

35. See Norbert King, *Mittelalterliche Dreikönigspiele*, Freiburg, 1979, pp. 16 and 195; concerning *Ordo Stellae* of the category A, see also pp. 2-3; see also Smoldon, *The Music of the Medieval Church Dramas*, pp. 127-8. For the two melodies: a) Davidson [ed.], *Hildegard von Bingen*, p. 1; Barth and Ritscher [eds.], *Hildegard von Bingen*, p. 165; b) from the *Ordo ad repraesentationem Herodem* from the Fleury Playbook, W. Thomas Marrocco and Nicholas Sandon [eds.], *The Oxford Anthology of Music*, London, 1977, p. 49.

36. See above, n. 22.

37. I refer to my unpublished Danish language doctoral dissertation on the genre of the liturgical drama (Institute of Church History, University of Copenhagen, 1994) which is presently being reworked for English publication. In briefer form I have also discussed this in a number of published articles, among which I here refer to three (which contain further references): "A Mutual Lamenting: Mother and Son in *Filius Getronis*," in Jacqueline Hamesse [ed.], *Roma, magistra mundi. Itineraria culturae medievalis. Mélanges offerts au Père L. E. Boyle à l'occasion de son 75e anniversaire*, Louvain-La-Neuve, 1998, pp. 687-701; "*Quem quaeritis in sepulchro?* The Visit to the Sepulchre and Easter Processions in Piacenza 65," in Pierre Racine [ed.], *Il Libro del Maestro: Codice 65 dell'archivio Capitolare della cattedrale di Piacenza (sec. XII), Atti del convegno Marzo 1997*, Piacenza, 1999, pp. 109-22; and "Les textes polyvalents du *Quem quaeritis* à Winchester au dixième siècle," *Revue de Musicologie* 86 (2000), pp. 105-18.

38. Clifford Geertz, "Religion as a Cultural System," in Michael Banton [ed.], *Anthropological Approaches to the Study of Religion*, London, 1966, p. 28. See also Flanigan, "Medieval Liturgy and the Arts," p. 10.

39. Cf. ritual readings of *Visitatio Sepulchri* ceremonies by C. Clifford Flanigan, both in his "Medieval Liturgy and the Arts" and in his early contributions, "The Roman Rite and the Origins of the Liturgical Drama," *University of Toronto Quarterly* 43 (1973-74), pp. 263-84; and "The Liturgical Context of the *Quem Quaeritis* Trope," *Comparative Drama* 8 (1974), p. 45-62.

40. Cf. the well-known answer of Hildegard to the question about the lavish dressing of her nuns during the office on feast days. See for instance Potter, "The Holy Spectacles of Hildegard of Bingen," pp. 315-7, where letters (in translation) to this effect are quoted extensively.

41. Cf. for instance the reading of the Gregorian Reform proposed in Norman F. Cantor, *The Civilization of the Middle Ages*, New York, 1993, pp. 243-49.

The Performed Book: Textuality and Social Space in the Cult of Sainte Foy
Kathleen Ashley and Pamela Sheingorn[*]

The impetus for this essay was a question: how do books or images of books function in the cult of Sainte Foy? In seeking to understand the multiple constructions of books in medieval religious culture we included the material representations of books and writing as well as the social implications of texts. The importance of books for the cult of Sainte Foy is evident from even a casual glance at the sculpture adorning monuments associated with the saint, for example, at Perse, an early twelfth-century priory church belonging to the nearby monastery at Conques, home of the cult of Sainte Foy.[1] The sculptors at Perse had obviously sought inspiration from the iconographic themes of the mother church. What the art historian Jean-Claude Fau calls "a Conques theme par excellence" is visible in the image of an angel holding with both hands an open book,[2] one of a number of such angels carved on the arches surrounding the tympanum of the south portal at Perse (Figure 1). The multiple images of angels with books that strike any visitor to the small church at Perse are visual icons of a theme we extend to the whole cult of Sainte Foy, that is, the performance of the book. We find it significant that the book is not closed, but open. The angels gaze out at viewers entering the doorway, as if insisting that they examine the open pages. This same insistence on the visitor's attention to texts characterizes many aspects of the cult of Sainte Foy. The various social spaces in which the cult of Foy was enacted are inscribed with a kind of insistent textuality that we explore here.

---

[*] We would like to thank Marilyn Deegan for her photography at Conques and Perse; Richard Swartz for helpful leads in the literature on literacy; Daniel Smartt for sharing portions of his unpublished discussions on Moissac and his extensive knowledge of medieval pilgrimage; Jody Enders and Cynthia Brown for inviting us to participate at the colloquium on "The Book in Performance" at the University of California, Santa Barbara. This paper was also read at the Indiana University medieval symposium in memory of C. Clifford Flanigan.

Figure 1: Angel with book from arch around tympanum at Perse church (Photo: Marilyn Deegan)

Our exploration requires that we interrogate modern assumptions about the book, moving back to a historical and cultic context in which a very different set of associations was triggered by texts. The contemporary model of the book often presumes that reading is an individual, silent, and usually private experience.[3] As figured in the eighteenth and nineteenth centuries, reading could be a means of escape from one's mundane life into a realm of fantasy. It could be seen as a refusal to participate socially, hence a selfish indulgence. This proto-modern reader is represented in the late medieval dream vision, where dwelling on the book often creates a solipsistic space, alienated from social obligation and community. An alternate but not totally incompatible view is that books belong in libraries built and used by specialized professionals such as librarians and scholars. Books are kept in separate, exclusive spaces, either aristocratic or professional, such as Duke Humphrey's library, the Duke of Berry's collection, or the monastic or university library. Access to the privileged book space is restricted to some elite, so that the book becomes a sign of privacy and cultivation. In the eleventh- and twelfth-century cult of Sainte Foy we see a very different model of the book, one which although especially apparent at Conques may well be more broadly applicable in similar cultic contexts. In these contexts, books are publicly performed; they are to be seen and heard.[4] At the various cult sites, in sculpture, manuscript illustrations, and texts, we see an insistent performance of the book that we interpret as deliberate self-representation by the monastic authorities. But what they are performing is a monastic literacy that, contrary to our modern expectations, does not display a private and exclusive textuality but rather dramatizes a public act of reading. The book is open, inclined towards the general viewer, not closed, accessible only to the specialized reader.[5]

Other scholars, of course, have pointed out differences between modern reading experience and medieval literacy. Rosamund McKitterick refined our understanding by directing attention to the many different levels of literacy she found in the Carolingian period,[6] and Michael Clanchy emphasized that people heard texts rather than reading them.[7]

Others have emphasized that even in monasteries silent reading was not the norm. The individual reader there probably uttered sounds, and texts were read aloud in the refectory and in liturgical services. Our point would be that books are not simply performed audibly, which has been generally acknowledged, but are performed visually as well. In fact the monastic book is positioned at the interface of hearing and seeing. The image of the open book both represents the monastery's claim to the power of literacy and (paradoxically) becomes the vehicle for the popular extension of the cult.[8]

To demonstrate the interrelations between textuality and the social space, we have found useful Brian Stock's notion of "textual community," even if our use of the idea goes well beyond his. Stock defines a textual community as a group of people "whose social activities are centered around texts."[9] However, he emphasizes that "[t]he text in question need not be written down nor the majority of auditors actually literate."[10] In other words a "literate interpreter" may verbally relate the text. Stock's most important point is that the group's "interaction must take place around an agreed meaning for the text," so that their understanding of the text provides a basis for their communal "thought and behavior."[11]

With due respect to Stock, we have extended the idea of a textual community to a much wider variety of cultural locations and social interactions, and here we see our work as paralleling that of Sharon Farmer's investigation into the multiple communities of Saint Martin.[12] The most obvious and best-known textual community associated with the cult of Foy is delineated in the first two books of the *Liber miraculorum sancte Fidis* written in the early eleventh century by Bernard of Angers.[13]

However, the textual community Bernard constructs is not found at the monastic site of Conques, where he collected stories of the saint's miracles from local oral informants, but rather back in his intellectual home at Chartres.[14] Bernard claims to have been a student of Fulbert of Chartres and a member of a close circle around him. Bernard dedicates his collection of Foy's miracles to that eminent scholar, and clearly intends the text to circulate among his highly educated and powerful friends in northern France, who form his intellectual cohort and patronize his act of scholarly piety. As Bernard dispatches his first collection to this northern textual community, he flatters their powers to judge literary accomplishment. He suggests for example (in a passage of labyrinthine logic) that his book be given to a John Scotus who

> would never indulge in heretical deception or uncritical admiration.... [I]n his close friendship he is so favorable toward my humble work that he dares to number me among the wise. ... For John Scotus displayed such favor towards me that he asserted I was not inferior to the genius of the writers of antiquity. But although his generous honesty may be exaggerated, I won't fall under this spell. I won't be so deluded as to think myself their equal, since, as I have said so often, I seem more like a monkey than a man in comparison to them. Nevertheless it is fitting that a teacher praise a student, because the encouragement increases mental abilities, but it is also fitting that the disciple see himself as less than he is, so that he does not come to grief through excessive praise. Moreover, some famous men have read my book and their opinions differ only a little from those mentioned above. (1.34)

In contrast to the portrait of a discriminating northern elite, Bernard's text represents the monastery and region of Conques as a backwater, populated by gullible rustics and naive monks. Bernard presents himself as educated outsider and privileged interpreter of the miraculous events that have happened around Conques, whose complete significance the actual participants are too ignorant to grasp. In Bernard's narrative, there is no textual community at Conques; he writes of his exasperation with the monks' failure to keep any written records of the miracles worked there – they were ignorant of the names of people who had received miracles, he says,[15] and in a devastating critique of their knowledge of Latin, he informs them that they do not even decline the name of their own saint correctly.[16] Bernard's significant textual community is, as we have said, the one in northern France, and the south is deliberately constructed as the illiterate antithesis to the cultivated, intellectual, and textualized north. For example, Bernard identifies a negative response to his work with the local populace and with illiteracy by placing the only critique in the mouth of a local peasant who, he says, was instigated by the Devil to ridicule the miracles Bernard redacted. Bernard characterizes this critic as an "ignoramus" and "a stranger to all wisdom." He "gives thanks to the Author of Truth … that the only man the Enemy sent for this wicked task was illiterate and ignorant of all good."[17] Many historians including Brian Stock have accepted Bernard's picture as a historical description of Conques in the early eleventh century, but we would argue that the antithesis between Conques and Chartres is very clearly a literary construction that fits Bernard's agenda and cannot be read as a simple reflection of the actual textual communities.[18]

There is evidence even within Bernard's own miracle collection that the monastery is not as unlettered as he implies in his address to Fulbert. Bernard chose to write most of his miracle stories in Latin prose but composed one passage in hexameter verse (1.6). And in the subsequent chapter Bernard attempts to rationalize this anomaly by telling the reader that "A monk named Arseus persuaded me to write [the hexameter verses] with his insistent pleas." Bernard reports that he gave in reluctantly but still chose to set those verses on the page like prose "lest the second half should seem to be out of harmony with the first." He says, "I feared that the meaning would be lost if the rhythmical measure of the scansion confused the reader's expectations."[19] Bernard's literary expectations may differ from those of Arseus, but the detail indicates a literary culture at Conques that Bernard ignores.

Bernard had visited Conques three times and compiled two books of miracles that helped to popularize the cult in the north. As he says in the letter that closes Book I, "many respected people have heard of Sainte Foy for the first time through my writing and through me her previously unknown miracles become known to many." No doubt aware of the utility of the miracle collection in spreading the fame of the monastery, after Bernard's death one or more monk-authors at Conques took up the task of redacting the miracle stories. In the prologue to Book III the monk-author is well aware of the *Liber miraculorum* as a book and of himself as an author. He is concerned that readers understand why a second prologue is appropriate (since Bernard had written such an elaborate first prologue). He thinks matters of authorship must be clear, since if they are confused, readers might abandon the book. To this subsequent author, these miracles "deserve to be widely known and written up in elegant style"– a clear indication of a literary community at Conques.

A variety of other evidence also points to the monastery's enjoyment of literary experimentation and its poetic self-awareness. Numerous passages in the non-Bernardian continuation of the *Liber miraculorum* are written in highly elaborate metered verse with classical allusions testifying to a textual community based not just on miracle stories but also on the antique poetic tradition. For example, a monk-author describes Foy's resurrection from the dead of one of her devotees in language dense with classical allusion:

> How often my Foy has broken the law of Avernus.
> The Thracian showed respect when he visited Pluto's kingdoms,
> But she shatters laws when she goes there and demands the return of her prize.
>
> The gates of Tenaria lie open and he departs from Erebos,
> Then they flee the shadows, the barred doors of Hell are opened,
> Death also quakes when it abandons its own laws in this way,
> Thus the victrix conveys supernal souls to the upper air. (L. 6)

It is quite clear, then, that not just a general textual community of monks existed at Conques but, more specifically, one formed around classical poetic texts, an identity which was then displayed in the efflorescence of metered verse in the non-Bernardian miracle collections.

Although for Bernard the collection of miracle stories about Foy formed the text for his ideal textual community, the *Liber miraculorum* was for the Conques community merely one of a collection of texts about their patron saint that formed the basis for the cultic community. That the monks were consciously compiling larger collections of texts about their saint, a type of manuscript called a *libellus*, is certainly indicated by the monk-continuator in the prologue to Book III where he describes his rewriting of another crucial text about Foy, the *Passio*:

> since it was clumsily composed on the basis of early descriptions of her torments and is highly confusing and far too short, even to the point of obscurity, it has been my task to straighten out some of its confusions and correct it by casting it in a more highly rhetorical style.[20] To the *Passio* I have added a few miracles chosen from many. And I have decided to call the whole volume Panaretos, by which I mean "the book of all of her powers."[21]

In a self-conscious display of sophistication, the assembler of this text uses a Greek rather than a Latin term for a collection of texts about a saint. The term *Panaretos* is repeated elsewhere in the book as the name of the text that will spread Sainte Foy's fame to the world (4.15).

A complete example of a *libellus* or *Panaretos* (that is a collection of texts about Sainte Foy) is preserved in Sélestat (Alsace). In the late eleventh century, a priory there was given to the monastery of Conques and the church renamed after Sainte Foy. Presumably as part of the establishment of this foundation, a *libellus* was composed, surely at Conques, and sent to the new acquisition, suggesting that the community in Sélestat was identified not just with land and buildings or personnel, but also with a set of cult texts. The manuscript, which exists today as Sélestat, Bibliothèque Humaniste 22, includes the *Passio*, the *Translatio* or account of the movement of the saint's relics, a hymn to Foy, the *Book of Miracles*, and two sermons for the feast of Foy on 6 October. To this collection sent from Conques, the monks at Sélestat added an Office of Sainte Foy for her feast day as well as a foundation legend specifically tailored to the new home of the cult, which provides legendary justification for its patronage by the Hohenstaufen family.[22] The manuscript with the addition of the foundation legend thus constructs a textual community at Sélestat that was influential in spreading the cult to Germanic lands.[23]

One of the most significant contexts for performing books was the liturgy. Without these texts, a new foundation could not have centered its ritual activities on its patron saint. Miracle stories may well have been read aloud at mealtimes; the rhymed text of the Office for the feast day of Sainte Foy is complete with the neumes necessary for its performance. The *Passio* as well as each of the sermons is divided into parts for reading during the liturgy, presumably on the feast day. The clearly separated sections of the *Passio* are designated by Roman numerals in red and colored initials, elements designed to enable the performance.

Most interesting is the large multi-colored and historiated initial S on fol. 5v, which introduces the *Passio* text.[24] Framed in the top loop of the S are three figures: Foy on the left, in the center her fellow martyr Caprais, who points towards the third figure, Dacian, the Roman prefect responsible for their martyrdom. Thus the initial represents the passion narrative whose text it initiates. However, the scene is not simply a representation of a historical event. Foy's gesture of blessing must be intended for the figure pictured in the lower loop of the S below. This figure, a tonsured monk, tilts his head back in order to direct his gaze on the three figures in the upper loop and holds a book aloft in both hands. Thus, the initial is reflexive of itself as text. The figure probably represents the writer, offering his book to his patroness. He may also embody the reader, since the scene is indicated as a liturgical moment by the pendant lamp between the two saints in the upper loop, a type of lamp normally hanging in a church in the high Middle Ages. The initial thus refers to the reading aloud of the *Passio* on the saint's feast day as a performance of the book for the liturgical community that owned it.[25]

A manuscript contemporary with Sélestat 22 contains a vernacular version of Foy's *Passio*, a song in Provençal that explicitly describes performance of the book for a non-monastic textual community. This *Chanson de Sainte Foy*, which has been translated and studied by Robert Clark, was presumably sung on Foy's feast day as a way of communicating the narrative of her Passion to a lay audience.[26] Such a performance would unite the Latin-reading monastery (who owned the manuscript) with the vernacular-speaking laity who heard the song. The opening lines of the song seem to reveal the writer's concern with authorizing the vernacular version, since it begins: "I heard a Latin book read under a pine tree. I listened to it in its entirety, to the end. There was no meaning that it did not render clearly." The *Chanson* thus explicitly describes the transfer of the Latin book from its liturgical space into the outdoor epic space marked by the pine tree, where it can be transformed into a vernacular song.

In addition to the vernacular *Chanson de Sainte Foy*, extensive and disparate types of historical documentation from Conques itself reveal various ways that the monastery formed a textual community with other sectors of society. A chief example is the cartulary compiled at the monastery in the early twelfth century, which records donations from the previous three centuries. It provides testimony to the importance of Conques as a pilgrimage site and to the monastery's economic and political power in southern France and also represents a community that includes lay men and women of many classes and the monastery – a community textualized by the cartulary.[27]

The swelling number of pilgrims in the eleventh century had outgrown the earlier monastic church at Conques on the site and the prosperity of the cult provided the means to replace it with a larger church in the Romanesque style, built between about 1050 and about 1120. The carving at this church bears out Jean-Claude Fau's claim that the angel holding a book is the "Conques theme par excellence." For us, these angels are only the most obvious example of the broad and pervasive performance of textuality both on the interior and on the facade of the building.

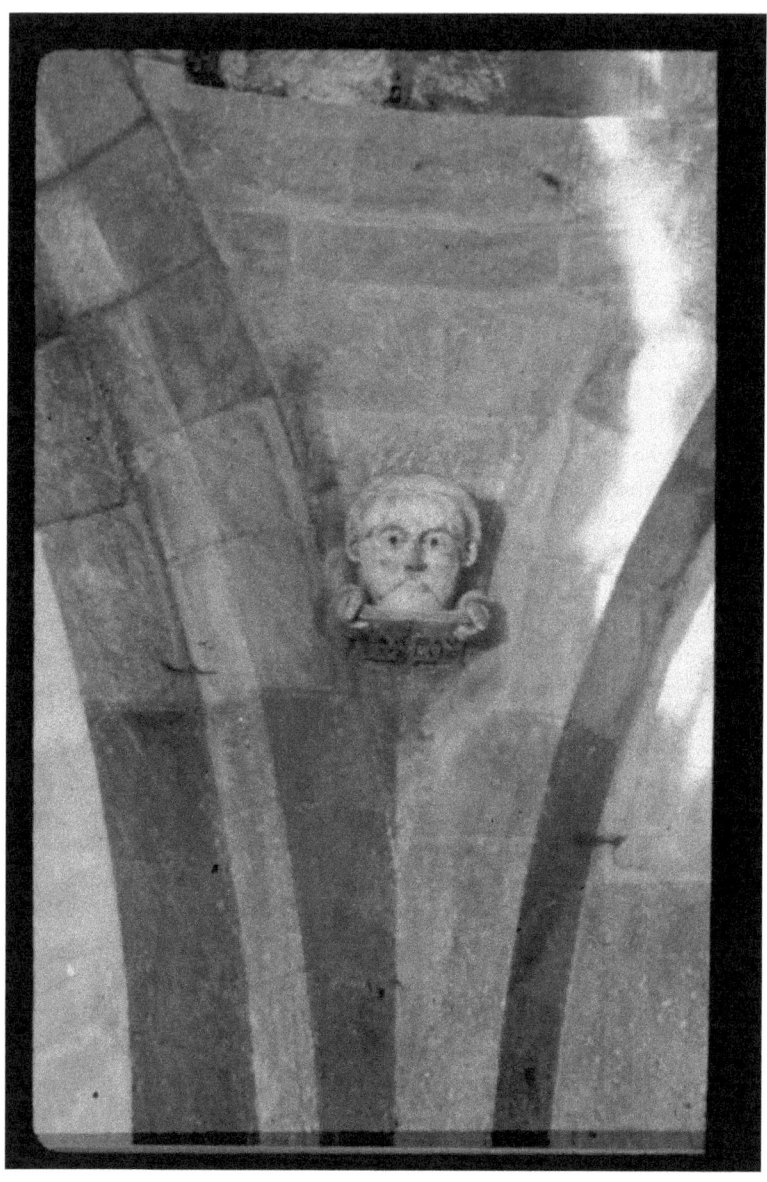

Figure 2: Sculpture of Peter or Paul with open book from crossing in monastery church of Sainte-Foy, Conques. (Photo: Marilyn Deegan)

The densest cluster of images of reading and writing inside the church is found at the crossing. The place where nave and transepts intersect, the crossing at Conques was covered by some kind of a dome that made it the highest point in the interior of the church. The capitals of the northwest and southwest piers are each carved with four angels, two displaying open books and two displaying scrolls that name them as evangelists and representatives of the angelic orders.[28] Above these capitals, framed in the four arches at the corners of the crossing, stand large figures of archangels displaying inscribed scrolls and busts of Peter and Paul with open books (Figure 2). Thus the composition includes apostles, evangelists, archangels, and the angelic orders of cherubim and seraphim. This grouping of celestial figures clearly indicates that it is a representation of the heavenly liturgy in performance. As Jacques Bousquet and Marcel Durliat have shown, these figures are grouped around the cupola, which signifies the dome of Heaven and implies the presence of the resurrected Christ.[29] Perhaps there was a painting of Christ in Majesty in the dome, as there often was in other medieval representations of the heavenly liturgy.

The open books and scrolls displayed by every figure in this composition signal that the heavenly liturgy is always in progress. In other words, in the celestial space, the book is continuously performed, and the monastic liturgy, though intermittent, aspires to that model. Although the sculptures are placed very high and in the sacred space of the building so as to indicate that they symbolize the divine realm, we also notice that the books are turned towards the earthly realm below, as if to strengthen visibly the bonds between the heavenly liturgy and its earthly performance.[30]

Just as in the Sélestat initial where the representation of hanging lamp and book-holding monk juxtaposed to the historical scene of martyrdom situate the social space of the Sélestat monastery in relation to the martyr's powers, here at Conques the social space in which the monks perform their liturgy is given celestial sanction by its participation in the cosmic performance of divine worship. The community addressed by these images is essentially the monastic, liturgical community, one of whose important functions is symbolized by this iconography. This is, therefore, the most exclusive set of textual images connected with the cult. However, there is a plethora of other images of texts and books that do not have that monastic self-referential function but are clearly addressed to a much larger and more diverse community that includes townspeople, visitors from the surrounding countryside, and pilgrims coming from a longer distance. Deciphering this broader textual community is in some ways the most challenging part of our task.

Figure 3: Tympanum, monastery church of Sainte-Foy, Conques. (Photo: Marilyn Deegan)

Given the conventional dichotomizing of literate from illiterate, literate from oral, learned from unlearned, elite from popular, or image from text, that occurs in much medieval historiography, it is somewhat surprising to see how densely the publicly oriented tympanum of the Conques church is inscribed with verbal text (Figure 3). Stylistic analysis of the sculpture reveals its easy accessibility to the unlettered viewer, since the naturalistic dynamism of the scenes would seem to demand little glossing. Furthermore the overall theme of Last Judgment was a totally conventional one for a western portal and the elements are arranged in a generally predictable configuration, from the large central figure of the judging Christ to the symmetrically arranged oppositions of saved and damned, Heaven and Hell. Given this sculptural lisibility, the insistent textuality of the tympanum cries out for some explanation.

Of course, Romanesque decorative schemes generally include some texts,[31] but Conques appears to have a peculiar density of these inscriptions, especially for a pilgrimage road church. There inscriptions occur not only on the tympanum, but also on capitals, reliquaries, tombs, and lintels of doorways. They can also be rather lengthy, as is the case with this lintel inscription: ISTE MAGISTRORVM LOCVS EST SIMVL PVERORVM MITTVNT QVANDO VOLVNT HIS RES QVAS PERDERE NOLVNT.[32] Conques thus provides a particularly convenient place for taking up the larger interpretive questions that apply to many Romanesque sites. What is the function of all this writing, the vast majority of it in Latin? Our sense is that a reception study of these texts will lead us to revise our understanding of saints' cults as cultural spaces.

Figure 4: The word DEMONAS, Conques tympanum, detail.
(Photo: Marilyn Deegan)

The Conques monastic community was poetically sophisticated and self-consciously literary, as the *Liber miraculorum* reveals. However, the inventiveness of the Conques community was not confined to their manuscripts but is emblazoned on their buildings. As Calvin Kendall points out, the verses carved on the monastic buildings at Conques are usually in dactylic hexameter and pentameter, most commonly in leonine rhyme,[33] and the tympanum has more verse inscriptions than any other existing Romanesque tympanum. The poetic term Tartarus, borrowed by Roman poets from Greek as a synonym for Hades, is used on the inscription near the top of the side at Christ's left and directly above scenes of grisly punishment in Hell. In addition, the Greek accusative plural, *DEmonas* rather than the Latin *DEmonES* is used in another inscription, in order to fit the meter (Figure 4).[34] Kendall notes that "Whether the Conques poet got it from classical Latin or from medieval sources, his assured use of the Grecism is indicative of the cultural level of the abbey of Conques."[35]

The linguistic eclecticism of the tympanum extends to an inscription on the robe of the angel who sounds a trumpet on the right-hand side of the cross, that is, above the scenes of Hell and its tortures. The Arabic inscription, which resembles a band of embroidery, repeats over and over in Kufic letters the word *al-youm* – happiness.[36] It is obvious that many visitors to the church would not be able to either read or appreciate this kind of linguistic display. One must therefore seek an explanation for these elements outside of direct communication of a simple verbal message. Rather they seem to perform the monastery's literary prowess and to proclaim it as a site of learning. They also display its technological expertise, as in the scene in Hell of the man who makes false coins with an anvil and a die (a tube the man holds in his hand). This scene is located in the upper part of the triangle at the far right of Hell, just below the I of MERSI. On the very top of the die, the scholar Paul Deschamps read the word, *cuneus*, that is, die or matrix.

Most of the inscriptions, of course, are easily readable by a literate person standing on the ground before the tympanum and communicate the significance of the carved scene they accompany. The overall message is explicitly spelled out at the bottom of the tympanum in direct address to the viewers: "O sinners, if you do not change your ways, know that a harsh judgment awaits you" (O PECCATORES TRANSMVTETIS NISI MORES: IVDICIVM DVRVM VOBIS SCITOTE FVTVRVM). For those who were not literate in Latin, the monastery may have provided a monk-explicator as a kind of textual tour guide, the "literate interpreter" posited by Brian Stock.[37] There is evidence from England that such functions were exercised; for example, St. Hugh, bishop of Lincoln, is reported to have explicated the images of the Last Judgment on the facade of Lincoln Cathedral in an attempt to persuade King John to mend his ways.[38] Certainly the monks at Conques today see their pastoral duties as including discussing the tympanum with groups of pilgrims. Whether there was such an interpreter or not, the tympanum with its pervasive literacy creates a textual community that includes the monks and their pilgrim visitors.

Our analysis of the complex textuality of the tympanum, however, suggests that the concept of a textual community as defined by Brian Stock should be much more nuanced. Taking what Mieke Bal calls "a reception-oriented perspective of cultural critique" enables us to focus on "the interaction between the visual and verbal 'behavior' of those who deal with, process, or consume" this work of art, the tympanum.[39] These interactions form textual communities, each of which may arrive at its own reading of the tympanum. Bal's semiotic approach calls for "letting go of a unified concept of meaning"[40] and recognizing the "validity of alternative or conflicting interpretations."[41] For example, the monks participate in multiple textual communities, as we have shown, which are overlapping but not necessarily congruent. Even within a textual community like the one joining the monastery and the pilgrims around the tympanum, one cannot, strictly speaking, identify one set of beliefs or experiences that structure everyone's behavior, as Stock suggests we should. Rather there appear to be multiple possible subject positions within one textual community such as that of monks and pilgrims reading the tympanum.[42] Even the monks, who would appear to be the privileged interpreters of the narrative, might occupy different subject positions on the tympanum. For example, an abbot displaying his crosier strolls confidently in the procession of the saved (Figure 5), while in Hell a devil ensnares three monks in a net.

Figure 5: Abbot leading a group of the saved, Conques tympanum, detail. (Photo: Marilyn Deegan)

Figure 6: In triangle, Hand of God granting Foy's intercessory prayers; in lower left corner, Wise Virgins holding open book, Conques tympanum, detail. (Photo: Marilyn Deegan)

As we have suggested, the cult of Foy at the Conques monastery functioned in a variety of ways for the local population.[43] A church portal was a common site for local judicial proceedings in France in the high Middle Ages[44] and the lay community at Conques gathered outside the church for religious rituals as well.[45] Among this lay population were witnesses to miracles, who brought their oral accounts to Bernard and other compilers for inscription in the *Liber miraculorum*. As agents in the translation of the cult from oral to written text, these local laypeople might well have seen themselves in a powerful relation to the open books represented at the church.[46] For example, these local people might have thought of their own roles in the creation of the *Liber miraculorum* when they studied the lower left corner of the tympanum, where two wise virgins display an open book, directly below the arches and altar representing the interior of the Conques church (Figure 6, lower left).

The once-in-a-lifetime experience of a pilgrim who had come from afar specifically to visit the shrine in fulfillment of a vow might have been entirely different. For such a person, the tympanum could convey a very personal message that might powerfully embed that seeker in a visual and verbal matrix of meanings. When those pilgrims looked at the tympanum and saw the top of the cross above the judging Christ, they could connect that image to the crosses marked on their own bodies at the outset of their pilgrimage.[47] On the bar of the cross itself are carved the words: "The sign of the cross will be in the sky when the Lord comes to judge" (OC SIGNVM CRVCIS ERIT IN CELO CVM [DOMINVS AD IVDICANDVM VENERIT]), clearly a crucial verbal echo of the message of the entire tympanum. But it was also specifically a liturgical verse chanted in connection with the Feasts of the Invention and Exaltation of the Cross and, even more pertinently, it was the verse of an antiphon chanted at the origin of the pilgrims' journey when they were blessed and marked with the sign of the cross.[48] Thus pilgrims who had had this liturgical experience were more likely to see their personal goal in cosmic terms when they read the anagogical promise inscribed on the tympanum at the end of their journey. In comparison to local inhabitants, who helped to write the books at Conques, the distant pilgrim was a particularly invested and close reader of the tympanum as text.

Another kind of pilgrim came specifically to ask for Foy's miraculous intercession. It is likely that such a pilgrim would come as an already instructed participant in the textual community around the *Book of Miracles*, having read or, more likely, heard of Foy's miracle-working powers. This pilgrim, looking up at the tympanum, would focus not on the future and the judgment theme, but rather on present time, as indicated by the image of Foy herself kneeling inside the very church the pilgrim is about to enter, its space adorned with the shackles of prisoners miraculously freed. (Figure 6, scene in triangle). Observing the haloed hand extended toward the interceding saint and thus reminded of Foy's success in persuading God to grant miracles to her devotees, such a pilgrim found in the tympanum renewed hope at the end of the long journey. Thus, whereas it might appear that as a text the overpoweringly structured tympanum conveys a completely coercive message, the viewer is actually invited to select a subject position. The person looking at the tympanum enters into an interpretive process, placing her- or himself not only into the narrative of the end of the world, but also into one of a number of textual communities that have a more specific set of shared understandings and behaviors.

Figure 7: Judging Christ with angel holding open Book of Life at his left, Conques tympanum, detail. (Photo: Marilyn Deegan)

The texts performed in all the aspects of the cult of Foy are, we would argue, open books. They are still in the process of being read and interpreted; they are in the midst of being performed by one or another textual community for its specific and historically contingent purposes. It is therefore important that they are open, that they hold a promise of continuing possibility. The message of the entire tympanum however is that the Last Judgment, in ending time, ends those possibilities. And that appears to be the significance of the book held by an angel to Christ's left, identified by its inscription as the Book of Life (Figure 7). Bernard of Angers refers to the Book of Life (1.4) when he pleads, "Christ, may I never be ashamed to acknowledge Your truth to people and to write it in my book, lest You are ashamed to acknowledge me before Your Father who is in Heaven and You delete me from the book that You have written." In the context of the tympanum, the Last Judgment becomes the final chapter of this book written by Christ's divine hand, for it is inscribed with the message, "The Book of Life is sealed." Paradoxically, as Jean-Claude Bonne has noted, this "sealed" book is held in an open position.[49] In its tantalizing contradiction this image of the angel performing the sealed book with open pages perfectly embodies the role of textuality in the cultural spaces associated with Sainte Foy. While gesturing towards a moment when the Book of Life will be sealed and new inscriptions will cease to be possible, the open book in its material visibility symbolizes the ongoing process of constructing social communities, a process to which the performance of the book is both crucial and central.

Notes

1. The priory of Perse was given to the monastery at Conques by Hugh of Calmont, his wife Foy, and their son, Begon. See the charter no. 572, dated 1060, in the Conques cartulary (Gustave Desjardins [ed.], *Cartulaire de l'abbaye de Conques-en-Rouergue*, Paris, 1879).

2. "La première voussure contient une série d'anges, assis ou debout, tenant des deux mains un livre ouvert, un thème conquois par excellence. A la troisième voussure, on reconnaît les archanges Gabriel et Raphaël, accompagnés d'un énigmatique personnage couronné, un marteau à la main." Jean-Claude Fau, *Rouergue roman*, Saint-Léger-Vauban, 1990 [*Zodiaque: La nuit des temps*, 17], p. 263.

3. For a rereading of the "complex iconographic history" of the solitary reader see Elizabeth Long, "Textual Interpretation as Collective Action," in Jonathan Boyarin [ed.], *The Ethnography of Reading*, Berkeley, 1992, pp. 180-211.

4. In regard to the monastery at Moissac, Daniel Smartt comments, "Since the abbey boasted a great scriptorium and library, the public probably could see a fair number of books in the church, at least from a distance." He adds, "In the frame of reference of the average twelfth-century European a book was still a relatively rare sight. To spy several in one place – particularly if they were luxury manuscripts with illuminations and rich binding, as were some of those at Moissac – was an experience that could happen to most people only on pilgrimage" (from chapter 4 of his dissertation-in-progress, "Pilgrims in the Moissac Portal").

5. In regard to the early ninth-century monastery of San Vincenzo al Volturno, John Mitchell, "Literacy Displayed: The Use of Inscriptions at the Monastery of San Vincenzo al Volturno in the Early Ninth Century," in Rosamond McKitterick [ed.], *The Uses of Literacy in Early Mediaeval Europe*, Cambridge, 1990, pp. 186-225, writes, "The second thing about the monastery, which would have struck a ninth-century visitor, was the display of script. An extraordinary number of inscriptions of various kinds were to be seen in the various parts of the complex. These were executed in a number of media, two of which were quite exceptional for the time. Each category merits our attention" (p. 192). Mitchell describes inscriptions running below paintings to identify them or convey a message about their content to the viewer: "Inscriptions of these kinds were commonly employed by artists in western Europe in the early middle ages" (p. 193). "Somewhat less usual, however, was the practice of writing legible texts in books held open by individual painted figures. In the crypt, both Christ and Mary are represented with open books, the one with the words spoken by God to Moses from the burning bush: *Ego sum D[eus] Abraha[m]*, the other with a passage from the Magnificat. These were clearly legible when they were newly written. While it is by no means unknown for figures to be depicted holding open books with legible texts in the early middle ages, it is certainly more usual for them to be shown with books which are closed, or which, if open, are either blank or covered with indecipherable script-like notations. The presence of two such fully inscribed books in a single small pictorial cycle, at this period, is exceptional. The written word was clearly a thing of some significance to the inventors of the pictorial scheme in the crypt" (p. 193). "The convention of introducing writing on scrolls or books was employed in the middle ages as a means of incorporating the act of speech into the mute medium of painting, and here the Prophets were represented calling out their prophecies in succession" (p. 194). "Figures holding open scrolls bearing legible inscriptions are not commonly found in the mediaeval west before the eleventh century" (p. 194). "In the west scrolls of this kind seem to have been of the utmost

rarity before the eleventh century, and it was only in the twelfth century that they are often put in the hands of Prophets and other figures, in wall paintings, mosaics, manuscript painting, ivory carving and in other media" (p. 194).

6. See Rosamond McKitterick, *The Carolingians and the Written Word*, Cambridge, 1989.

7. Michael T. Clanchy, *From Memory to Written Record: England 1066 – 1307*, Cambridge, 1979. See also Harvey J. Graff, *The Legacies of Literacy: Continuities and Contradictions in Western Culture and Society*, Bloomington and Indianapolis, 1987, on the "essentially oral environment, wherein writing represented an extension in time and space of the spoken word – not its replacement.… Religious education and whatever degree of popular participation was achieved came through the ears, the eyes, and the voice" (pp. 48-9).

    There has been strong opposition among literacy theorists and historians like Harvey Graff to an "autonomous model" of literacy which, Brian V. Street, *Literacy in Theory and Practice*, Cambridge, 1984, p. 2, argues, "assumes a single direction in which literacy development can be traced, and associates it with 'progress,' 'civilization,' individual liberty and social mobility.… It isolates literacy as an independent variable and then claims to be able to study its consequences. These consequences are classically represented in terms of economic 'take off' or in terms of cognitive skills." For Graff, Street, and others, "literacy" is a term that may name a complex variety of social practices and must always be historically situated.

    For another "complex weave of orality, literacy, and ritual practice that runs counter to the evolutionary approaches to the development of literacy," see Dianna Digges and Joanne Rappaport, "Literacy, Orality, and Ritual Practice in Highland Columbia" and Nicholas Howe, "The Cultural Construction of Reading in Anglo-Saxon England," in Boyarin [ed.], *The Ethnography of Reading*, pp. 139-55 and pp. 58-79 respectively.

8. In writing about a similar display of inscriptions and open books in the early ninth century at the monastery of San Vincenzo al Volturno, John Mitchell, "Literacy displayed," pp. 224-5, emphasizes only "how a large and enterprising religious community, situated in a highly sensitive location, in the border marches between Carolingian and Beneventan territory, deployed these cultural symbols to its own advantage. Painted decoration and prominent inscriptions not only gave the monastery an air of splendor and superiority, but they also doubtless served to attract the interest of benefactors from the region, whose support was vital to the continued prosperity and success of the community. The paintings, which were to be seen in almost every room at San Vincenzo, and the prodigal display of writing, in inscriptions of every kind in all parts of the complex, reveal the abbot and the monks as masters of an apparatus of cultural control, which was being developed and deployed by the most aggressive and successful powers in the contemporary world."

9. Brian Stock, *The Implications of Literacy: Written Language and Models of Interpretation in the Eleventh and Twelfth Centuries*, Princeton, 1983, p. 522.

10. Ibidem.

11. Ibidem. Most of Stock's examples are connected to his thesis about the rise of heretical movements.

12. Sharon A. Farmer, *Communities of Saint Martin: Legend and Ritual in Medieval Tours*, Ithaca and London, 1991; see also the review by Sherry L. Reames in *Speculum* 68 (1993), pp. 1111-3.

13. For an edition of the Latin text see Luca Robertini [ed.], *Liber Miraculorum Sancte Fidis*, Spoleto, 1994. For a translation into English see Pamela Sheingorn [ed.], *The Book of Sainte Foy*, Philadelphia, 1995; all translations in this paper are taken from this book.

14. On this point, see A. G. Remensnyder, "Un problème de cultures ou de culture?: la statue-reliquaire et les *joca* de sainte Foy de Conques dans le *Liber miraculorum* de Bernard d'Angers," *Cahiers de civilisation médiévale* 33 (1990), pp. 351-79.

15. 1.31: "And when I chided the senior monks because they had not kept written records of the freed prisoners – their names, families, homes – they said that it would have been very difficult. Furthermore, they had not expected a writer like myself just now, for whom they would have kept brief descriptions of these things that could have been used to write a fuller text. And, as they shamelessly admitted, all these miracles happened daily, to the point where they loathed them – in short, they had become completely indifferent. They were even completely ignorant of the name of the man whose fetters – a huge quantity of them! – I myself have seen hanging below the carved panelling of the ceiling."

16. 1.34: "A controversy has been produced by certain people that greatly confuses a clear reading of the word 'Fides,' for they want it to be inflected in the fifth declension. But I have paid attention to the long tradition of the ancient writings and I say that it ought to be 'Fides, Fidis,' as, for example, in 'nubes, nubis' and 'soboles, sobolis.' Unless I am mistaken, Master Fulbert, bishop of Chartres, most learned of almost all mortals in this our age, will agree with this assertion. At Fulbert's altar of the martyr Sainte Foy, on the day of the birth of that same virgin, I myself have seen and I have read that 'Fidis' not 'Fidei' was expressed as the genitive two or three times. For if we change this rule, it will seem that we mean the virtue named Faith, or the Faith who was martyred with her two sisters, Hope and Charity, at Rome under the emperor Hadrian. And so I admonish you amiably that you abandon the practice you have followed up till now and make the name of our Faith a word of the third declension."

17. Bernard relates in 1.7 that a local peasant was instigated by the Devil to ridicule the miracles Bernard wrote up, but that the attack was ineffective because the peasant was illiterate: "This same Devil had tried to impede me from setting out for Conques in a thousand ways, but he failed to thwart me since God was defending me. Nevertheless, he regained his strength somehow and used this man to raise doubts in the minds not only of inexperienced people, but also in my own, even though I ought to have been an unconquerable defender of this truth. He was trying to deflect me from my plan of writing the remaining miracles. With the subtle skill of his crafty trickery he even diminished my resolve a little. But I give thanks to the Author of Truth for this, that the only man the Enemy sent for this wicked task was illiterate and ignorant of all good.... If this ignoramus still doesn't understand for what reason or necessity God worked this miracle, he should look it up in the old texts. But if he is illiterate and can't verify it there, he should understand that in comparison to wise men he is a brute animal wholly unworthy to dispute concerning divine reasons."

18. On this point Jacques Bousquet, *Le Rouergue au premier Moyen Âge (vers 800-vers 1250)*, vol. I: *les pouvoirs, leurs rapports et leurs domaines*, Rodez [*Archives historiques du Rouergue*, 24], 1992, p. 282, comments, "Il serait peut-être excessif de penser que l'abbaye n'avait pu trouver sur place un rédacteur convenable. Le relevé des scribes du Cartulaire montre une remarquable continuité pendant tout le Xe siècle, avec le plus souvent plusieurs moines disponibles dans la

même période, et il en sera de même pendant tout le XIe siècle." For a more complete discussion of Bernard's ideological agenda in the *Liber miraculorum* see our *Writing Faith: Text, Sign, and History in the Miracles of Sainte Foy*, Chicago, 1999.

19. *Hujus miraculi medietas inferior, quod contra morem versibus constat exametris, quidam monachus nomine Arseus, orando ac pene violenter a me extorsit. Verum ne a precedentibus subsequentia disonare videantur, versus ipsos ad prosaicas posituras distinguere malui, veritus absurdum fore, si statum lectionis turbaret modulatio scansionis.*

20. In spite of this claim, scholars do not assign the writing of the *Passio* to the author or authors of Book III of the *Book of Miracles*.

21. *omnium virtutum liber.*

22. For the important role of the Hohenstaufen see our "'Discordia et lis': Negotiating Power, Property, and Performance in Medieval Sélestat," *The Journal of Medieval and Early Modern Studies* 26 (1996), pp. 419-46. The multiple implications of moving the cult to a new location are explored in our "Translations of Sainte Foy: Bodies, Texts, Places," in Roger Ellis [ed.], *The Medieval Translator*, Turnhout, 1996, vol. V, pp. 29-49.

23. The textual community at Sélestat seems to have generated other manuscripts with similar contents; for example, Lyell 64 in the Bodleian Library, a fourteenth-century manuscript, opens with the foundation story of the Sélestat monastery in German, and contains revised versions of selected miracles. This manuscript was originally from Melk, and there is a copy of it at Stift Klosterneuburg (Codex Claustroneoburgensis 1080). The absence of much historical documentation beyond these cultic collections makes it difficult to generalize about the relations between the monastic community and the surrounding societies.

24. This frequently reproduced image appeared on a .60 euro postage stamp commemorating the Bibliothèque humaniste in 2007. For reproductions see the library's website.

25. "'On saints' days, the customaries prescribed that nocturns during matins, which were normally given to the Psalms, should consist of the vitae sanctorum" (Stock, *Implications of Literacy*, p. 72).

26. See the translation of the song by Robert L. A. Clark in Sheingorn [ed.], *The Book of Sainte Foy*, and the bibliography there. Clark's note to the first laisse of the song reads: "This Latin book, the contents of which are briefly indicated here and developed in laisses 44-55 of the poem, is almost certainly Lactantius, *De mortibus persecutorum*. The unique manuscript of this text (now Paris, Bibl. Nat., Colbertinus, 2627) was in the abbey of Moissac. The pine as a place of assembly is a commonplace in Old French epic poetry (Chanson de Roland, ll. 114, 165, 168, etc.)."

27. See Barbara H. Rosenwein, *To Be the Neighbor of Saint Peter: The Social Meaning of Cluny's Property*, 909-1049, Ithaca and London, 1989, which deals with the gifts of land, specifically land that was repeatedly in circulation, as a way of forming bonds of community between lay donors and the monastery. See also Rosamond McKitterick's chapter on charters and literacy.

28. Inscriptions identify the pairs on the northwest pier as Luke and John, a seraphim and a cherubim, and the pair on the southwest as the archangels Gabriel and Raphael and the evangelists Matthew and Mark; see Robert Favreau, Bernadette Leplant and Jean Michaud [eds.], *Corpus des inscriptions de la France médiévale*, vol. 9: Aveyron, Lot, Tarn, Paris, 1984.

29. Jacques Bousquet, *La sculpture à Conques aux XIe et XIIe siècles: essai de chronologie comparée*, Thesis, Toulouse, 1971 (photographically reproduced in 3 volumes, Lille, 1973, 2 vols. of text; 1 vol. of plates), insists on the underlying influence of Byzantine art for representations of celestial beings in the high parts of the building. Marcel Durliat, *La Sculpture romane de la route de Saint-Jacques: de Conques à Compostelle*, Mont-de-Marsan, 1990, p. 442, argues for a unified theme to the capitals and other sculpted figures on the crossing in that all belong to the following of the resurrected Christ.

30. On representations of the heavenly liturgy in religious art, especially in church interiors, see Pamela Sheingorn, "The Te Deum Altarpiece and the Iconography of Praise," in Daniel Williams [ed.], *Early Tudor England: Proceedings of the 1987 Harlaxton Symposium*, Woodbridge, 1989, pp. 171-82 and plates 1-4. But see also St. Augustine, *Ennarationes in Psalmos*, in J.-P. Migne, [ed.], *Patrologiae cursus completus* […] Series Latina, vol. 36-37, col. 1602 and in Corpus Christianorum, Series Latina, vol. 40, p. 1783, who sees no need for books in Heaven: "There are all the righteous and holy, who enjoy the word of God without reading, without letters; for what is written on pages for us, they see on the face of God" (Ibi omnes iusti et sancti, qui fruuntur Verbo Dei sine lectione, sine litteris; quod enim nobis per paginas scriptum est, per faciem Dei illi cernunt).

31. For a list of examples see the "Catalog of Romanesque Verse Inscriptions," in Calvin B. Kendall, *The Allegory of the Church: Romanesque Portals and Their Verse Inscriptions*, Toronto, 1998. See also Kendall's "The Voice in the Stone: The Verse Inscriptions of Ste.-Foy of Conques and the Date of the Tympanum," in Patrick J. Gallacher and Helen Damico [eds.], *Hermeneutics and Medieval Culture*, Albany, 1989, p. 164 and p. 178, n. 12.

32. Kendall, "Catalog," no. 37. Favreau, Leplant and Michaud, *Corpus des inscriptions de la France médiévale*, record fifty-two inscriptions for the department of the Aveyron, of which twenty-three are at the abbey of Conques, whereas there are only six at Rodez. The number of twenty-three for Conques omits the captions to the paintings on the sacristy wall (Cf. Auguste Bouillet and L. Servières, *Sainte Foy, vierge et martyre*, Rodez, 1900, pp. 146-7).

33. Kendall, "The Voice in the Stone," p. 165.

34. "The regular accusative plural form of the word for demons (demones) is cretic (long, short, long) and therefore cannot be used in a hexameter or pentameter verse. In order to get around this problem and to secure an initial dactyl, the poet adopted the Greek accusative plural in (short) -as" (Kendall, "The Voice in the Stone," p. 168).

35. Kendall, "The Voice in the Stone," p. 167.

36. For other Romanesque inscriptions in Arabic in southern France see Louis Balsan, "L'inscription arabe du tympan de l'église de Conques," *Procès-verbaux des séances de la Société des Lettres, Sciences et Arts de l'Aveyron* 37 (1954-58), séance du 17 octobre 1957, p. 339.

37. The *Liber miraculorum* indicates that monks did not strictly separate themselves from the spaces of the surrounding community but rather mingled with the laity. See for example, 2.1, which describes a vicious fight between the monk Gerbert and a townsman which occurred while "Gerbert was walking around in the open space in front of the church … holding a lambskin in his hand and playfully waving it in the air."

38. "Then the bishop pointed to the left hand of the Judge, where kings in their regalia were being consigned to damnation…. The bishop turned to his companion and said, 'A man's conscience ought continually to remind him of the lamentations and interminable torments of

these wretches. One should keep the thought of these eternal pains before one's mind all the time.... Let the memory of these pains remind you how severe will be the charge against those who are set for a short time to rule others in this world, but fail to govern themselves. In this life we still have a chance to avoid this terrible fate, and to do so we ought to dread it in our whole being....' He said that images like this were very rightly placed at the entrance of churches. For thus the people going inside to pray for their needs were reminded of this greatest need of all.... If only [King John] could be warned in time of the wrath so soon to come! That even so late he might endeavor to escape eternal punishment, and remove himself from the left hand to the right of that Eternal Judge!" (Life of St. Hugh of Lincoln, as quoted in A. Caiger-Smith, *English Medieval Mural Paintings*, Oxford, 1963, pp. 40-1).

39. Mieke Bal, *Reading "Rembrandt": Beyond the Word-Image Opposition* (The Northrop Frye lectures in literary theory), Cambridge, 1991, p. 8.

40. Idem, p. 13.

41. Idem, p 9.

42. For a general feminist approach to the practices of reading which argues for the crucial roles of gender see Elizabeth A. Flynn and Patrocinio P. Schweikart [eds.], *Gender and Reading: Essays on Readers, Texts, and Contexts*, Baltimore, 1986.

43. Kathleen Ashley and Pamela Sheingorn, "An Unsentimental View of Ritual in the Middle Ages or, Sainte Foy was no Snow White," *Journal of Ritual Studies* 6 (1992), pp. 63-85.

44. On this practice see J.-F. Lemarignier, J. Gaudemet, and Msgr. G. Mollat, "Les institutions ecclésiastiques," in Ferdinand Lot and Robert Fawtier [eds.], *Histoire des institutions françaises au Moyen Age*, Paris, 1962, vol. III, p. 261.

45. See, for example, 3.17 of the Book of Miracles: "Because the senior monks did not have the resources to stand up to [Siger's] audacious wickedness with force, they persevered in praying to the holy martyr to help them; they implored her to free them from this incredibly cruel plague. In addition, they unfurled the banner of the Lord's victory and displayed it in the public square, along with a cross, the reliquary boxes, and the blessed martyr's holy image. They aroused all the people assembled there so that the holy virgin would be moved to stir up God's wrath against the tyrant and preserve her own territories from the violence of this cyclops."

46. For the idea that the witnesses of miracles would form a distinctive textual community with the Conques representations of open books, we are grateful to Sharon Kraus.

47. "When his enemies had been placated and his creditors satisfied, the pilgrim sought out his parish priest or, occasionally, his bishop, and received a formal blessing. Texts of these blessings for travellers survive from the early eighth century, though they did not pass into general use until the eleventh. Blessing ceremonies reflected the growing feeling among pilgrims that they belonged to an 'order' of the Church, distinguished from other men by a uniform and by a solemn ritual of initiation." (Cf. Jonathan Sumption, *Pilgrimage: An Image of Medieval Religion*, London, 1975, p. 171.)

48. After indicating the ultimate source of this text in Matthew 24, Favreau, Leplant and Michaud, *Corpus des inscriptions de la France médiévale*, continue, "Mais la source directe du texte gravé à Conques se trouve dans la liturgie. Aux vêpres des offices de l'Invention et de l'Exaltation de la sainte Croix sont chantés, après le *Vexilla Regis*, le verset et le répons suivants: *Hoc signum erit in caelo, alleluia, cum Dominus ad judicandum venerit, alleluia*. C'est également ce même texte qui

formait le verset d'une antienne que l'on chantait lorsque le pèlerin était marqué du signe de la croix: *Adoramus te, Christe, quia hoc signum crucis erit in caelo cum Dominus ad judicandum venerit"* (p. 24), which cites as a source for this text A. Franz, *Die kirchlichen Benedictionen im Mittelalter*, Graz, 1960, vol. II, p. 283.

49. SIGNATUR: LIBER VITE. Jean-Claude Bonne, *L'art roman de face et de profil: le tympan de Conques*, Paris, 1984. Bonne notes that this is one of the liturgical angels, as is the one below it who holds a censer. He says that the most eminent quarter of this group of four angels is reserved for the angel carrying the Book of Life, "ouvert en son milieu en un diptyque dont la forme réplique les destins opposés des hommes et/ou la symétrie des lieux; par là se trouve à nouveau produite une équivalence entre le champ du tympan et celui de l'Écriture" (p. 55).

Contributor Biographies

Kathleen Ashley is Distinguished Professor at the University of Southern Maine. With Pamela Sheingorn, she has published numerous articles on the cult of Sainte Foy and one book, *Writing Faith: Text, Sign and History in the Miracles of Sainte Foy* (Chicago, 1999). She also publishes in pilgrimage studies in collaboration with photographers: *Being a Pilgrim: Art and Ritual on the Medieval Routes to Santiago* (with Marilyn Deegan, Lund Humphries, 2009) and *The Way of Saint James: A Journey Within* (with Jean-Pierre Rousset, forthcoming).

Amelia J. Carr (B.A. The Ohio State University 1976; Ph.D. Northwestern University 1984) is a Professor at Allegheny College in Meadville, Pennsylvania, teaching ancient, medieval, and Renaissance art history and serving as chair of the Art Department. Her current research interests include *Ut Mos Habet. Easter Dramatic Liturgy and the Church at Klosterneuburg* (with Michael Norton) and NWPa Heritage, a collaborative public history project utilizing mobile and web applications.

Robert L. A. Clark is Professor of French at Kansas State University. He has published broadly on medieval theater, devotional practices, and gender as well as on opera. He is co-editor with Kathleen Ashley of *Medieval Conduct* (Minnesota, 2001) and with Pamela Sheingorn has published seven articles on the performative reading of illuminated manuscripts. He is currently working on a monograph on Jacques Copeau and the Middle Ages.

Lawrence M. Clopper[†], late emeritus professor of English at Indiana University, published on English medieval theater, Langland, and Chaucer. Among his many publications were *Drama, Play and Game: English Festive Culture in the Medieval and Early Modern Period* (Chicago, 2001); *"Songes of Rechelesnesse": Langland and the Franciscans* (Michigan, 1997); and *The Dramatic Records of Chester, 1399-1642* (Records of Early English Drama, Toronto, 1979). Professor Clopper died shortly before this volume went to press.

Claus Clüver, an Indiana University professor emeritus of Comparative Literature, has also taught at New York University and UC Berkeley and in Brazil, Portugal, Germany, Sweden, and Denmark. His publications include a book in German on 20th-century theater and over forty essays on interarts studies. He is co-editor of *The*

Pictured Word (1998), *Signs of Change: Transformations of Christian Traditions and their Representation in the Arts, 1000 – 2000* (2004), and *Orientations: Space / Time / Image / Word* (2005).

Thomas Goodmann is Associate Professor of English at the University of Miami, where he offers courses on medieval language, literature, and culture. A board member of the International *Piers Plowman* Society, he serves as the current Vice President of The Consortium for the Teaching of the Middle Ages (TEAMS). He is currently editing a collection of essays to support teaching William Langland's *Piers Plowman* poems.

Jesse Hurlbut is a former student of C. Clifford Flanigan. He has taught in the French Departments of the University of Kentucky and Brigham Young University. His specialty is fifteenth-century court spectacle and culture in Burgundy.

Eric Metzler is the Instructional Support and Assessment Specialist at the Kelley School of Business at Indiana University. There, he oversees learning outcome assessment for the School's eleven degree-granting programs and consults with faculty members about all aspects of teaching, helping them maintain Kelley's national reputation of teaching excellence. Eric satisfies his interest in the Middle Ages by reading Middle High German poetry. He lives with his husband in Bloomington, Indiana.

Ignacio Navarrete received a Ph.D. in Comparative Literature from Indiana University in 1985. Since 1987 he has been a professor of Medieval and Early Modern Spanish literature at the University of California, Berkeley. His research interests center on poetry, poetics, narrative, and the history of the book. In addition to articles, he is author of *Orphans of Petrarch: Poetry and Theory in the Spanish Renaissance*.

Michael L. Norton (B.M.Ed, James Madison University 1974; Ph.D., The Ohio State University 1983) is an Associate Professor of Computer Science and Affiliate Faculty for the School of Music at James Madison University, Harrisonburg, Virginia. He is currently working on two books: *Liturgical Drama and the Reimagining of Medieval Theater* and *Ut Mos Habet. Easter Dramatic Liturgy and the Church at Klosterneuburg* (with Amelia J. Carr). His research also includes studies on women's liturgy at Klosterneuburg (with Amelia J. Carr), the Tours *Ludus Paschalis*, and Austrian liturgical manuscripts.

Nils Holger Petersen is Associate Professor of Church History, University of Copenhagen, focusing on music, drama, and medieval liturgy. He is leader of an international project on medieval saints and collective identity, *Symbols that Bind and Break Communities* (European Science Foundation). He is main editor for the book series *Ritus et Artes: Traditions and Transformations* (Brepols) and area editor for music for the *Encyclopedia of the Bible and its Reception* (De Gruyter, 2009 –).

Pamela Sheingorn is emerita professor of History at Baruch College, City University of New York and of History, Theatre, and Medieval Studies at The Graduate Center, CUNY. She is co-author (with Kathleen Ashley) of *Writing Faith: Text, Sign, and History in the Miracles of Sainte Foy* (Chicago, 1999). With Robert Clark, she has published a series of articles that center on the performative reading of illustrated French manuscripts.

Claire Sponsler is Professor of English at the University of Iowa, where she teaches medieval literature, with a focus on performance studies and cultural history. She is the author of *Ritual Imports: Performing Medieval Drama in America* and *The Queen's Dumbshows: John Lydgate and the Making of Early Theater*, as well as other books and articles.

The Medieval and Renaissance Drama Society (MRDS)

The Medieval and Renaissance Drama Society is an academic association of scholars, artists, and other individuals interested in Medieval and Renaissance drama. The Society's activities include organizing annual meetings, sponsoring long-range research projects, and publishing material of interest to the membership. The annual journal ROMARD, and the Early European Drama in Translation Series (EEDTS) are publications affiliated with MRDS. The MRDS business meeting is held annually each May at the International Congress on Medieval Studies at Western Michigan University in Kalamazoo, Michigan. Members and non-members are invited to attend. Each year MRDS sponsors conference sessions at the Medieval Congress in Kalamazoo, the Modern Language Association Convention, and the Medieval Congress in Leeds, England.

MRDS members receive the Society's Newsletter twice a year and the annual issue of ROMARD. To join MRDS, please visit the Society's website (http://mrds.eserver.org/) or contact the MRDS Secretary/Treasurer Carolyn Coulson-Grigsby at ccoulson2@su.edu. Dues Structure: Regular Member (US $25); Student (US $10); Friend (US $50); Benefactor (US $100).

www.ingramcontent.com/pod-product-compliance
Lightning Source LLC
Chambersburg PA
CBHW050105170426
43198CB00014B/2463